How to Get and Keep
Good Clients

Global Third Edition

Preface to the Global Third Edition

This Global Third Edition has been written because there is a need for it. Non U.S. Lawyers throughout the world have asked for many years for the ability to buy just the information that is appropriate to their national and local practices and ethical standards from this book and from the all time ABA bestseller, *How to Start & Build a Law Practice*.

Through the miracle of the Internet, one may now pay electronically and instantly receive electronic digital delivery anywhere in the world 7 days a week, 24 hours a day. One may download the entire book or select just the chapter one wishes to read from anywhere on this globe.

The reader may supplement this Global Third Edition book at any time with newly written information simply by visiting the FoonbergLaw (**www.FoonbergLaw.com**) or the National Academy of Law Ethics & Management, Inc. (**www.nalem.org**) web site. ABA section members may be eligible for discounts by visiting the American Bar Association Bookstore.

Many other of my works can be obtained digitally, in various formats, via the Internet. A partial list of these products can be found on the overleaf of this page.

Jay G Foonberg
Beverly Hills, California
July 2008

An 8-Hour Audio CD version of this course is available.
Visit: www.Foonberglaw.com

Library of Congress Catalog Card Number: 90-060704

ISBN: 978-0-9818541-0-6

Printed in China by www.lithopak.com

Table of Contents

CHAPTER C
THE LAWYER IN THE OFFICE

CHAPTER D
THE LAWYER'S CONDUCT OUT OF THE OFFICE

CHAPTER E
ADDRESSING THE NEEDS OF CLIENTS AND POTENTIAL CLIENTS

CHAPTER F
GETTING BUSINESS FROM OTHERS IN THE OFFICE

CHAPTER G
GETTING BUSINESS FROM OTHERS OUT OF THE OFFICE

CHAPTER H
ETHICS: USING ETHICS TO CREATE NEW OPPORTUNITIES TO GET CLIENTS

CHAPTER I
GETTING WORK FROM LARGE OR PUBLICLY HELD COMPANIES

CHAPTER J
THE OFFICE AND OFFICE PROCEDURES AS A FACTOR IN KEEPING CLIENTS

CHAPTER K
BOMBARDING YOUR CLIENTS WITH PAPER

CHAPTER L
YOUR INVOICE - A FACTOR IN SATISFYING OR ANGERING CLIENTS

CHAPTER M
GETTING PAID FOR WHAT YOU DO

CHAPTER N
BIG FIRM TECHNIQUES THAT CAN WORK FOR A SMALL FIRM

CHAPTER O
ASSORTED MARKETING TIPS

CHAPTER P
TAKING CLIENTS WHEN LEAVING THE FIRM

CHAPTER Q
A QUICK REVIEW OF YOUR CURRENT MARKETING PRACTICES

CHAPTER R
THE INTERNET AND THE FUTURE

Foreword to Third Edition

Reader reaction to the Previous Editions of *How to Get and Keep Good Clients* has been overwhelmingly and enthusiastically favorable. The publisher surveyed buyers and found that 98.2 percent of the readers felt that the book was helpful to them and that they would recommend it to another attorney.

The book reviewers were also overwhelmingly favorable.

There were a few bona fide criticisms of the book which I've addressed in this edition and a few comments which I'll defend. I've also added and updated some earlier chapters and added chapters on elementary planning, the internet, and cross-marketing. The chapter on cross-marketing was added in response to my doing seminars at private law firms and discovering that the lack of planned coordinated cross-marketing needed immediate attention.

In a soul searching, difficult decision I've decided to re-write parts of the chapter on "How To Take Clients With You When You Leave The Firm." Many of my close friends in some of the most important law firms in the world objected to that chapter as originally written. I must present a truthful and accurate picture if I am to be of service to the profession and the public. I feel that by presenting *both* sides of the problem I've also helped the firm. Accordingly, I've not bowed to pressure and I have presented a balanced treatment.

The chapters intended for women lawyers have also received both positive and negative reaction. The positive reactions were thanks from women attorneys for being honest and helpful as well as comments from male lawyers who, reading the chapters, became aware of, or more sensitive to, unintentional gender bias. The negative comments have come primarily from well intentioned attorneys who feel that by explaining differences I was creating or exacerbating perceived differences where differences in fact did not exist. I respect those who would have me remove the chapters from the book but I feel an obligation to present realism as well as idealism.

Lastly, there have been some comments that the book contains too much of Jay Foonberg and is self aggrandizing. It is true that many of the examples are from my personal experience. I'm simply trying to emphasize that I personally have practiced what I preach and that it works.

I've continued to utilize the writing style of delivering valuable information in "bite size" pieces. This does result in some duplication but allows the reader to read just the parts they're interested in without having to read the chapter before or the chapter after.

Lastly, there are now multiple new versions of this book available. There is a PDF download version, an 8 hour CD version, a one hour DVD and a one hour CD version intended for brand new lawyers with no practical experience. All of these versions can now be downloaded from the internet or will be in the future. Lawyers and other professionals anywhere in the world can gain instant access to this information to be read or listened to or watched. This has been done in response to the large demand for this and other books from lawyers throughout the world. English has become the acknowledged Lingua Franca of the world of law and lawyers.

Chapter A
About This Book and How to Use It

A-1
Why This Book Has Been Written

I have written and re-written and updated this book because I know there is a continuing need for it. I sincerely believe in the role the sole practitioner and small law firm can and should play in fulfilling the legal needs of the American public. This role has been greatly impaired by the creation of huge "mega-firms," which are taking the bigger clients, and the trend toward the "clinic atmosphere" and do it yourself books and CDs, and internet downloads or the "cheapest way," which is taking away many of the smaller clients.

I am not convinced that the entire American public is benefiting by these trends or that these trends are a natural and proper evolution in the delivery of legal services in all cases. I believe that these changes are basically the result of good practice development and good marketing techniques used by the megafirms and clinics and poor marketing effort (or no marketing effort) on the part of most solo practitioners and smaller firms. With affirmative marketing techniques, solo practitioners and small firms can stop the trend and, indeed, reverse it.

Through my book, *How to Start and Build a Law Practice,* published by the American Bar Association in 1976 and updated in 1984, 1991, 1999, and 2004, and through my articles and programs, I believe that I have done more than any other lawyer alive to convince lawyers and the public that the world is changing and that active marketing is essential.

Surprisingly, many of the buyers of my books are lawyers with 3 to 5 years experience, who love law and love client contact but are not happy being "lab rats on treadmills" (their term, not mine).

The buyers want to leave their firms, and start a practice alone or with others. They want to practice law, make a decent living, and be happy. This book receives many compliments from those lawyers.

In 1968, I began participating in programs intended for *new* lawyers on practice development. To my surprise, a great number of experienced lawyers attended these programs.

Although I was initially aiming my program at new admittees and those beginning a practice, the greatest appreciation for the techniques came from the more experienced lawyers. Over and over again, these experienced lawyers came over to me and said, "I wish this information had been available years ago." Many times lawyers with 25 to 50 years of practice experience came to me personally to express their appreciation. The more experienced the lawyer, the more enthusiasm for marketing the attorney showed. Law students and law schools, however, were skeptical of the need for, or the success of, marketing techniques, believing that somehow clients would automatically discover these techniques because they received an "A" in "Future Interests" in law school. Experienced lawyers knew that if you want to develop a practice, you must take the initiative and do something, but they didn't know what to do to achieve successful practices.

In 1976, I began participating in practice-development programs intended for experienced lawyers and Bar Associations, and have participated in more than 300 programs in every state in the union, from Vermont to Florida, from Oregon to California, and even Hawaii to Alaska, as well as every province in Canada and on every one of the seven continents. I've also participated in programs for architects, accountants and doctors and have found that the techniques of practice development are universal for all professions (naturally, with some modifications from profession to profession).

Many, many lawyers asked me to write this book, believing I was uniquely qualified due to my personal experience. In 1980, when I was elected simultaneously to the Chair of the State Bar of California Economics of Law Practice Section (9,000 members) and then to a third two-year term on the council of the American Bar Association's Economics of Law Practice Section (22,000 members), I determined to conclude the first edition of this book.

I wish to state that I did not invent or create all or even most of the techniques in this book. Although I did create or pioneer many of these marketing techniques, many more of them came from other lawyers throughout the United States and other countries.

I have written this book because I am convinced there is a need for this reference material in the personal library of every professional in America. It should be read, and periodically re-read, by every person who works in a firm rendering professional services.

In the 1990s and into the 21st Century I began doing programs for more international groups and learned that the process and techniques for getting and keeping good clients was universal to lawyers and clients from hundreds of countries and cultures in every language and on every continent. Certainly there were some differences based on local custom and culture, but the basic questions were the same and the basic answers were the same.

I served in the House of Delegates of the American Bar Association and on the council of the Senior Lawyers Division of the ABA and as chair of the Senior Lawyers of the State Bar of California. Sadly, I learned of lawyers in their 50s and 60s being forced out of the firms they started or built. Those lawyers had to re-learn the lessons of this book in order to survive.

The commercialization of large law firms and the quest for profits has proven to be critical in terms of law firm competition and competition within law firms.

A client following has become the only security for a lawyer. This book can help provide that security.

A-2
Marketing - An Acquired Skill
Which You Must Learn –
You Can Do It!

Professional practice development is not a skill genetically inherited. It is a skill which we must learn to use and perfect.

Reading books on how to ski will not make you a skier. Hiring skiing coaches and consultants will not make you a skier. The book on skiing or coaches can only provide you with help. You still have to put on the skis and get out on the slopes. You will fall a few times in the learning process. It is the same for readers of this book. You must *use* the tools. You will make some mistakes, but after a while you will find those techniques or tools that work best for you.

This book presents specific techniques for the professional. The professional can adopt any techniques that he or she feels comfortable with or can realistically utilize. On the other hand, if the professional doesn't feel comfortable using the technique or feels that the technique won't work, that individual can simply ignore it.

I have found that no matter how successful a technique might be, some people just won't feel comfortable using it. I've also found that many marketing instructors and workshop leaders are insensitive to this fact. When an instructor or workshop leader doesn't feel comfortable with a technique, the technique will be ignored or downgraded even though it might have been a good one for one of the participants.

Accordingly, I have included as many techniques as I can in this book with the hope that you'll use the ones you like and that you feel have potential for you. Don't be afraid to experiment. Don't be discouraged if you have some failures. Look upon "failures" as learning experiences. You will find the techniques that work best for you. Eventually you will capitalize on your strengths and work on, or eliminate, your weaknesses. As Shakespeare wrote, "This above all: to thine ownself be true." *(Hamlet,* Act 1.)

In several places in this book you will find a quotation from Thackeray.

"Successful people weren't born that way. They became successful by adopting the habits that unsuccessful people don't adopt."

You can learn from this book. You can do it!

A menu in an excellent restaurant may include some items you adore and others you abhor. Similarly with the techniques you will learn in this book you should go for the ones you adore and leave the other techniques to other people.

A-3
This Book Is Based on Actual Successful Experiences of Myself and Others

This book contains practical, time-proven information from:

1. My own personal experiences in successfully building law firm clientele and CPA firm clientele; and
2. Tips and techniques I learned from other lawyers and other professionals while participating in more than 300 programs on practice development. The techniques come from every state in the union and several foreign countries.

This book is not theoretical. It is based on real-life experiences of real-life attorneys and their clients. Most of the techniques are based on my personal practice-building techniques. Some of these techniques I invented. Some I learned from clients.

In 1958, I successfully started my own accounting practice. In 1964, I successfully started a solo practice right out of law school and, using these techniques, built a firm with 20 lawyers and 50 non-lawyers. In 1978, I joined a 12-lawyer firm and built it into an 18-lawyer firm. Each time I was successful because I used the techniques that are in this book.

Many of the concepts expressed in this book were invented by me, others were not.

I have been helping young lawyers start law practices since 1964. I've participated in approximately 1,000 law office economic programs in every state in the union and on many foreign countries. At these programs I was generally the principal speaker, but I was usually preceded or followed by other speakers or panels. By listening to those speakers I learned many, if not most, of the things you will find in this book. Thus, if someone in New York, Chicago, Seattle, Rapid City, Tampa, Paris, Rio or Budapest claims to be the inventor or originator of a concept found in this book, he or she may be right.

I have had the good fortune to be exposed to these ideas over a period of more than four decades, covering about 3 million miles. In this book, I am simply putting all of the various concepts together in one place at one time.

This book will provide the tools (techniques) which a professional must use for both long range and immediate practice development success. It is not a book dedicated primarily to long-range planning, which to be most effective may require the assistance of outside consultants and a substantial immediate investment of time and money with results in the future.

Once you have mastered some of the low-cost and no-cost techniques of this book, you should give serious consideration to your long range planning. I highly recommend long-range marketing studies and planning but they are beyond the scope of this book. I feel that immediate success and survival is the first step to long-range success. I know that long range planning for success includes the lessons of this book consistently practiced.

A-4
Partial List of Sponsors of Programs Where I Have Participated to Learn the Techniques of This Book

I have indicated that most of the information in this book originated with lawyers (and others) located throughout the U.S. and indeed throughout the world.

The following list is simply a partial compilation of some of the bar associations, continuing legal education organizations, law schools and other professional organizations for which I have lectured or participated in programs as a speaker, member, etc. I have indicated the place of the program so that you can get an indication of the places where the participants practice. In some cases there is an overlap of the sponsors or locations. In some cases I may have incorrectly identified the exact name or section of the sponsoring organization, for which I apologize.

I have indicated the sponsors to establish the credibility of the subject in today's environment.

Lastly, in case you ask "When do you practice law?" please remember that these programs were done over a period of more than three decades. I try to limit myself to about two programs per month.

In most cases, I do not charge a fee. On some occasions when a program takes me away for more than a day, I must be compensated for my time out of the office while expenses continue. I have received some referrals from these programs, but I could easily earn more money staying behind my desk. I have participated in these programs because I enjoy sharing experiences with other lawyers and I enjoy traveling.

I have flown more than 3 million miles and estimate that I've been away from my home and my office about more than 1,000 days of billable time over the years. The list does not indicate where I have participated in multiple programs for the same sponsor at the same city. If I have inadvertently omitted a program where you heard me speak, please drop me a note and I'll correct the list when the book is updated.

PARTIAL LIST OF SPONSORING GROUPS

Country/State	Sponsoring Group	City
Alabama	Alabama State Bar	Birmingham
	Auburn University Law School Alumni Assoc.	Auburn
	BBA-Women Lawyers Section-Parenting & Lawyering Comm.	Birmingham
	Birmingham Bar Association	Birmingham
	Birmingham Bar Assoc. Young Lawyers Section	Birmingham
	Najjar Denaburg, P.C.	Birmingham

Alaska	Alaska Bar Association	Juneau
		Anchorage
Arizona	American Assoc. of Atty. –CPAs	Phoenix
	American Assoc. of Atty. –CPAs	Scottsdale
	American Assoc. of Atty. –CPAs	Tucson
	American Bar Association	Scottsdale
	Arizona Bar Assoc. Annual Convention	Scottsdale
	Arizona Chapter of the Assoc. of Legal Admins.	Phoenix
	Commercial Law Affiliates	Scottsdale
	Connecticut Society of CPAs	Phoenix
	Connecticut Society of CPAs	Scottsdale
	Pennsylvania Bar Association	Scottsdale
	State Bar of Arizona	Phoenix
	State Bar of Arizona	Scottsdale
	State Bar of Arizona	Tucson
	Strategic Media Counselors	Scottsdale
Arkansas	Arkansas Bar Association	Hot Springs
	Arkansas Bar Association	Little Rock
California	ABA-Criminal Justice Section	San Francisco
	ABA-Economics of Law Practice Sect.	San Diego
	ABA-Economics of Law Practice Sect.	San Francisco
	ABA-General Practice/Solo & Small Firm Div.	Olympic Valley
	ABA-Law Practice Management Section	Olympic Valley
	ABA-Law Practice Management Section	San Francisco
	ABA-Law Student Division	San Diego
	ABA-Section of Taxation	Los Angeles
	ABA-Young Lawyers Division	San Diego
	ABA-Young Lawyers Division	San Francisco
	Amer. Medical Assoc. – Long Beach Chap.	Long Beach
	American Assoc. of Atty-CPAs	Beverly Hills
	American Assoc. of Atty-CPAs	Monterey
	American Assoc. of Atty-CPAs	Palm Springs
	American Assoc. of Atty-CPAs	San Francisco
	American Bar Association	San Francisco
	American Bar Association	Santa Barbara
	American Bar Association	Monterey
	American Bar Association – ELP	San Francisco
	American Immigration Lawyers Assoc.	Los Angeles
	American Indian Lawyers Assoc.	Los Angeles
	American Institute of Architects	North Hollywood
	American Institute of Architects	Studio City
	Apartment Owners Association	Van Nuys
	Arab-American Lawyers' Assoc. of Southern CA.	Los Angeles
	Assoc. of Real Estate Attorneys	Los Angeles
	Assoc. of Legal Administrators, Legal Secretaries, Inc.	Monterey
	Association of Continuing Legal Education	San Diego
	Association of Legal Administrators	Sacramento
	Bailey Law Firm	Long Beach
	Bailey Law Firm	W. Los Angeles

Bay Area General Reporters Assoc of the Peninsula	San Francisco
Barristers of the L.A. County Bar Assoc.	Los Angeles
Beverly Hills Bar Assoc. Int. Law	Beverly Hills
Beverly Hills Bar Association	Beverly Hills
Beverly Hills Bar Association	Los Angeles
Beverly Hills Bar Association	Pacific Palisades
Brazil California	Los Angeles
Brazil California Trade Association	Beverly Hills
Brazil California Trade Association	Los Angeles
Brazil California Trade Association	North Hollywood
CA. State Polytechnic University	Pomona
Cal. Western School of Law	San Diego
California Assoc. of Attorney-CPA's	Beverly Hills
California Assoc. of Attorney-CPAs	San Francisco
California Cont. Educ. of the Bar	Westwood
California Cont. Educ. of the Bar	Santa Barbara
California Cont. Educ. of the Bar	Beverly Hills
California Cont. Educ. of the Bar	Anaheim
California Cont. Educ. of the Bar	Irvine
California Cont. Educ. of the Bar	Los Angeles
California Cont. Educ. of the Bar	Santa Barbara
California Cont. Educ. of the Bar	Westwood
California Rental Association	Anaheim
California Rental Association	Los Angeles
California Rental Association	Oxnard
California Rental Association	San Diego
California Rental Association	Sacramento
California Rental Association	Palm Springs
California Rental Association	Oakland
California Rental Association	Bakersfield
California Rental Association	San Jose
California Rental Association	Fullerton
California Rental Association	Laguna Hills
California State Polytechnic University	Los Angeles
California State Society of CPA's	Beverly Hills
California State Society of CPA's	Inglewood
California State Society of CPA's	Los Angeles
California Trial Lawyers Assoc.	Palm Springs
Century City Bar Association	Los Angeles
City of LA Economic Devel. Corp.	Los Angeles
Consulate General of Brazil	Los Angeles
Contra Costa County Bar Assoc.	Concord
Contract Staffing of America	Long Beach
Daily Journal Corporation	Los Angeles
Desert Bar Association	Palm Springs
Economics of Law Practice Section	Monterey
Export Managers Association	Long Beach
Export Managers Association	Los Angeles
Foonberg Client Seminars	Beverly Hills
French American Chamber of Commerce	Los Angeles
Greater Los Angeles Waste Management Assoc.	City of Commerce
Group, Inc.	San Diego

Howard University Law Alumni Assoc.	Los Angeles
ICLE	San Francisco
International Bar Association	San Francisco
Kansas Bar Association	Salina
LA County Bar Assoc.-Bridging the Gap	Los Angeles
LA County Bar Assoc.-Sole Practitioner Sect.	Los Angeles
LACBA-Small Firm & Sole Practitioner Sect.	Los Angeles
LACBA-Lawyer Referral & Information Srvc.	Los Angeles
Law School Advisors of Southern CA.	Costa Mesa
Law Offices of Procopio, Cory, Hargreaves & Savitch	La Jolla
Lawyers Club of Los Angeles	Los Angeles
Lawyers' Mutual Insurance Company	Costa Mesa
Lawyers' Mutual Insurance Company	Eureka
Lawyers' Mutual Insurance Company	Fresno
Lawyers' Mutual Insurance Company	Goleta
Lawyers' Mutual Insurance Company	Los Angeles
Lawyers' Mutual Insurance Company	Monterey
Lawyers' Mutual Insurance Company	Palm Springs
Lawyers' Mutual Insurance Company	Pasadena
Lawyers' Mutual Insurance Company	Petaluma
Lawyers' Mutual Insurance Company	Redding
Lawyers' Mutual Insurance Company	Sacramento
Lawyers' Mutual Insurance Company	San Bernardino
Lawyers' Mutual Insurance Company	San Diego
Lawyers' Mutual Insurance Company	San Francisco
Lawyers' Mutual Insurance Company	San Jose
Lawyers' Mutual Insurance Company	San Luis Obispo
Lawyers' Mutual Insurance Company	San Rafael
Lawyers' Mutual Insurance Company	Santa Barbara
Lawyers' Mutual Insurance Company	Santa Clara
Lawyers' Mutual Insurance Company	South Lake Tahoe
Legal Education Institute	San Diego
Legal Secretaries Inc.	Los Angeles
Long Beach Bar Assoc.-Barristers	Long Beach
Long Beach Bar Association	Long Beach
Long Beach Women Lawyers Assoc.	Long Beach
Los Angeles County Bar Assoc.	Los Angeles
Los Angeles County Bar Assoc. Barristers	Century City
Los Angeles County Bar Assoc. Barristers	Beverly Hills
Los Angeles County Barristers	Pasadena
Los Angeles County Barristers	Los Angeles
Los Angeles County Medical Assoc.	Los Angeles
Los Angeles County Medical Assoc.	Los Angeles
Los Angeles Daily Journal	Los Angeles
Los Angeles Daily Journal	Ventura
Los Angeles Legal Secretaries Assoc.	Beverly Hills
Los Angeles Waste Management Assoc.	Los Angeles
LPM Lawyers Mutual Insurance Company	Santa Barbara
MAPS	San Diego
Marin County Bar Association	San Rafael
Mexican-American Legal Defense Fund	Los Angeles
MICHIE Company	San Diego

Mount Diablo Bar Institute	Walnut Creek
Mt. Diablo Bar Association	Concord
NationAir Insurance Agency	Long Beach
NationAir Insurance Agency	Santa Monica
NationAir Insurance Agency`	W. Los Angeles
Natl. Assoc. of Law Firm Marketing Admin.	San Francisco
National Association of Mfgrs. Reps.	Los Angeles
National Law Firm Marketing Association	Los Angeles
National Practice Institute	Los Angeles
Newport Bar Association	Newport Beach
Newport Beach Conference & Visitors Bureau	Newport Beach
North Orange County Bar Assoc.	Fullerton
Oakland Bar Association	Oakland
Orange County Bar Association	Costa Mesa
Orange County Bar Association	Santa Ana
Orange County Bar Association	Tustin
Orange County Bar-Corporate Law Sec.	Tustin
Orange County Barristers	Orange
Orange County Barristers	Santa Ana
Orange County Medical Assoc.	Santa Ana
Pacific Bell Tele. System (Mgrs.)	San Diego
Pepperdine Univ. School of Mgmt.	Malibu
Pepperdine University School of Law	Buena Park
Phi Alpha Delta Law Fraternity	Los Angeles
Phi Alpha Delta Law Fraternity International	Studio City
Phi Alpha Delta Law Fraternity International	Westwood
Plant Engineering Society	Los Angeles
Pomona Valley Bar Association	Claremont
Power Rentals	Los Angeles
Riverside county District Attorney's Office	Riverside
Ropers, Majeski, Kohn, Bentley, Wagner & Kane	Santa Cruz
San Bernardino County Bar	San Bernardino
San Bernardino County Bar Association	Ontario
San Diego Apartment Association	Palm Springs
San Diego County Bar Association	San Diego
San Fernando Valley Bar Association	Encino
San Fernando Valley Bar Association	Van Nuys
San Fernando Valley Bar Association	Woodland Hills
San Francisco Bar Association	San Francisco
San Luis Obispo County Bar	Lompoc
Santa Barbara Bar Association	Goleta
Santa Clara County Bar Association	Santa Clara
Santa Clara County Bar Association	San Jose
Santa Clara University	Santa Clara
Santa Clarita Bar-Lawyer Referral Srvc. Exec. Committee	San Jose
Santa Fe Railway Company	Los Angeles
Santa Monica Bar Association	Santa Monica
Santa Monica Bay District Bar Assoc.	Marina del Rey
Society of California Accountants	Beverly Hills
Sonoma County Bar Association	Los Robles
Southwestern Univ. School of Law	Los Angeles

	State Bar of CA.-Economics of Law Practice Sect.	Los Angeles
	State Bar of CA-Law Office Management Sect.	Los Angeles
	State Bar of CA-Law Office Management Sect.	Monterey
	State Bar of CA-Law Practice Management Sect.	Anaheim
	State Bar of CA-Law Practice Management Sect.	Los Angeles
	State Bar of CA-Law Practice Management Sect.	San Francisco
	State Bar of CA-Standing Comm. on Senior Lawyers	Anaheim
	State Bar of CA-Standing Comm. on Senior Lawyers	San Diego
	State Bar of California	Fresno
	State Bar of California	San Francisco
	State Bar of California	San Diego
	State Bar of California	Monterey
	State Bar of California	Los Angeles
	State Bar of California-Economics of Law	Monterey
	State Bar of California-Economics Section	Monterey
	State Bar of California-General Practice Sect.	Los Angeles
	State Bar of California-General Practice Sect.	Sacramento
	State Bar of California-Senior Lawyers Sect.	Monterey
	State Bar of California-Senior Lawyers Sect.	San Diego
	State Bar of California-Senior Lawyers Sect.	Long Beach
	State Bar of Florida	Los Angeles
	South Bay Bar Association	Torrance
	Southern CA. Society of Assoc. Executives	City of Industry
	Southern CA. Society of Assoc. Executives	Newport Beach
	Southern CA. Society of Assoc. Executives	Pomona
	Superstars	Los Angeles
	Superior Educational Advancement Co.	Los Angeles
	Tri-County Court Reporters Assoc.	San Luis Obispo
	US Department of Commerce	Los Angeles
	United States Court Reporters Association	San Diego
	Univ of Calif. Santa Barbara Alumni	Santa Barbara
	Univ. of California. Los Angeles	Westwood
	University of California Extension-CLE	Beverly Hills
	University of Southern CA. Law Center	Los Angeles
	Van Camp & Johnson	Sacramento
	Ventura County Bar Association	Oxnard
	Ventura County Bar Association	Ventura
	West Orange County Bar Assoc.	Huntington Beach
	Western Conference of Association Executives	Anaheim
	Westwood Bar Association	Westwood
	Whittier Law School	Costa Mesa
	Women Lawyers of Long Beach	Long Beach
	WORLDPORT L.A.	San Pedro
Colorado	ABA-Law Practice Management Section	Keystone
	American Bar Association	Vail
	American Association of Attorney-CPAs	Aspen
	American Association of Attorney-CPAs	Vail
	Colorado BA Nat'l. Practice Inst.	Denver

	Colorado Bar Association	Colorado Springs
	Colorado Bar Association-CLE	Denver
	Colorado Bar Association-Sole/Small Firm Section	Denver
	Colorado State Bar	Golden
	Continuing Legal Education in Colorado, Inc.	Denver
	Denver Bar Association	Denver
	Lawyers Mutual Insurance Company	La Jolla
	National Practice Institute	Denver
	Network Affiliates, Inc.	Vail
	Professional Education Institute	Golden
Connecticut	Connecticut Bar Assoc. Law Office Economics Committee	Meriden
	Connecticut Bar Association	Meriden
	Hartford County Bar Association	Hartford
District of Columbia	American Bar Association	Washington
	College of Law Practice Management	Washington
	D.C.Bar-Law Office Management & Economics Section	Washington
	District of Columbia Bar	Washington
	Georgetown University Law Center	Washington
	Hispanic National Bar Association	Washington
	U.S. Chamber of Commerce & Department of State	Washington
Delaware	Delaware Bar Association	Rehovett Beach
	American Corporate Council Association	Dover
Florida	ABA-Comm. on Opportunities for Minorities in the Profession	Orlando
	ABA-Commission on Inter-American Affairs	Miami
	ABA-ELP	Orlando
	ABA Economics of Law Practice Sec.	Miami
	ABA Economics of Law Practice Section	Tampa
	ABA Law Practice Management Section	Lake Buena Vista
	ABA Law Practice Management Section	Miami
	Academy of Florida Elder Law Attorneys, Inc.	Long Boat Key
	Association of Legal Administrators	Orlando
	Carlton, Fields, Ward, Emmanuel, Smith & Cutler, P.A.	Naples
	Florida Bar	Orlando
	Florida Bar Solo & Small Firm Special Committee	Clearwater
	Florida Bar Solo & Small Firm Special Committee	Miami
	Florida Bar Administrators & Managing Partners	Orlando
	Florida Bar Association	Miami
	Florida Bar Association	Tampa
	Florida Bar Association-Elder Law Attorneys, Inc.	Long Boat Key
	Florida Bar CLE	Orlando

www.Foonberglaw.com

	Florida State Bar Assoc.-Economics & Management of Law Practice Section	Tampa
	Henderson, Franklin, Stames, & Hold	Fort Meyers
	Inter-American Bar Association	Miami
	Sarasota County Bar Association	Sarasota
	State Bar of Florida	Clearwater
	State Bar of Florida	Tampa/Miami
	Transportation Lawyers Association	Orlando
	The Group	Lake Buena Vista
Georgia	ABA-House of Delegates	Atlanta
	ABA-Law Practice Management Section	Atlanta
	ABA-Senior Lawyers Division	Atlanta
	ABA-Section of Economics	Atlanta
	American Assoc. Of Attorneys/CPAs	Atlanta
	American Bar Association-ELP	Atlanta
	American Bar Association	Atlanta
	Atlanta Council of Young Lawyers	Atlanta
	Institute of CLE in Georgia	Atlanta
	Balch & Bingham Firm	Calloway Gardens
	State Bar of Georgia	Savannah
Hawaii	ABA-Economics of Law Practice Section	Honolulu
	American Assoc. of Attorneys/CPAs	Kamuela
	American Assoc. of Attorneys/CPAs	Kahuela
	American Assoc. of Attorneys/CPAs	Kamuela
	American Bar Association	Honolulu
	Hawaii State Bar Association	Honolulu
	Hawaii State Bar Association	Kona
	Hawaii State Bar Association	Maui
	Hawaii State Bar Association	Waikiki
	Hawaii Bar Association CLE	Honolulu
	Hawaii Inst. Continuing Legal Ed.	Honolulu
	Maui County Bar Association	Maui
	West Hawaii Bar Association	Kona
Iowa	Iowa State Bar Association	Ames
	Iowa State Bar Association	Des Moines
	Iowa State Bar Association	Wes De Moines
Idaho	Idaho Bar Association	Boise
	Idaho Bar Foundation	Sun Valley
	California Rental Association	Sun Valley
	State Bar of Utah	Sun Valley
Illinois	ABA Assoc. of Professional Responsibility Lawyers	Chicago
	ABA General Practice, Solo & Small Firm Section	Chicago
	ABA Law Practice Management Section	
	ABA Law Student Division	Chicago
	ABA Section of Economics of Law Practice	Chicago

	ABA Senior Lawyers Division	Chicago
	ABA Special Committee on Solo & Small Firm Practitioners	Chicago
	ABA Young Lawyers Section	Chicago
	American Assoc. of Attorneys/CPAs	Chicago
	American Bar Association	Chicago
	American Medical Association	Chicago
	Decalogue Society of Lawyers	Chicago
	Illinois Assoc. of Attorneys/CPAs	Chicago
	Illinois Bar Association	Chicago
	Illinois State Bar Association	St. Charles
	Institute of Continuing Legal Education	Chicago
	John Marshall Law School	Chicago
	Lake County Bar Association	Lake Forest
	National Association of Bar Counsel	Chicago
	Northwest Suburban Bar Association	Des Plaines
	Young Lawyers Section ABA	Chicago
	University of Michigan Law School	Chicago
Indiana	Barrett & McNagny	Fort Wayne
	Indiana BA Continuing Legal Educ.	Indianapolis
		Bloomington
		French Lick
	Indiana Continuing Legal Education Forum	Indianapolis
	ISBA Women in the Law Committee	French Lick
Iowa	Iowa State Bar	Des Moines
Kansas	Kansas Bar Association	Overland Park
		Wichita
	KBA Law Office Economics	Overland Park
	KBA Young Lawyers Section	Overland Park
Kentucky	Chase College of Law	Covington
	Cincinnati Bar Assoc. Young Lawyers Section	Covington
	Greenebaum Boone Treitz Maggiolo Reisz & Brown	Louisville
	Lawyers Mutual Insurance Company of Kentucky Inc.	Louisville
	Northern Kentucky Univ. Sch. of Law	Covington
	University of Kentucky	Lexington
	Univ. of Kentucky College of Law Office of CLE	Lexington
Louisiana	ABA Center for Professional Responsibility	New Orleans
	ABA Consortium on Legal Services & Public	New Orleans
	ABA Law Practice Management Committee	New Orleans
	ABA Law Practice Management Section	New Orleans
	ABA Law Student Division	New Orleans
	ABA New Orleans National Organization of Bar Counsel	New Orleans
	ABA Section of Economics of Law Practice	New Orleans

	ABA Section of Family Law	New Orleans
	ABA Young Lawyers Division	New Orleans
	American Assoc. of Attorney CPAs	New Orleans
	American Bar Association	New Orleans
	American Bar Association-ELP	New Orleans
	Law Firm Profit Report	New Orleans
Maine	Economics of Law Practice Committee	Augusta
	Maine State Bar Association	Augusta
	Maine State Bar Association	Bangor
Maryland	ABA Law Practice Management Section	Baltimore
	ABA Young Lawyers Division	Baltimore
	American Bar Association	Baltimore
	Bar Association of Montgomery County	Rockville
	Daily Record	Baltimore
	Maryland State Bar Association	Baltimore
	Whiteford, Taylor & Preston	Baltimore
Massachusetts	Maine State Bar Association	Bangor
	ABA Section of Economics of Law Practice	Boston
	American Assoc. of Attorney-CPAs	Boston
Michigan	Detroit Bar Association	Detroit
	Detroit Bar Association	Southfield
	Detroit Bar Association Lawyers Weekly	Southfield
	ICLE	Ann Arbor
	Institute of Continuing Legal Education	Grand Rapids
	Michigan Institute for CLE	Detroit
	State Bar of Michigan	Detroit
	State Bar of Michigan	Lansing
	State Bar of Michigan Economics of Law Practice Com.	Detroit
	State Bar of Michigan ICLE	Detroit
	State Bar of Michigan Law Student Section	Lansing
	State Bar of Michigan Young Lawyers Section	Detroit
	State Bar of Michigan Young Lawyers Section	Lansing
Minnesota	Minnesota Lawyers Mutual Insurance Company	Minneapolis
	Minnesota State Bar Association	Duluth
	Minnesota Stat Bar Association	Minneapolis
Missouri	ABA Law Practice Management Section	Kansas City
	ABA Section of Economics of Law Practice	Kansas City
	American Bar Association	Kansas City
	Assoc. of Professional Responsibility Lawyers	Kansas City
	Eastern Jackson county Bar Association	Blue Springs
	Missouri Bar Association	Kansas City
	Missouri Bar Association	Springfield
	Missouri Bar Association	St. Louis
	National Institute	Kansas City

	Paule, Camazine & Blumenthal	St. Louis
	University of MO, K.C.	Kansas City
Mississippi	Hinds County Bar Association	Jackson
Montana	CLE Student Bar Association Law School	Missoula
Nebraska	Nebraska State Bar Association	Lincoln
	NSBA Law Practice Management Section	Omaha
Nevada	American Assoc. of Attorney – CPAs	Las Vegas
	American Bar Association	Las Vegas
	California Rental Association	Las Vegas
	Economics of Law Practice Section/Young Lawyers Div.	Las Vegas
	Law Firm Profit Report	Las Vegas
	Live Oak CLE, Inc.	Las Vegas
	National Academy of Law, Ethics & Management, Inc.	Las Vegas
	Natnl. Affiliation of Durable Medical Equipment Companies	Las Vegas
	State Bar of Nevada	Las Vegas
	State Bar of Nevada	Reno
	State Bar of Nevada	Sparks
	State Bar of Nevada – CLE	Las Vegas
	State Bar of Nevada – CLE	Reno
	State Bar of Nevada – Young Lawyers Section	Las Vegas
	State Bar of Nevada – Young Lawyers Section	Reno
	United State Court Reporters Association	Las Vegas
	UNLV Boyd School of Law	Las Vegas
	Washoe County Bar Association	Reno
New Hampshire	NHBA Economics of Law Practice Committee	Concord
	NHBA Task Force on Small Firms & Solos	Waterville Valley
New Jersey	Essex County Bar General Practice Committee	West Orange
	ICLE Law Office & Management Committee	Atlantic City
	ICLE Law Office & Management Committee	Saddlebrook
	New Jersey ICLE	New Brunswick
	New Jersey SBA Resource Center for Law Office Mngmt.	New Brunswick
	New Jersey State Bar Association	Atlantic City
	New Jersey State Bar Association	Jamesburg
	New Jersey State Bar Association	Morristown
	New Jersey State Bar Foundation	New Brunswick
	NJSBA Young Lawyers Division	New Brunswick
	Philadelphia Bar Association	Atlantic City
New Mexico	ABA Section of Economics of Law Practice	Santa Fe
	American Bar Association	Albuquerque
	New Mexico Hispanic Bar Association	Albuquerque

	State Bar of New Mexico – CLE	Albuquerque
	State Bar of New Mexico – LPM Section	Albuquerque
	State Bar of Texas - Business Law Section	Santa Fe
	State Bar of Texas - Corporate Counsel Section	Santa Fe
	State Bar of Texas - Intellectual Property Law	Santa Fe
New York	ABA Economics of Law Practice Section	New York
	ABA General Practice, Solo & Small Firm Section	New York
	ABA Law Practice Management Section	New York
	ABA Senior Lawyers Division	New York
	ABA Young Lawyers Section	New York
	American Bar Association	New York
	Assoc. of the Bar of the City of NY – Comm. On Small Law Firm	New York
	Association of the Bar of the City of New York	New York
	Erie County Bar Foundation	Buffalo
	International Assoc. of Young Lawyers	New York
	Monroe County Bar Association	Rochester
	Nassau County Bar Association	Long Island
	Nassau County Bar Association	New York
	New York City Bar	NY
	New York State Bar	Syracuse
	New York State Trial Lawyers Institute	New York
	NYSBA Law Office Economics & Management	New York
	NYSBA Law Office Economics & Management	Syracuse
	Onondaga County Bar Associations	Syracuse
North Carolina	Campbell Univ.-North Carolina Bar	Pinehurst
	Campbell University Kenelm Foundation	Southern Pines
	Campbell University School of Law	Bules Creek
	No. Carolina Bar Association	Cary
	No. Carolina Bar Association	Raleigh
	Univ. of No. Carolina Law School	Chapel Hill
	Univ. of No. Carolina School of Law Student Bar Assoc.	Chapel Hill
	Wishart, Norris, Henninger & Pittman, P.A.	Bald Head Island
North Dakota	North Dakota Bar Association	Dickinson
	North Dakota Bar Association	Medora
Ohio	ABA Economics of Law Practice	Cleveland
	Bar Assoc. of Greater Cleveland	Cleveland
	Cincinnati Bar Association	Cincinnati
	Dayton Bar Association	Dayton
	Ohio CLE Institute	Cincinnati
	Ohio CLE Institute	Cleveland
	Ohio CLE Institute	Columbus
	Ohio State Bar Assoc. – CLE Institute	Cleveland
	Ohio State Bar Assoc. – CLE Institute	Columbus
	Ohio State Bar Association	Cleveland
	OSBA General Practice Section	Cleveland

	OSBA General Practice Section	Columbus
	OSBA Litigation Section	Huron
Oklahoma	Oklahoma Bar Association	Oklahoma City
	University of Oklahoma Law School	Norman
		Salem
		Salishan
Oregon	Multnomah County Bar Association	Portland
	National Practice Institute, Ins.	Portland
	Oregon BA Nat'l. Practice Institute	Portland
	Oregon State Bar Association	Portland
	Oregon State Bar Association	Vancouver
	Oregon State Bar Continuing Legal Education	Portland
	Premier Legal Education, Inc.	Portland
Pennsylvania	ABA Economics of Law Practice	Philadelphia
	ABA General Practice Section	Hershey
	ABA Law Practice Management Section	Philadelphia
	ABA Lawyers Alert Magazine	Hershey
	ABA New Lawyers in Practice Committee	Philadelphia
	ABA Solo & Small Firm Practitioners Division	Philadelphia
	Allegheny County Bar Association	Pittsburgh
	American Assoc. of Attorneys/CPAs	Philadelphia
	American Bar Assoc Law Student Div.	Lancaster
	American Bar Association	Philadelphia
	Law Student Division	Lancaster County
	National Bar Association	Philadelphia
	Pennsylvania BA Mid-Year Meeting	Scottsdale
	Pennsylvania Bar Institute	Hershey
	Pennsylvania Bar Institute	Hershey
	7th Natl. Cont. on Women in Law	Philadelphia
Rhode Island	Hinkley, Allen, Snyder & Comen	Providence
	Justinian Law School	Providence
	Rhode Island Bar Association	Providence
South Carolina	American Bar Association	Charleston
	American Bar Association – ELP	Charleston
	American Bar Association – SLD	Charleston
	College of Law Practice Management	Charleston
	NC State Bar Association	Myrtle Beach
	SCB Continuing Legal Education Division	Columbia
	SCB Real Estate Practices Section	Columbia
	SCB Section & Tax Law Section	Columbia
	SCB Senior Lawyers Division	Charleston
	SCB Solo & Small Firm Section	Charleston
	So. Carolina Assoc. of Legal Administrators	Columbia
	So. Carolina Bar Association	Charleston
	So. Carolina Bar Association	Columbia
	Univ. of So. Carolina Law School	Columbia

South Dakota	American Bar Association, ELP	Rapid City
	SDBA Committee on Continuing Legal Education	Rapid City
	SDBA Committee on Continuing Legal Education	Sioux Falls
	South Dakota Bar Association	Rapid City
	South Dakota Bar Association	Sioux Falls
	South Dakota Bar Association	Vermillion
	South Dakota Bar Association CLE	Rapid City
Tennessee	American Bar Association	Knoxville
	American Bar Association	Nashville
	American Bar Association	Memphis
	NALFMA / NALEM	Nashville
	Nashville Bar Association	Nashville
	Professional Education Institute	Nashville
	Supreme Court of TN – Board of Prof. Responsibility	Memphis
	Supreme Court of TN – Board of Prof. Responsibility	Nashville
Texas	ABA Section of Economics of Law Practice	Dallas
	ABA Standing Comm. on Solo & Small Firm Practitioners	San Antonio
	American Association of Attorney-CPAs	Dallas
	American Association of Attorney-CPAs	Houston
	American Bar Assoc.-ELP	Dallas
	American Bar Assoc. Law Student Div.	Dallas
	American Bar Association	Houston
	American Bar Association	San Antonio
	American Corporate Counsel Association	Houston
	Austin Young Lawyers Association	Austin
	Baylor University	Dallas
	Baylor University	Houston
	College of Law Practice Management	San Antonio
	HBA Assoc. of Legal Administrators	Houston
	HBA Law Practice Management Section	Houston
	Houston Bar Association	Houston
	Houston Bar Young Lawyers Assoc.	Houston
	Houston Young Lawyers Association	Houston
	Institute of Continuing Legal Education	Dallas
	Live Oak CLE	Corpus Christi
	Live Oak CLE	El Paso
	Live Oak CLE	Laredo
	Live Oak CLE	San Antonio
	SMU	Dallas
	So. Methodist Univ. School of Law	Dallas
	So. Methodist University	Dallas
	So. Texas College of Law	Houston
	St. Mary's University CLE	Corpus Christi
	St. Mary's University CLE	Laredo
	St. Mary's University CLE	San Antonio
	State Bar of Texas	Austin
	State Bar of Texas	Dallas
	State Bar of Texas	Fort Worth

	State Bar of Texas	Houston
	State Bar of Texas	San Antonio
	State Bar of Texas – Professional Development	San Antonio
	State Bar of Texas Convention – PEER Comm.	Houston
	Texas Rental Assoc. Annual Convention	San Antonio
	Texas Rental Association	Corpus Christi
	Texas Rental Assoc. Annual Convention	San Antonio
	Univ. of Texas Law School CLE	Austin
	Univ. of Texas School of Law	Austin
	University of Houston Law Center	Houston
Utah	ABA Law Practice Management Section	Salt Lake City
	ABA Young Lawyers Division	Salt Lake City
	State Bar of Utah	Salt Lake City
	Utah State Bar CLE	Salt Lake City
Vermont	Vermont Bar Association	Burlington
	New York State Bar Association	Manchester Village
Virginia	American Bar Association	Williamsburg
	Potomac Assoc. of Attorney CPAs	Alexandria
	Virginia State Bar	Virginia Beach
	Virginia State Bar – General Practice Section	Virginia Beach
Washington	ABA Law Practice Management Section	Seattle
	ABA Law Practice Management Section	Stevenson
	King County BA Natl. Practice Inst.	Seattle
	National Practice Institute	Seattle
	Premier Legal Education, Inc.	Seattle
	Univ. of Wash.-Women's Law Caucus	Seattle
	Washington State Assoc. Attys/CPAs	Seattle
	Washington State Bar Assoc. ABA	Seattle
	Washington State Bar Association	Seattle
	Washington State Bar Association	Spokane
	Washington State Bar Association	Tacoma
	Washington State Trial Lawyers	Seattle
Washington, D.C.	ABA ELP	Washington, D.C.
	ABA Young Lawyers Economics Committee	Washington, D.C.
	ABA Young Lawyers Division	Washington, D.C.
	ABA Young Lawyers Section	Washington, D.C.
	American Bar Association	Washington, D.C.
	American Bar Association	Washington, D.C.
	D.C. Maryland Bar Association	Washington, D.C.
	Georgetown University Law Center	Washington, D.C.
	Hispanic Bar Association-ABA	Washington, D.C.
	U.S. Chamb. Comm & U.S.Brazil Bus.	Washington, D.C.
	Washington, D.C. Bar Association	Washington, D.C.
West Virginia	Univ. of W. Virginia Law School	Morgantown
	W. Virginia Bar Association C.L.E.	Charleston

	W. Virginia Bar Association C.L.E.	Morgantown
	West Virginia Bar Association	Charleston
	West Virginia Bar Association	Morgantown
Wisconsin	State Bar of Wisconsin	Eau Claire
	State Bar of Wisconsin	Madison
	State Bar of Wisconsin	Milwaukee
	State Bar of Wisconsin – Law Practice Section	Madison
	State Bar of Wisconsin – General Practice Section	Madison
	Wisconsin Association of Legal Administrators	Madison
	Wisconsin Bar Association	Madison
	Wisconsin Lawyers Mutual	Eau Claire
	Wisconsin Lawyers Mutual	Madison
	Wisconsin Lawyers Mutual	Milwaukee
Wyoming	Univ. of Wyoming Law School CLE	Laramie
	Wyoming Bar Association	Laramie
AFRICA	International Bar Association	Nairobi, Kenya
	International Bar Association	Durban, South Africa
ALBANIA	American Bar Association	Tirana
ANTARCTICA	Antarctica Sports Federation	King George Island
	Antarctica Sports Federation	Orm Bay
ARGENTINA	Argentine American Chamber of Commerce, Inc.	Buenos Aires
	1st Natl. Congress/North Amer. Business	Buenos Aires
	Inter American Bar Association	Buenos Aires
AUSTRIA	Greiter, Pegger, Kofler & Partner	Innsbruck
BAHAMAS	American Bar Association	Nassau
	Inter American Bar Association	Nassau
BARBADOS	Inter American Bar Association	Georgetown
BELGIUM	American Assoc. of Attorney/CPAs	Brussels
	Claes & Partners	Brussels
BERMUDA	Daniel J. Cantor & Company	Southampton
BRAZIL	Brazil U.S. Business Conference	Sao Paulo
	Rio Internacional	Rio de Janiero
	Inter American Bar Association	Sao Paulo
BULGARIA	American Bar Association	Sofia
	Balkans Law Forum	Sofia
	Bulgarian Bar Association	Sofia
	International Bar Association	Sofia

CANADA	ABA-ELP	Banff Springs, Alberta
	American Assoc. of Attorney-CPAs	Vancouver, BC
	American Bar Association	Toronto, Ontario
	American Bar Association	Montreal Quebec
	British Columbia CLE	Vancouver, BC
	California Court Reporters Association	Vancouver, BC
	Canadian Bar Association	Calgary
	Canadian Bar Association	Halifax, Nova Scotia
	Canadian Bar Association	Montreal, Quebec
	Canadian Bar Association	St. John, New Brunswick
	Canadian Bar Association	Toronto, Ontario
	Canadian Bar Association	Vancouver, BC
	Canadian Bar Association – P.E.I. Branch	Charlottetown
	CLE Society	Vancouver, BC
	College of Law Practice Management	Toronto, Ontario
	ICLE Law Office & Management Committee	New Brunswick
	Legal Education Society of Alberta	Calgary, Alberta
	Law Society of British Columbia CLE	Vancouver, BC
	Law Society of Newfoundland CLE	St. John's Newfoundland
	Legal Education Society of Alberta	Banff, Alberta
	Law Society of Manitoba	Winnipeg
	Law Society of New Brunswick	St. John, New Brunswick
	Law Society of Saskatchewan	Regina
CHINA	Peking University School of Law	Beijing
COSTA RICA	United Nations Space Conference	San Jose
FRANCE	IBA General Practice Section	Paris
	International Bar Association	Cannes
	International Assoc. of Young Lawyers	Vichy
	International Bar Association	Paris
	International Space University	Strasburg
MEXICO	ABA-Law Practice Management Section	Cancun
	American Bar Association	Cancun
	Inter-American Bar Association	Acapulco
	American Immigration Lawyer Association	Mazatlan
NETHERLANDS	American Assoc. of Attorney CPAs	Amsterdam
NEW ZEALAND	New Zealand Law Society, Auckland Charter	Auckland
PANAMA	Inter. American Bar Association	Panama City
PUERTO RICO	American Assoc. of Attorney CPAs	San Juan
	ABA ELP	Bayamon

SOUTH AFRICA	All Africa Law Forum	Durban
UNITED KINGDOM	ABA Common Law Common Bond	London
	American Assoc. of Attorney CPAs	London
	Law Society of England	London
	Interntl. Bar Assoc. – General Practice Section	London
U.S. VIRGIN ISLANDS	American Bar Association	St. Thomas

A-5
Defining Practice Development
and Lawyer Marketing

The terms, "lawyer marketing" and "practice development" are relatively new terms applied to relatively old concepts. It will probably require a generation or two before lawyers can agree on definitions for these two terms.

Some people use the terms lawyer marketing and practice development interchangeably. Some people use the two terms to describe two totally different things to different lawyers or different professionals or different clients.

I believe there is some value in recognizing that in the English language the same word or words can have many different meanings, depending upon the context in which they are used.

For purposes of this book and, indeed, for purposes of using the techniques of this book, it is probably helpful to give these two terms slightly different meanings, although you could interchange the words if that makes you feel more comfortable. Over simplified, practice development is deciding where you want to go, and lawyer marketing is the things you have to do to get there.

Practice development is the "overall picture." It is the *process* of thinking about where you want to go with your practice and how you get there. It includes obtaining the necessary information about yourself and your practice, your clients and potential clients, and the people in your office and out of your office. It is both historic and futuristic. It includes market forces and trends, supply and demand, and the known and estimated.

If you were in college studying economics, you might call practice development macro economics.

The practice development concepts and techniques of this book are basically valid for all professionals. I have given practice development programs for physicians, dentists, architects, health-science professionals, office administrators for various professions, CPAs and attorney-CPAs. The basic concept of practice development is fundamentally the same for all professions simply because we are dealing with human beings and those who render important personal services to those human beings. Although this book is intended primarily for attorneys, the reader could lend it to another professional (or give it as a gift) and the other professional would tell you that almost everything in the book also applies to his or her profession.

Lawyer Marketing, for purposes of this book, would be considered "micro economics" rather than "macro economics." Lawyer marketing includes the *techniques* for developing our practice. Lawyer marketing is *HOW* we develop our practice. It is *WHAT* we do and *WHERE* we do it and *WHO* does it and *WHEN* we do it and *WHY* we do it.

It may also be helpful for you to think of *SELLING* as trying to convince new and old clients to buy more of the services you already provide and to think of *MARKETING* as trying to modify your existing services or to create new services to meet the actual or perceived present or future needs of new and existing clients.

For the purposes of this book, it is helpful to think of practice development as the overall process of systematically using the techniques which lead to more and/or better clients.

It is also useful to think of *TECHNIQUES* as being the tools or methods which people consciously and intentionally use for successful practice development. The techniques are oral and written and visual. The techniques taught in this book are either oral, written, or visual, and will consist of doing something or refraining from doing something.

Again, you may, if you wish, use the terms interchangeably or use them as I have in this book.

Use of the word "Sales" in practice development.

I personally do not like the use of the word "sales" in the process of client development.

To me (and many clients and professionals) the word "sales" may connote hustlers, con-artists, fast-buck high commission sleazy sales people and a host of other absolutely negative connotations.

The word "sales" may or may not be appropriate in the world of used cars, and refrigerators, but it does not belong in a profession.

The word "sales" is often used by non lawyers to appeal to those who look upon the practice of law as a business to make money any way legally permissible, rather than a profession putting the client's interest first.

On the other hand, you may feel that the word "sales" accurately describes the way you practice law and you may be perfectly comfortable using it.

A-6
More on Why This Book Has Been Written

Again, I have written this book because there is a need for it.

This book contains a large variety of specific techniques and tools for increasing and upgrading any professional practice.

This book is not theoretical. It is a compendium based upon real-life experiences of real-life attorneys and their clients. Most of the techniques are based upon my personal practice-building techniques. Some of these techniques I invented. Some I learned from my accounting practice and some from my law practice. Many I learned from other lawyers and professionals in the course of my lecture activities over the past three decades in more than 300 programs in every state and many foreign countries.

From the 1960s to the present, I've been helping Bar Associations and law schools with programs on "How to Start and Build a Law Practice." In the late 1970s, more and more experienced lawyers began to come to these programs originally intended for new lawyers. I then began to recognize the need for materials for lawyers who needed to, or who wanted to, upgrade and/or increase their practices. In the late '70s, I began participating in Bar programs on lawyer marketing. Previously, there was nowhere for the practicing lawyer to get help based on proven techniques which would be applicable in small law firms. In the 1980's, 1999's and into the 21st Century, I have presented programs entitled as this book, "How to Get & Keep Good Clients."

The techniques that work for a small firm are always doable for a large firm, but not vice versa. I've seen lawyers who never started a law practice give well-intentioned but meaningless advice on starting a law practice. I've seen mega-firm lawyers give well intentioned but worthless advice to small firms on getting and keeping clients. The larger firms were preoccupied with which clients *not* to take. The smaller firms were preoccupied with getting whatever good clients they could.

I've seen books on how lawyers should market, written by people who themselves never were lawyers nor did practice development for a law firm. I've seen self styled legal marketing experts who, in reality, were learning from the lawyers rather than teaching them. Some "consultants" have any little or no interest in helping sole practitioners or small firms because the fee potential isn't high enough.

Because the small firm and sole practitioner had been left to flounder, I decided to write this book.

Many lawyers came up to me following my talks on practice development to share their successes (and failures) with me. I quickly made notes of these conversations in order to use them where appropriate in my talks and to include them in this book. I would also test these techniques in my practice to determine whether they worked for me.

I have had the good fortune to be exposed to these ideas over a period of four decades. In this book, I am simply putting these various concepts together in one place for the busy lawyer to read, learn and put to use.

A-7
How to Start and Build
a Law Practice

My first book, *How to Start and Build a Law Practice*, now in the 5th edition, contains about 150 chapters. It covers most of what a brand new lawyer needs to know, ranging from how to file papers in a file folder to how to set fees to cash flow management.

The book contains a large section on getting clients, and many of the basic precepts set forth for new lawyers also apply to experienced lawyers. Accordingly, some of what is contained in that book is carried over to this book. That book is intended as an over-all practice management book for new lawyers, with a small section on getting clients. This book is purely a practice development or marketing book. Many of the things touched upon in that book are more fully developed in this book.

How to Start and Build a *Law Practice,* has two most interesting distinctions:

1. It is the all-time best seller of the American Bar Association, having been first printed in 1976 and updated in 1984, 1991, 1999 and 2004; and

2. It is the most stolen book from law libraries in the United States. It can be obtained from the American Bar Association, Law Practice Management Section www.abanet.org or www.Foonberglaw.com.

It is also available as a PDF download on the internet.

A-8
How to Use This Book

This book was designed to be read and used by busy people. Each chapter of the book is designed to stand alone as a self-contained "bite sized" unit. You can read any single chapter of this book at one sitting without having to read any chapter before or after the chapter you are reading.

In order to do that, there is unavoidably some repetition of information, but the end result is a meaningful and useful tool for practice development rather than a book to be stuck on a shelf and read "when I find time."

You can easily read a single chapter (or more, if you wish) over a cup of coffee or during TV commercials. Each chapter can be photocopied by you for your personal reading and can also be distributed to others you wish to inform. I wrote the book *How* to *Start and Build* a *Law Practice* and the prior editions of this book in this format and received many compliments and no complaints. Accordingly, I am using the same format for this edition of the book.

What This Book Will And Will Not Cover

If you use this book, you will get more clients, more fees and have better cash flow. You will have fewer bad cases and fewer bad accounts receivable. You will have fewer or no Bar complaints and fewer or no malpractice complaints.

You still have to produce the legal services after you get the clients and cases.

This book will not convert gross fees into net profits. To produce good legal work and net profit requires good people, good systems and good equipment or, in short, good old fashioned practice management. This aspect is beyond the scope of this book. Therefore, be careful to realize that just bringing in new clients and business may not produce net profits if you can't economically handle the business. You may do much better financially by sending some of your newly acquired business to other law firms. You may or may not receive a forwarding or referral fee, depending on your particular local rules and regulations.

A-9
The Format of This Book

This book is structured so that you can read just the part(s) you are interested in at any particular time.

This book is intended for use by busy people who don't have the several hours it would take to read and study this entire book leisurely in one sitting. They don't have the many hours to think about which techniques they want to use and how and when to use them.

I have used the same format for the prior editions of this book as I used for my book, *How to Start and Build* a *Law Practice.* Each chapter is intended to stand on its own, without prior knowledge of or reference to other chapters. The reader can read a single chapter or several chapters at a time. In a very few instances, there is a close connection between one chapter and another, and I have tried to place such chapters close to each other in the book. In order that each chapter might stand alone, it is sometimes necessary to refer briefly to a concept or technique which is explained in greater detail in another place in the book. This necessitates a limited amount of duplication of information.

This book is available in two printing formats-traditional hard binding and soft cover.

This book is also available as a download and is also available as an 8-hour CD series which can also be downloaded.

Visit www.Foonberglaw.com or www.abanet.org for more information.

A-10
Getting Maximum Value from This Book
From Others in the Firm by Allowing Them
to Use the Techniques They Want to Use

This book won't be of help to anyone if it sits on a shelf. This book should be used by:

1. You.
2. Your secretary/assistant.
3. Your partners and their staff.
4. Your associates and their staff.
5. All staff of the firm whether or not they have client contact.

You should adopt those concepts which you like and ignore those which you don't. Others in your firm should do the same. These concepts can be used by an individual or by many different people in the office. It is not necessary for every person to adopt all of the concepts. One size will not fit all. You could probably use all of the concepts of this book without conflicts. You can even add concepts as you go along.

By allowing others to use the techniques they enjoy using, you will be observing the old adage: "If it ain't fun, it won't get done."

I predict that after a while most of the people in the office will be using most of the ideas. They will want the personal feeling of pride when they learn they can do it. If you try to force the people in your firm to use only those techniques which appeal to you, they may not use any of the techniques.

A-11
Feminism and the Author's Writing Style

Professionally, I am a feminist. I believe in equal pay for equal work and for equal advancement opportunity. I am also a realist. There are law firms and, indeed, clients who do not give female lawyers equal pay or equal opportunity. Feminism cuts both ways. Women may prefer a female lawyer for a divorce case. This is a fact of life. My personal views (or yours) on the role of males or females in the home or anywhere outside of the legal profession is beyond the scope of this book and is irrelevant to the purposes of the book.

If you are a feminist, I would advise that you not preach your points of view to judges, clients or potential clients. If they are not in sympathy with your point of view, you may lose a client, a potential client or a case by preaching to them. There are some exceptions, of course (see chapters on "Minorities" and "Lawyers' Reference Service").

Notwithstanding my admittedly feminist point of view, my writing style may appear to some to be sexist. I may refer to a client or a lawyer as he or she. I use the word that looks or sounds best to me in the presentation. Please do not infer any sexism or other bias based on my language usage. For the record, the masculine includes the feminine, and vice versa.

A-12
The Price of This Book

I have absolutely no qualms about charging for the information in this book. I attended a summer course at Harvard Law School. On the last day of class, the professor (who is well known) announced: "This concludes the course. I am no longer available as a professor to answer questions for free. From this moment on, I am available as a consultant at my usual hourly rate."

Over the years I have given, and continue to give, many thousands of hours of my time to the profession and to individual lawyers for free. I have written and given away many books and articles over the years in my sincere attempt to raise the level of legal services for both the public and the lawyer. I will continue to do so. This book, however, is not for free. There is no reason why it should be. This is a book which can produce huge fees for you or your law firm over the years. The information in this book took almost four decades to acquire and is the result of many hours "on the road" in every state of the United States and many foreign countries and on every continent. It also is the result of hundreds of hours of writing time. The concepts in this book work. These techniques are of great value and the book is priced accordingly.

My son graduated from Massachusetts Institute of Technology. MIT is consistently the most expensive college in the United States. Occasionally it falls second to Bennington College in Vermont.

When my son was interviewing at prospective colleges, I asked if the tuition price at MIT was so high as a matter of prestige. The reply was "No." I was told that each year the school surveys the starting salary of its newly graduated students. The tuition for the next year is set at 50% of the average starting salary of their graduates. There was a direct relationship between cost and benefit. There is also a direct relationship between cost and benefit in the price of this book.

This book probably cost you between 20 and 40 minutes of your time at your hourly rate or even less if you purchased the downloadable version. Each technique in this book will cost you a tiny percentage of its potential value. Anyone of these techniques could produce one or more clients that will benefit you and your family for a lifetime. It is worth many times the price charged.

A-13
Reproduction of Chapters of This Book

It is a condition of the agreement between the author and the publishers of this book that material in this book may be reprinted in Bar Association journals and other professional and legal publications, on the following terms:

1. No more than one chapter may be reproduced in any publication in anyone publishing period of that publication.
2. The publication reprinting the chapter must be the official publication Journal, bulletin, newsletter, etc.) of one of the following:

   a. Bar Association
   b. Bar Association subdivision (committee, section, etc.)
   c. Law Schools, Universities or other educational or professional institutions qualified under Section 501 (c)(3) or 501 (c)(6) of the Internal Revenue Code

3. Written permission must be obtained from either the author or the publisher.
4. The reprint must acknowledge the copyright and indicate that permission has been received.
5. The reprint must indicate "available from www.Foonberglaw.com as a download or CD series."

How to Get and Keep Good Clients, Copyright 2007
Jay G Foonberg, Beverly Hills, Calif.
www.Foonberglaw.com

Chapter B
Why and How the Lawyer Must Consider Practice Development

B-1
Use Marketing Techniques That
You Are Comfortable With
"If It Is Fun, It Will Get Done"

A menu in a *fine* restaurant may *list* dozens, even hundreds, of individual items on it. Each of the *selections* may be superbly prepared and reasonably *priced,* but you will select the items you like or think you will like within the *price* range you wish to pay. Other people with different tastes may select other items to suit their particular tastes. You can analyze the techniques in this book as you would a menu. Choose those techniques that appeal to you and leave the other techniques to other people. Eventually, you or others in your *firm* can try all the available items.

In this book I have recommended hundreds of simple, inexpensive things you or your staff can do for practice development. Some of these techniques may intrigue you; some may simply be reinforcement of what you are already doing. Some of these techniques may actually be distasteful or unsettling to you. Some may seem like fun.

You are unique, your clients are unique, your practice *is* unique. You are a special person; your clients are special people. You don't want to do anything to alienate your existing clients or potential clients.

For purposes of this book, let's assume that all of the above is 100 percent accurate.

As already stressed, you should use only those techniques you are comfortable with. Don't do anything that you really don't want to do, or that makes you feel "funny" or uncomfortable.

Similarly if a member of your staff expresses a feeling of uneasiness or distaste, respect it. An unhappy staff member or lawyer who does not want to do what they have been ordered to do will find a way to sabotage your efforts.

Some lawyers may feel uncomfortable sending Christmas cards to clients but not feel uncomfortable sending "season's greetings" cards.

Lawyers have told me that they would feel uncomfortable doing full blown television *advertising* but would not feel uncomfortable sponsoring a "grant" making possible a program of the Boston Symphony Orchestra on the local public television station.

A lawyer with 55 years of practice experience attending one of my programs told me that he would not feel comfortable sending out a formal engraved announcement to potential clients of a seminar on new laws to be held at a hotel ballroom. The same lawyer told me that he would not feel uncomfortable sending a simple postcard to existing clients inviting them to a Saturday morning seminar on new laws at the public conference room of a local savings bank.

I can only recommend that you start by using those techniques which you have successfully used in the past but which might have gotten lost in the shuffle of a busy law practice. After you have begun thinking in a practice development mode, you can try a few new techniques which seem comfortable and natural or even fun for you. Then you should experiment with a few new techniques which might seem "avant-garde" and see if you like them. Discontinue the ones that don't work for you or are too much effort, and then continue the ones that do work for you.

Remember, the application of only *one* marketing technique may get you the one client or the one case which will dramatically increase your net income.

B-2
Why Practice Development
Is Essential

1. To ensure firm stability and survival anticipating the death or retirement of the firm's "client-getter" or "rainmaker."
2. To ensure the firm's client-getters or rainmakers that they or their estate will get paid what they have coming when they retire or die.
3. To be able to compete in an environment where there is less and less legal work available for more and more attorneys.
4. To compete for clients and survive in the face of exponential expansion by the large law firms.
5. To ensure firm stability and survival in the event of the loss of a principal client or referrer of clients.
6. To upgrade the practice so that you can do the kind of legal work you really prefer to do for the kinds of clients you really prefer to do work for.
7. To be able to get rid of the clients and work you really don't like.
8. To be able to get the clients who pay their bills.
9. To enable you to get the kinds of clients and cases which give you more free time and money.
10. To ensure replacement clients for those clients who cease to be clients for a variety of reasons not caused by the lawyer.
11. To provide security to the lawyer with a client following. Lawyers without client followings are vulnerable in an age of brutal economic competition within law firms and between law firms.

B-3
Practice Development Leads to a Higher Level of Professional Practice

"If I do all these things you recommend, when will I practice law?" Often a lawyer will ask "How can you devote so much time to marketing?"

"When do you practice law?" When I hear that question, I know I am dealing with a lawyer who has never successfully marketed himself or his firm to the maximum potential.

In my opinion, a lawyer who devotes time to practice development need not sacrifice much practice time and, while doing so, also practices a higher level of law. The lawyer is in the process of meeting the new clients and getting the facts on the new cases, and then outlining the tentative issues and tentative problems and the tentative solutions.

True, I don't get to do much original drafting of lengthy complex documents anymore, or much library research (which I leave to law clerks), but on the other hand, I get to work with the highest level of people at the initial stages of both simple and complex cases. You will need "coverage," however, for times when you must go out of town or be out of the office. By devoting time to marketing, you will necessarily have to delegate much of the document drafting, legal research and other routine functions that you used to do; at the same time, you may be practicing a much higher level of law than before.

In my case, as with most lawyers I know, practice development is an ongoing part of my normal law practice. The amount of time sacrificed from the practice really need not be great.

"Where will find time for practice development?"

This is a bona fide question.

Many lawyers feel they're simply too busy practicing law for clients to have time available or "left over" for practice development.

The answer is to use your existing time more effectively and to make other people in and out of the firm as part of your team to do some of your practice development work for you.

For example, you don't have to do the work of examining incoming mail from your clients. You don't have to take the calls when you are in the office. Your secretary or receptionist or another lawyer can. You can use your own time more effectively by collecting and handing out cards and having lunches with your clients and potential clients, and sending clients copies of new cases as you come across them.

Many of the techniques of this book can be done for you by others in the office. It is incumbent on you to teach the others in the office to do the right things and to avoid the wrong things. You must educate them. They will not self-educate and you should accept the fact that they won't do it as effectively as you.

A major part of client retention success is to conduct your law practice on a client pleasing level and be sure that your entire office follows your systems of client communication.

Remember the old adage, "Nothing is hard to do if you don't have to do it."

B-4
Increasing Your Net Profit by Getting More Clients and Cases

There are only two ways to increase net profit:

1. Increase income; and/or
2. Decrease expenses

Every management expert will agree that the time spent increasing income is much better spent than the time spent in controlling or reducing expenses.

While the experts may differ as to whether management expansion time is worth two times or three times (or some different multiple) the value of expense reduction time, no one would contend that expense reduction is more valuable to a lawyer than increasing income.

Accordingly, you as a practicing lawyer should devote your time to increasing income if you want or need more profits.

If you can raise your prices (hourly rate or fixed fee) or if you can pay your people less money, then, of course, you can increase profits without getting more clients and cases. If you can't raise prices, then you will simply have to get more clients and cases within your ability to properly do the work.

B-5
Why You Should Upgrade Your Practice

Upgrading your practice should accomplish one or more of the following five goals:

1. You make more net profit;
2. You do the kinds of work you like to do;
3. You don't do the work you don't like to do;
4. You get more leisure time for family, recreation and personal goals; or
5. You are a happier person, enjoying life more, and you are more of a pleasure to be with.

When you are starting or building a practice, you tend to take whatever you can get. You will take cases that are marginally profitable, at best, because you have the excess capacity at the time the case comes in. You will take "garbage work" and money-losing work in the faint hope of getting more profitable work or referrals in the future.

At some point in your practice, you will begin to realize that you can't be all things to all people. You can't be equally competent in Medical Malpractice, Taxation and Anti Trust. You will find that you like some kinds of work and clients and don't like other kinds of work and clients. You will find that you are more profitable with certain kinds of clients and cases because you enjoy what you are doing and can do it well.

You will want to turn down or refer out work or clients to other lawyers in or out of your firm.

Upgrading your practice occurs when you make a conscious attempt either to turn down certain types of work or clients and/or aggressively seek certain types of work or clients. The process of upgrading is not always based purely on economic considerations. There are often psychological factors involved. Early in my career, I turned down entertainment clients because they have huge egos. Their huge egos clashed with my ego and I just didn't like them. I know criminal lawyers who left lucrative criminal law practices when their clients began coming back for a second, third and fourth time. The lawyers involved simply couldn't rationalize putting the accused people back on the streets to commit more crimes.

The techniques in this book will help you upgrade your practice to get the targeted clients and types of work you want by getting more clients and cases so you can get rid of, or delegate, the cases you don't want.

B-6
Work Generates Work Generates Work
(Foonberg's Third Rule)

With apologies to Gertrude Stein, this is Foonberg's Third Rule. Another way to phrase this is to say that the more work you do for clients, the more work they want you to do for them. Most clients appreciate your doing a large amount of work on their cases, and if you gave them a choice they would ask you to do all the work they could afford. When they know you are working conscientiously on their case, they will ask you to do more work for them. They will ask you to do legal work on cases they have been deferring.

I can assure you from first-hand experience that if you will project to a client that you are working hard on his or her case, the client will ask you to do more legal work.

When you finish legal work in a timely, efficient manner, clients will bring to you the next case they have and will brag to others what a great lawyer they have, thus increasing referrals.

B-7
The Importance Of Planning
or
"Woodsman, Sharpen Your Ax"

People don't plan to fail-they fail to plan. If there is anything that distinguishes successful people from unsuccessful people, it is that successful people plan and unsuccessful people don't plan. Unsuccessful people go through life reacting to the most recent emergency that crosses their desk, whether it be a small emergency or a large one. Unsuccessful people leave working on major problems in order to work on the minor problem that just interrupted them.

I have been told but not independently verified that the average person can only plan 30 days into the future. Successful business owners and managers can plan a year into the future. The most successful leaders in Finance and Government and private management can plan up to 5 years in advance.

You must spend some time and energy planning the kinds of cases and clients you want. You must draw up a plan on how to attract those cases and clients, and how to get clients and client sources to refer you similar clients.

The story is told of the woodsman who had a market for an unlimited amount of firewood during a blizzard. As the woodsman chopped down tree after tree, his ax became duller and duller. Finally, the ax was so dull that he was making very little progress. He was swinging harder and harder yet cutting less and less wood. A young boy tapped the woodsman on the shoulder and asked him, "Mr. Woodsman, why don't you sharpen your ax?" Without looking up, the woodsman continued swinging his ax with the dull blade and muttered to the boy, "I can't. I haven't got time. I'm too busy trying to cut down trees."

Don't find yourself in the position of that woodsman. Don't be so busy trying to cut down trees with a dull ax that you have no time to sharpen the ax. Spend some time sharpening that ax. The time you spend thinking about where you are going will pay off handsomely.

My father said it very simply, yet very accurately, in just six words. He never went to college or took courses in psychology or industrial planning, but he summed it all up when he said, "Jay, plan your work, work your plan. "

Ask yourself some questions, as follows:
1. Do I like the work I'm doing and the fees I'm earning?
2. What are the kinds of clients and cases I like?
3. Where are those cases and clients located?
4. How can I let the people in my target areas know that I'm a lawyer and want their work?

The time you spend thinking about these questions will be well spent.

B-8
Analyze Your Existing Practice Strengths, Weaknesses and Client Sources and Work On Them

Where do your clients now come from? In the long run and the short run, existing clients and existing client sources are always your best source of new business if you want more of the same kind of practice.

Are your clients coming as the result of referrals from a specific person? If so, devote some time and energy to that person to know him or her better. At least take client referrers to lunch. Ask them why they refer you clients. If they don't refer you clients, ask them if there is anything you are doing wrong that prevents them from doing so. You may be surprised at the answers.

Are your clients coming from a particular industry? If so, make it a point to attend as many industry-wide meetings as you can. Learn about the trade associations. Speak to meetings and conventions and workshops of the association. Write articles for the trade association journals and publications. Put copies of those journals in your reception room. In time you will develop a reputation for expertise in that area of work and people in the industry will think of you as "the expert" in that area of law.

Are clients coming to you because of your particular geographic location? If so, emphasize your location wherever and whenever you can. For example, I live in Beverly Hills, California, and I make it a point to tell people that I am really just a "small town lawyer," because Beverly Hills has only 29,000 residents. I'm being facetious and the people know it, but they will remember where I live. I also ask them if they remember who Betty Grable was; if they answer "yes," I tell them that I live in Betty Grable's former house. I also tell them my house was once owned and lived in by Edgar Rice Burroughs, the creator of Tarzan. I tell people that my little town of 29,000 people has 3,500 lawyers and 3,000 doctors. I tell them that Wilshire Boulevard, where my office is located, runs the entire length of Los Angeles from downtown to the ocean. I tell them that my office is within a few minutes of the finest shopping in the world, the finest restaurants in the world and the finest hotels in the world.

Learn something about where you practice or live and tell people about it so that they will identify you with the place when they need a lawyer in that location.

Do clients come to you because of a particular lawyer in your firm? If so, do everything you can to push that lawyer into the public and into those places where his or her presence will be felt so that the lawyer can generate even more practice growth.

Relieve that lawyer of nit-picking administrative duties and give him or her plenty of staff to do lesser chores so that he or she can devote time to the greater profit of the firm.

Is there something negative about your firm which has to be overcome? If so, either devote time and energy to attacking and correcting that weakness or bypass the weakness, conserving your strengths and resources for other work. For example, if several clients have expressed dissatisfaction with the way you handled their divorce cases, you should either:

A. Improve the quality of what you are doing by getting the appropriate people, equipment or systems to do the job -correctly; or
B. Stop doing divorce work

In either case, you should communicate your decision to those unhappy clients so that they will regain respect for you and become sources of business again.

Chapter C
The Lawyer in the Office

C-1
Do It Right - How Turning Down My
First Case Led to 19 Cases

My very first client was the man who installed my telephone. He saw my CPA certificate on the wall and asked me to "review" his tax return for $5 (1964 prices). I told him that I couldn't "review" it unless I prepared it. I told him that $35 was the minimum fee (1964 prices) for an income tax return. I told him that I would need about an hour of his time for an interview to ascertain whether the income tax return was correct. He begged me "please" to look it over for $5 and said he wouldn't hold me responsible for any mistakes. I told him that I wouldn't do anything unless I did it right and that $35 was my minimum fee. He said he wouldn't pay that much and we talked about something else until he finished his work.

Two days later the phone rang. It was the installer. I said "hello" and told him that the phone was working fine because my wife had already called twice. He said he was calling me for professional help and asked if I could see him that evening in the restaurant of the building. I asked him the nature of the problem. He explained that his wife had a daughter by a prior marriage and that the father was a drunken bum. He had promised the wife that if anything happened to her he would do his best to keep the child away from the natural father. He had not adopted the child. His wife had just died in an accident and he wanted to do whatever was necessary to keep the child from the natural father.

I discussed the case with a couple of lawyers in the building who told me the case was an absolute loser because the natural father would get the child unless it could be conclusively proven that the natural father was unfit. They also told me that, in those days, $2,500 would be a reasonable fee, and to be sure to get another $2,500 for investigators, deposition costs, child psychiatrists, etc (1964 Dollars).

I met the client that night in the restaurant and told him that he had a losing case and not to waste his money, and that, if I were to take his case, I needed my fee and costs paid in advance before I would begin work. Truthfully, I was trying to dissuade him from proceeding with the case. He told me he had already been to see another lawyer who told him essentially the same thing but who was a little more optimistic and who would charge less. I said nothing. He said he would drop by the next morning.

The next morning he came by with a cashier's check for $2,500 and 14 $100 bills and asked if I could wait a few days for the next $1,100. As a phone company employee, he had accumulated a large amount of AT&T stock and was borrowing against it to get money for my fees. I could have waited six months.

I then got cold feet and told him that I had never handled this type of case before and, in fact, had never handled any kind of case before. He told me that he knew this was my first time but that he had promised his wife that if anything happened to her he would do his best. He said that I had told him when I refused to review his tax return for $5 that I wouldn't do anything unless I did it right. Therefore, he was confident that, even though the case was a loser and I had no prior experience, I would do whatever could be done and he would have fulfilled his promise to his late wife.

I won the case (by default) after lining up all sorts of witnesses and devoting all of my time day and night to the case. The other lawyer caved in when he and his client saw the huge array of evidence I had prepared.

I got a $2,500 fee on the custody case and a $3,000 fee on his wife's industrial accident case, all within a short time of opening my practice, and all because I turned down a low fee and told a prospective client that I would not do something unless I did it right.

I eventually received 19 cases with a value (at 2007 prices) of $357,000 from that first client and the recommendations from that client. A diagram and a chart following this chapter graphically display the chain of clients and fees.

Believe me, over the years you'll do better and get more clients and fees if you make it clear that you'll only do things the right way. Always do your best. Even when you underestimate the fee, do your best. When the client is not worthy of your best, give your best anyway.

How My First Case Led to 19 Cases

Anatomy of a Client Referral

		CLIENT SOURCE				
Year	Nature of Case	Client #1 (My Very First Client)	Client #2 (Referred by Client #1)	Client #3 (Referred by Client #2)	Client #4 (Referred by Client #3)	Client #5 (Referred by Client #4)
1964	Child Custody	$ 15,000				
1964	Worker's Comp. of Wife	9,000				
1964	Will of Friend		$ 300			
1965	Probate of Wife	600				
1967	Probate of Mother-in-Law	1,500				
1965	Guardianship of Stepdaughter	3,000				
1968	Drunk Driving Defense	3,000				
1970	Estate of Client	2,000				
1970	Partition Proceeding of Land		60,000			
1972	Negotiate Lease with Oil Co.		4,000			
1974	Form California Corporation		3,000			
1977	Will of Friend of Friend			$ 700		
1978	Estate Contest for Friend			40,000		
1982	Estate Tax Problems of Client #1				$ 68,000	
1982	Preliminary Estate Tax Planning				6,000	
1982	Preliminary Estate Tax Planning					$ 6,000
1982	Corporate Problems of Unrelated Corporation					6,000
1983	Renegotiate Oil Company Lease				56,000	56,000
1983	Advise on Subchapter S Laws				3,000	3,000
	TOTALS	$ 34,100	$ 67,300	$ 40,700	$ 133,000	$ 71,000

NOTE: All fees have been translated into 2007 dollars.

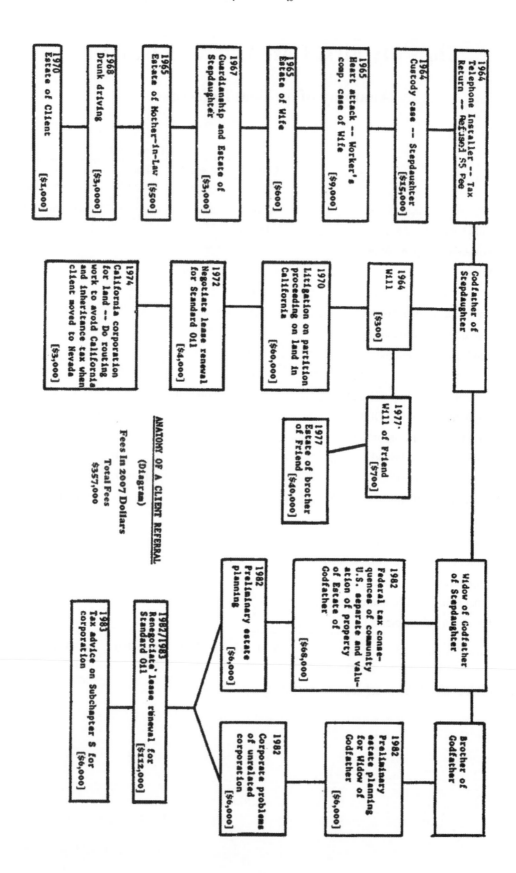

ANATOMY OF A CLIENT REFERRAL

(Diagram)

Fees in 2007 Dollars
Total Fees
$357,000

C-2
The Importance of the Client Interview
In Marketing Yourself and Your Firm

Interviews are extremely important opportunities in the process of attracting and keeping clients both on a short range and long range basis. The client or potential client who doesn't use your firm at the conclusion of the interview may use your firm or refer someone to you many years later. Alternatively, you can unintentionally "turn off" or alienate potential clients and their referrals

Many of the things which are briefly commented on in this chapter are developed in great specificity in other chapters. This chapter can be referred to just prior to every interview you have as a check list.

A. Before the interview begins, you or your secretary or another lawyer in the firm should pre-screen the client to find out a little about the facts and probable area of law involved. You may wish to update yourself on the area of law involved or alert another associate or partner to be available if needed. It's embarrassing when the client wants to discuss an area of law you know absolutely nothing about and the other lawyer in the office who is the expert in that area is not available because you didn't ask him or her to be.

B. Get a check list questionnaire, prepared or downloaded or copied from form books or the internet, before the client arrives. Your pre-prepared list of questions will establish you in the client's mind as expert in the area of law involved because you're asking the right questions.

C. Notify the receptionist of the interview so that when the client arrives the receptionist can say something like, "Good morning, Mr. Smith. Mr. Foonberg is expecting you for your ten o'clock meeting. I'll tell *them* (Note-not *him)* you're here." The fact that the receptionist is expecting the client is a mark of efficiency. By saying "I'll notify *them"* rather than "him" (or "her"), the client won't be upset if you're on the phone and can't get off or if you're having difficulty ending an earlier meeting. If the receptionist refers to you by your first name, the client will wonder what's going on in the office.

D. Have your receptionist offer the client a cup of coffee or tea, or bottle of water, or a cold drink. Clients have a high anxiety level and often are nervous and/or thirsty. The drink may wet a dry mouth and give the client something to do with their own hands. Even if they don't want the drink, the offer will be taken as a gesture of hospitality.

E. Learn what you can about the client before the meeting. If the prospective client is a famous person or a significant company, you can run Google or other computer searches of newspapers, trade journals, SEC filings and other sources to learn a lot about that client. The prospective client will be impressed that you know so much about his or her activities. He may think that you are genuinely interested in him or the company or, at the very least, he'll appreciate how well prepared you are. If the client comments about your preparation or knowledge, you can say something like, "When I practice law, I insist on being well prepared with all the facts I can get. I don't want to lose a client's case in the conference room or court room through lack of preparation." The client will be favorably impressed.

If you want to spend the effort, there are literally hundreds of data bases you can access through the internet. If you don't have access to a computer or LEXIS or NEXIS or WESTLAW, you can hire a law student to do the data base accessing on the law school computer or you can hire commercial research companies. Some law school master agreements may prohibit the site being used for commercial purpose.

F. Have the receptionist tell the client, "You can have a seat, if you wish," so the client won't feel awkward hovering over the receptionist, not knowing where to go next.

G. Be sure that you have one or more hard back, simple chairs in the reception area. Some seniors and injured people have difficulty getting up out of stuffed chairs. This difficulty can cause a client to become confused, disoriented or even hostile, which is a bad way to start a relationship.

H. Be sure that the receptionist keeps the reception area clean and neat with periodicals neatly arranged, and ashtrays empty and clean (where permitted), if there are ashtrays, and prior clients' drink cups removed.

I. Be sure that the periodicals in the reception room reflect the kind of clients and practice you want clients and potential clients to think you have. Technical, legal and trade journals are good.

J. Go out to the reception area to greet the client.
1) If this is your first meeting with the client, ask: "Mr. Jones?" It's embarrassing for both of you to find out that the person in the reception area is Mr. Smith and your client, Mr. Jones, just went to the washroom.
2) Offer your hand to the client (including female clients) as a gesture of friendship and introduce yourself. "I'm Jay Foonberg." Don't call yourself "Mr. Foonberg" or "Ms. Jones" or "Attorney Smith" or "Dr. Foonberg". Giving yourself a title in oral communication is interpreted by some people as being self-aggrandizing and a sign of insecurity. A handshake can be important to the client as a sign of friendship.
3) If the client has packages or a briefcase or files or a drink, you should offer, "Can I help you with your things?" This will relieve the client of the confusion of

having to get out of the chair with all the items he or she is carrying and may save you the cost of cleaning a carpet if the drink is spilled.

4) Say to the client, "Please follow me."

5) When you get to the door of your office or of the conference room, stop. Say, "Won't you please go in?

6) When the client goes in, follow close behind and gesture toward the chair you want the client to occupy and say "Won't you please sit down?"

7) You are now ready to begin the formal interview.

All of the above steps are designed to relieve the client's anxiety in being in a strange location and to indicate your desire to be friendly and helpful, which are important factors in the attorney-client relationship. Additionally, each of the above steps begins the process of putting you in command of the situation and the interview process. This aura of command helps establish the client's assurance of your competency.

K. Begin the interview by asking simple questions such as name, business and home address and phone numbers.

L. Ask where the client wants his or her mail sent for that particular matter. Some clients don't want their office people to know what's happening on a legal matter, and some don't want their spouse or family members to know what's happening. More than one client has told me not to send mail anywhere, that they'd come pick it up from the office. Correspondence concerning a possible sale of the business can unnerve the employees. If you're handling a divorce case, you don't want the other spouse or the family members to know the status of your negotiations for alimony. Some clients get a P.O. Box for their legal correspondence. Some clients tell me to call and advise of a fax and they will be at the fax machine to receive it.

A client once came close to firing me because of my stupidity in handling mail. I sent a letter to him in which I related that I had just reviewed the company's financial statements and that the profits were so high that he should consider installing a pension plan to get the profits to the key share holders/officers. The client's secretary copied the letter and circulated it throughout the company. The employees decided that they should be getting some of those profits and brought in a union to organize the employees. Be careful how sensitive mail is handled. Email poses confidentiality problems.

M. Be sure you have phone numbers and all addresses including email to contact the client at night and on weekends. When the client is reluctant to give you a home address, remind the client you can't bring papers to a post office box or a closed factory on a Sunday when you need documents signed for a court motion on Monday morning.

N. Ask the client if it's all right to call him or her at work or home by telephone. Some people don't want co-workers or family members to know they've got a legal matter requiring a lawyer. They may be concerned that co-workers or family members will incorrectly guess why the person is using a lawyer.

O. At the beginning of the factual interview state, "It will be easier for you and easier for me if I ask questions and you answer them. Don't worry, at the end of the interview *you'll* have an opportunity to ask me anything you want to ask me or tell me anything you want to tell me." This will prevent the client from talking too much at first, and will establish that you are in control of the situation and are experienced because you know what questions to ask.

P. Be sure you discuss fees and follow up the discussion with a fee and representation letter.

Q. If you are interrupted during the interview by a client emergency, be sure you indicate to the client in the office that he/she is not being charged for that time.

R. When you feel you have all the information you want be sure to ask, "Is there anything I forgot to ask or anything you want to tell me?" This will obviate your client getting upset with you for controlling the interview to the point that they felt they couldn't communicate with you and that you accordingly were aloof and didn't really care about him and his case.

S. Be sure that you communicate to the client in the interview the following:
1) You are interested in the client and want to help;
2) You understand the client has an important case;
3) You will be available (or someone in the firm will be reasonably available) whenever the client needs help;
4) You are competent and experienced in the area;
5) You are ethical;
6) You have a good reputation;
7) You will keep the client informed;
8) Your opinion of the case;
9) You want the case or the client. (It always surprises me how few attorneys tell a prospective client that they want the client's business.)

T. Set an "action date." Tell the client or prospective client that you will call them if they don't call you by a certain date. You can say that it's easier and cheaper to leisurely prepare a case than to rush-rush at the last minute. Set the action date as soon as possible to reduce the lawyer shopping the client might otherwise do. Tell the client that beginning after that action date you or the firm are expecting a heavy commitment of time to a major matter. This also tells the client that you are in demand and they must act quickly to get you. It's the same philosophy as a maitre d' asking you if you have a reservation when the restaurant is empty. They want you to think that normally they are so busy that a reservation is necessary.

U. Your office should be neat. If you are a believer in the theory that there should be nothing on the desk but the client's file, then I suggest you meet the client in a conference room. Some clients will equate a clean desk with a lawyer with no clients who therefore is not a good lawyer. Suit yourself in this matter of clean vs. cluttered desk.

V. When the interview is over, stand up and say, "The interview is over. Won't you please follow me?" Escort the client back to the reception area. Don't let the client wander unescorted through the office where he can see computer screens or other clients' papers on desks and overhear other people discussing other cases by telephone. The client may believe that others can see his papers on desks and overhear his matters being discussed.

The subtleties of the office interview cover a myriad of subjects. In this one chapter, I've simply tried to highlight and summarize some of the more important aspects.

C-3
How To Handle the Friend of a Good Client When the Friend Has No Money for Legal Fees

What should you do when you are informed by a good client (or a good former client) that "Old Joe" has been recommended to you because you are such a great lawyer, but please try to take it easy on Old Joe because Old Joe hasn't got much money to pay for the legal work he needs. Old Joe may or may not have a lawyer who is perceived to be overcharging Old Joe.

I advise you to do the following:

1. Give Old Joe a royal welcome.
2. Send the referring client a thank-you note.
3. Don't take Old Joe's case unless it stands on its own economically.

This is one of those areas where, over the years, I've had a remarkable lack of success. I've rarely earned a decent fee on a matter when it started out up front that someone came to me because they did not have money to pay another lawyer for the work they needed. The important thing here is to maintain a good relationship with your referring client.

I usually say the following when I talk to Old Joe by telephone, and again when I see him in the office and again when I write the fee and engagement letter:

"My referring client is a very important person to me, as are all my clients. Anybody he recommends gets very special treatment. We will do whatever we can to help you." This royal treatment will usually be reported to the referring client, who will feel flattered and will try to refer you more (and hopefully better) matters in the future.

You can suggest that Old Joe borrow the needed legal fees from the referring friend. On rare occasions, Old Joe has been able to do just that; in most situations, however, you'll find out that the referring client isn't that good a friend to Old Joe.

You also can simply consider making a "cluster concept" analysis. That is, you take into account the profitability or non-profitability of the work being sent by the referring client to decide whether you want to absorb the loss of Old Joe.

Normally, you'll have to accept or reject the new client and new case purely on its own merit, having no regard for the source. The referring client will get enough "ego stroke" from your compliments. It is unlikely that the referring client would want you to increase the fee he or she pays you to cover the fee you lost on the referred case.

C-4
How to Tell a Client He or She Has Lost The Case (or Has No Case) and Still Keep the Client

It is simultaneously both difficult and easy to tell a client that he or she has lost the case, or has no case, and still keep a good client who will both use you and refer you legal business and clients over the years.

It is difficult because no one likes to be the bearer of bad news. It is easy because all you have to do is to tell the truth. Believe it or not, clients want the truth. Your job is to tell them the truth in an appropriate manner. (Besides which, lying to a client is possibly a breach of your fiduciary relationship and could result in disciplinary problems for you.)

When the client's case is legally meritorious but not economically meritorious, you might try one of the following approaches:

A. When the case is simply too small or non-economical:

"John, you are right. The other person is wrong. The problem is that it is not economical to pursue your legal rights. You may spend dollars to get back pennies, If the moral principles of the case are so important to you that you are willing to spend dollars to recover vindication, plus pennies, then I'll be glad to be your lawyer, but please don't come back to me and say that you didn't expect the cost to be so high."

In this situation, you have told the client that he or she is legally in the right, which may be 90 percent or all the client really wants.

If you gently let the client down, you won't have lost a client; on the contrary, the client will still like you and refer you business.

Don't be flippant or comical when dealing with a case that's been lost. Tell the client in person or by phone, rather than by letter. Bad news should be given simply and quickly. A good thing for you to say might be, "I'm sorry the case was lost as I know how important it was to you. We can appeal, but I don't think it would be successful."

B. When the client has no case:

"Mary, legally you have no case. You eventually will lose if this goes to court. I don't mislead clients or give them false hopes just to get a client or fee. The money and effort you spend on legal fees will be wasted. Save that money for other good uses."

If appropriate, add:

"You can and should check with another lawyer for a second opinion, and I'll certainly cooperate with that attorney."

Put this in a written letter to the client so you don't get sued for malpractice when the person claims that you undertook the prosecution of the case.

C. When the case is lost:

1.   Be the first person to tell the client. Do it immediately by telephone & follow up with a letter (not an email). If the client first finds out they have lost from the other side, or a third party, you probably will lose the client and future work from the client and their referrals.

2.   Be honest. Don't lie. Tell the client if you can, why you think the case was lost. "I'm sorry to tell you that the case is lost. The judge (or the jury) decided against you. We don't know why he (they) decided as he (they) did. Perhaps he (they) just didn't believe our witness. (Don't say, "they didn't believe *you*. ") Perhaps the judge sees the law differently from the way we do. I just don't know. I'll send you a letter as soon as I have more information and we can discuss whether or not to appeal. I'm sorry, because I believed in your case when it began and I still believe in your case."

        If you gently let the client down, you won't have lost a client. On the contrary, the client will still like you and refer you business.

3.   Remind the client that the client participated in the choices made.

4.   Suggest the possibility of appeal and your estimate of the chances of success. Tell the client that appeals are usually not a good investment of time & money because 85% are not successful.

5.   Suggest that you will help them find another lawyer for the post judgment motions & the appeal if they wish a second opinion.

6.   Do not abandon the client. Stay in touch. Take or answer all calls immediately.

C-5
Office Checklist for Closing the Deal with New Clients and Cases

(To be filled out for each new matter or case.)

YES   *NO*

1. Did you communicate your availability?

    A. Did you give your home telephone number or cellular mobile number on a slip of paper or back of your card? (Possibly except for family law)   _____   _____

    B. Did you tell the client that if you personally are not immediately available, the client can bring the problem to another member of the firm who will help?   _____   _____

2. Did you communicate your reputation?
    Did you specifically communicate to the client that you have a good reputation with the courts or insurance adjusters or administrative agency or adverse party involved, or other areas where your good reputation can help the client?   _____   _____

3. Did you communicate to the client that you have experienced attorneys in the firm, or available to you, in the area of law involved and/or clients in a similar business or situation as the client's?   _____   _____

4. Did you communicate to the client that the case at this point does/does not appear to need a specialist and that you have in-house specialists or can bring in specialists, if and as needed?   _____   _____

5. Price and Fee Arrangements:

    A. Did you give the client your best estimate of the range of the fee, based on experience in handling similar cases?   _____   _____

B. Did you state to client that your estimate of the fee range is based on the facts as known to you to this point, and that it might be necessary to adjust the fee estimate up or down, based on additional facts as they become known?   _____ _____

C. Did you explain how much cash is required *up front* in advance of doing work, and that the firm will extend reasonable credit, subject to limitations?   _____ _____

D. Did you explain evergreen trust accounts?   _____ _____

6. Did you expressly communicate to client:

A. That you are concerned about his or her problem?   _____ _____

B. That- you want to help the client to the maximum extent possible?   _____ _____

C-6
Client Personal Data File

I've never done this, relying instead on my memory in most cases, but I've talked to lawyers who told me that a personal data card file or client relations management program is a tremendous client pleaser. It projects that you really care about the client. In a Rolodex or card file or in a computer, if you have a video display at your desk, you have a client card for *each person* with whom you have contact, including some personal data. A typical card might read:

Jones, John
   b.Oct. 29, 1940.
Wife: Mary
Children: Alan-born Sept 27,1963
David-born May 6, 1967
Steven-born June 12, 1969
Hobbies: Tennis, pro-football (Raider fan)
Last Meeting: Jan 1, 1986, Rookies Restaurant
June 15, 1985: Office meeting re Smith case
July 20, 1985: Office meeting re Thomas case
(was proud of new Mercedes)

Obviously, when the client calls, it is easy for you to make conversation on one or more people or subjects that the client cares about. Although I've never set up such a file, lawyers who do use one tell me that it is very worthwhile. You should also add the name of the client's secretary to the card or to the file system so you can mention him or her by name when you talk to him or her or the client.

Chapter D
The Lawyer's Conduct Out of
The Office

D-1
Every Person You Meet Is a Potential Client
Or Potential Recommender of a Client

If you were to ask (and you should) lawyers whom you meet at Bar meetings "What are some unusual sources of clients you have had over the years," a few of the answers would amaze you, and most would simply confirm what you are reading in this book.

If you are an outgoing person, you will meet many people in many different situations and will have many opportunities to obtain clients if you handle yourself correctly. In my personal practice, I have obtained new clients or client referrals from many sources, some of which are common place and some of which are almost bizarre.

The list of possibilities is endless. I only wish to point out that every person you meet or know is a potential client or referrer of clients. All of these people became my clients though none of them was looking for a lawyer when we met.

1. The man who installed my telephone.
2. Cleaning people in my office building.
3. My doctor.
4. My dentist.
5. Airline flight attendants.
6. People I've met on planes.
7. People who have heard me speak.
8. People who have read my books or articles or have seen my videotapes or DVDs or listened to my CDs.
9. People I've met at weddings and other social gatherings.
10. Active judges.
11. People I've met on package group tours.
12. Foreign lawyers whose offices I've visited.
13. People I've met while scuba diving (actually, while on the diving boat).
14. People I've met while jogging.
15. The book representative who sold me my tax service.

The list of possibilities is endless. If you treat people as potential clients or referrers of clients, you'll be greatly surprised at the number of cases which actually develop.

D-2
You Must Tell People You're a Lawyer

People can't use you as their attorney or refer people to you for legal work if they don't know you're an attorney. You have to communicate your profession to them. You somehow have to work the fact that you're a lawyer into your oral or written communications with them.

Be positive! When people ask you what you do, be enthusiastic when you respond!

In our society, people are often categorized according to their job or profession.

As soon as you entered law school, people who knew you began thinking of you as a lawyer and were proud of you and of the fact that you would become a lawyer.

New acquaintances will modify their initial opinion of you as soon as they find out you're a lawyer.

It is my personal opinion after more than 40 years of practice that people who react favorable to you being a lawyer are nicer, more educated, and more sophisticated than those who react with an unfavorable comment. Don't' waste your time arguing with people who don't like lawyers. You won't change their mind.

People actually have a very high opinion of lawyers, generally. We as lawyers think that the public has a lower opinion of us than is the reality. This phenomenon has been studied quite extensively. People may say that lawyers are not nice people but their lawyer is a wonderful person.

You should enthusiastically communicate the following whenever you can:

1. I'm a lawyer.
2. I help people.
3. I like to help people.
4. I'm a good lawyer.

D-3
Joining Clubs and Organizations to Get Clients

I have always advised against joining clubs and church groups solely to get clients. I have always felt that the "animal clubs" (the Moose, Elks, Lions, Eagles, etc.) are no longer a good source of clients. At a time when there were far fewer lawyers, one could join one or more of these service clubs, show up at a meeting now and then and get clients. People who belonged to your clubs or church groups would seek you as a lawyer simply because they didn't know any other lawyers. This has all changed with the internet and the large number of lawyers today, and in many organizations lawyers constitute a very large number of the members. Accordingly, the possibility or the probability of getting legal business from these organizations is very small.

If you want to work hard for an organization because you believe in the organization and its goals, then by all means you should do so. When people see you working hard for the organization, they will realize that you are capable of hard work and will trust you with their legal work, believing that you will work hard for them on their legal matters. On the other side of the coin, however, if you do a poor job in your clubs and organizations, potential clients and referrers of clients will think that you will do a poor job with their legal work and they won't use you or refer clients to you. Accordingly, for many years I have advised people not to join clubs and organizations for the sole purpose of getting clients.

In recent years, however, I have been doing work among minority lawyers, and I have been told by many minority lawyers that they still meet a lot of clients in service clubs and church groups, because there is little competition among the members for clients. In many of these clubs, the minority lawyer is the only attorney member and, accordingly, does get clients, simply because the people involved don't know any other lawyers. This is similar to the situation as it existed for most lawyers 20 years ago.

This being the case, I would rephrase my advice concerning joining service clubs and church groups to get clients. Investigate the prospective group. If there are few or no attorneys in the group, go ahead and join and see what happens. If after a year or two you haven't picked up any clients, then move on to other clubs. If there are already a lot of attorneys in the group, don't join for the purpose of getting clients. Join because you care about the organization, or don't join at all.

If you are a member of a minority group in which there are not a lot of attorneys relative to the population of the group, then by all means seek out these minorities at church, civic and social clubs as places where you can get a high return on your time in terms of new clients and worthwhile legal matters. Join as many as your schedule will permit you, and be most active in those where you care about the goals of the organization.

There is a technique called "cause related marketing" involving charitable organizations, which I recommend and which is covered in a separate chapter.

D-4
Be Visible to Your Banker

Bankers are an excellent source of business. Bank managers have opportunities on an almost daily basis to refer many different kinds of clients and cases to a lawyer. Most bankers know many attorneys to whom they could refer legal work.

A lawyer should go out of the way to be visible to the bankers. Make it a point to drop by the bank at least once a week on some pretense or other. Make your own deposits. Drop by to cash a check instead of using that Automated Teller Machine. Offer to take the manager to lunch. Always drop by and say hello, if the banker is on the phone at least wave to him or her. Tell the banker how you're doing. Let the banker know the kind of work you want and can do.

With the huge increase in branch banking, and the continued takeovers and mergers and failures, managers keep changing jobs. You'll have to make it a point to cultivate each new manager who comes into the bank. You may wish to follow the banker to the new bank.

The manager often is required to recommend only lawyers on a list approved by general counsel or by house counsel. The list may be based on reciprocity for client accounts or referring clients on the list may be based on lawyers deemed to be non-competition for the bank's existing counsel or may be based on any number of other factors. A new manager is often ignorant of the list or may not wish to use it in an attempt to develop branch business or his or her own personal following.

The visits to the bank will never be a waste of time. Even if you don't get clients and business you will get more favored treatment for loans when you need them. Bankers tend to be favorable toward customers whom they know.

A Utah lawyer once told me that the only marketing training he ever got in law school was a professor who told him: "When you've got nothing to do, go hang around the bank. They'll always eventually have something for you." The Utah lawyer told me that 30 years later he still follows that advice by dropping by at least once a week to make the deposit and over a period of time the bank has referred him a lot of business.

Be visible to your banker-you'll get business or loans or both.

D-5
The Importance of
Correct Verbal Identification
("What Kind of Law Do You Practice?")

When someone asks you "What kind of law do you practice?", you have a unique opportunity to do good or to do harm to your practice growth. Be careful how you answer the question. The right or wrong answer to this question can make you a lot of money or cost you a lot of money over the years. You should think carefully before answering this question. It probably is worth your while to practice the answer to this question with a prepared answer and to have multiple prepared answers available, depending on when and where the question is asked and depending on who asks it and their reason for asking. Your staff and other lawyers in the firm should also be trained in how to answer this question.

Every lawyer has been shocked when a client went to a different lawyer for legal work the first lawyer could have done and would have done if given the opportunity. Often the client just didn't know the lawyer did "that kind" of legal work. This is usually the fault of the first lawyer.

If you tell people you practice "civil litigation," you shouldn't be surprised that they go somewhere else for their "accident case" or "will" or "probate" or "criminal" matters.

When you give a narrow answer to the question "What kind of law do you practice?", you are telling people that you don't do other kinds of work and that you don't want other kinds of work.

One approach to answering the question "What kind of law do you practice?" is to answer with the question: "What kind of lawyer are you looking for?" or "What kind of legal problems do you have?" The person may then be specific and say a lawyer for shopping centers (or, whatever) and you can then answer something like, "I do that kind of work. Here's my card. Give me your phone number and we can get together if you wish." Or, "I personally don't do that kind of work. I specialize in accidents (or, whatever), but one of the lawyers in my firm (my office, my suite, my building) does do that kind of work. I'll give you his name and number and ask him to call you as a courtesy to me to see if he can help." (You then call the referred lawyer so he or she knows where the client came from in the event you want referrals back, or you want the next case this client has, or you want a referral fee, or you want this lawyer sending this client's next case back to you.)

Another way to respond is to say, "I personally don't do that kind of work. I specialize in accidents (or whatever), but I'll find you someone who does specialize in what you need. I can probably find the right lawyer for you more easily than you can find one yourself." Here again you want to be the source of the client to the attorney finally selected. You want to be the gate keeper for this client's legal matters.

If the answer to your question "What kind of lawyer are you looking for?" is non-specific, such as, "At the present time I don't need any lawyer, but I was curious about what kind you practice," you can revert to a general response.

You must project a capacity of being able to help the client in many different kinds of legal work.

The telephone company lists more than 64 different areas of law in its directory. You obviously can't say, "I practice admiralty, bankruptcy, civil litigation, domestic relations, etc." You would be standing there all day and the client or potential client would doze off.

If you say, "I'm in general practice," you'll lose a lot of potential clients who need, or think they need, a specialist.

One good way to answer the question "What kind of law do you practice?" is to respond along the following lines: "Look, the phone company lists 64 different areas of law. No lawyer or firm could possibly handle all 64 areas. When you have any kind of legal problem, bring it to me. If I can't handle it, there are other lawyers in my firm (or the suite where I practice, or the building where I practice) who practice other areas of law.

If you need a specialist, I'll help you pick the right one for your particular case. You won't be able to select the right lawyer for the case as well as I can. I'll bring in a specialist." (Note, you did not say you would "refer out" the client. You said you would "bring in" a specialist. This reassures the client that you won't abandon him or ignore him.)

If you want to, you can answer, "I personally do a lot of litigation trials and business transactions, but I work with others who handle many other areas. "

You want to be the "traffic manager" or gate keeper for all their legal work. You want the referral fee, if there is to be one, and you want to be sure that the lawyer who finally gets the case outside of your firm is a lawyer who owes you a referral. Additionally, if you refer the client, the attorney will be more likely to refer the client back to you for future legal work rather than accept the client's work as they would do if there were no lawyer referring the client.

Additionally, it's true that you *may* do a better job of finding the right lawyer for their case than they could directly.

You must describe your legal practice in terms your audience or questioner can understand. You should also keep in mind how the telephone company classified areas of practice since some clients look for lawyers in the Yellow Pages. (See Exhibit D-5A.) Law practice areas are very technical and it is often difficult for lawyers themselves to define what they do. Sometimes lawyers mislead or confuse clients and potential clients with poor descriptions of their practice areas. Some examples of alternate word choices are:

Lawyer's Vocabulary	*Common Vocabulary*
Dissolution	Divorce
Private international law	International law
International law	International government relations
Probate	Estates
Estate planning	Wills
Negligence	Accidents
Warranty law	Defective products
Litigation	Trials
Driving under influence (DUI)	Drunk driving
Literary or intellectual property	Copyright and licensing

These are some simple examples, and I'm sure that you can think of other instances in your career when a prospective client simply couldn't understand just what kind of law you do practice.

When a prospective client asks "What kind of law do you practice?", be sure to answer in such a way that the person understands that they should send you almost anything as it arises.

Obviously, you can sometimes tailor your answer to fit your audience or your questioner. Here are some "one liners" that are effective and that I have often used over the years.

When I am with a group of foreigners, I will often say I do general business work, including international work, especially representing foreigners in California. This is much more likely to lead to business than if I say only that I do general business work. On the other hand, when I am with a group of CPA's, I'll say that I do tax and international work and practice in the civil and criminal tax fields.

You must describe and define your legal practice in terms your audience or questioner can understand.

"I personally specialize in architectural sex tax law." This especially gets a raised eyebrow or two. Then, I say, "I design and construct ways to screw the government out of taxes"; or, "I personally specialize in loopholes and technicalities and fine print." This says nothing but interests the listener. Or, I say, "I personally do a lot of work in the criminal tax and white-collar crime fields."

If you are at a party of middle-income people between the ages of 20 and 30, and you tell them you do estate planning, don't be surprised if you don't get a lot of business from them or their parents, who are in their 40s and 50s. You'll have more referrals if you can truthfully say that you are in general practice and do divorce, accident cases and house closings. It is, of course, better to indicate that they should initially come to you with any kind of legal problem.

On the other hand, if you are talking to an 80-year-old man at a brokerage office, you're more likely to get business if you say you do estate planning than if you say you do child custody work.

If you are with a group of bankers, don't be surprised if the atmosphere chills a bit if you say you represent defendants in repossession and debt collection cases. On the other hand, the atmosphere may warm quickly if you can say that you chase dead-beat flakes who don't pay their bona fide debts.

When I am talking to a small business person, I mention that I specialize in taxes and do a lot of work in connection with the purchase and sale of businesses. This will create a good rapport with the small business person, who is always considering buying or selling a business and who will need and want tax advice when there is a purchase or sale of a business.

Naturally, if you are told directly or indirectly what kind of lawyer they think they need, this should be taken advantage of. For example: when a man says, "My uncle just died with a big estate. What kind of law do you practice?", you should somehow get that person to understand they can (and should) bring you that case.

Verbal identification describing your practice can create or defeat much new business over the years.

D-5A
64 Wrong Ways to Answer the Question, "What Kind of Law Do You Practice?"

Administrative
Admiralty Law
Adoption
Agency Law
Antitrust & Unfair Competition
Appellate Practice
Aviation Law
Banking Law
Bankruptcy Law
Business Law
Civil Litigation
Civil Rights Law
Commercial Law
Computer Law
Condemnation Law
Condominium Law
Conservatorship Law
Constitutional Law
Construction Law
Consumer Claims & Protection
Copyright Law
Corporate Finance & Securities Law
Corporation & Partnership Law
Criminal Law
Customs Law
Discrimination Matters
Divorce, Adoption & Family Law
Entertainment & Sports Law
Environmental Law
Estate Planning
Family Law
Franchise Law

General Practice
Guardianship Law
Health Care & Hospital Law
Immigration & Naturalization Law
Insurance Law
International Law
Juvenile Law
Labor Law
Landlord & Tenant Law
Legislative Practice
Licensing Law
Malpractice Law
Maritime Law
Military Law
Mortgage Law
Motion Picture & Television Law
Municipal Law
Patent, Trademark & Copyright Law
Pension & Profit Sharing Law
Personal Injury & Property Damage
Probate Law
Public Utility Law
Real Estate Law
Social Securities Law
Sports Law
Taxation Law
Trademark Matters
Transportation Law
Utility Law
Veterans Law
Wills, Trust & Estate Planning
Worker's Compensation Law

The above 64 "specialty areas" were listed in the Greater Los Angeles Yellow Pages. You should keep in mind that potential clients using the Yellow Pages may rely on these descriptions of "specialty" areas of practice.

D-6
The Role of Clothing in Marketing Yourself

I am a firm believer in the role of clothing in marketing yourself for several reasons:

1. The effect of clothing on potential clients and recommenders of clients.
2. The effect of clothing on your own demeanor, and
3. The effect of dressing to be different or to be similar.

    1. *The effect of clothing on potential clients and referrers of clients.*

People get their first impression of you as soon as they see you. Later, they will have a chance to talk to you and, possibly, to be charmed by your wit and intelligence. Remember that we are discussing new or potential clients and referrers of clients. After people have known you for some time, they will or won't use you or recommend you clients for all sorts of reasons including but not limited to your alleged wit and intelligence and ability to lose close games at tennis or golf. Sometimes people may actually use you as a lawyer because of your legal skills, or at least your perceived legal skills. Therefore, your clothing mayor may not affect existing clients. (The same is true of your office address and furnishings.)

New or potential clients, however, will form an opinion of you based on the way you look. That first impression is a critical one. A negative first impression, even though subliminal, lessens your chance of success with the potential client. Imagine yourself going to see another lawyer for a consultation or, possibly, to associate that lawyer into a case you are handling. Imagine that the lawyer is wearing a shabby, dirty suit of clothes and scruffy tennis shoes. Your confidence in that lawyer has to be affected, no matter how great his or her reputation might be. If you'll admit that your confidence in that potential lawyer was affected, then you will admit that your potential clients could have a similar reaction to you in similarly inappropriate dress. If you wear inexpensive, poorly tailored clothing on the grounds that your clients are plain, simple people who wouldn't recognize or appreciate fine clothing, then you are subconsciously telling yourself that you want these plain, simple clients. If, on the other hand, you want to upgrade to higher-income, more-profitable clients, you must realize that these people may recognize and appreciate fine clothing and that they will make a first judgment of you long before you have a chance to impress them with your wit and intelligence. Low-income people won't be "turned on" by fine clothing, but high-income people will be "turned off" by mediocre clothing.

Whether you want to admit it or not, your clothing has a very definite effect on whether you attract or repel potential clients.

Priests wear collars and robes; doctors drape a stethoscope around their neck, even though 80% of doctors can't use a stethoscope correctly.

2. *The effect of clothing on your own demeanor.*

Your opinion of yourself and your own self-confidence is greatly affected by the clothing you wear.

When you meet people and you are wearing good clothes, you feel more confident. You feel more sure of yourself. You automatically increase both your and your client's perception of "taking command" of the situation, which is what clients want. I have five expensive suits. I rotate the suits, wearing one each workday. I buy some of my suits, shirts and ties on Rodeo Drive in Beverly Hills. I know I could get suits "almost as good" or "just as good" somewhere else at one-half the price. When I buy my suits or have them tailored, I know that I might be "overdressed" for the occasion but I will never be "underdressed." The feeling of self-confidence I gain is well worth the difference in cost. This difference in cost is an investment, not an expense. It pays. I even wear "name brand" clothing when I jog, when I swim and when I'm doing yard work. I simply feel more confident of myself when I do so. *Knowing* that you are well-dressed may give you the same feeling of confidence that I have. I am not so much concerned about "looking good" as I am concerned about not "looking bad." If you feel that your clothing has absolutely no effect on people's opinion of you, then you can, of course, ignore this entire chapter.

3. *The effect of dressing to be different or to be similar.*

There are specific situations where clothing makes a difference. I do a lot of work with and for foreigners. Non-Europeans generally wear shoes without laces (loafers). I frankly don't know why they do. Perhaps it is the Asian or Muslim custom of taking shoes off when entering homes and temples. Perhaps it is simply a matter of style. I don't know. Since I do a lot of work with and for foreigners, I consciously began wearing loafers when I was with them. I thought this was one way to make them less self-conscious of their own clothing difference.

One day one of my friends, a Brazilian banker, told me "Jay, when we Brazilians meet with Americans, we have a joke. We say, 'Look at the shoes. The American with the thickest soles is the most important person in the room.' After hearing that, I looked around and observed that he was usually correct. I went out and bought a pair of thick-soled, wing-tip, laced shoes which I now wear whenever I am with Brazilian business people and bankers, and I feel more confident with them.

Scuffed dirty shoes and dirty worn clothes mark you as a "loser" before you open your mouth.

As another example, I once went to Dallas to "do a deal" involving an overseas export of agricultural products. Four of us flew in to the hotel at the Dallas airport. I flew in from Los Angeles, one man flew in from Houston, one from Missouri and one from Argentina. I knew that my clients (the Americans) were not sophisticated, so I wore a Levi pantsuit and jacket instead of a suit. We spent three days at the airport putting the deal together. I noticed that all of the others wore boots while I wore loafers. I asked my clients why they wore boots when we never left the hotel. My clients told me, "Jay, when you do an "ag deal" (agricultural or farm transaction), you have to wear boots or no one will trust you. You will be an outsider. The boots can be inexpensive but they must be boots." I went over to Fort Worth and bought an expensive pair of alligator boots. I wear these boots whenever I have an "ag deal" and feel I am more accepted. The "ag" clients often comment on the boots, so I know they observe them.

When I gave a lecture to the South Dakota Bar Association, I wore a three-piece expensive suit (to preserve my image as a high-priced Beverly Hills lawyer-expensive but worth every cent) and I also wore my alligator boots. More than half of the lawyers in the audience were wearing three-piece suits and boots. I pointed out my boots at the beginning of the talk and immediately gained their acceptance and good will.

A good general scouts the terrain before attacking; a good lawyer also finds out what is waiting for him or her and dresses for the event, feeling more confident by doing so.

Saving money on clothing is a false economy for someone who deals with the public and wants to influence people. The amount you "over pay" for the brand name of the clothing or the name of the store where you buy the clothing should be considered as an insurance premium against making a mistake and an insurance premium for feeling more confident.

Whether you want to "dress up" or "dress down" to a particular group of potential clients or referrers of clients is, of course, your decision. But you are foolish if you ignore the effect of your clothing on potential clients and sources of clients.

Perhaps one way to decide what *you* should wear to the office, or to meet a client, is to ask yourself . . . "How would I want my lawyer to dress if I were paying that lawyer a fee?" You should then dress up or down to the level of what you would expect of your lawyer if you were paying a fee.

Clients may also get an impression of the firm from the way your staff dresses. Clients will assume you approve of the way they dress.

D-7
General Practice vs. Full Service

Lawyers and doctors use the words "general practice" to describe their ability to accept a wide variety of clients or patients with a large variety of needs, referring the client or patient to a "specialist" when needed.

When you inform a client or potential client or recommender of clients or potential recommender of clients that you are in "General Practice" or that you are a "General Practitioner," you may be doing yourself and the client a disservice.

The term "General Practice" may communicate to a non lawyer that you only handle the following types of legal matters:

1. Small fee
2. No fee
3. Small cases
4. Unimportant cases
5. Unimportant clients
6. Cases where no significant money is involved
7. Cases where no complex or sophisticated legal issues are involved
8. Cases done as a favor to someone

The client or potential client will want to go to a "Specialist" when the case is big, either in terms of money or in terms of importance.

Think of your own situation. Assume that you or a family member had an important medical problem. Would you prefer to go to a "General Practitioner" or to a "Specialist." Obviously you'd rather go to a specialist. Your client is no different. Given an important legal matter, clients often don't want "General Practitioners."

Rather than informing people that you are in "General Practice," tell them that you have a "Full Service Practice" or that your firm is a "Full Service Firm." Explain if questioned further that clients should call you with any legal problem and that if you can't handle the problem you network with other lawyers in and out of the firm who have various specialties so that you can help the client find the "right specialist for their case." Clients and prospective clients want to hear the magic word "Specialist."

Try using "Full Service" instead of General Practice. After awhile you'll like it and you'll never go back to saying "General Practice."

D-8
Personal Hygiene and Cleanliness

Lawyers who don't care how they look won't care about how their work looks.

It seems incredible that people who are high school graduates, college graduates and law school graduates have to be reminded to be aware of their personal hygiene and cleanliness and the effect of lack of hygiene upon clients and potential clients.

Judges tell me that it is easy to tell the successful attorneys from the others just by looking at them. The judges are right. If you doubt me, go down to any courthouse and go to the master calendar call and look at the lawyers and their clients. You, too, will be able to pick out the winners and losers by looking at them.

Some of the obvious things which any attorney should double check every morning are:

1. Clean shave. Beard stubble on men and facial hair on women can be negative factors when people judge you.
2. Neat, clean hair. Expensive "hair stylings" are preferable but not essential. Neatly trimmed, clean hair free of tobacco or other odors is important.
3. No dandruff. Dandruff is disconcerting to clients, judges and juries and is indicative of a lawyer who may be oblivious to the obvious.
4. No mouth odor. Lawyers talk a lot, which dries out their mouths and is conducive to mouth odor. An occasional mint or other breath freshener may help.
5. No tobacco odors. Tobacco smells disgust and repel many people, especially former smokers, who may undergo a negative physical reaction to the smell of tobacco.
6. No alcoholic odors. The slightest mumble or mispronunciation may be taken as the sign of an alcoholic if the odor of alcohol is also present.
7. Clean shoes. There is no excuse for dirty and scuffed shoes. Your firm should have a shoe buffing machine and you should use it.
8. Clean fingernails. Fingernails should be cared for and any dirt under or around them removed. Whether you manicure them or not is up to you, but ragged fingernails with dirt under them or fingernails chewed down to the bed of the nails is not acceptable.

9. Clean suit. There is a high incidence of soiled, wrinkled suits among the losers and a small incidence among the winners.

10. Clean, crisp shirt collars. Shirt collars show signs of being worn two and three days in a row even when the shirt is otherwise clean.
    People will think you are poor and cannot afford to wear clean shirts.

11. No body odor. Some people just don't realize how bad they smell. There is no substitute for routine showers or baths. I've seen lawyers jog or play tennis at lunch time and then come back to the office or go to court unbathed and smelling terrible. Excessive perfume or cologne or shave may indicate a "cover up" of bad odors.

D-9
How Do You Look from Behind?

I am making a separate chapter out of this very short topic because it is totally new to me and to almost every lawyer I've discussed it with. It may also be new to you.

Lawyers don't realize how often clients, potential clients, judges and jurors see "them from behind." In the office, you most often face the other lawyers and staff. In court, you are visible from behind to the client, the judges and the jurors when you approach and leave the witness stand or the judge or the clerk, or when you leave or return to your counsel table.

People are negatively impressed by clothes that hang poorly in the back, frayed collars, unkempt hair, scuffed shoes, worn-down heels, dirty clothes, etc., that the lawyer can't see or overlooks. Occasionally a woman lawyer's dress or skirt clings to the back of her thighs due to static electricity.

When the salesperson adjusts the clothes in the mirror in front of you have someone with you tell you how the clothes look in back.

Sit down and stand up with the jacket both buttoned and unbuttoned so your friend can observe how the clothes look and hang from behind.

Before you leave your home in the morning, have someone examine you front and back. Repeat the examination before going to court and before meeting. a client.

How we look from behind is something we ourselves seldom think about but which our clients and potential clients observe.

D-10
Wearing Jewelry

The wearing of jewelry by an attorney is at best of minimal value and at worst of major harm. Trial lawyers have very fixed opinions about the effect of jewelry on jurors and, accordingly, normally avoid all but the simplest of jewelry, if they wear any.

Expensive jewelry, particularly lots of it, can lead a client or potential client to question who's paying for the expensive name brand gold watch or the big diamond ring. Even those clients who react favorably to high quality clothing may react unfavorably to expensive jewelry. In some circles, a Rolex is a *sine qua non* for acceptability. In other sets, it is a big turn off and symbol for a flake. If you're going to wear expensive jewelry, be careful where you wear it.

I would avoid religious jewelry. Not wearing it is unlikely to cost you a client or potential client, and wearing it may or may not offend or concern clients. One attorney told me of losing a major divorce client because the client saw a photo of him with the Pope and was concerned that the lawyer was Catholic and wouldn't represent a divorce client with zeal. As it turned out, the attorney was Jewish, but by the time the attorney found out why the client had left, it was too late.

Fraternity jewelry, school rings, pins, etc., really should be worn only if the wearer feels an absolute need to advertise his or her affiliation to the whole world.

Some single women lawyers tell me they put on a wedding ring when interviewing a male client. They tell me doing so helps keep the meeting focused. Some married women lawyers tell me they take off their wedding ring when interviewing a male client as they want to use every advantage they have when getting clients. I express no opinion on either practice.

Suit yourself in this area, but I don't see any great advantage in wearing jewelry and I do see disadvantage out of proportion to any possible benefit.

D-11

Getting and Keeping Business Clients and Other Clients by Visiting the Prospective Client's Place of Business or Scene of an Accident

Offering to visit the place of business of a prospective client, a new client or an existing client is a very, very effective technique of gaining and keeping a client's confidence in you as a lawyer. I've gained a lot of new clients with this technique. I've used this technique many times over the years and 'the clients have always been impressed with the offer to visit. The usual reaction to the offer is, "You're the first lawyer who ever cared enough about me to find out about my business."

By nature I'm a curious person. I like to learn about other people's businesses. Typically, if a client has any interest in using you as a lawyer, somewhere in your preliminary conversations the client will ask something like, "How do we get started?" or "How do you work?"

At this point I'll usually say something like, "If you don't mind, I'd like to visit your place of business. I'd like to see your product line or your factory or meet your key people. When I understand a client's business I can do a better job of representing the client."

I truly believe that a lawyer should at some point visit the client's place of business in order to understand and represent the client better.

Meeting the client's key people is very important. In addition to your meeting them, they are meeting *you*. By meeting *you*, they will think of you as the firm's lawyer and automatically call you when a legal problem comes up rather than ponder whom to call. It is important to meet the telephone receptionist who can find the key person when you call (or call you when a lawyer is urgently needed); the secretary who will get you access to the key person; and the bookkeeper who will pay your bill. The bookkeeper is more likely to pay you quickly, perhaps first, when that person can identify your name or your invoice with your face.

Be very pleasant to these people. A display of arrogance, aloofness or superiority will cost you a lot of potential good will from people who are extremely important to your selection or success as the company lawyer and their lawyer.

Most people like to talk about their job or their company. Providing them with a willing audience (yourself) is a good way of beginning your relationship with the client.

From time to time during your professional relationship with the client, you should offer to meet at the client's place of business rather than at your office. The client will enjoy taking you to a local restaurant for lunch and showing you off to all the "regulars."

If you have a targeted prospective client, this technique is a good one for getting the potential client as an active client.

At your first opportunity, including even the first time you meet the potential client, you should state something along the following lines:

A. "I know a little (or, a lot) about your industry, but I'd like to learn about your company. Could you arrange a 'nickel tour' for me? I'd love to see how your company operates. I'll even buy you lunch as payment for the tour."

In addition to showing the potential clients your interest in them, you've also demonstrated some prior knowledge of the industry which can help establish you as an expert or specialist in the industry, or at least as being knowledgeable in the industry.

B. "Your business really sounds interesting. I'd love to come out and see:

1. Your factory
2. Your offices
3. Your computers
4. Your store
5. How you operate
6. Other (depending on what the prospective client talked about).

"Do you think you could arrange a nickel tour for me? I'd even buy you lunch as payment."

Try to get introduced to the key officers in the company while you're there. Your "tour guide" will probably introduce you to a lot of the people as you go through the facility. Try not to interrupt unduly the people who are working.

I've used this technique for getting new clients other than business clients. A few examples are:

1. Accident Cases. In a case where the client had not yet decided on which lawyer to use, I've offered to visit the scene of the accident with the prospective client. I'll tell the prospective client that the case sounds very significant, but that I'd like visit the scene of the accident before accepting the case. (It is true that I'd probably accept the case without having seen the place of the accident, but is nonetheless true that I'd also like to see the place before committing to accept the case.)

In more than one case, the potential client chose me rather than another lawyer because I showed that I liked to be fully prepared to represent the client.

I know of a lawyer in Hawaii who represents clients who have mainland accidents. He does an internet video conference with the client and they look at satellite photos to describe the accident in great detail.

2. Estate Planning. I often indicate that I want to see the assets involved, especially the business and, whenever possible, the land. By seeing the property I can get better insight into how to value it. Understanding the age and condition of the improvements, the neighborhood and surrounding properties can give me an idea for using a creative approach with the estate plan (such as partioning the property before or after death).

3. Domestic Relations. If property division is the issue, say you want to see the property. If custody is the issue, say you want to see the neighborhood, school location, etc., of the parent.

4. Other Situations. The list of possibilities where you can visit the business, property or other facility of a client or potential client is endless.

Obviously these techniques will require some of your time, so you want to use them only where you truly want the client or the case.

Try these techniques at your first opportunity and you will be pleased with the good results.

D-12
Attending or Teaching Classes
to Get Clients

A. *Attending.*

Back in the early 1970's, I did some work in the Peoples' Republic of China which was just beginning to open up after the death of Mao Tse Tung. A friend of mine was working for a major international CPA firm. He told me that he was enrolling in a course at UCLA in Chinese. I told him that I thought he was wasting his time. Friends of mine who lived in Beijing (then Peking) in an embassy told me that it takes a minimum of two years to learn enough to maintain the simplest of communications. The CPA friend told me that he really was not interested in the class at all. The marketing committee of the firm had told him to enroll in the class and to attend for three or four sessions and then drop out. They wanted him to meet the students who were interested in China trade because these people, or their companies, were potential clients for the International Tax Section of the firm. If he could find some "qualified" leads, he was to develop them further. The CPA told me that this was a regular marketing technique of the firm. They regularly monitored the catalogues put out by the extension or evening divisions of local universities, looking for classes which might attract people and companies who were potential clients. They sent the CPA to the first few meetings to meet the students, and then the CPA dropped out in time to get a refund of the tuition. The firm used the classes to identify and qualify good leads for later sales.

B. *Teaching.*

Almost without exception, lawyers report to me that they pick up a lot of good clients by teaching either in an evening law school course or an undergraduate or graduate university course. By teaching the subjects likely to attract the decision-makers they were looking for, they got a good return for the time invested. The "students" often worked full time for companies that paid their course tuition, and the students regarded the teacher as being "the expert. "

C. *The* XY *Experience in Hard-Core Selling.*

Mr. XY is the fictitious designation of a real attorney who is extremely successful in plaintiff's personal injury litigation. He taught an evening course on contracts at a non-accredited law school. He taught first year contracts. Every semester about 10 to 12 doctors would enroll in law school for a variety of reasons. Most if not all of the doctors dropped out of both the class and the school after four or five sessions when they learned how much work is involved in becoming a lawyer.

The PI lawyer who taught the course would "hard sell" the doctors. He invited them to dinner before the class and to coffee after the class. He invited them to his home for a Sunday barbeque. He told them how he was the greatest PI lawyer who ever lived. He told them about the great cases he had handled. He told them that he would protect their medical fees on any case they sent him.

The PI lawyer told me that 60-70 percent of the doctors he "sold" to were disgusted and revolted by him and his tactics. But one or two doctors became convinced that he was as good as he said he was and sent him their PI cases. This lawyer is a well-known lawyer with a huge profitable personal injury practice built up from clients sent to him by these doctors. One doctor can be the source of a lot of personal injury practice. The lawyer wasn't concerned about the doctors he alienated because they weren't sending him any business to begin with. As the lawyer said to me, "You can't lose what you never had."

In each of the examples above, the fact pattern is more or less the same:

1. Pick a class to attend or teach where the students who are interested or involved in the subject matter are likely to use lawyers or refer others to lawyers;
2. When you enroll as a student, you can move into and out of many different classes;
3. As a teacher, you will be classified as an instant expert by your existing clients (once you communicate to them that you are teaching);
4. You have to decide how and when to make the sales pitch, ranging from a super soft sell (do nothing, let the students come to you) to the hard sell, as exemplified by the personal injury lawyer.

D-13
Speaking Engagements

Speaking engagements are a most important way of reaching the specific targeted group of potential clients you want to target. I have successfully utilized this method extensively in my own practice development. As of the writing of this book, I have spoken several hundreds of times in every state in the union, every province in Canada, several foreign countries, and on every continent, including Antarctica over a period of three decades.

Speaking to Bar Associations, law students or young lawyers for the sole purpose of getting business is not cost-effective, considering the time spent, unless you target a local audience. Getting clients and cases is simply one of the benefits which justifies to the other members of my firm the amount of time I spend on speaking engagements. At the same time, I speak to the Bar Associations and young lawyers and law students out of a sincere desire to help them and the profession.

I probably have been somewhat careless in not utilizing Bar speaking engagements more aggressively for practice development.

On the other hand, my speeches to non-lawyer groups are almost exclusively for the purpose of client development. I devote a lot of time and effort both before and after the talks to preparation and follow-through.

Maximize the Effectiveness of Speaking to Groups

Remember that public speaking is more beneficial on a long-range, repetitive basis rather than on a short, hit-and-run, immediate-result basis.

I get a call about once a month along the following lines: "Mr. Foonberg, I heard you speak in Chicago about five years ago," or "Mr. Foonberg, my lawyer, John Jones, heard you speak in Dallas last year. I have a problem (my client has a problem) and we want to know if you can help us find someone who can help us."

In a given year, I will get 10 to 20 of these calls. About half are simply requests for free advice. A few involve a small matter that I will handle for a small fee (or no fee) just to establish a good contact. About three or four involve a reasonable fee ($1,000-$2,500), and about every two years I might get a substantial matter with a very substantial fee (over $25,000 and as high as $200,000). I once received a $100,000 fee matter and a $250,000 fee matter in a two-month period and then nothing substantial for one year from speaking.

1. DECIDE EXACTLY WHAT KIND OF CLIENTS AND CASES YOU WANT

You don't want all the legal work. You want only work that you can handle competently and profitably; otherwise, you must realize, you will be wasting your time and efforts.

For example, giving talks to college students on "How to Represent Yourself Without a Lawyer in a Landlord-Tenant Dispute" is not likely to do much to bring you immediately profitable legal business. On the other hand, a talk to plastic surgeons on "Tax Advantages of Professional Corporations," or a talk to residents of an exclusive retirement home on "Is Your Will Up to Date," might result in immediately profitable legal business.

Certain kinds of practices are usually immediately profitable.

Examples: A. Taxes or any tax-related item
          B. Purchase or sale of a business
          C. Personal injury (if properly selected)

These cases don't usually require significant outlays of working capital for costs and can result in fees over a fairly short period (three months to one year) from the date of the talk.

2. DECIDE WHERE THE BUSINESS COMES FROM (NETWORK THE NETWORKERS)

A. Certain types of businesses and professions can feed or refer people to you other than themselves. Examples: CPAs for clients' wills and taxes and sales of businesses; doctors and insurance agents for personal injury cases; real estate brokers and bankers for their clients for sales or exchanges of businesses or real estate. Other lawyers can send you specialty work beyond their expertise. Large firms can refer to a small firm where they don't want the client going to a competitive, large firm. I call these firms and people "networkers." You are not seeking the "networker" as a client you are seeking the networker's clients as clients.

B. Direct approaches to the "consumer or end user groups" are, in my opinion, the most immediately profitable. For example, a talk to a medical association or dental group on "Tax Advantages of Professional Corporations" may be more profitable, in terms of direct contact, than trying to reach these people through their professional advisors.

About half of all new legal business comes from new and repeat work from existing and former clients. About 1/3rd comes from referrals from existing friends, relatives and professional acquaintances. Therefore, speeches directly to the "potential clients" (if you can reach them) are not quite as valuable as speeches to existing clients, friends, relatives and professional acquaintances who advise or recommend to the potential client. In my opinion and experience, speeches directly to the potential clients are slightly better than speeches to their advisors.

3. DECIDE THE MOST COST AND TIME-EFFECTIVE WAY TO GET TO THE GROUPS OF POTENTIAL CLIENTS OR THEIR ADVISORS

Some examples are as follows:

A. Ask an existing client to recommend you to the group as a speaker.

B. Contact the group "cold" by telephone or letter or email (telephone is recommended) to get the name, address and phone number of the President, the Program Chairman, the Educational Chairman, the Convention Chairman, Executive Secretary or Executive Director. You must do this to find out who the decision-maker is. After you find that person, you should call the individual and explain that you want to address the group.

Usually these trade associations or groups are looking for legal expertise in their industry or profession. They may want an address on a topic that you would never have considered. One group wanted me to give an address on "How Lawyers Compute Their Fees." The address was very well received, but I never got any business out of the address that I'm aware of. Generally speaking, you should stick to a subject that shows that you know the law in the area of the industry or profession which you are addressing, so that it is apparent to members of the audience that they can call you or use you.

4. CONTACT THE GROUP YOU WISH TO ADDRESS

You must take the initiative. Most of the officers are volunteers. They are taking time from their families or their businesses to be involved with the professional group. When you take the initiative and contact them, you are doing them a big favor. They have the burden of finding speakers and subjects and you have saved them a lot of their valuable time. They will often take the path of least resistance and use you rather than seek someone else who mayor may not be available or who might turn them down.

5. CONTINUING LEGAL EDUCATION (CLE) SPEAKING ENGAGEMENTS

Speaking at CLE programs has the same general results and effectiveness of speaking to any group of client advisors. The lawyers who are attending want to learn how to do the work themselves. If they wanted to refer the work to a specialist in the area, they wouldn't be spending their time at the seminar. Occasionally, however, one of the lawyers who attends may decide to bring you in if the matter is simply too complicated for that lawyer to handle. Interestingly enough, you sometimes get work from the lawyers who don't come to the CLE seminar. They identify you as a specialist when they receive the program announcements (assuming they read the announcements). If they have a problem in their office when the announcement comes, they may call you then. (Remember, if they wanted to handle the matter themselves, they'd attend the seminar.)

6. SIZE OF THE AUDIENCE

The size of the audience is totally unrelated to the amount of legal work you might get as a result of the speech or the announcements of the speech. The smallest group I ever addressed was nine people and I got a $40,000 fee from someone who meant to come but didn't. The lawyer called me at my office after the speech to give me the work because he needed a California lawyer. On the other hand, the largest audience I ever addressed was 2,000 lawyers and spouses. I never got any business from that group.

7. DON'T EVER CANCEL A SPEECH!

Two lawyers here in Los Angeles, one male and one female, who were and still are trying to become known at the State Bar and American Bar Law Practice Management levels, once cancelled a speech because only 29 people were coming. In addition to showing more concern for themselves than their fellow attorneys, they disappointed the Bar Association, which had spent a lot of money advertising the program. The Bar Association asked me to "bailout" the situation. About 120 people came to the program after it was advertised that I, and not these two, would be speaking. I have since refused to speak on the same program with either of these lawyers and this has cost them several good opportunities. I also got a small referral matter out of the speech. Please don't ever cancel a speech after you commit to give it.

8. CLE DIRECTORS

Most bar associations have a CLE director. Most CLE directors belong to ACLEA (The Association for Continuing Legal Education). This person may ask you for a DVD or video tape or both (tapes are normally used when there are multiple venues in a small room). They may or may not offer a fee. Many lawyers and consultants have gotten a bad name for themselves by turning CLE into "infomercials" fishing for business. Don't oversell when you do CLE. Try to project yourself as a lawyer willing to share information with other lawyers. Don't forget that the CLE component may be secondary to the wishes of what the program chair or President wants.

9. SPEAKERS' BUREAUS

I have never used a speakers' bureau to seek speaking engagements. I find that many consultants and lawyers use them to get infomercial exposure. Some require a fee. Try one and come to your own conclusions.

D-14
How to Maximize the Effectiveness
Of Speaking Engagements

The most effective use of your speaking engagement will be the impression you create on the people who see and hear you speak and some who read the program announcement. There is also some benefit to be obtained from your pre- and post-speaking activities. You should do the following:

1. Ask the group to publicize your talk in their mailings to their members, identifying yourself, your firm, the city in which you practice, your qualifications, your photo, and a description of the speech. If they don't want to do it, offer to do it for them. They may not be willing to give you access to their email list.

2. Send the same information to the local newspapers where you practice, labeling the handout a "press release".

3. Send the "press release" to the local newspapers in the area where the talk will be given.

4. Be sure that there is a handout of some nature at the talk with your name, address, including website, speech title, and date on it (if you give the same talk to different groups, simply change cover sheets).

5. Leave some vital information out of the handout. Tell the audience that you will be glad to send them the missing information, if they'll give you their card. Then promptly send the missing information to them. They will be impressed with your efficiency and that you care and you will have their name on your mailing list.

6. Tell the people that if they will leave their card you can put their name on a client and colleague mailing list.

7. If you are speaking to a group, ask for a copy of the list of attendees and add them to your mailing list. If they won't give you the list offer a door prize to be drawn from their professional card. Keep the cards for your mailing list. It is a cheap trick and you may never be asked back again.

8. If you are speaking to lawyers, ask for a list of the attendees and add them to your mailing list.

9. Show up at least one hour before the speech (preferably more if possible) to be sure that everything is set up properly. Use that time to introduce yourself to the group members who arrive early. Ask them if there is any thing special they wish to hear covered.

10. Stay around for as long after the speech as possible. Do not just give the speech and run away. Ask various people if the speech covered what they were interested in knowing and if they have any suggestions for improving the talk. This is a valuable source of clients.

11. Send thank you letters to all the people whose names and addresses you acquired. Tell them how much you enjoyed speaking to the group and meeting them. Follow up on any leads you obtained.

12. Review all evaluations to look for ways to improve your presentation.

D-15
Getting Admitted to Multiple Courts and Joining "Prestigious" Legal Societies

Clients and potential clients are sometimes impressed by the number of courts and number of "prestigious legal" societies to which a lawyer belongs. Lawyers know that many of these organizations require only a license to practice law, membership dues and an interest in the society to join or to be admitted to the court. Some clients think that you are somebody special when you belong to these courts and groups. There are various ways of indicating your multiple admissions to clients and potential clients including: certificates on the walls of the office, listing in the firm brochure and website, listing on professional cards, listing in a biography, listing on announcements.

Typical courts which are relatively easy to gain admission to in addition to your state court include:

A. Your Federal District Court
B. Other Federal District Courts in your state
C. Federal Circuit Court of Appeals for your Circuit
D. Supreme Court of the United States
E. Tax Court of the United States
F. Claims Court of the United States "
G. Circuit Court of Appeals for the Federal Circuit

Many professional societies and associations which have prestigious-sounding names have little or no requirements for admission. (Naturally, you'll have to pay membership dues.) If you come across such an organization, don't be afraid to contact them to inquire about membership.

Almost every Bar Association has sections or committees in substantive areas of law as well as *ad hoc* committees to study specific needs. All you have to do to list yourself as a member is to ask to join the committee.

If your local Bar Association doesn't have a committee to meet your needs, you should ask the President of the Bar Association or the Board of Governors of the Bar Association to appoint you as a temporary or *ad hoc* chair to get the committee functioning. In addition to serving a worthwhile function to your fellow lawyers, you'll be able to tell clients and potential clients that you're such an expert in the area of law that you are the Chairman of the Bar Association's committee or section. If you do international work, you'll get a double benefit in being "Chairman" since many foreign languages don't have a word for "Chairman" and you become "the President" in translation.

D-16
Going Back to Where You Came From

If you are a transplanted person, that is, you moved to where you practice law from some other place, then it can be worthwhile to go back periodically. This is especially true if you are licensed to practice law in both places.

It is important, however, to organize your trip from a marketing point of view before you go. It is also important that you make your "marketing trip" at least once a year, if possible.

Let me give you a successful case in point. A lawyer from upstate New York who had been in practice a few years was compelled to move to Florida because of the health of one of his children. He didn't know a single person. It was necessary for him to study for the Florida Bar. I advised him to go back to upstate New York and speak to whatever Bar Association would let him speak on the subject of "What to Do for Your Client Who Moves to Florida." He spoke at countless local Bar Association lunches and meetings and also to CPA society lunches and meetings. On my advice, he also began to attend all of the New York State Bar Association conventions and personally introduce himself to all the lawyers he could, being sure each received his Florida business card. Other lawyers and CPAs began to think of him as the New York lawyer who moved to Florida. They began to refer him the work for their clients who had moved to Florida for the winter or permanently. Typically, their clients have real property interests and personal property in both states. The Florida lawyer worked with the New York lawyers whenever possible. The end result is a very successful practice in Florida. The Florida lawyer goes back to New York twice a year-once for the Annual Meeting of the State Bar Association and once for the "lecture circuit," combining the meeting of the local Bar Association, CPA Society meetings and innumerable lunch meetings with individual attorneys.

You can and should go back to college seminars, fraternity reunions, law school reunions, Bar Association conventions, etc. These can be good sources of legal work. Don't start, however, unless you are willing to make a commitment of at least two or three trips just to reinforce their memory of you and their association of your law practice to where you now live.

D-17
Be Careful About Going to Funerals, Hospitals or Accident Sites

Acts that you intend as gestures of friendship and helpfulness can be interpreted as solicitation or ambulance chasing.

When I was a brand new lawyer, the father of one of my lifelong friends died in a tragic swimming pool accident. I went to the funeral out of a sense of honor to the man whom I knew and friendship to my friend as well as to offer condolences to the widow. After the funeral there was a memorial service at the home. I went to the service and said to the widow, "Mrs. X, I am truly sorry. Let me know if there is anything I can do to help." She said she would be calling me in a few days for some help on filling out the insurance forms and asked if I would please give her a card with my office number on it. I did so. Several days later I got a call from her other son, whom I knew, but not well. He said his lawyer had said I was unethically hustling a grieving widow at a funeral to get legal work and that he (the lawyer) would be happy to handle the estate in an ethical manner. My explanations were to no avail. The widow had no memory of anything that she or I did or did not say. I lost out on a good probate because of my offer, sincerely made, to be of help.

The moral is to be careful about how and where you make contact with widows, widowers and others at funerals or memorial services. You're probably better off waiting a couple of days and then calling to offer your help (if you really want to).

I have had similar negative feedback when I've visited accident victims in hospitals or at accident sites.

I know of at least one incident where newspapers reported that accident lawyers called an airline after a plane crashed to learn at which hotel the victims' relatives would be staying. One law firm opened a "temporary office" in the hotel to sign up the families of the victims. To their chagrin, they found that three other firms had gotten there earlier and had already signed up most of the relatives as clients.

Representatives of the airlines were angry that witnesses had been interviewed before being told not to talk to anyone but airline representatives.

Apparently, the families were not in the same frame of mind as the widow to whom I gave my card. The lawyers laughed at their critics when the lawyers got their clients and their fees. In some jurisdictions, going to the hotel to sign up the survivors is apparently not unethical. Perhaps times have changed since my incident with the widow. Perhaps the survivors welcomed the fact that they didn't have to seek out an expert lawyer to help them. Perhaps they appreciated the opportunity to arrange for the burial and the lawsuit at the same time.

I personally try to avoid any contact with my potential client at funerals, hospitals, accident sites, etc. I do not recommend that the reader sign up cases under these grieving circumstances. I wouldn't do it. On the other hand, some lawyers do go out and find the victims of tragedy and the survivors and they apparently do so with a high degree of success. Perhaps they are simply delivering door -to-door service to people who need it and want it. These are often big cases with big money and big fees, and the people often need immediate legal advice before they are contacted by agents of the other side. Perhaps you should distinguish between those situations where you do have a pre-existing relationship with the client and those situations where you don't. I leave it to you to make your own decision.

I have been told, but have never verified that airlines and others do not give information about the victims to stall for time in order that their lawyers and investigators can get to the families before plaintiff's lawyers or investigators can do interviews or photograph evidence.

Some states prohibit plaintiff's attorney or their investigator from contacting victims or families of victims for a certain number of days. Defense representatives and their investigators on the other hand are given carte blanche to contact victims and tell them not to talk to plaintiff's lawyers or to try to convince families or the victims that they will get less money if they use a lawyer to deal with the defendant.

Whatever decision you make about going to funerals, hospitals accident sites or talking to victims or their family, be prepared to act as quickly as your rules allow because you may find yourself going into territory already occupied by large defense firms or large plaintiff firms or both.

D-18
Political Activity and Running for
Political Office to Get Clients (and Experience)

The effectiveness of running for political office in order to get legal business is, at best, questionable. I've spoken to many established practitioners who have run for political office to get their opinion of the effectiveness of this technique. They uniformly tell me that if you run and lose, it's a disaster. The candidate and the candidate's family spend tremendous amounts of time and money, all to the detriment of the practice of the loser. When the election is over, there is no increase in clients because no one wants to go to a loser. Additionally, good clients are lost when the practice is neglected because of campaign commitments.

On the other hand, I've talked to new practitioners who ran for office before they got their practices started. Typically, they moved into a community where they knew no one. They ran for political office simply to get their name out to the public. They reported getting some clients and contacts. They reported that the time and money spent was very cost effective.

Accordingly, I would reconcile the two results by saying that if you already have a practice, it probably *would not* be cost effective to run for political office to get legal business. On the other hand, if you are starting from ground zero, with little or no practice which will be neglected during the campaign, it may be a worthwhile endeavor.

Political activity as a means of getting clients is, at best, questionable in terms of cost and time effectiveness. Lawyers, however, historically and currently, are expected to have and express opinions on political candidates, judicial candidates and pending legislation. When a lawyer has no opinion on these subjects, some people equate lack of *knowledge* or opinion on pending laws to a lack of knowledge of law generally. If you want to avoid expressing an opinion because of a lack of knowledge or fear of offending a client, in the event of disagreement you can beg off by commenting, "I feel that the difference in the candidates or in the issues is as much a matter of your personal opinion as anything else. I recommend that you study the candidate's expressed positions on the issues you consider important and then form your own independent opinion."

I've been told that in rural areas and small towns, lawyers are especially expected to have and express firm convictions on issues and candidates. The failure to do so is a serious negative attribute.

I personally do my best to avoid heated political discussions with clients for fear of my confusing my reaction to their political views with the merits of their case.

Former President Gerald Ford is one of the nicest most charismatic human beings I have ever been blessed to know. He opined that running for office was excellent training for a new lawyer because lawyers and politicians did the same thing.

To paraphrase President Ford:

"Good lawyers are like good politicians. They go out into the public and meet people. They listen to and learn the people's old problems and new problems. They help people to solve their problems. Law is an excellent training for politics and politics is an excellent training for law."

I would unhesitatingly recommend President Gerald Ford to be my lawyer on any matter. One cannot argue with success!

I am willing to modify my advice as follows: We live in a rapidly changing world. By getting out into the public you might learn of areas needing legal solution that you never knew existed. This knowledge can be of great help in functioning in modern society when you meet potential clients with the new problem. Accordingly, it might be a good investment of your night and weekend time to run for office and knock on doors or go to political club and other meetings to meet new people and learn of new problems facing them.

D-19
Going to Conventions and Trade Shows
When You Are Not the Principal Speaker

There are pluses and minuses to this approach. Time spent at annual meetings of groups can be worthwhile but it is usually time that you have to take away from actively practicing law, and for that reason alone, you might not want to do it. If you truly are interested in the activities of an organization, then you can and should use the time you spend at these meetings to do practice development at the same time. The best point to emphasize is that you are a lawyer who understands the industry and who has clients in the industry. (Don't assume that your presence alone makes this point obvious. You should orally state it as often as you can.)

For most solo practitioners and small law firms, I don't consider annual conventions and trade shows to be the best investment of your limited time and funds unless you are a speaker at the program or unless you wish to combine marketing with a vacation.

On the other hand, these shows are a good way to learn about an industry you want to get into as a lawyer because of the growth potential of the particular industry. When you subsequently try to develop clients in the particular industry, you can "name drop" that you were at the annual convention or show. This will give you credibility with the client or potential client.

Don't waste time with anyone who obviously can't help. For example, don't make a dinner date with a small retailer from upper Maine if you practice in Southern California. On the other hand, a dinner date at the convention or a lunch date after the convention could be worthwhile if the person is the CEO of a large distribution company in your area.

Try to get the convention registration list of names and addresses for both pre-attendance study and for follow-up letters to the people you wish to pursue at a later time. Two sample letters follow.

Be sure you bring and give out and collect as many cards as possible.

SAMPLE POST CONVENTION LETTERS

A. People you didn't meet at the convention:

Re: Annual Convention of Widget Makers

Dear Mr. _____:

I had hoped that we could meet at the annual convention of the Widget Makers Association in Las Vegas. In the activity of the convention, we missed each other.

I was particularly interested in your views on how the new interpretations of the new tax laws affect your business practice. We have many clients in the industry and are always seeking information on cost-effective techniques that work and which comply with the tax laws. You are welcome to attend my firm's seminar where we will cover the new tax laws, including the laws affecting the Widget industry. You may come alone or bring a friend or advisor, if you wish. In any event, I would truly enjoy getting your opinions either by phone or by letter or email.

I will be calling you in a few weeks to try to get together for lunch if you have the time. (This follow-up call may be an aggressive technique with which you are not comfortable. On the other hand, you have nothing to lose if the company or person is not your client and you really want them as a client or contact in the industry.)

You may wish to visit our website at www.widgetlawyer.com

Sincerely,

B. Lawyers you met at the convention, especially house counsel:

Dear Mary:

I very much enjoyed meeting you at the annual meeting of the Widget Makers Association in Las Vegas. It is always professionally challenging to meet with other attorneys who have a common interest in Widgets.

If I can be of any help to you or to your clients here in California, please give me a call at any time.

You can find information about the firm at www.widgetlawyer.com

Sincerely,

Be sure to put the attorney on all your mailing lists. There are no ethical prohibitions on your contacts with attorneys.

C. Non-lawyers you did meet at the convention:

Mr. John Doe
Widget Makers of California

Re: Annual Convention of Widget Makers

Dear John:

I very much enjoyed meeting you at the Widget Makers Convention in Las Vegas.

I wish we could have spent more time together. I was particularly interested in your views on how the interpretations of the new tax laws will affect your business practices. We have many clients in the industry and are always seeking information on cost-effective techniques that work and which comply with the tax laws. You are welcome to attend my firm's seminar where we will cover the new tax laws, including the laws affecting the Widget industry. You may come alone or bring a friend or advisor, if you wish. In any event, I would truly enjoy getting your opinions, either by phone or by letter. You may wish to visit our website at www.Lawyer.com.

I will be calling you in a few weeks to try to get together for lunch if you have the time. (This follow-up call may be an aggressive technique which you are not comfortable with. On the other hand, you have nothing to lose if the company or person is not your client and you really want them as a client or contact in the industry.)

Sincerely,

D-20
How to Handle People Who Hate Lawyers
or the Legal System

From time to time you may be verbally attacked by some person who doesn't like lawyers or the legal system.

Typically, the person makes his or her comments as loudly as possible and when there is an audience of other people to hear the attack.

The reasons for this attack are numerous and may include:

1. Someone who confuses lawyers with the law and who blames the lawyer or a judge or the system for bad results in his or her own private legal matter.
2. Someone who truly has been abused by a lawyer or judge or the system (these people are rare, but it sometimes happens).
3. Some people who are very vocal when the moon is full, and quiet the rest of the month.

It is a mistake to argue with this person. This person is baiting you and would like nothing better than for you to go on the defensive. This person wants to embarrass you or the system publicly in order to get personal attention.

On the other hand, you can't just ignore the person, as this might be taken as an admission of the correctness of the charges and would leave you looking foolish in the eyes of the others present.

I have found the following "lines" to be successful in handling this person by seeming to agree with him to satisfy his ego and then putting him into an impossible corner that he can't get out of.

A. When the person accuses lawyers of "stirring up litigation" by bringing non-meritorious suits (usually this person or company has just been sued for something and is now paying legal fees for a defense):

> "You know, Mr. Jones, you might be right, but you have to understand our system. Our legal system gives access to all people to air their complaints and grievances in court, even when the complaints and grievances are not meritorious or are only imagined. Anybody who can afford a filing fee or find a lawyer who is willing to handle the case can file a complaint and the case must be defended. Well managed companies considered this as just cost of doing business like electricity. Insurance can normally be obtained at low or reasonable cost to protect yourself. I do sympathize with you."

You have just shifted the "fault" to the attacker for not properly managing his company or offices by not carrying proper insurance coverage. You have also expressed sympathy for the individual without agreeing or disagreeing with his allegation.

Another response is:

"You know, Mr. Jones, the world is changing and the legal system is simply reflecting these changes. When I was a boy, if I were to come home from school crying and my father were to ask me why I was crying and I were to respond 'I was a bad boy in school and the teacher hit me,' then my father would also hit me. Today, if *YOUR* (emphasize the word "your") child came home from school crying and told you that he had been a bad boy and the teacher hit him, you would sue the school board."

Here you have shifted the attack back to your attacker and left him in the no-win situation of agreeing he would sue the school board (thereby becoming part of the problem), or of saying he wouldn't take legal action to redress the wrong done to his child.

B. When the person accuses lawyers or judges of being "dishonest" or "on the take" or in collusion with each other, the response here should be first to ask the person what he does for a living (assume he is a widget maker, for this example). Then say,

"Mr. Jones, doctors and lawyers and teachers and judges and widget makers and priests and rabbis and policemen are just human beings. In every group of people there are some bad apples. No profession is perfect. No group is 100 percent anything. It is theoretically possible that something was improper in your case, but it is not likely. Besides, if you have any real belief that somebody was dishonest, you can file a complaint with the state bar and the police and there will be a very thorough investigation. Dishonesty is a very serious allegation and a lawyer would be risking his or her license to do that. Was there enough involved in your case for a lawyer to risk his career? Call my office and I'll get you the proper numbers for you to file police reports and bar complaints."

Here again, you have pushed the burden back to the accuser to say or do something. The person will probably be embarrassed to admit that his case wasn't big enough for a lawyer to risk losing a license. You have also lumped his business or occupation with yours, and he's placed in the awkward position either of fabricating an explanation of why his group is different from lawyers, doctors, judges, policemen, etc., or of acknowledging that there is also a percentage of bad apples in his group, occupation or profession. You have offered to help him file a police complaint. He is boxed.

C. When a person complains that society is too complex due to all the laws and rules and regulations and that lawyers have created these rules to make money for themselves, I like to respond,

"Mr. Jones, if the human race simply obeyed the Ten Commandments, starting with 'Thou shall not steal' and 'Thou shall not commit adultery,' 90 percent of all legal work would disappear and few would need lawyers. Most of these rules and regulations are simply refinements of the Ten Commandments, so I guess as long as people won't obey the Ten Commandments, these rules will be necessary. When people obey the Ten Commandments, we won't need all these rules and regulations.

God told Adam & Eve to leave the apple alone. They didn't. Ever since then people have been breaking the rules. Perhaps you have a solution to this problem."

Making reference to the Ten Commandments and Adam & Eve puts the person in an awkward situation. The reference to adultery is something people identify with because of the soap operas and the news. Offering to hear this solution leaves him looking foolish regardless of what he does or does not say.

D-21
How to Explain Defending Criminals to Clients and Potential Clients

How can you defend people who are obviously guilty or how you can plead "not guilty" for your client when 34 eyewitnesses saw the client do the criminal act captured on 4 video cameras? Or, how can you be part of a system that puts convicted rapists and child molesters and killers and armed robbers back onto the streets so they can commit their acts on yet other innocent people before they are sent to jail?

The person who asks that question may have a prejudice against all lawyers. The person may believe that the defense of accused people who are ultimately found guilty is not in the public's best interests. If you can properly "field" that question, you may be the one lawyer in whom that person may have confidence.

The above questions (or similar questions) have often been asked of me by all levels of people from the poorly educated to the well educated and the rich and the poor. It is possible that you yourself may have similar reservations about representing defendants in criminal proceedings in some situations. Whether or not you practice criminal law, you should have an answer to these questions, as your response (or failure to respond) to the question could easily cost you a potential client or legal matter, even though the people who ask the question may never have a criminal or other matter themselves.

There are multiple "short answers" and a few long answers that can solve the problem of how to respond. Some of them are as follows:

1. It is our system of criminal laws that every person accused of a crime is legally innocent until a judge or jury finds him or her guilty. Our whole system is built around this fundamental concept. Once you assume people are guilty until proven innocent, we have a police state.

2. Joseph Stalin once characterized the difference between the Soviet Penal System and the U.S. Penal System by saying that in America we would rather let 99 guilty people go free than execute one innocent person for a crime he did not commit. In the Soviet Union they would rather execute 99 innocent men than allow one guilty man to go free. You (the person you're speaking to) have to decide which system you would rather have and then you will be able to answer your own question. Perhaps this is one of the many reasons the Soviet Union collapsed.

3. It is a fundamental part of our legal system that every person is entitled to a fair trial. In order to defend himself, a person has to be able to prepare his defense by finding witnesses or evidence. For this reason, we let the defendant out on bail to assist in the preparation of his defense. Sometimes, we let people back onto the streets who use their freedom to commit crime instead of prepare their defense. There is no perfect system and we just don't have any alternatives that would protect innocent people.

4. The practice of law is something like the practice of medicine or being a minister. When someone is shot by the police while being arrested the doctor is ethically bound to get the injured person well enough to stand trial, even though the person may subsequently be found guilty and executed. It is the job of the judge or jury, not the doctor, to decide who shall die. Similarly, the lawyer is bound by ethics to help an accused person receive a fair trial. Doctors must heal bad people, Priest must comfort bad people, Lawyers also must help people. It is part of being a profession rather than being employees of a business.

    It is a fundamental part of our American history that people accused of crimes are entitled to a fair trial, and that the defense lawyer tries to be sure that the accused gets a fair trial. One of the earliest examples is the famous Boston Massacre case where the English soldiers were accused of murdering the colonists on Boston Common. John Adams, a future President of the United States, along with Josiah Quincy, Jr., helped defend the British soldiers.

    Each of these two great patriots to the Revolutionary cause received a lot of personal abuse from family, clients and other revolutionaries for undertaking the defense.

    On March 20, 1770, Josiah Quincy wrote to his son:

My Dear Son,

I am under great affliction at hearing the bitterest reproaches uttered against you for having become an advocate for those criminals who are charged with the murder of their fellow-citizens. Good God! Is it possible? I will not believe it.

. . . I must own to you . . . as one destined to be a savior of your country . . . the representation will be destructive of your reputation and interest . . .

Your anxious and distressed parent,
Josiah Quincy

The answer clearly sets forth Josiah Quincy, Jr.'s position:

Boston, March 26, 1770
Honored Sir:

. . . If they [the reproachers] had been friends, they would have surely spared a little reflection on the nature of an attorney's oath and duty . . . and discharge of his office.. . . these criminals charged with murder are not yet legally proved guilty, and therefore, however criminal, are entitled, by the laws of God and man, to all legal counsel and aid; that my duty as a lawyer strengthened the obligation. . . people will one day rejoice that I became an advocate for the aforesaid "criminals" *charged* with murder . . .

. . . There are honest men in all sects-I wish their approbation; there are wicked bigots in all parties-I abhor them.

I am truly and affectionately,
Your son
Josiah Quincy, Jr.

Frankly, the reason for repeating so much of these two letters is not so much to explain criminal defense to clients and potential clents but rather to express some of my personal philosophy.

5. The "legal technicalities" complainers. I frequently use this response when a person complains about non-admissibility of evidence due to "technicalities."
    My response: "Right now you are objecting to 'legal technicalities' but if it's your son or daughter who is being prosecuted, what you now call these legal technicalities will suddenly become 'constitutional rights.' "

D-22
Using Foreign Language Ability

We now live in a global economy. English is the worldwide common Lingua Franca of the legal profession. Almost without exception lawyers and other professionals and executives in all countries learn English as part of their education. I have lectured on every one of the seven continents to English speaking lawyers from hundreds of countries where hundreds of local languages are spoken.

Foreign language ability however, can still be immensely valuable in attracting and keeping local and specific clients. America has traditionally been the land of refuge for people from all over the world. There are no signs that this will change in the future. There are an estimated 250,000 to 350,000 Koreans in Los Angeles alone and only a' few lawyers who can speak Korean, including a Caucasian lawyer who tells me he is doing quite well with Korean clients.

There is no accurate count of the number of illegals who do not speak English but may need a lawyer for a large variety of cases.

I personally speak Spanish, Portuguese and German, in various degrees. Over the years, I have obtained many clients who feel more comfortable speaking with someone who can communicate with them in their own language. I tell them to bring an interpreter with them just to be sure that I understand their exact legal situation.

At the time of writing this chapter in 2007, no English is spoken at all in 59% of the huge San Fernando Valley, a large part of Los Angeles. If the San Fernando Valley were a city (which might happen) it would be the 6th largest city in the U.S. Spanish, Farsi, Arabic, Hebrew, Russian, Chinese and many other languages are the only language spoken in 59% of the homes.

It can be worth your time and effort to learn at least one foreign language if you don't already know one. It is also worthwhile to brush up on your high school or college language. Obviously, there should be some relationship between the language you decide to learn and the needs of your community. Immigration can be a very lucrative field, especially if you are dealing with a businessman who wants to immigrate. He will have corporations to form and relatives to bring in and investments to make. A single immigration client can become a five-figure legal fee. Immigrants also have their share of accidents and criminal problems.

Just being able to make simple conversation is adequate. No one will expect you to be able to expound philosophically in the foreign language.

Of course, you must communicate your language ability. The best place for media advertising, if you want to do it, has been reported to me to be the classifieds of the local foreign language newspaper and radio and television. Some immigrants are illiterate both in English and their native language. They can be reached by TV and radio. Belonging to the local Chamber of Commerce or cultural club of the foreign country is also a good place to meet these people. I would caution you not to get involved in these chambers and cultural clubs unless you really care for their purposes and motives. If you join just to get business, you probably won't and you will have wasted time and money. On the other hand, if you really care about the groups involved, then these groups are excellent sources of clients.

If you can't or won't learn the appropriate foreign language, then you should consider having an associate who has foreign language capability. You should also consider having secretaries and other non-lawyer people who can speak a foreign language since they can both bring you foreign language clients and translate for you. To put it another way, if two secretarial applicants or two associate applicants are otherwise equal in ability, hire the one with foreign language ability.

It may or may not be worthwhile to set up an office in the same building or near a foreign consulate where your foreign language is spoken, if that is the business you want.

D-23
Learn to Say "Lawyer" in Foreign Languages for Your Contacts with Foreigners

The practice of law is now global. Almost all lawyers throughout the world have standard English in school.

While traveling, I have met many foreigners who do not know English. If you travel for business or pleasure, you also will meet foreigners. Inevitably, at some point in the conversation, the subject of occupation will come up. You should be able to say something like, "I am an American lawyer," or simply "I lawyer" (pointing at yourself). Then hand the person a card and point out the words "attorney at law" on your card. This procedure has produced a couple of clients over the years. There really is not much investment of time or money involved. If you had the ability to study for and pass the Bar exam, you should be able to learn how to say "lawyer" in the language of the foreigner you meet here or in the language of the foreign place you visit.

D-23A
The Word "Lawyer" in Foreign Languages

Language	*Spelling*	Phonetic (English) *Pronunciation*
English	lawyer	lawyer
Afrikaans	procureer	procureer
Arabic		al-muhawmee
Armenian		pasdahpahn
Bulgarian	advokat	uhdvokuht
Chinese		liuhshy
Czech	pravnik	prahv-nyeek
Danish	advokat	ahdvookaht
Dutch	avocaat	ahvokaaht
Farsi/Persian	vakil	vakeel
Finnish	asianajaja	ahseeanahjahja
Flemish/Belgian	advocat	ahdvokat
French	avocat	avo kat
German	rechtsanwalt	rektsahnvalt
Greek	dixnyoqos	dheekeegoros
Hebrew/Israeli		o'rekhdin
Hungarian	jogasz or ugyesz	yogahs
Indian		avokaht
Indonesian	abugado	ahboogahdo
Italian	avvocato (m)	ahvokahto (m)
	awocatessa (f)	ahvocahtessa (f)
Japanese		bergo-shi
Korean	pyenho-sa	pyenho-sa
Norwegian	jurist	yureest
Pakistani		wakeel
Philippino	abugado	ahboogahdo
Polish	advokatas	ahdvokahtahs
Portuguese	advogado	ahdvogahdo
Romanian	avocat	ahvokat
Russian	jurist	yureest
Serbo-Croatian	advokat	ahdvokaht
Spanish	abogado	ahbogahdo
Swahili (Kenya)		wakeelee
Swedish	advokat	ahdvookaht
Turkish	avukat	avukat
Ukranian	advokat	ahdahkaht
Vietnamese	luat su	looaht-suh

D-24
Giving Testimony to Federal or State Committees or Commissions to Establish Yourself as an Expert Who Has Good Connections and Influence

Many clients and potential clients think that if you are asked to give your opinion on pending legislation, you are some kind of expert in this area.

Clients don't realize that the reason you appear or give testimony is because you volunteered to give it, not because they approached you and asked for your opinion.

Often you can send in an unsolicited letter to the clerk of the appropriate legislative or administrative committee with your opinion and ask that the letter be circulated to the members of the committee for their consideration. The clerk usually is happy to do this. If, however, the clerk will not do it for you, mail the letter directly to the committee members. Ask the clerk the date of the next scheduled committee meeting and include references to that date in your letter.

The opinion can range from one sentence setting forth your personal opinion to an article worthy of publication in a law journal. If you wish, you can sign the letter under penalty of perjury or in affidavit form and ask that it be considered "evidence" for the committee.

If you wish actually to appear in front of the committee to state your opinion, simply ask to do so. A committee will rarely refuse to grant its permission, especially if you are insistent. They may limit you to two or three minutes, but they will normally let you speak.

After the committee meeting is over, you can send your clients and non-clients a press release about your appearance. You can also post this press release or a letter on your website. Alternatively, you can simply send a letter to your clients and potential clients.

Whatever you do, don't send the press release or the letter *before* you go, as the clients or potential clients may think you have a lot of influence with the committee and they may ask you to assert some position you know nothing about.

If you actually go to the committee meeting or hearing, try to get there before it commences or after it adjourns so that you can mumble a few words to the chairman and the key people with whom you agree. They won't be difficult to identify as they normally have signs at their seats with their names. You can mumble a few words like, "Just want you to know we're following this closely." These few words will be referred to as "personal conversations" in your press release. If the person has a few moments available (not likely), you should also introduce yourself by name and city; but this really isn't necessary since your name will already appear in the records of the committee and you may not have enough time to give *both* your name *and* comments. You can put your scheduled appearance on your website under "future appearances."

Naturally, you should pick the committee carefully to coincide with your marketing plans. As indicated, the purpose of this exercise is to establish yourself as an "expert" with "connections and influence" in Congress or the State Assembly, etc. Accordingly, the committee actually chosen must be an important committee to those clients and potential clients you want to hold or acquire.

There are many committee activities which easily tie into the kind of clients and/or cases you have or want. These activities almost always have one committee or another studying bankruptcy (creditor or debtor); taxation; health care; banking (interest rates are always being considered); worker's compensation; counterfeiting of goods; debt collection activities; litigation (the judicial system); high tech (copyright and patent problems), etc.

The list of "tie-ins" between the kinds of clients and cases you want to keep or get and the various committees which are continually studying them is endless. You have to use a little ingenuity to find the connection and then exploit it.

If you personally don't have the time to search for the appropriate committees, have a law student or college student majoring in government get you a list of all of the standing and *ad hoc* committees at the particular legislative body with which you are concerned, along with a description of the scope of the committee's activities. You then must link that committee's scope of activities with your marketing plans.

In all honesty, I should advise you of one possible negative aspect to this plan of sending unsolicited comments or giving testimony to those committees. You may find your name on the contribution list of every member of the committee. They may bombard you incessantly with requests for contributions for campaign funds, fund raising dinners, ad books, etc. Apparently, there appears to be a mentality among some legislators that if you want their time to express your views or your client's views, they can ask you to give them money for their campaign funds. When I testified on behalf of a client concerning pending legislation, I was besieged by telephone calls and letters asking me for money. This siege lasted for years. These people are persistent. You have to say no without insulting them, as you may need them in the future-unless, of course, you or your client are willing to pay the money.

A sample "Press Release" and a sample "Letter" follows.

D-25
Sample Letter to be Sent After Giving Testimony to a Federal or State Committee or Commission

Re:

Dear Clients and Colleagues:

On January _____, 20XX, I gave testimony to (I appeared before) the House Ways and Means Committee of the United States Congress to express my opinion on:

1. Pending litigation concerning reinstatement of the full investment credit; [or]
2. The need for legislation concerning reinstatement of the full investment credit.

In a personal conversation with the Chair, Rep. Jones of New York, I assured him that our offices and clients were following closely the activities of the Committee in this area of high concern to our clients (optional: and that we approved of his ongoing efforts.)

We know of your interest in (the subject under consideration by the Committee) as well as of the interest of other clients with the same problem.

Your comments would be of great help toward the goal of getting the legislation we need.

Very truly yours,

Jay G Foonberg

D-26
Sample Press Release After Giving Testimony Before a State or Federal Committee or Commission

To be sent to targeted clients and targeted potential clients as well as to newspapers, TV, etc. You may also wish to put it on your website under the "Press Releases" link along with other "press release."

FOR IMMEDIATE RELEASE:

Jay G Foonberg has appeared before the House Ways and Means Committee. [Optional]

Jay G Foonberg, a noted Beverly Hills tax attorney, gave testimony on January____, 20XX, before the House Ways and Means Committee to express his views on the need for reinstatement of the full Investment Credit on used as well as new equipment purchases. Mr. Foonberg reported that his views have been submitted as part of the permanent records of the Committee and are being studied in depth by the Committee. Mr. Foonberg also indicated that in a private conversation with the Committee Chairman, Mr. Jones, he communicated that the Committee's proceedings are being followed closely.

No date was given as to when the Committee would vote on Mr. Foonberg's proposals.

D-27
Name Tags

If you are at a meeting where people have name tags, you should wear your name tag on the right side so people can see your name when you shake hands. Men often erroneously wear names tags on the left because historically men wore military decorations on the left side and they continue to do so to the present.

I personally carry in my brief case an extra name tag on which my name is printed in large legible letters so that I can switch name tags if the one I'm given is too hard to read. (The extra name tag can also get you into a party in your hotel when you're not a guest. No one questions where you got your name tag. They assume that the host ran out of the "regular" name tags.)

I normally add the words "attorney" or "atty." or "Esq." on the tag, as I don't verbally inform such strangers that I am a lawyer. I've seen people replace the name tag they were given with their professional card by inserting their card into the name tag holder. Since they now have a name tag different from that of others in the group, people look carefully at the tag and "discover" the person is a lawyer.

Women sometimes avoid "pin on" name tags because of concerns that the pin will damage the fabric of their clothing. The name tag can be pinned unto the strap of their purse or they can keep empty name tags that clip on or hang around the neck and then insert whatever name tag insert they want to use.

D-28
Why You Should Travel First Class

When I was in law school, one of my professors told the class, "Always arrive at the courthouse by taxi, never by subway," and he was right. There are several valid reasons for first-class travel.

1.) HOTELS

Your clients and potential clients will be more favorably impressed when you tell them you can be reached at the Ritz rather than at the "Happy Cockroach" motel. I live in Beverly Hills, California, where there are about 10 hotels in the immediate area. People are often judged by their hotel, as follows: (These are one person's ratings, and other people might disagree; additionally, these ratings might not apply in other cities.)

A.) HOLIDAY INN-RAMADA INN

Salesmen on limited expense accounts and per diem, low-level employees and low-income tourists.

B.) BEVERLY HILTON-CENTURY PLAZA

Department managers, upper income tourists and middle-level management.

C.) BEVERLY HILLS HOTEL

Movie stars, corporate presidents and wealthy tourists.

D.) BEVERLY WILSHIRE HOTEL

Kings, Queens, Princes, Princesses, Chairmen of the Board, highest level people.

You won't impress anyone, least of all your client or potential client, by staying at "El Cheapo" hotel or "with friends." On the other hand, they'll be flattered when you suggest a breakfast meeting or dinner meeting or drinks at your fine hotel.

If you truly can't afford a good hotel, tell people that you couldn't get into the good hotel, or that your travel agent fouled up. Whatever you do, don't start bragging about how you saved money by staying at a cheap hotel.

In foreign business and travel, it is especially important to use the prestige luxury hotels so that you can have email and other communications with your clients and office and you can get your telephone messages in proper English.

The Hilton Hotels, the Westin Hotels, the Ritz Carlton and the Hyatt Regencys are, generally speaking, good hotel chains to work with when you don't know anything about the local hotels. If you already have a client in the city, ask the client to recommend the "best" hotel.

You can stay at a moderate price or cheap hotel and meet your clients in the lobby of the better hotel.

2.) AIRLINES

It is worthwhile to travel first class by air, but by no means is it as important as staying in first-class hotels. If you have to choose between first-class hotels and cheap air fare, or first-class air fare and cheap hotels, then by all means choose the better hotel. First-class travel has the following advantages:

A.) Contacts

The people you meet are more likely to be influential or in positions of power. You may be able to contact them years later (I have done so), reminding them that you happened to meet on a plane from A to B, and then seek a contact you need. It is not likely that you will make a client of many people you meet on airplanes, but it does happen on occasion and you sometimes are able to make contact through the people you have met on the plane.

B.) Working Conditions

If you are going to work on an airplane, then by all means travel first class. You can spread your papers and files and turn your notebook screen without the person in the adjoining seat reading your documents and jeopardizing the attorney client confidential relationship. You will arrive ready to do business. If you are going to dictate into a recorder while you travel, there is much less engine noise in first-class to interfere with the tape recorder transcription.

C.) Lounge

Unless you travel a lot, paying annual dues for a lounge probably isn't worth the money. The lounges are often over crowded, loaded with screaming running children and often full of litter, but they are better than the airport lobby if you want to contact clients from an airport. Many of these lounges have conference rooms that can be reserved for free or for a fee for meeting with clients and potential clients.

D-29
How to Handle a Potential Client With a Good Case Who Already Has a Lawyer

It is exceptionally difficult for me to write this chapter for reasons which will become apparent as the information develops.

Most, if not all, Bar Associations or groups have a rule to the effect: "You shall not give legal advice to a client already represented by a lawyer in a matter."

The motivation and background for this rule is probably well intentioned. A lawyer with full knowledge of the facts of the case and who is current on the law of the case is theoretically better able to give legal advice than one who is getting five minutes of the client's version of the facts at a cocktail party and who has had no opportunity to research the law of the case.

On the other hand, I find that lawyers, especially young lawyers, are less and less experienced. As the number of lawyers increases and the number of cases handled by each lawyer decreases, there is sometimes a corresponding lack of experience and therefore lack of good advice or lack of good client relations.

I often hear "horror tales" from clients of other lawyers about a case in progress that the client wants to talk about. Sometimes, as a result of hearing the client's version of the case, I can conclude the case seems to be badly handled. I become tempted to tell the potential client that the case is being badly handled and, at least, that the case could warrant review by a second or third law firm (including yours).

On the one hand is the professional rule which may prohibit your getting into the case, and on the other hand is your sincere desire to help someone who appears to need help.

Over the years, I have attempted to stick by the rules, but I have lost good clients and good legal matters to lawyers who don't stick by the rules.

A dissatisfied client who is confused enough or unhappy enough with the way his or her case is being handled indicates a lawyer who is already in danger of having a client go elsewhere. If the client and lawyer had a good relationship, the client probably would not be discussing the case with another lawyer to begin with. The only question is whether you, as the third-party lawyer, should get involved and, if so, on what basis.

Let me illustrate possible courses of action in response to a given situation. Someone meets you at a cocktail party and relates the following:

"My manager just walked out on me and went to work for my biggest competitor as a sales manager. He is calling all of our accounts and stealing them for the competitor. I went to our lawyer and he said, 'There is probably nothing that can be done. Judges feel sorry for little guys and there is no point in filing a law suit because you will probably lose.' All I know is that this sales manager is hurting us badly and I can't do anything about what he has done."

You have several possible responses:

1. "My ethics as a lawyer prohibit my giving you advice on the case while you are represented by another lawyer. I'm sorry, I can't help you." (This is also good when you really just don't want the case). Unfortunately, this may create suspicion in the client's mind that the case is being mishandled (a conspiracy of silence among lawyers).

2. "Your lawyer may have given you good advice. I don't know enough about 'the facts of the case to question his or her decision. On the other hand, I've handled many of these cases. Sometimes the judge rules in favor of the former employer if there are trade secrets involved such as knowing your confidential customer list, your supplier, sources, your pricing terms both for purchasing and for sales, or confidential special selling or purchasing techniques you may have. It really is a question of fact. The judge might not be sympathetic to an employee's stealing the guts of a business. Besides, in your suit, you can sue both the former employee and the new employer on a conspiracy or agency theory. Even if you lose, you will have taught a lesson both to your existing employees and potential employees that you won't take this lying down, and if they want to do this to you they had better be ready for a good fight."

3. Again, I can't advise you without knowing all the facts. If you like, I'll be glad to go contact your lawyer and see if he has any objection to a second opinion.

The latter response has two levels: The first level is a literal explanation of the ethics and an offer to consult the prior lawyer; the second level shows the potential client that his or her present lawyer may not really have the experience to handle the case properly. If all of this has been explained and explored by the prior lawyer, you will simply reinforce the client's view of the lawyer's value on the case and the client will be even more confident knowing that the lawyer really knew what the law was and what could be done. If none of this was explained by the lawyer to the client (whether or not the lawyer knew it), then you will probably have a new client.

I have lost clients to other lawyers during my representation of the client (perhaps I deserved to lose them). I have also gained clients from other lawyers because these clients were unhappy enough to seek my opinion (perhaps they deserved to lose the client).

In the final analysis, it may be a reasonable rationalization to say that a lawyer should be willing to take over the case from another lawyer when the client is dissatisfied, but the second lawyer should not create the dissatisfaction with a view toward getting a new client.

There are other possible responses which might be along the following lines:

4. "I am most concerned by what you are telling me. Possibly there is bad communication between you and your lawyer. Possibly the case is being handled incorrectly. The ethics of my profession prohibit my advising you on this case. If you wish, I'll make a thorough study of your case, and if I feel there is a mishandling of your case, I'll tell you so and you could seek another lawyer. In no event will I undertake the case, so you'll know that what I tell you is not intended to get you as a client."

5. "It is impossible for me to express any opinion of the case without relearning what your current lawyer already knows, and then I might or might not give you the same advice you have already gotten. If I agree with your current lawyer, you will have wasted your money."

If a client is dissatisfied enough with his or her lawyer to discuss a case with you, then the first lawyer may be on the verge of losing the client no matter what you do or don't say. I would say that you should be honest in what you say, but don't kindle or fan the flames of discontent, and do leave the door open for the client to come to you or back to you at a later time. Be sure that you have read and understand your local rules on the subject because there is a good chance that the lawyer who lost the client may commence a proceeding against you for violating the rules (he'll do this if the case was a good one). If the case or client was a bad one, you will probably have the files in minutes by special messenger and you will get a bottle of booze at Christmas time.

D-30
Personalized License Plates for Lawyers

My license plates make no reference to my being a lawyer. Other people do have personalized plates referring directly or indirectly to their being a lawyer. When personalized plates first came out, I thought the people with these plates were simply trying to get a tax deduction for their car as a sort of moving billboard. A few lawyers with these plates told me that the plates were a factor in getting new business, typically in parking lots.

I personally have my doubts about the amounts or kinds of legal clients one could get or keep as a result of having personalized plates. If you're interested in personalized plates, the following list might give you ideas. They might be available in your state or in California if not renewed.

These names are from a seven letter state. Some states allow up to 7 letters and some states have symbols.

Many states have "special plates" and you may be able to get the word or letters you want on a "special plate" series that might otherwise not be available on regular plates.

LAW	LAWEELS	LAWFOLK	LAWHON
LAWISE	LAWMAAM	LAWRBIZ	LAWA
LAWEEZR	LAWFONE	LAWHOOO	LAWISEl
LAWMAJR	LAWREP	LAWAND	LAWELEE
LAWFOX	LAWHORN	LAWIZ	LAWMAKR
LAWRESS	LAWANNA	LAWELLS	LAWGAL
LAWHORU	LAWJAM	LAWMAM	LAWRICK
LAWCME	LAWENDY	LAWGAME	LAWHYME
LAW JAW	LAWMAMA	LARWRIZ	LAWCML
LAWENGR	LAWGIRL	LAWIEBE	LAW JEAN
LAWMAN	LAWRKR	LAWCO	LAWENGl
LAWGIVR	LAWIFE	LAWJF84	LAWMANl
LAWRLTY	LAWCOC	LAWENG2	LAWGNHO
LAWII	LAWJM	LAWMD	LAWRMGR
LAWCONV	LAWEN2M	LAWGUY	LAWIII
LAWJUR	LAWME	LAWRMOM	LAWCORP
LAWERED	LAWH	LAWILD	LAWLADY
LAWMEN	LAWRNC	LAWCPA	LAWERL
LAWHAIR	LAWIMPY	LAWLAND	LAWMGR
LAWRSKI	LAWCR	LAWERSC	LAWHARE
LAWINB	LAWLASS	LAWWMN	LAWRUB
LAWD	LAWER2B	LAWHAT4	LAWINC
LAWLAYD	LAWWMNI	LAWDAW6	
	LAWRX		
LAWESK	LAWHAWK	LAWINCO	LAWLER

LAWNASZ	LAWS	LAWDDA	LAWETC
LAWHEAD	LAWINES	LAWLESS	LAWOFFS
LAWSAAB	LAWDEAN	LAWETSU	LAWHEAT
LAWING	LAWLESl	LAWOFIC	LAWSAGE
LAWDOC	LAWEWIN	LAWHEED	LAWINGS
LAWLEY	LAWOK	LAWS CAR	LAWDOCI
LAWEWON	LAWHEEE	LAWINKS	LAWLEYJ
LAWONE	LAWSECS	LAWDOC2	LAWEZEE
LAWHER	LAWINNE	LAWLEYl	LAWORDR
LAWSFUN	LAWDOG	LAWEZZ	LAWHERl
LAWINNER	LAWLIBR	LAWORK	LAWSKY
LAWDOGG	LAWEl	LAWHER2	LAWINO
LAWLIFE	LAWPFSR	LAWSOME	LAWDOGS
LAWFEE	LAWHEl	LAWINR	LAWLINC
LAWPRES	LAWTOO	LAWDP	LAWFEM
LAWHIMZ	LAWINS	LAWLINE	LAWPROF
LAWTYME	LAWDST	LAWFIRM	LAWHIT
LAWINTU	LAWLM	LAWR	LAWUCLA
LAWDUCK	LAWFISH	LAWHITE	LAWINUS
LAWLOR	LAWRAT	LAWURE	LAWEDA
LAWFIVE	LAWHIZ	LAWIRTZ	LAWLYON
LAWRAZE	LAWUSC	LAWWIFE	LAWYRET
LAW4YOU	SUEBOY	SUEM4U	ARBITR8
LAWWIMN	LAWYRZ	LAW43	SUEBRAT
SUE ONE	ACQUIT	LAWWITZ	LAWYRl
LAW5	SUEBRIG	SUEOOl	CRIMLAW
LAWWIZ	LAWYR2	LAW66	SUEBRV
SUEPWR	CPAATTY	LAWWL	LAWYR2B
LAW82	SUEBUGG	SUE STAR	JDCPA
LAWYA	LAWYR4U	LAW88	SUEBZ
SUESTA	CPA JD	LAWYAH	LAWYR85
SUECA	SUE4FUN	LAWYAIB	LAWYUR
LEGALET	SUE CAR	SUE4lT	JGFESO
LAWYARl	LAWZDRY	LEGALEZ	SUCARR
SUE4ME2	LAWYAR2	LAWZME	LEGALHI
SUCARl	SUE4YOU	LAWYA2B	LAWZOOT
LEGALl	SUCHEF	LAWYER	LAWZTHR
LEGALIX	SUECITY	WHIPLSH	LAWYERA
LAWl	LEGALKD	SUECO	JGFLLB
LAWYERD	LAW2	LEGALLY	SUEFLY
JGFJD	LAWYERl	LAW2B	LEGALMR
SUEFLYS	LAWYERR	LAW28	LEGALMS
SUEFOX	JURIS	LAWYERS	LAW4
LEGALRX	SUE GAL	JURISl	LAWYERX
LAW4ALL	LEGALTV	SUEHAPY	LAWYERZ
LAW4LOR	LEGAL!	SUEHITAXES	LAWYER2

LAW4ME	LEGAL2	SUEHIGH	TAXMAN
LAWYER3	LAW4MR	SUE HPPY	TAXLAW
LAWYNNR	LAW4PAY	SUEBIG	SUE LADY
TAXLAWR	LAWYORR	LAW4REL	SUEBILL
SUEME	TAXLWYR	LAWYOUR	LAW4STU
SUEBIZ	SUEME2	LAWYRE	LAW4U
SUEBMW	SUEYOU	SETTLE	LAWYRES
LAW4U2	SUEBOON	SUEYOU2	

D-31
Visit Other Lawyers' Offices

Try to go to other lawyers' offices whenever you get the chance. Alternatively, try to get other lawyers to your office. Try to meet or be introduced to as many of the lawyers as possible whenever you visit other lawyers' offices.

Over the years, I have visited many other lawyers' offices. As a managing partner and because of my activities in the Economics of Law Practice Section (now Law Practice Management Section) of the American Bar Association, I was genuinely interested in how other offices were run. I always had an innate curiosity in "how the other fellow does it." I wanted to see (among other things):

1. What kinds of offices could be gotten for how much per square foot;
2. The comparison of size and location of partners' and associates' offices;
3. The types of furnishings in the lawyers' offices;
4. The proximity of secretaries, libraries and word processing and other equipment to the lawyers' offices;
5. How clerks and paralegals were accommodated; and
6. The equipment in each lawyer's office.

These and other interests brought me in face-to-face contact with associates and partners in their offices. The associate or partner will usually remember the visit for may years. Over the years, other lawyers have visited my offices. Practice development was never in my mind during these visits.

While organizing my experiences for writing this book, I've realized that I've received many good clients and cases from these lawyers. I've received many cases and clients from associates after they left the firm where I met them and later started their own practices or joined other firms.

For some reason, the fact that we spent a few moments together discussing office management was enough to leave them with a memory of my name and that I was from California. They have referred to me many of their clients who needed a lawyer in California.

Accordingly, I would recommend that you visit other lawyers in their offices when you can, or have them visit your office.

When I have a lunch meeting with another lawyer, I do not meet the other lawyer at the club or restaurant. I meet him or her at my office or their office, then go to lunch. When I'm at another lawyer's office, either for a short meeting, conference or deposition, I ask the other lawyer for a "quick tour" of the offices. These lawyers normally are happy to show off their offices and I try to say hello and introduce myself to the other lawyers we see. I don't linger. I usually give out and collect a card and go on. I put the information about the other lawyer and the circumstance of the meeting into my database and communicate with them by email, with announcements and other communications I would send on to clients. These few moments with each lawyer have been very rewarding both from a management and a practice development point of view.

D-32
How to "Work a Room" and Make Small Talk
To Get New Clients

After reading this chapter you need not fear going into a room full of people you do not know.

You will be able to make contacts and perhaps even get a new client or two initially or eventually by following these steps

1. Where to sit.

    Get there early. Try to decide where you will want to sit. You may chose to sit up front or on a side where people looking at the speaker or a stage will also see you. The front row seats at basketball games typically sell for a huge price because they are the seats where TV cameras are likely to include them in the game play and where others at the event can see them. Many front row seats are owned by theatrical agents who want to put their clients where they can be seen. If you opt for front seats, make it a point to take your seat late even though you arrived early, and leave early so everyone can see you.

    You may wish to sit at the rear or close to the exit (my preference). I can step out to talk to a prospective client, one on one, in the hallway outside the room.

2. Name tags.

    Determine if the name tags have colors or other designations (ribbons, stick-ons, etc.), so that you can identify a person's position in the sponsoring organization by their name tag.

    Always wear your own name tag on your right.

    When people shake hands their line of sight is usually drawn to the right shoulder. If you carry a purse you may wish to pin the name tag to a shoulder strap to avoid damaging the fabric of your clothing.

    Bring your own name tag with both your first and last name in big bold letters for those who have poor eyesight. Have your own name tag holder with a clip and a name card in it which may be better than the one you were given.

    If questioned about your having a different name tag you can respond: "Yes this is a different name tag. I wear it for the benefit of my clients with poor eyesight. The large lettering makes it easier to see and remember the spelling of my name." This may impress the questioner to think that you are a loving caring lawyer considerate of seniors.

3. Table seating place cards.

    When you get there early look at the seating arrangements to determine if there is someone at a table where you also would wish to be. Try to switch place cards or seating assignments if you can.

4. Carry your drink in your left hand. You don't want to shake hands with a cold wet right hand.

5. Only drink clear drinks, water, club soda, white wine, etc. In the event you spill it on yourself or another person or someone bumps into you, there won't be red stains and you will be able to stay without changing clothes or trying to get the stain out before it dries.

6. Skip the finger foods or only use your left hand for finger foods. You don't want to shake hands with a greasy right hand.

7. Carry any plates in your left hand. Put the beverage container on the plate not in your right hand. As pointed out in 4, 6, & 7 always leave your right hand free for shaking hands or for writing if right handed.

8. Carry a lot of professional cards and at least 2 or 3 working pens. Hopefully you'll give out the cards. Also bring a small pad of plain white paper with your name printed on each sheet if possible. If you have pens with your name on them tell the person who borrowed it, "Keep it I have more."

9. Starting a conversation.

    The best way is to stand directly in front of and close to the person and say, "Hello Mary (or whatever her name might be). It looks like your name is Mary Lotzacrakers did I pronounce it correctly?" Everyone likes to have their name pronounced correctly and will correct you if you mispronounced it. By standing close you may block her view of another person which might cause her to leave you.

10. Look at the name tag again (to reinforce your memory).

    If the person's organization and position are apparent on the tag, you can say, "I see from your name tag that you are the vice president of Widget Productions. It sounds like an interesting position or 'challenging' position, is it?"
    Hopefully the other person will then go into a good explanation that gives them a chance to expound their own importance.

    If the person's organization and/or position are not there or if the answer to your previous question was not illuminating, you can also ask, "What brings you here?" The person will usually answer giving you valuable information for a client contact. Be prepared to answer the question "and what brings you here?" when the other person has finished their answer and asked of you.

11. Never never ask a person, "What do you do?" or "What kind of work do you do?" This can be a difficult question to answer especially if the person is a stay at home person who has not been otherwise working. This question will also mark you as a "user," someone who wants to take more than they put in, and who wants to use the other person.

12. Pick out some item of their jewelry or clothing and say, "That's an interesting pin (or whatever). Is there a story that goes with it?

    Note you never said it was pretty nor that you liked it. You just said it was interesting and inquired if there was a story.

    The person will normally tell you if they also think it is interesting and if there is a story behind it. They obviously like it or they wouldn't be wearing it.

13. At this point announce yourself as sincerely as you can.

    "Well you can see from my badge my name is Jay Foonberg. I'm a lawyer and represent some of the people in this room (in this industry)" or "I support this charity" (if true.)

14. Ask for a card.

    Simply say, "May I have one of your cards?" If they ask, "Why?" tell them the truth. "I would like to send you some information and I need your number and address." They may or may not ask you for one of your cards. Don't be concerned if they don't ask you for a card. You will have their name and address and know a little about them in order to send them a follow up letter or make a follow up call (if you wish).

    If they don't have a card offer them one of yours and a pen (letting them keep it) and ask them to jot down their email address on the back. It takes very little of their time to do this and they may also give you the address and the number(s) etc.

    As a last effort you can ask them to jot their email address on the plain white paper small pad. The person will see your printed name on the pad when they add their name and email address. Tell the person to keep the pen you gave them, especially if it has your name on it. It will be a reminder of you.

15. Breaking away.

    Just tell the truth. "Mary, I would like to stay and chat a bit longer, but I'm supposed to meet as many people as possible because I may be working with them (in the charity), (as their lawyer), (whatever). I've got to go but I will call you or write you in a few days."

16. As soon as you can, jot down the name of the event, the place and the date on the back of the card you received or on your own card or a piece of paper. You will need to remind yourself and the other person of where and when you met, as well as the item of clothing or jewelry, and how they answered the question about what brought them there.

17. When you get back to the office send a short follow up note as follows:

> Dear Mary:
>
> It was nice meeting you Saturday evening at the Starving Artists Organization at the Beverly Hilton Hotel. I enjoyed your story about - the jewelry (whatever).
>
> I am enclosing some information about my firm and if I can ever be of any assistance to you please let me know. I have also added your name to our VIP list of people whom we update from time to time about what is happening in our office.
>
> Sincerely,
>
> Jay G Foonberg
>
> Enclosure: Firm Brochure

18. Put that person on your mailing list and send them the usual announcements, and emails. Call that person if you really see them as a potential client.

19. Circulate the name(s) of the people you met throughout your office to determine if others also know the person or their organization.

20. If you are going to be photographed with an important person, put your drink away out of the picture and try put your arm around the person at the shoulder so that your hand is visible. If an object such as a plaque or trophy is in the photo, get your hand onto the object. By having your hand in the picture on the important person or on the object you are not likely to be cropped out of the picture.

21. Using your cell phone camera or button mike recorder.
    I have never done either of these, but I have seen others doing so. You may wish to have a small voice recorder in your pocket with a small non observable button mike. You can then put your hand in your pocket immediately after meeting someone and dictate everything without stopping to write or relying on your memory. I have also seen others using their cell phone cameras to surreptitiously take photos of the person with whom they have just met or to pose for a photo with them.

22. If you found the event or the sponsors worthwhile, send a thank you note to the organizers, complimenting them on the guests and ask to be placed on their mailing list so you can come to their next event.

D-33
Lawyer's Conduct Out of The Office

When you are out of your home or office you are still in public. What follows are a few miscellaneous tips. Some of the tips have been expanded upon in other chapters.

1. Responding to "First thing, let's kill all the lawyers."

    Responding to people who claim that Shakespeare said: "First thing, let's kill all the lawyers."

    These morons are easy to handle if the lawyer is prepared with a nonstop barrage of talk, not allowing the other person a chance to interrupt.

    I respond as follow; in a loud voice for all to hear: (I really do)

    "You must have gone to a school that didn't teach English literature. It's obvious you never read the play and are just repeating something you heard someone else say. You are repeating the words of a murderer who wanted illiteracy in order to cause rebellion.

    That statement is a complement and tribute to lawyers, Shakespeare never said that.

    Shakespeare wrote a play called *Henry IV* in which one of the characters said that.

    The Character was Dick the butcher. Dick the butcher was a co-conspirator of John Cade. John Cade had that name because his father had stolen a cade of herrings. A cade at that time was a small barrel. John Cade, the son, was also a thief and he was a revolutionary who was hired to try to stir up a rebellion in England against the King.

    He declared himself to be king, promising that food would cost a third of the current price and that the sale of weak beer would be a felony. He declared that everyone would dress in clothing he designed and that all food and drink would be free when he was king.

    He said that everyone would have to worship him as their lord.

    His co-conspirator, Dick, then said: 'The first thing we do, let's kill all the lawyers.'

    The first overt act of their conspiracy was to immediately murder Emmanuel, the town clerk, by hanging him because he admitted that he could read and write.

    Shakespeare knew that lawyers could protect the innocent against crimes, like the murder of the innocent town clerk. Shakespeare was using his characters to pay a great compliment to lawyers.

    Perhaps, before you repeat those words, you should read the play. Shakespeare's plays can be found on the internet or in a library.

    It's a shame your school probably didn't teach English literature."

    You will have put him on the defensive with nothing he can say in return.

If you say or do nothing in response you will have allowed him to insult you and your chosen profession. You may not win any friends, but you will be respected.

2. Responding to anti lawyer jokes.

   I usually say: "The next time you tell a lawyer joke, you should give thanks to the lawyers of America who protect your 1st amendment right to tell that joke."

3. The clothes you wear.

   When you are outside your home of office you are still in public.

4. Taking cell phone calls when in the presence of others.

   Tell the caller: "I'm with other people and I can take your call. I don't want to discuss your legal matters in front of other people. I'll call you back in 15 minutes (or whatever)." Tell the people around you, "I'm sorry about that. As a lawyer (if they don't know you are), I must be available to clients when they have serious emergencies, but I don't discuss client matters in public, so I'll call him back after the 9th hole (or whatever). I apologize for the interruption." Your reputation will be increased by both the caller and those who were near you when the caller called.

5. If you decide not to charge for your services, send a bill showing nothing due.

   If you don't send the "no bill" bill, the client may think you forgot to charge. The client might not call you in the future when they have a fee paying matter for fear you forgot to bill and might discover your error when starting a new matter for that client.

6. Carry a photo of your family members in your wallet or in your cell phone. The photo will remind you to discuss fees and payment at your first meeting. Clients want you to discuss fees and costs at the earliest possible opportunity.

7. Send appropriate copies of client communications to their accountant or insurance agent or others whom the client wishes to keep informed. These people may send you more clients with the same or similar problems.

8. Suggest mediation or arbitration with potential clients when the matter does not warrant the costs or delays of a trial.

9. Accurate error fee time records are critical in maintaining client trust in the financial aspects of the case.

10. Be polite but never friendly with the opposing counsel in the presence of a client. The client may think that friendship is the sign of a deal or sell out of their case.

11. Be prompt and exact with all meeting times for clients If you are early they may think you had nothing to do. If you are late they may think you are arrogant or disrespectful.

12. Shake hands with anyone you meet, and especially with the client, when you say hello or goodbye. Appropriate touching is a sing of friendship and confidence.

13. Make bank deposits in person and wave or make small talk with the manager. Bank managers can send you clients.

14. Keep your car clean inside and out. If a client or potential client associates you with a dirty automobile, they may think you can't afford a car wash or don't care about your appearance.

15. Carry a visible yellow pad when you go to a meeting. It will identify you as a lawyer and you may be approached by potential clients.

16. Keep a voice recorder in your car to record sudden brainstorms for your clients and their cases.

17. If you have a lot of clients in a given industry, go to that industry's trade show to understand their interests and concerns.

18. Speaking engagements to targeted groups almost always provides good results.

19. If you are asked by a potential client what differentiates you or your firm from other lawyer, be prepared with a rehearsed answer.

20. Pick an office location with or near where successful lawyers have their offices, typically in a successful first class building. If you are in a second or third class building, some clients may think you are a second or third class lawyer.

D-34
What To Call Yourself – Attorney? Advocate? Lawyer? Counselor? Esq.? J.D.? Shark? Or What?

Hopefully this chapter will prompt some original thinking on your part.

What you call yourself is primarily a matter of personal choice, local custom and local ethics rules. It may be helpful to understand the background of your choices as part of the history of our legal profession.

You have many choices, and most, if not all of them, are proper. The practice of law is a continuum, not always a series of stops and starts. Many changes are gradual, taking place over centuries.

If you don't care about history skip over to Current Practice.

Under the Roman legal system, lawyers went to court. That's all they did. They went to court. Non lawyers did the transactional work. The court lawyers were called "advocates" or "those who were called." They were called by the court or by the litigant to help the litigant. The word "advocate" stems from the Latin Advocare, which means to "call" or "call out" for help. In England and the Commonwealth countries today, lawyers are "called" to the bar rather than "admitted to practice."

The Roman Legal System was codified by the Emperor Justinian in 535. Included in the codification was the Civil Code. Included in the Civil Code was a position called the Notary. The Notary did most, if not all, of the documentation and registration of anything which involved money or business. Conveyances, mortgages, loans, company formations, family law if money was involved, inheritances and other transactional work. Since most of the world was illiterate, they also drafted the documentation. Notaries were not then, and still today, have no loyalty to any client. They are loyal to the transaction and sometimes to their government. They are not allowed to represent any of the parties or even all of the parties.

England developed the common law, rather than the civil law. The division between civil law and common law was sealed by the Magna Carta, which created the right to trial by jury, something which has never been part of the civil law. The creation and use of the common law trust is unknown to the civil law. The concept of the rental or the hire was also a rarity in the civil law until recently.

While England did not follow the Civil law, it did follow the system of lawyers who only went to court and notaries who did the transactional work. In 1538, Henry the Eighth wanted a divorce from Catherine of Aragon. The Pope in Rome refused to give the divorce and Henry broke away from the Church of Rome to create the Church of England (also called the "Anglican Church") and got his divorce from the archbishop of Canterbury. Henry also took away most of the powers of the notaries, who had been appointed by the Vatican.

After the split with the Church of Rome, lawyers still only went to court and were called Barristers. The work formerly done by the notary was now done by the Solicitor. both the barrister and the solicitor were regulated by the court system.

In colonial America, which was part of England, the practice of law was still divided into the two parts, barrister and solicitor.

After the American revolution, there was westward expansion and a critical shortage of lawyers to write laws; to help the often illiterate people; and create the structure for the industrial and agricultural enterprises of America as they grew westward. The frontier and early lawyers did not have the luxury of only practicing court work or office work and they practiced both. In America. there never has been a distinction between the licensing of the lawyer who never went to court and the lawyer who only goes to court.

The Roman concept of Notary and Advocate developed into the English concept of Solicitor and Barrister which developed into the American unified concept of "Lawyer."

CURRENT PRACTICE

Some American lawyers prefer to call themselves "attorney and counselor at law," indicating they practice both courtroom law and non courtroom law. You also may wish to call yourself "attorney and counselor at law." You may also wish to call yourself "lawyer" or "attorney at law" or indicate "Law Offices" on your card.

The designation "Esq." at one time had gender connotations, but now is use by both male lawyers and female lawyers. Historically, any one with an education or money called themselves Esq. or Esquire. The term is now synonymous with the practice of law.

Only a person with a valid license to practice law at the address on their card or letterhead may call themselves Esq.

Although you have the right to add only your degree(s) to your name, I recommend against it. Anyone who in fact has a J.D. or LL.B. or other Law Degree may so indicate on their card or letterhead. Since so many degrees can be purchased by mail order with no courses of study, some holders of bona fide degrees indicate the institution from which they obtained the degree. They may not add Esq. or Attorney or Lawyer unless they also hold a valid license to practice. People with only a degree indicated after their name either never did hold a license to practice law in the jurisdiction, or were disbarred or gave up the license during disciplinary proceedings to avoid disbarment, or for some other reason gave up or never had a license to practice. Accordingly, I would recommend against using only a degree on your card.

You may call yourself by a fictitious name such as "The Legal Eagles" or "The Litigation Bunch" or the "Tax Loophole Group" or "The Showbiz Firm," in some states. In many states, if you are a sole practitioner, you cannot indicate that you are a "firm." One of my favorite fictitious names of a law firm is "The Four Bitches From Hell." I leave to your imagination what kind of law they practice. Keep in mind that you may wish to use one name on your card or letterhead and other names for your website or email address. You might use the name Mary Doe, Attorney at Law on your card and letterhead. You might with to also use the name MaryImmigrationLaw@aol.com as an email address and USImmigrationLawyer.com as your website.

I personally prefer "Lawyer" or "Attorney at Law," as these terms are well understood in the United States. Calling oneself "Attorney" without using the words "at Law" may be problematic outside the United States.

Whatever you decide to do, you should double check the Ethics with your local Bar and you should feel comfortable with the name.

Chapter E
Addressing the Needs of Clients
And Potential Clients

E-1
The Importance of Being Available

"I needed a lawyer.
I couldn't get hold of you.
I reached another lawyer.
I don't need you anymore."

A lawyer must be available if the lawyer expects to be hired. The lawyer or another person must be available personally or electronically.

Lawyers often hide from prospective clients and then are surprised when the client goes to another lawyer who is available.

When a client decides which lawyer to hire, there are several factors that the client considers. A joint survey sponsored by the American Academy of Advertising and the American Bar Association revealed the factors clients consider important when *deciding to use* a lawyer after trying to contact a specific recommended lawyer.

(In order of importance)
1. Availability
2. Reputation
3. Experience
4. Specialty
5. Price
6. Helpfulness

In today's electronic digital age, availability typically is accomplished one of three ways.
1. Your local area:
   a. The telephone is the primary form of initial communication.
   b. Email is increasingly important.
   c. Walk-in (in resorts and smaller communities, etc.).
2. Nationally:
   a. Telephone
   b. Email and Website
   c. Walk in
   d. Mail
3. Internationally:
   a. Telephone
   b. Email and website
   c. Mail and Fax

The subject of telephone availability and answering techniques will be covered in a separate chapter. However, the lesson to be learned here is that if you want to attract business outside your immediate area, you should invest in a website and facsimile and put the email address, website and fax and telephone numbers on your stationery. The website on your stationery will both advertise your availability to potential international clients and indicate to domestic clients that you do international work.

When you meet a new client or a potential client, write your home or mobile cell telephone number on the back of your card. Say something like, "This is my home number (or my cell number). I'm always available to you in a bona fide emergency, but please don't use the number unless it's really an emergency. I value the time I spend with my family. They are the most important people in the world to me, so use it only in an emergency."

The client will be really appreciative. You will have satisfied his or her major concern: availability. Don't worry; the clients almost never use the cell or home number. If in fact, clients call you at home when there is no emergency, (sometimes a problem with family law and divorce clients) simply repeat what you said and tell them, "This is not an emergency. Please call me at the office tomorrow (after the weekend). I'll alert the receptionist to find me immediately when you call. In the meantime, don't worry, there is no time urgency. Call me tomorrow," and hang up. In most cases the client will call you at the office and apologize. Some family lawyers feel that family law clients will abuse this privilege.

Have a second cell phone. Do not give this personal cell number to clients. Give it only to those who need to talk only with you (family) and your secretary or assistant for bona fide emergencies.

It is possible to "design" your office or home phone to call your cell after a message is left on your office phone.

E-2
Ask Your Present and Past Clients Why They Do or Don't Refer You New Clients

The people who refer you clients may have varied reasons for doing so. The motives or reasons that one person has for referring clients may be totally unrelated to those of other persons who do or do not refer you new clients.

Obviously, if you can identify the specific reasons a particular person refers you clients, you may be able to do whatever is required to get still more clients from him. On the other hand, if you find out what the referrer *doesn't* like (perhaps the reasons for the referrer's not sending business to you), then you can consciously avoid alienating or antagonizing the referrer.

People are sometimes sensitive about disclosing why they do or don't refer you clients. The best way to find out why people send you business is to ask the source at a thank-you lunch or by telephone, or by asking the referred client at the initial meeting.

It requires a certain amount of courage for you actually to bring up the subject and ask the question. If you don't have the courage to do this, don't try it. If you bungle the process through nervousness or fear, you may create the impression that you or your practice are in trouble and that you need business.

After selecting the right time and place to ask the question, you might use words along the following lines:

A. To a client or person who does refer you clients.

"Joe. . . I'd like to ask you a personal question. I consider you both a client and friend, so I don't feel awkward about asking this question.

First, let me tell you that my practice is booming, business is good, but I always can make room to handle more good cases and clients. (This reassures him that you are a successful lawyer.)

I am curious about the specific reasons you refer us work. Is it our good service? Our high-quality legal work? Our interest in you and your case? Our fees? Our results? Our availability? Our returning calls? Or keeping you informed? Just what is it that appeals to you, causing you to send us more legal work?"

You have made a sales pitch to the person by assuring him that you can deliver the very things you asked about. The response may be helpful to you.

B. To a client or person who does not refer you work.

"Joe. . . I'd like to ask you a personal question. I consider you both a client and friend (if true), so I don't feel awkward asking you this question.

First, let me tell you that my practice is booming, business is good, but we are always looking for more good cases and clients and we can handle them well (again reassuring him that business is good).

Most of our business comes from referrals from well-satisfied clients. They like our good service, our high-quality legal work, our interest in their cases and themselves and our fees and results. Some like the way we return calls. Some like our availability. Some like how we communicate. (You have just made a sales pitch.)

Yet, we don't receive any referrals from you. Is there a specific reason? Are you unhappy with us? Is there something you could tell us that would be helpful to us?"

You have put this person on the defensive. Either he will or won't open up to you as to why he hasn't sent any business. You've lost nothing because this person has not been referring you anything.

If you have the courage to ask these questions, the answers will be very rewarding.

E-3
Understanding How Clients Find a Lawyer
The Importance of Being Recommended

We tend to look at our law practices through our eyes rather than through the eyes of a client or potential client. The American Bar Association and The American Bar Foundation spent several years surveying clients of lawyers and others to determine the client's perception of lawyers. This study" *The Legal Needs of the Public,* by Barbara Curran, took several years to do and analyze and was published in preliminary form. The work, published by the American Bar Association, is extremely well done and is worth reading. Although it is a bit dated, it is still reasonably accurate. I have referred to it indirectly at many different times in this book and in my programs.

As with any survey, the survey for *Legal Needs* can be affected by the questions asked, how they are asked and how the results are interpreted, but it is more or less a reasonably accurate picture of how clients and potential clients see us; how they find us and why they do or don't use us.

Among people surveyed who had used a lawyer, 12 percent had a blood relative who was a lawyer and 30 percent had a friend or social acquaintance who was a lawyer. I would imagine that this part of the report may be dated in that it seems today as though everybody has a friend or relative who is a lawyer.

Among the survey respondents who had a friend or relative who was a lawyer, a majority of them in fact went to a lawyer who was recommended by a friend or relative. The key word is "recommended." The lawyer they went to was recommended by:

1. Friend, neighbor, fellow worker,
   business acquaintance, etc.   39%
2. Relative   23%
3. Bank   3%
4. Realtor   4%
5. Employer   4%
6. All other sources   27%
                               Total: 100%

Thus, the Curran study showed us statistically what we always knew intuitively, which is that clients find a lawyer by being recommended to one by a friend or relative who knows of a lawyer. These referrers of clients are obviously the key to expanding any practice base.

Where people did know a lawyer, they found the lawyer they used as follows:

1. They had used the lawyer in business   1 %
2. They knew the lawyer in some context
   other than using him/her   33%
3. They were recommended to the lawyer
   they used   52%
4. Other ways   <u>14%</u>

Total: 100%

Thus, we see that even where people knew a lawyer, they still relied on recommendations 52 percent of the time, compared with 62 percent of the time when they didn't know a lawyer.

The process of recommendation is also referred to as "word of mouth."

E-4
How to Get Recommended and Used For Legal Work
The Barbara Curran Report and
The Temple University Report

The seminal American Bar Association study, still valid, *The Legal Needs of the Public,* authored by Barbara Curran in 1976, clearly demonstrated that people go to a lawyer recommended by a friend, relative or social acquaintance. Where the client already knew a lawyer, 33 percent went to the lawyer they knew and 52 percent went to a lawyer recommended by someone. Where the client didn't know a lawyer, 62 percent of the people went to a lawyer recommended by a friend or relative.

We now know that more than a half of our clients are recommended to us and about one-third of our business comes from someone we know whom we have not represented (referred).

The logical procedure is for us to do those things which will cause people to recommend us and to avoid doing things which will deter clients from recommending us. What people considered in recommending us or not recommending us can be categorized in order of decreasing importance as follows:

1. Personal interest in the client and the client's case as proven by good *communication* with the client (office demeanor, bombarding clients with paperwork, telephone availability)   19.9%
2. General reputation (clients want a lawyer with a good reputation)   18.1 %
3. Ethical standards, honesty and integrity   16.2%
4. Professional skills, including specialty and experience   15.2%
5. Personal characteristics personality, appearance, etc.-and location   14.3%
6. The fee-amount and perceived reasonableness   11.0%
7. Work habits   2.9%
8. Other factors   2.4%

TOTAL: 100.0%

Any individual could be encouraged to recommend you or be discouraged from recommending you through any single factor or combination of factors. It is, of course, worth your while to try to adapt your marketing techniques to meet the perceived needs of all those people who collectively, by recommendation, will account for more than one-half of all your new business contacts.

This chapter is the basis of a book I am writing entitled "9 Steps To A Successful Law Practice – From Womb to Tomb," if interested, see www.Foonberglaw.com.

The two important reports produced with funds provided by the American Bar Association provide insight into why and how people choose and use lawyers.

Another American Bar Association study was conducted by Temple University, again analyzing clients who had in fact used a lawyer to determine what pleased or displeased clients. The results were slightly different between moderate income clients and low income clients but the order of important traits was the same. I have paraphrased the descriptions.

		Satisfied Clients	Dissatisfied Clients
1.	Explained the applicable law and my position.	96%	50%
2.	Was honest and truthful in dealing with me.	95%	51%
3.	Listened to me and paid attention to what I said.	93%	47%
4.	Demonstrated and communicated interest and concern in my matter.	91%	47%
5.	Kept me informed of what was happening on the matter.	84%	34%
6.	Promptly returned calls.	83%	42%
7.	Promptly prepared documents and did the work.	83%	42%

It should be readily apparent that how & what you communicate as seen and heard by a client is the critical aspect of client satisfaction, practice success, and not being the subject of non meritorious complaints.

E-5
Cross Marketing

For purposes of this book I shall define Cross Marketing as educating existing and potential clients to use the firm for additional legal work which the client potentially needs.

As law firms grow in size and scope of practice, the opportunity for cross marketing increases. I have found in my consulting work very few firms understand their own cross marketing capacity and opportunities. Most law firms are not cross marketing anywhere near their potential.

Cross marketing has been defined by some attorneys as also including the activities whereby an attorney or department tries to get a client for another attorney or department in the firm whether the target is not a client of the firm. This subject can be treated purely as an extension of getting new clients and not included in cross marketing.

I believe that one of the reasons that firms do not effectively cross market is that they are unwilling to put in the effort necessary to successfully cross market. The compensation system may actually discourage cross marketing.

Effective cross marketing requires input from every attorney and non-attorney in the firm on a periodic organized basis. The information concerning available services and resources must continually be updated and the information must be acted on in a deliberate systematical way. This is more than most firms are willing to do.

Accordingly, this section will include some techniques that are simple and require very little effort and some additional techniques that will require significant time and effort.

E-6
Marketing and Cross Marketing
Opportunity Matrix – Getting Started

I've invented this marketing and cross marketing opportunity Matrix to help a firm of any size identify specific opportunities to do more work for existing clients or to do work for new clients. Obviously it's easier to learn about the needs of your existing clients than the needs of potential clients, but when you can obtain information about the client's needs you can match that information with the information you already have about your own firm and its ability to fulfill those needs.

The Matrix will help you see in graphic form in a few moments what might otherwise be difficult to put into a narrative format.

Each individual lawyer in the firm should prepare a personal Matrix form based on the clients known to him or her. Based upon the size of the firm each lawyer can act upon the form they prepared, the individual forms can be combined into a departmental Matrix for departmental action or the Matrices can be further combined into a firm Matrix for firm action.

The steps for developing the Matrix are as follows:

1. Each lawyer starts with a blank Matrix form.
2. The areas in which the individual lawyer practices are added by the lawyer across the top.
3. The areas of law for which the client uses other firms or in-house counsel are added across the top.
4. Other areas in which the firm practices are added across the top if they might pertain to the client, even if the areas are not practiced by the individual lawyer.
5. Areas of law the firm does not practice but for which the client uses in-house or outside counsel can also be added across the top.
6. The clients for which the lawyer or department or firm does work are listed along the side, preferably in fee income rank since these clients are currently the most important to the firm, and the clients are listed again by sales or number of employees or asset size since those clients may represent the greatest future potential to the firm.
7. The key or legend to the Matrix is as follows:
   a.   x = We do their work
   b.   0 = Others do their work

    c.   w = We and others do their work.

    d.   n = They need or will need the work. No one is currently doing it.

    e.   N/A = Not applicable. They don't need this type of work.

    f.   ? = Unknown.

8. 0, x and n represent cross-marketing and marketing opportunities.

9. A decision is made as to whether the firm could service the client's needs in the 0, x and n categories with existing firm resources or whether additional personnel, offices, equipment, etc., would be required.

10. If additional firm resources would be required to service the client or potential client's needs then a decision must be made to add these resources on a speculation basis, hoping to get the business or on a contingent basis, i.e., the resources will be added if the firm gets the business.

11. The decision is made how to approach the client or potential client to inform them of your ability and availability to do the work in the 0, x and n categories.

12. Remember-o, x and n represent Opportunities.

E-6A
Marketing and Cross Marketing Opportunity Chart

PRACTICE AREAS

SYMBOLS

x = we do their work

o = other outside counsel does the work

w = we and others do their work

i = in house corporate counsel does
     their work

n = they need or will need
     work-no one is doing it

Biggest Clients to Firm
in Fee Income Client

1.	
2.	
3.	
4.	
5.	
6.	
7.	
8.	
9.	
10.	
11.	
12.	
13.	
14.	
15.	

	PRACTICE AREAS														
Biggest Clients in Absolute Size Not Listed Above															
1.															
2.															
3.															
4.															
5.															
6.															
7.															
8.															
9.															
10.															
11.															
12.															
13.															
14.															
15.															

E-7
The S.E.X. Approach of Increasing Your Practice

The S.E.X. method recognized three types of clients:

| S | E | X |

S   Are the Satisfied clients. These clients have paid your bill and if they need you in the future they'll use you, but they never refer new clients.

E   Are the Enthusiastic clients. These clients or referrers of clients are ones who will do everything they can to go out and get you more business and will use you in the future for their own legal work.

X   Are the Ex-clients. These clients or referrers of clients are ones who will never use you again and/or never refer you any business.

In the S.E.X. approach, you realize and accept that clients and referrers of clients typically fall into one of these categories, and you have to analyze why clients are in one of these categories. The best way to find out is to simply ask clients directly or indirectly why they do or don't use you or refer you clients. You can use the techniques of this book to help modify your clients' and referrers' behavior.

E-8
Foonberg's Upside Down Pyramid
Of Client Recommendations

```
32  F F F F F F F F F F F F F F F F F F F F F F F F F F F F F F F F
   16  E E E E E E E E E E E E E E E E
      8  D D D D D D D D
         4  C C C C
            2  B B
               1  A
```

It has been estimated that every satisfied client you have will recommend two new clients to you at some time during your career. Each of these new clients will also recommend two new clients to you, and so on, for a pyramid effect. Assuming that a client has an opportunity to recommend a lawyer once every two years, then in a period of 10 years, a satisfied client will lead to 62 new clients, 124 clients in 12 years, etc (this is an arithmetic progression). This "upside down pyramid" phenomenon is one of the reasons older practitioners usually have more business than they can handle and why the older, larger firms tend to continue to grow and flourish. Obviously, depending on many factors, the time interval may be longer or shorter, but the theory remains constant.

E-9
Ask Your Clients What They Want
From You *Before* You Set Your Fees

During the first interview involving a new matter, the lawyer should take charge and ask pertinent questions. Typically, the lawyer overlooks a most important question, which is, "Just what is it you really want in this case?"

You should always ask clients this question. Once you know what they want or are expecting from you, you'll be in a better position to discuss and set fees, and either to come to a mutually agreeable relationship with the client or, alternatively, to encourage the client to make some other lawyer rich and famous by taking the case elsewhere to a lawyer possibly picked by you.

Listen carefully to the client's response. Just by your having asked the client, "What do you really want?" the client will appreciate you. Additionally, you will be able to assess the case realistically in terms of what the client wants or expects rather than dealing in abstract legal principles. The client will be happier if he perceives that you are giving him what he wants.

Obviously, you can't always give the client what he or she wants, but often you can shape your handling of the case to try to give him some of the things he wants.

For example: When your client is the plaintiff in litigation, you could ask your client:

1. What do you want?
2. Do you want money?
3. Do you want revenge?
4. Do you want to impress the defendants that they are making a big mistake getting into a fight with you?
5. Are you really seeking money or are you trying to teach the defendant a lesson, or both?
6. Do you want to deter the defendant from doing this to you or others in the future?
7. Do you want to 'get even' for some wrong done you?
8. Do you simply want the cheapest possible resolution regardless of how long it takes?
9. Do you want the fastest possible resolution regardless of how much it costs?

10. Do you want to convince the other side that it's cheaper to pay you than to pay lawyer fees?
11. Do you care how much this is going to cost?

When your client is the defendant in litigation, you could ask:

1. Do you owe the money and are simply trying to buy time?
2. Do you want to make the plaintiff sorry that he ever started this fight with you?
3. Do you want to convince him that he should accept less than he is suing you for, in order to save legal costs or to save time?
4. Or simply ask, "Why are you fighting this? You owe the money."

In a matrimonial matter, you might ask, "Do you really want custody of the child or are you just using the child custody issue to get revenge or negotiating advantage from your spouse?"

When representing a corporate client, you might ask, "Are you simply interested in the cheapest way out? If so, we should discuss settlement or mediation or arbitration before going very far with legal fees. Or are you concerned over setting a precedent or the effect on others if you pay their blackmail?" (It is interesting that many, if not most, business clients really believe in the moral honesty of their position and frequently regard the other side as "blackmailers." They frequently denigrate litigation by calling it "frivolous" to be contested even when it is meritorious litigation which should be settled.)

Always try to determine the dollar value of the case to the client. Every case has some value which can be expressed in dollars, even though it may not be readily apparent. When you know the value of the matter to the client, your legal fees will or will not seem appropriate. The client will also realize that what he wants has a dollar value to him, which makes it easier to reach a decision on spending or not spending money on lawyers.

In some cases, the amount of money involved in the case is relatively easy to determine. Promissory notes, breach of contract, rent, etc., are rather easily determined. In other cases, the value is more complicated such as the value of a piece of real estate.

In some cases the amount of money is less apparent but it is nonetheless there. An example that comes to mind is a man who was being divorced by his wife and who was living with another woman during the pending divorce litigation. The other woman was pregnant and the man desperately wanted the divorce in time to marry his girlfriend before the baby was born. The man was willing to pay almost any price within his financial ability to get the divorce finalized.

Criminal cases also have a dollar value. Businessmen have come to me in criminal tax cases. In willful failure to file cases, the businessman often wanted to clean up his affairs so that he could come into the open. So long as he was "hiding" from the IRS and keeping a low profile, he could not go into deals with other people who were clean, or he could not get bank financing. It is worth a lot of money to such a client to clean things up!

In criminal tax fraud cases or other white collar crimes, it is often worth large sums of business and profit for the client's customers or sources of supply not to be contacted by IRS agents. Such contacts would or could result in the loss of lucrative contracts or relationships. (It is an unfortunate fact that people, even sophisticated business people, still believe "Where there's smoke, there's fire!")

A professional such as a lawyer or doctor may lose his or her professional license and livelihood if he or she were to be convicted of or even charged with certain crimes. The dollar value of the case accelerates immediately when a client is reminded of this fact.

NON-MONETARY CONSIDERATIONS IN EXPENDING MONEY ON LAWYERS

The "You've done everything that you could do" syndrome is often a valuable one when a third party is going to pay the legal fees. For example, a parent paying a child's legal fees (or vice versa) or a relative paying legal fees for an elderly aunt or uncle.

I recently had a case in which an elderly woman (85) was being evicted from her apartment. She had little or no money. Her nephews were wealthy. When her nephews went to one lawyer, they were told, "Look, your aunt will probably lose this case. She's 85 and ready for a home, anyway. Let's spend as little as possible on legal fees and drag it out as long as possible while you look for a new home." This lawyer was analyzing the case from a *purely* dollar-and-cents point of view, giving no consideration to the non-economic factors.

When the two brothers came to me I told them, "Look, your aunt will probably lose this case. If you want, I can keep the fees and expenses as low as possible while you look for another place for her. On the other hand, I can fight like hell for her. If you're willing to spend the money, I'll put up a fight that's immense. I'll depose the landlord, I'll depose the manager, I'll depose every tenant in the building. Your aunt will probably still lose, but you'll have had the satisfaction of knowing that you did everything that could have been done. At least you will go down fighting. No one can fault you, saying that you deserted your aunt to save legal fees. Besides, there's always the possibility that the discovery process will yield information that neither you nor your aunt knows about, and which will give your aunt a defense. Again, I want to tell you that you'll probably lose, but at least you'll know you did everything you could have done. It may cost you $20,000 or more (2006 amount), but you'll have done what could be done."

The two nephews decided that they owed it to their aunt to do everything they could, and then at least their consciences would be clear.

We won the case when after deposing 14 tenants, we discovered evidence previously unknown to the aunt. We now have a very happy client and we have a very happy bank account. Even if the case had been lost, the money would have been well spent to satisfy the nephews' sense of obligation.

SETTING A FEE IN LITIGATION MATTERS

Usually, you should say something like, "I can't give you a guarantee on the amount of the fee. That is determined to a large extent by how hard the other side fights, which is beyond my control."

Another approach is, "Don't start a fight unless you make the other side think you're serious about winning it." In the early stages, do everything you possibly can to convince the other side you mean business. Then, after seeing their response, you can decide whether you want to slow down or increase the pace.

E-10
Why Clients Change Lawyers

Clients don't always stay with the same lawyer for their repeat work. The American Bar Association's *Legal Needs of the Public,* authored by Barbara Curran, attempted to analyze the reasons clients change lawyers. I believe that the statistics given are accurate in terms of the questions asked and the answers given, but I'm not comfortable that the survey asked enough questions, or possibly the respondents didn't give complete answers. People often give one reason for not doing something, when, in fact, they may have another reason. In any event, the information developed by the above survey and my comments are presented for your guidance. Perhaps in going through this list you'll think of specific situations where you lost a client you wanted to keep. Perhaps the list can make you more sensitive to clients' given reasons for changing lawyers.

1. Prior lawyer not available. Couldn't reach   27%
    him/her or client moved.

[JGF Comment: They can't use you if they can't get hold of you. You must be available by telephone and email.]

2. Prior lawyer didn't handle this type of   15%
    case or new lawyer was better qualified.

[JGF Comment: It's possible that the prior lawyer did handle this type of case, but the client didn't know it because the prior lawyer never communicated the fact he/she could handle it. Certainly, client couldn't know if the other lawyer was, in fact, better qualified. A brochure or website reference could possibly have caused the client to know that the lawyer could handle it.]

3. A third person suggested or recom-   11 %
    mended that the client contact the new
    lawyer.

[JGF Comment: Here again we see the power and influence of recommendations. The client went to a recommendation rather than the first lawyer.]

4. Prior lawyer referred client to the new   7%
    lawyer.

[JGF Comment: Note that in 93 percent of the cases where the client changed lawyers, the first lawyer may have lost control of the client for future business and may have lost fee income which might have been earned by referral fee or division of fees or by some other method of working with a new lawyer selected by the first lawyer.]

5. Prior lawyer turned down case because   11 %
    prior lawyer had conflict of interest or
    was too busy.

[JGF Comment: In 89 percent of the cases, it was the *client,* not the *lawyer,* who decided the client should not use the lawyer again.]

6. Client was dissatisfied or uneasy with   10%
    prior lawyer.

[JGF Comment: Quite possibly the chemistry just wasn't there. No lawyer can be all things to all people.]

7. New lawyer's office more conveniently   6%
    located.

[JGF Comment: This problem is usually not controllable by the lawyer unless the lawyer demonstrates a willingness to go where the client is. On the other hand, the lawyer may be in a community that is changing, or the lawyer's office may be located in a place that once was fashionable but is no longer fashionable for clients. A lawyer who has been in the same location or area for a long time may be losing clients that wouldn't be lost if the lawyer changed office location. Email and teleconferencing can reduce this client loss somewhat.]

8. Client wanted to give the business to a   5%
    new lawyer for personal reasons. The
    typical reason was to give the business
    to a friend or relative who had just set up
    a practice in order to help the relative.

[JGF Comment: Don't be upset. This is probably how you started your practice, with business from your friends and relatives.]

9. Client felt prior lawyer's fee was too high.   3%

[JGF Comment: No matter how many times I preach the same lesson, lawyers just don't want to believe that the fee is not the predominant consideration in lawyer selection. If you needed a doctor or hospital, you would not intentionally select the cheapest. You would get the best doctor or hospital you could afford. Legal clients are no different.]

10. Other factors   <u>5%</u>

                          TOTAL: 100%

E-11
Personal Qualities Clients *Dislike*
in Lawyers and Doctors

One lawyer claimed to have made a personal survey of clients and claims the following lists appropriately present 1) personal qualities that his clients dislike in lawyers, and 2) lawyers' perceptions of what clients dislike. I'm not sure that these two lists are complete or accurate. On the other hand, it is worthwhile to review the list with a view toward self improvement. I pass them on to you for what value they may have.

What clients dislike:
1. Superior attitude toward client
2. Bored and indifferent attitudes toward client or case
3. Impatience with client
4. Insincerity
5. Lack of personal interest
6. Rudeness
7. Unsure of self
8. Failure to inform
9. Brusque manner

What lawyers think clients dislike:
1. Procrastination
2. Failure to inform
3. Failure to explain basis for fee at earliest opportunity.
4. Lack of frankness concerning merits of case
5. Lack of courtesy and consideration
6. Neglect and indifference to client's case
7. Unethical conduct

A lawyer's friendliness is one of the most important things cited among satisfied clients.

A large medical health plan surveyed patients in 2006 to determine which doctors to reward financially based on patient satisfaction. I do not know the relative importance of the 9 aspects of communication and listening skills but the plan asked about the patient's primary care physician.

A common cause of dislike was interrupting the patient. On average, un-liked doctors listened only 18 seconds before interrupting the patients.

The 9 questions asked by the plan asked if the primary care physician:
1. Is easy to talk with.
2. Is very familiar with my medical history.
3. Gives helpful advice.
4. Is easy to make an appointment with.
5. Listens carefully to me.
6. Seems genuinely concerned about my health.
7. Takes time to answer my questions.
8. Follows up when I feel it's necessary.
9. Is someone I feel I can trust.

How would you rate yourself using the doctor's questions as criteria?

E-12
Make Something Happen Now – The Instant Gratification Approach to Impress a New Client

The way you begin to handle your first matter for a new client sets the tone for the client's impression of you and your firm.

We live in a world of instant gratification. People want everything *now*. They often have no patience for waiting. You can get off to an excellent start to a great relationship with a new client by doing some part of the case *immediately* so the client sees instant *action,* thereby satisfying the client's desire for instant gratification.

People go to a "convenience store" next door to a supermarket where they knowingly pay 10 to 15 percent more for everything they buy because they don't have to wait.

Think of the photo developing and photo finishing business. It used to take a week to get pictures developed through a drugstore. Then people began to pay a little extra to get three-day service, then one-day service, and now there are major companies opening chains of hundreds of one-hour photo finishing stores. One chain is advertising 59-minute photo service. Another is advertising 30 minute service.

New cleaners and laundries offering same-day or one-hour service are flourishing while other established stores go out of business because they don't adjust. Traditional restaurants often are having a difficult time surviving while instant service fast food restaurants are flourishing.

The American public wants speedy service. Give it to them, at least in beginning the very first matter you handle. You want the new client referring you more cases and clients immediately without waiting until after the case is over.

It's a very traumatic situation for a client to bring a legal problem to a lawyer, especially to a lawyer whom he or she has never used before. Clients want to feel that they have found someone who knows how to solve their problem. An obviously impressive and rapid handling of their case gives them a high opinion of you and is likely to result in referrals of other clients long before their own legal problem is solved.

A legal problem may have gathered dust on the client's desk for two or three years before the client finally decided to see a lawyer. The matter may take another three to five years to get to trial. You know and I know that there is no great rush to do anything unless a statute of limitations is involved, as the case is going to languish in the legal system for another three to five years.

On the other hand, the client wants to see something happen *now*. This is a golden opportunity for you to impress your client with your capacity to get a job done quickly.

If it is at all possible, you should accomplish *something* immediately. Don't do the entire job, just the first step. Prepare the complaint for the client's review in hours rather than days or weeks. Form the corporation the same day or the next day. Send off a letter to the government or the opposing party or opposing counsel while the client is in your office.

You can say to the client, "This one-day service really isn't necessary in your case, but I just want you to know that we have the capacity to handle a client matter immediately when the case requires it, although we often have to charge a slightly higher fee because of the extra night and weekend work required."

In summary, you will accomplish the following by doing *something* immediately:

1. Satisfy the client's needs for instant gratification;
2. Start getting new referrals and recommendations from the client immediately instead of waiting until the case is over; and
3. Demonstrate your ability and willingness to do emergency work (on a premium fee basis) when needed.

In applying this chapter, you should also keep in mind the chapter entitled "How to Lose Clients by Being Too Competent or Too Efficient," and the chapter entitled "Building a Practice with One-Day Service."

E-13
Building a Multi-Million Dollar Business By Offering "Same Day" and "Next Day" Service for Routine Matters

I created and built a multi-million dollar bank collection litigation practice by providing and delivering next-business-day litigation service on all routine matters when properly documented by the client.

In the 1960's, I hired a law student named Bob Frandzel as a law clerk. In 1967, I got Union Bank of Los Angeles to try me for collection work. (See the chapter on "Getting Selected by the Client by Recognizing the Five A's of Lawyer Marketing"). I used my Air Force supply experience and my CPA knowledge to design routine litigation transmittal forms to give one-day service. When things got rolling, I hired Bob as an associate and we specialized in doing simple routine collection work with one-day turn around service. In 1970, I made Bob a partner and he specialized in getting the work out while I got the clients in. We hired Richard Share to moonlight for us on nights and weekends because he was experienced in using non-lawyers for finance company collections. Eventually Dick left the finance company to supervise the non-lawyers. It worked beyond our wildest dreams. I got the clients by emphasizing one-day service. Dick got the non-lawyers to get the cases prepared in one day and Bob supervised the lawyers in those cases which were contested. I continued marketing and designing systems.

Banks are no different from any other clients except that they can and do pay well and quickly. Each bank recommended us to other banks. I was able to use each bank as a lever to open the next bank.

Union Bank was well satisfied. They recommended us to Bank of California, where a man I played cricket with at UCLA was instrumental in getting us chosen. The two banks recommended us for Security Pacific National Bank, where the house counsel in charge of collections was someone with whom I had served in the Air Force. I used these three to open the doors to Crocker National Bank which was our own bank. In each case, I emphasized one-day litigation service, which was unheard of at the time.

The firm eventually broke up under rather bizarre circumstances. We were making so much money that the spouses created discontent over the profit sharing plan receiving cash the spouses felt would be better spent by them. It was bizarre, but I learned a lot about "balance" of life. However, before the breakup, I had 19 major banks and financial institutions all built up in a period of a decade.

I was able to grow rapidly, handling profitable business for major clients by giving the clients one-day service on their routine collection matters after the loan had been, gathering dust, in default in the bank for a year or two before bringing it to me. The case might be enmeshed in the court for one to three years or more after gathering dust for years, yet the clients loved and paid for one-day service. Other law firms just didn't see any urgency to the cases and, from a case result point of view, they were correct. The clients, however, wanted fast service and gave us an ever-increasing share of their legal work. They gave us larger & larger and more complex matters because nothing gathered dust in our office. Other firms were bigger, more prestigious and frequently had ties into the various boards & committees of the bank, but we were the firm where everything moved and that's what the clients wanted.

I had to invest a lot of my time, my money and my energy in systems which made it possible to assemble a case from an instruction form and to prepare all the litigation documents, etc., for the court in a few hours.

If there is a type of practice which you have (so that you're familiar with the processing and legal problems involved) and which you want to increase, you should devise systems to give same-day and next-day service and you'll get a large increase in that kind of business.

E-14
What to do When a Good Client
Needs a Big Job You Can't Handle

This chapter should be read with chapter E-17 Getting a Good Client When You Have No Experience in the Legal Area.

When you have a good client, you want to do everything you can to retain that client. Every time you bring in an outside law firm (especially a larger one), you create the risk of the client comparing you with the new firm and possibly preferring the new firm, or going to the new firm for all work because the new firm can do everything you do plus things you can't do. It took me a long time to realize that, often, when I sent a client to a "specialty" firm, I ended up losing the client. I also learned that my experiences were not unique; other lawyers had had the same experiences. "Entertainment," "copyright" and "international" firms suddenly developed tax and corporate and litigation sections, using as a client base the referrals sent to them for specialty work. Litigation defense firms developed plaintiff's practice and tax and corporate sections. Many of the larger firms became big by getting a reputation for doing specialty work and then using that specialty work as an entree to get the client away from the lawyer who had referred the client for the specialty work.

Some "specialty" firms flatly state that they consider it unethical not to accept the subsequent general work from the specialty client. Whether they are ethical, sincere, correct or wrong is beyond the scope of this book. The plain truth is that every time you bring in an outside law firm you risk losing the client. If the client is important enough to you and/or the matter is profitable in and of itself, you should consider one or more of the following:

1. Hire another law firm at your expense (the one you would have referred the client to) to educate you so that you can handle the matter. Insist that all communication with the client be through your firm. This is possible in some non-litigated areas such as tax, entertainment, labor, foreign, copyright, patent, etc. All documents would be drafted and reviewed by the "specialty" law firm but would come from your office on your stationery. Some "specialty" firms won't do this, for various reasons. Some will. (In this situation, the client won't know the name or the identity of the "specialty" firm but the client will still receive the needed quality legal care.) This is sometimes referenced to as "ghosting."

We paid another specialty big law firm to ghost 3 matters for us until we felt confident we could do the work in the newly developing area of fractional jet ownership. We then increased our penetration in this field until we had 4 lawyers doing this work which we didn't refer out for fear of losing the client.

2. "Associate in" the other law firm at your expense. (Here again, the "specialty" firm educates you so that you can handle or help handle the matter.) Insist that all office

meetings with the client take place in your office, not at the "specialty" firm, and that all written communication and documents be sent to your office for your review and your transmission to the client. Insist that all communications from the client go to your office so that you can review them and send them on to the "specialty" firm. (In this situation, the client knows the name and identity of the "specialty" firm, but you keep all control.)

3. Hire a lawyer to work for your firm who has the ability to handle the work. Tell the client that you think so much of him/her or the case that you added this new lawyer primarily to service his/her needs and possibly other clients in the future, but initially to serve the particular client.

4. Hire a retired lawyer or a new lawyer or a law professor or a house counsel on a part-time or moonlighting basis to work on the case. (The concept of the "K Lawyer"-contract lawyer-has been well developed by Kathryn Marshall of Waukegan, Illinois.) It is a good way for a sole practitioner or small firm to get the expertise it needs. (See ad of "Of Counsel", a company which provides these lawyers.) Although the company called itself "Of Counsel" it was providing contract lawyers rather than Of Counsels.

5. Enter into an "Of Counsel" relationship with a lawyer who has the expertise you need. I have done extensive research and written several articles in the area of the "Of Counsel."

6. Charging for your time in these cases: Don't unnecessarily add to the client's economic burden, just because you don't want to lose the client. If you feel it is important to be involved in the specialty case, then by all means charge for your time including the Of Counsel's time. (For example, your review time is beneficial to the client because you don't want the specialty firm to do something through ignorance that could prejudice your client in other areas the specialty firm knows nothing about.) If your participation in the specialty case does not protect the client's interests but rather only your interests, then don't charge for your time.

Currently, there is a very competitive marketplace for legal clients, especially the good ones. Do not send the client to another law firm if there is any way you can competently handle the matter "in house." Don't worry about the economics of that one case. Keep the cluster concept in mind, taking into account all of the work you do for that good client. (In the cluster concept, you aggregate the profitable and the non-profitable cases from a single client or client source to make a decision as to overall profitability.)

LAW FIRMS   SOLE PRACTITIONERS   LEGAL DEPARTMENTS

DISCOVER . . . . .

OF COUNSEL
INCORPORATED

PART-TIME AND PROJECT ATTORNEYS

A **NEW SERVICE** is now available for law firms, sole practitioners, and corporate legal departments of Los Angeles and Orange Counties. Part-time and project attorneys will be supplied upon your request by OF COUNSEL INCORPORATED.

These are experienced attorneys with strong educational backgrounds -- specialists in the areas your project requires. Comparable attorneys are usually billed in private practice at hourly rates much higher than rates paid to OF COUNSEL.

Many attorneys have already joined OF COUNSEL, and more are joining every day. They have elected to work on a part-time basis. Call us and discover that they can work for you!

ADVANTAGES

Flexibility: The ability to hire only what you need and when you need it. Call OF COUNSEL when your firm is overworked or understaffed.

Targeted Expertise: Different levels and types of experience -- hire exactly what you need -from new admittee to 25 years expertise.

Easy to Use: Just give us a call. We will have an attorney at your office when you need him/her.

Cost Effective: These attorneys are independent contractors and work by the hour. You pay only for productive time, not for continuing education, administrative activities, vacation time, sick pay, etc.

Fair Rates: Hourly rates range from $25.00 to 65.00, depending on the amount of relevant experience and educational background.

Reliability: OF COUNSEL verifies the background and experience of each of its attorneys. We monitor their performance on each assignment.

WE WANT OUR SERVICE TO WORK FOR YOUR LAW PRACTICE!

For more information, call OF COUNSEL at (213) 470-7958. We can answer your questions and react quickly to your requirements.

10801 NATIONAL BOULEVARD • THIRD FLOOR • LOS ANGELES • CALIFORNIA 90064 • (213) 470-7958

www.Foonberglaw.com

E-15
When to be a Mean, Rotten S.O.B.
With a Potential Client

There are times when, in order to get a client or case, it will be necessary for you to portray yourself or another member of your firm as a really rotten person. I apologize if I offend anyone by my use of language.

Recent studies by the American Bar Foundation indicate that when a lawyer projects himself as being a nice guy, a friendly helper, likeable, cooperative, broad-minded, accommodating or fair, then that lawyer may be in danger of losing a potential client because the potential client believes the lawyer will be taken advantage of by other lawyers who are aggressive, competitive, tricky, cold, etc. (called the Hero in the ABF study). When faced with a potential client who has a dispute or a present client who has a potential dispute or negotiation, you must feel out the client very carefully as to the nature of the client and what the client perceives his/her needs are.

Some clients or potential clients look upon litigation as a lawyer's fee getting intransigent substitute for peaceful and constructive negotiation and resolution of problems. Other people look upon litigation as a substitute for violence or self-help and as a means of providing social justice which gives the "little guy" equality with the "big guy" in the eyes of the law.

Some people truly enjoy fighting. They can be more competitive and vicious than their lawyer. They want a mean, hard, rotten fight. They want you, as their lawyer, to hurt the other side. They want you to inflict pain, personal embarrassment and humiliation, heavy expenses and unfavorable publicity on the other side. This type of a client can often be persuaded to write a huge retainer check on the spot if he is convinced that you or another lawyer in your firm has that ability. With these people, the lawyer is their hired gun fighter. The lawyer vicariously inflicts pain for him.

You can have as much fun as a pig in an ice cream store litigating the hell out of a case with unlimited funds to take depositions, interview witnesses, hire outside lawyers for second and third opinions on the law involved, etc.

I've often said to a client, "Look, I can be a M.M.F. if you want it and if you can afford it." The client will then ask what a M.M.F. is. I answer a M.M.F. is a Mean Mother F--ker. I can be the rottenest S.O.B. who ever lived when I work on this case. (Alternatively, I'll say that my partner is a Board Certified M.M.F.) If this terminology offends you, you may wish to use "junk yard dog."

This approach undoubtedly will frighten all the potential clients who regard litigation as an expensive interference with their normal business routine and who are more interested in good net profit than good law suits. Some types of persons will do almost anything to avoid litigation, including signing confessions to judgments or consent decrees or other stipulations or agreements that could have horrendous future effect.

If the lawyer comes on with the approach that litigation or extensive negotiation is costly and destructive, then the client may fear that the lawyer (especially if he or she is a sole practitioner) doesn't have the skill or resources to fight or negotiate to protect the client's interests effectively and the lawyer may lose the potential client to another lawyer.

Middle-of-the-Road-Approach

Until the client commits himself to just what he or she wants or what kind of person he or she is, the lawyer should use a middle-of-the road approach along the following lines.

"Look, I want you to tell me the kind of person we are dealing with on the other side. If he will respect only force, then let's come on like a herd of angry elephants. Let's show them you mean business and are determined to do whatever you have to do to win, regardless of the cost. If, on the other hand, the other side will treat this as simply a difference of opinion, then let's try to keep costs down and vengeance and ego out of the case. Tell me which approach is most likely to get you what you want."

It is a sad but true fact of life that if the client will devote the resources, any law firm can "grind" away limitlessly with discovery and various motions.

Let the client know that you or your partner has the ability to be a really mean, rotten S.O.B. if needed for the specific case.

E-16
Tell Your Client When You are Working Nights and Weekends on His or Her Case

I am not a workaholic, but when I work, I work hard. I frequently work at the office until 7:00 p.m. I live 10 minutes from my office, and I frequently will go in on Saturday mornings to see if there are any checks in the mail and I like to use these "irregular hours" to contact a client. What is the point of spending time at night or on a weekend for a client unless the client "knows" you were working on the case on a night or weekend or holiday?

I like to call clients from the office at night or on weekends (if I am at the office). I like to start the conversation with something like this:

"I'm sorry to bother you at home, but I am working of! your case at night because it is important."

(This will raise your esteem in the client's eyes by several percentage points.)

Or,

"Sorry to bother you at night, but I'm working on your case and I need some information from you."

When you call a client, phone them at night. They will be devoted to you and a friend for life.

Additionally, on some occasions, one time in a hundred, the client will say "I don't care what it costs, I want to be first to proceed with the filing of a lawsuit. Go ahead." When the response is given, give your client 110 percent, work nights or weekends; be sure he knows you are working on *his* case at night. Tell the client that since the case requires weekend or night work, you'll have to charge a premium rate because of the additional expenses you have such as overtime, dinners, taxis, etc., and also because overtime work causes morale problems due to the conflicts created between your people and their families.

On those occasions when the client wants and needs night and weekend work and is willing and able to pay for it, you can earn a premium fee and have a very happy client. Just be sure that you've communicated to the client you're working nights and weekends.

E-17
Getting a Good Client When You Have No Experience in the Legal Area

This chapter should be read with chapter E-14 "What to do When a Good Client Needs a Big Job You Can't Handle"

I started and built a very successful 70-person law practice, primarily representing banks in litigation.

At my first meeting with the bank's chief in-house counsel, I said frankly, "I've never represented a bank before or done bank litigation before. But I want to. I 'want the prestige of listing you as my client in the attorney directories. I'll kill myself to do a good job. I won't discount my prices, but I'll work hard. I, personally, will be involved in every case."

At the second meeting, I was faced with an examining board of five people, who asked me a series of questions for several hours about general law and about banking principles and financial terms. I had previously worked nights in a bank to work my way through high school, and I knew something about banking. My experience as a CPA helped me on the financial terms. Since I had no experience in bank litigation, I was very weak in the legal area, especially with respect to court procedures.

At the third meeting, the bank's chief counsel said, "Mr. Foonberg, we'll try you and see what happens. Our present litigation counsel takes us for granted and is giving us poor service at high prices. The top partners never return our calls or get involved in the cases. They keep sending the matters to the new lawyers and the new associates." (All of this may or may not have been true, but it certainly was the client's perception of the then existing facts.)

The chief counsel continued, "We understand that you are inexperienced in banking litigation," my interviewer continued, "We'll start you on small cases if you won't charge us for your learning time. You came to us seeking work. You're aggressive. In the litigation cases which we will give you, aggressiveness will be a necessary factor. You'll be dealing with 'hard core' people, and our general counsel doesn't seem to be aggressive anymore. They're fat and satisfied. They don't push the cases along. We want to keep the pressure on so we can get paid what's due us, so we can lend the money to other people. We've been thinking of a change in lawyers for these types of cases for some time, and we'd like to try you."

In this case, the client was more concerned with perceived willingness to work hard and general all-around ability than experience in the specialty area itself. They were willing to pay full prices for an inexperienced lawyer, although they didn't want to pay for the learning time.

I believe this example is important because it demonstrates that even a new lawyer without experience in a particular legal area can get good clients by demonstrating an awareness of the five A's of lawyer marketing. (There is another chapter on this subject.)

1. *Anxiety:* I recognized the client's anxiety level. Their other lawyers were perceived to be uncaring because the top partners were not involved in the cases and the lower associates returned the calls. The lower associates were inexperienced and asked stupid questions which disclosed that they were not getting supervision from the firm, or from the partners in the firm. The associate wouldn't have had to ask the questions or the answers to the questions were already in the file.

2. *Affordability:* Affordability was only indirectly a factor. The bank didn't mind paying high prices. They minded paying high prices for slow service. In the banking world, recovery of bad debts is extremely important because the new loans can be made at highly profitable interest rates with the cash received when old loans are collected. Defaulted loans often earn only "legal interest." (The rate of interest awarded by courts.) Therefore, the bank recognized the affordability factor in terms of profit and loss. That is, they didn't mind paying a high price, but they wanted their money back as soon as possible so they could re-lend it to earn a higher interest factor.

3. *Availability:* I made myself available for meetings and assured the bank personnel that I would be personally involved in the cases and available to them.

4. *Affability:* I did my best to be friendly.

5. *Ability:* Here, legal experience was not the determining factor. However, ability to get the job done was an important factor. I had to convince them that I had the *capacity,* if not the actual experience, which, when combined with the other factors involved I would be sufficient to get the job done.

Although I had only two-and-a-half years' general experience as a lawyer, I went to a major financial institution and sought their work although I had no experience in their particular area of law. It is to the credit of this institution (Union Bank of Los Angeles) that they gave me the chance subsequently to develop a practice in this area representing 19 banks and financial institutions. I went from being a sole practitioner with a part-time law clerk who was in law school, to building what was then one of the largest law firms in the state and the only law firm with offices in both Los Angeles and San Francisco. As a result of many different factors, I have been extremely handsomely paid for my partnership interest in this banking firm. The firm continues today as specialists in bank collection work, a specialty of law which I created with absolutely no experience.

E-18
How to Lose Clients by Being
Too Competent or Too Efficient

This is a difficult chapter for me to write and is an area even more difficult to give constructive advice on. All I can do here is to point out the problem and the possible solutions and leave the decision to you to apply in a given situation.

Several stories circulate about famous, excellent lawyers who supposedly charged huge fees for a single telephone call or single letter that got the client the desired result. One such lawyer is reported to have sent a letter to a defendant threatening to commence litigation simultaneously in the 40 states where the defendant did business and to seek a receiver in each of the 40 states to take possession of the defendant's warehouses there unless a sum of approximately $500,000 was paid in 24 "hours. The defendant paid the $500,000 on receipt of the letter and the lawyer reportedly billed the client $10,000 for the one letter and the results obtained.

Another of these lawyers reportedly billed a law firm $10,000 for a single telephone call to the Department of Defense which got the desired result.

In both cases, the famous lawyers reportedly got their fees yet lost the client, who probably would have been happy to pay many times that amount had the cases been dragged on for years. The clients felt that although they had gotten the desired results, the lawyers hadn't worked hard enough for the fee.

On occasion, I've made one or two telephone calls while the client was sitting in my office and solved their problems in front of them. I used my contacts and/or knowledge of the law which I've acquired over many years at a cost of many gray hairs. I often knew the exact pressure point to touch

and I didn't waste the huge amounts of time that another less-expensive, less-experienced lawyer might have.

In every such case, the client was the happiest person in the world until he or she received the bill. In every case, the client thought the fees were too high because "all it took was a few phone calls."

I believe that had I dragged the matter out for a month or two (assuming no prejudice to the client in the delay) and done extensive research, which I would have communicated to the client, and then made the important telephone call, the result would have been a happy client rather than an unhappy client. Whenever possible, I try to solve my client's problems as quickly as possible, but I still have the fee problems and sometimes lose a client for being too efficient.

I can only point out the problem. You will have to reach your own individual decision as to whether you should drag the case out and do more work to please the client and get the client the same result.

Internet, Email and Advertising Availability

E-19
Getting Chosen by the Client Using the Five A's of Lawyer Marketing

What I'm saying here has been said in other chapters in this book in other ways, and in more detail. In this chapter I am simply setting forth a "short form" summary which I heard somewhere from someone else. You may find this "short form" helpful. When a lawyer is dealing with a potential client on the- other side of the desk, he or she must address the "Five A's" in order to be chosen by the client. These "Five A's" are as follows:

1. Anxiety
2. Availability
3. Affability
4. Ability
5. Affordability

ANXIETY

The client has (or believes or she/he has) a legal problem. There is an anxiety level which may be low (this problem is a nuisance to me) or high (my life, my liberty, my property are at stake). The anxiety problem must be identified by the lawyer and dealt with so that the client feels you either are sharing the anxiety burden ("Together we'll solve this problem") or are removing the anxiety burden ("You go off and have a good weekend and leave the problems to me").

AVAILABILITY

You must be available to help the potential client and you must give the potential client the impression that you are available. A potential client can't use you if he or she can't reach you. Similarly, a client who perceives that you are not available, or will not be available, will not return to you and won't refer other clients to you. Clients want to know that they have access to their professionals when they need them. Accordingly, availability-both at the initial stage and at subsequent stages-is a major factor in getting selected by the client for particular work and getting referred by the client to others for work. Writing your home phone number on the back of your card is a demonstration of availability. Email and teleconferencing on the internet can sometimes solve this problem.

Internet, Email and Advertising Availability

Any well run practice has systems in place to respond to emails, voice mails, and internet contacts. The systems can be very simple or very complex. A simple system would include a person reviewing all incoming emails and voice mails to at least twice a day, noon and 4:00 p.m., for example, or 9:00 a.m., 1:00 p.m. and 5:00 p.m. All evening contacts would get a response, a simple response might be:

"Your email inquiry, voice mail (what ever) has been received and you may expect a response within 72 hours, between the hours of 9:30 a.m. and 5:30 p.m., Monday through Friday. If your matter is an emergency, please call again to this number and leave a message."

The "emergency" number could be a lawyer's cell phone.

Staff must be trained on how to handle calls resulting from the internet or yellow pages or other media source.

Your system could be more complex including a 24 hour duty person. Ask your dentist or physician or other lawyers what local systems they use.

AFFABILITY

Being a successful lawyer is not just a matter of winning a popularity contest. People will not use you or refer clients to you solely because they like you. On the other hand, they won't use you or refer clients to you if they despise you.

I have clients who have told me they didn't like me but that they used me because I was the best (that was their statement). I frankly got very little professional satisfaction out of doing their work even though they paid well, and these people rarely referred any other clients to me. I relate this to you to demonstrate that it is NOT a *sine qua non* that clients must like you before they use you. However, you must be sure they don't despise you. Additionally, I don't think you should prostitute yourself by trying to be everybody's friend. You should not simultaneously be trying to convince conservatives that you are conservative and liberals that you are liberal as this will eventually catch up with you. Simply accept the fact that some misguided souls simply may not like you and that this may be the reason, stated or unstated, for their not using you or their not referring people to you. If you won't go out of your way to be affable, at least try *not* to be unfriendly. You should ask yourself during the client interview if you think you are projecting yourself as being affable.

ABILITY

It is simplistic to say that people don't want incompetent or inexperienced people as their doctors or lawyers. Many people automatically equate inexperience with incompetence and equate experience with competence. Would you want to be operated on for an appendectomy by a brilliant medical graduate who had never done an appendectomy?

You have to communicate to the potential clients or referred clients that you have experience or ability in the matter involved. If you don't have experience in the matter involved and you want the work, you have to be careful about how you communicate your inexperience to the client. (There is a separate chapter in this book on "How to Get Legal Work in Areas Where You Have No Experience.") You might try something like the following:

> "I've never had a case *exactly* like this before (emphasize the word "exactly"); however, I've handled many *similar* cases (assuming this to be true), and if anything unexpected comes up," I'll bring in a specialist or combination of specialists to help if necessary."

By assuring the client that you either are experienced or you will bring in experienced people, should it be necessary, you can overcome this obstacle of the client's wanting somebody with ability where the client equates experience and ability.

AFFORDABILITY

Although law is a profession, not a business, a lawyer or law firm must be managed efficiently.

Good clients do not want to undertake financial obligations beyond their ability. Well-run businesses don't want to sell their products or services to people who can't pay for them. A well-run business must pay its own bills for salaries, equipment, rents, telephones, etc. A well-run business may choose to give away some of its services or products, but it must limit what it gives away or it will itself go under.

In corporate America, affordability is normally a matter of price and profitability for the expenditure.

With small businesses clients and in personal legal work clients, affordability is usually a matter of both price and terms. Many smaller businesses and private individuals are not equipped to pay a large, once-in-a-lifetime legal fee in a lump sum. They often are willing to pay the price, but need terms. The lawyer must tailor the cash flow to pay the bill on a realistic schedule or lose the client or potential client. The lawyer should also understand that the bad debt factor on deferred payments from private individuals is usually very high. It is my personal belief that a lawyer should never undertake any large amount of legal work for a new client without all the cash up front, if possible. If 100 percent cash up front is not feasible, then the lawyer must get about 50-60 percent of the fee up front or else feel very comfortable about the collectability of the deferred payments.

Be realistic. If the client can't pay sufficient cash up front or make credit or payment arrangements that are realistic, then the client can't afford the lawyer, and the sooner they both find that out the better off they'll both be.

Many times in my career I've said to a client, "I'm sorry. I'd like to help you but you just can't afford it." Many times these same people will come back years later and say something like, "Mr. Foonberg, when I was here three years ago, I wanted you as my lawyer but I couldn't afford you. Now I can afford you and I want to hire you."

Your fee normally won't be the problem. The client's ability to pay your fee will be the problem.

Affordability, not price, is normally the problem which must be solved in order to have a good attorney-client financial relationship.

Again, these "Five A's" are a short form summary of the process wherein the client chooses you to do the work after having met you.

E-20
Who Will Handle the Client's Case
When You are Sick or on Vacation

The solo practitioner and smaller law firm lawyer often doesn't realize that a potential client, especially a larger client, may be negatively affected by your being in solo or small firm practice.

In the back of their mind they may consciously or subconsciously be asking themselves:

"Who is going to take care of me and my case if this lawyer is in court or on vacation or sick?"

Ask yourself if you would want to use a doctor who had no "back-up" coverage. People have come to expect doctors to have back-up coverage but don't know whether lawyers have it.

You have to be prepared to answer the question, or possibly even to anticipate the question, by raising the subject yourself. It's a calculated risk whether raising the question yourself removes the question from the subconscious and puts it on the conscious level. You might be creating a problem where none previously existed. I recommend not raising the issue unless the client raises it.

Somewhere in the conversation with a potential client, the solo practitioner or smaller law firm lawyer could, if felt appropriate, bring up the subject of "coverage" so that the potential client's subconscious concerns can be satisfied. Don't make a big issue out of it, just casually mention it, such as:

"Because I'm a sole practitioner, I keep very extensive notes and memoranda of everything that happens on the case so that if necessary (a) my partner (b) my associate (c) another attorney can step into the case temporarily.

You also have a duplicate file on everything that happens on your matter. With your copies of documents and letters, you could go to any lawyer in America for help. It would be like traveling with your own medical records.

Putting the customer first is as important in law practice as it is in business. Consider these words of wisdom from sporting goods company L. L. Bean, Inc.

A CUSTOMER IS THE MOST IMPORTANT PERSON EVER IN THIS COMPANY-IN PERSON OR BY MAIL.

A CUSTOMER IS NOT DEPENDENT ON US, WE ARE DEPENDENT ON HIM.

A CUSTOMER IS NOT AN INTERRUPTION OF OUR WORK, HE IS THE PURPOSE OF IT.

WE ARE NOT DOING A FAVOR BY SERVING HIM, HE IS DOING US A FAVOR BY GIVING US THE OPPORTUNITY TO DO SO.

A CUSTOMER IS NOT SOMEONE TO ARGUE OR MATCH WITS WITH. NOBODY EVER WON AN ARGUMENT WITH A CUSTOMER.

A CUSTOMER IS A PERSON WHO BRINGS US HIS WANTS. IT IS OUR JOB TO HANDLE THEM PROFITABLY TO HIM AND TO OURSELVES.

L. L. BEAN, INC.

FREEPORT, MAINE

Chapter F
Getting Business from Others
in The Office

F-1
Marketing Is Not Hard to Do If Someone Else Has to Do It

This book was written to help the busy lawyer, or at least the lawyer who wants to be profitably busy. This book can even help the lawyer with little or no time available for marketing.

This book recognizes that many lawyers can't, or won't, make a commitment to ongoing marketing on a regular basis. This lack of commitment may stem from a feeling of being overburdened with too many time obligations from clients and others.

Frankly, some lawyers don't like to think of themselves as being actively involved in marketing. They prefer to think clients come to them because of their great technical skill rather than because of their conscious or unconscious successful use of proven marketing and client satisfaction techniques.

Most of the marketing techniques in this book can be done by non-lawyers, associates or others in and out of the office. Many of the techniques could be done by part-time law clerks.

To set in motion many of the techniques in this book, the lawyer simply has to photocopy the techniques described and hand them to someone else to do, with the instruction: "Please do this," or "Please be aware of this."

Naturally, some techniques can only be done by a lawyer. (For example, only lawyers can say they've handled a legal matter before. Only a lawyer can identify himself or herself as a lawyer in the courtroom or office in a social setting. Only a lawyer can give legal advice or make statements that appear to be legal advice.) Many techniques can be done by either a lawyer or a non-lawyer, and obviously, everybody should refrain from doing things that will alienate a client or potential client.

A lawyer could easily turn to an associate or non-lawyer in the office and say, "Here's the book on how to get clients. You do it." The lawyer would have to provide moral support to that person and help him or her do the marketing work. The lawyer would, at a minimum, refrain from doing those things which alienate clients and potential clients but, beyond this, could look to non-lawyers and associates to help increase the worthwhile practice through marketing.

As the lawyer or non-lawyer reads the techniques in this book, he or she should be thinking, "To whom can I give this technique to do?"

F-2
Marketing is a Learned Skill
For the Entire Firm

There are hundreds of things that every person in the office can do, or refrain from doing, in order to increase the number of good cases and clients. These techniques can, and must be, learned.

We are not dealing with "gimmicks" or manipulation of people. We are dealing with. teaching all people in the office what they must know and do to assure the firm's growth and stability.

No one was born with these marketing skills. Marketing techniques must be learned and then applied by the people who are going to do the marketing and these techniques must be reinforced periodically.

Although much of the "direct" or "heavy" marketing is done by the professional, the professional cannot do it alone.

Marketing is very much a team effort. The file clerk who misfiles documents which can't be located for a client; the associate who asks a client questions which the client has already answered; the receptionist who doesn't keep the reception room clean; the abusive, overprotective telephone receptionist; the secretary or associate who misspells a client's name; the office manager or billing clerk who keeps making mistakes on the bill- all of these people can undo the image of competence and availability and pride in work that the lawyer worked so hard to develop. All of these people must be taught what is expected of them in terms of client satisfaction, and even then there must be reinforcement.

It is not sufficient to say to them, "Use common sense and be liked." The reality is that the firm must take affirmative steps to teach and monitor.

Even under the best conditions, the non-professionals (and the professionals) in the firm will at times make mistakes that affect marketing. The professional must be aware of this and know how to repair the damage when it does occur.

The skills and techniques necessary for successfully getting and keeping good clients can be learned.

Remember. Successful people weren't born that way. They became successful by doing the things that non successful people don't do.

F-3
How to Convince Your Partners to Try Marketing and Practice Development

The managing partner of one of the largest law firms in the world once told me, "Jay, it is easy to explain things to my partners, but it's almost impossible to convince them to do anything." In some cases, it is difficult to motivate your partners to try something which is new to them. In many cases,. it is impossible to get them to *do* anything new.

I have a sign on my wall which only I can see and which says: "Either lead, follow, or get the hell out of the way." Unfortunately for the public and for the law firm, many partners will refuse to lead, refuse to follow and refuse to get out of the way. They will predict failure for any innovative concept and then do their best to ensure failure by covert, subtle sabotage. At the first opportunity they will quickly proclaim, "See, I told you it wouldn't work! "

When I told my father that I had decided to go to law school and become a lawyer, he said to me, "Jay, if you're going to be a lawyer, be a good lawyer not a bad lawyer." I asked my father, "Dad, what's the difference between the two?" My father responded, "Jay, a good lawyer has a solution for every problem; a bad lawyer has a problem for every solution." These "bad lawyers" will actively oppose practice development and have a problem for every solution.

The causes of this reactionary and self-destructive behavior are complex and it would take a qualified psychologist several volumes to describe the problems and the causes. I am going to set forth some of the more common causes of partners' resistance to change. My purpose in relating the causes is to help you to recognize and anticipate some of them in your own firm. Some reasons your partners resist change in the firm might include:

1. They are ready for retirement (the age is about 55-65). Kids educated. House and car paid off. Do not want the firm to invest money on long-term improvements because of the fear they won't be around to get the profits but will have to pay for the investment. (Such people also try to stop new equipment. new systems, new technology and hiring the people for them). Because of their age and lack of seniority with the firm, younger attorneys are afraid to disagree with them. The ready-for-retirement group just want to hang around and keep everything "status quo" until they retire.

2.   They have no desire to do anything different from what they have been doing for the last quarter century.

3.   They are afraid that they can't adapt to the change and they will become obsolete.

4.   They are afraid that implementing the marketing concepts in a formal manner may backfire and cause loss of existing clients.

I suggest you give a copy of this book to your partners to read. Then suggest that the marketing concepts of this book be the subject of part of a partners' meeting or retreat. Whatever you do, don't present the concepts of this book as your concepts. Make some bland statements such as, "Those are Foonberg's ideas, not mine. What do you think?"

Remember the maxim of Bud Orren of Minneapolis: "Nothing is difficult so long as you don't have to do it." Make it clear that to start the concepts, partners don't have to participate unless they want to, but you'd like their help in starting a few of the ideas. Emphasize that much, if not most, of the actual work will be done by the secretaries and non-partners.

Start with the concepts that are easy to install, cost very little money and are most likely to produce immediate results such as:

1.   Sending Christmas or season's greetings cards to clients.
2.   Sending thank-you letters to clients and other who refer you new clients.
3.   Sending copies of all correspondence, pleadings, documents, etc., to the clients.
4.   Getting a web site and putting the email address on your cards and stationery.
5.   Sending year-end tax reminders.
6.   Having an open house to coincide with a bar convention.
7.   Returning phone calls in less than two hours by allowing others to do it.

Vote to allow any individual partner to implement any of the concept she or she wants to try.

The results will speak for themselves. If your partners won't lead or follow or get out of the way, then you have serious problems. If your partners don't want to implement any of the concepts in this book or don't want to allow others to implement any of the concepts, then you should consider giving this book to a lawyer under the age of 50 and sharpening up some quill pens for the partners who won't change. They will soon find themselves obsolete and possibly involuntarily self employed especially if there is a marketing administrator with help and support in a modern world.

John Wooden, The UCLA Basketball Coach is one of my heroes. When asked what he thought of the many changes in sports, he responded, "You can't have progress without change. This does not mean that all change is progress, but you cannot have any progress without change."

F-4
Do Your Partners Bring in Business?
If Not, Why Not?

A small law firm cannot afford the luxury of a partner who never generates business through client referrals or totally new clients. In the smaller firms where interaction of people and a sense of pulling together is essential, there must be a perception of everyone's contributing to the survival and longevity of the firm. A partner who does not generate new business creates doubts as to the firm's longevity among the associates and staff, with a resultant attitude of "there's no future here." This causes the good people to leave to look for a place where growth and its opportunities are apparent.

It is my experience that partners who don't generate new business or clients are typically capable of practice development but often feel held back by their partners for one of two reasons:

1. They believe the compensation system doesn't reward client origination. Possibly the firm currently has essentially all the business it wants to handle and is more interested in getting work out than getting more work in. Accordingly, no direct measurable credit is given to the originating partner. Profit-sharing formulas are beyond the scope of this book, but I can suggest the following allocation for the first few years of a new client:

1.) ¼ of fee to partner who originates client

2.) ¼ of fee to partner who supervises and is responsible for the work

3.) ½ of fee to firm for associates' salaries and overhead.

Obviously, there are hundreds of possibilities, but I suggest this primarily to put some part of the fee into the pocket of the client originator as a direct reward. The part paid to the originator can diminish or gradually self-destruct over a period of time.

2. The partner who doesn't generate new business often perceives himself or herself to be overworked with inadequate attorney support and doesn't want to be overworked further. He or she may say or think, "What's the point of bringing in more work? I'll just have to do it myself and have even less time for myself and my family."

This situation should be corrected by other partners helping out with the new clients or by hiring more associates or paralegals. If the "overworked" partner does get the help, then everyone in the firm benefits. If the partner doesn't get help, he/she will be a "bad apple" in the firm, causing discontent, or he/she will make a lateral transfer out to another firm which will provide the help the partner needs in order to bring in new clients.

I recently had a situation in my practice where I had to refer out a potentially huge litigation matter because of conflict of interests. The first lawyer I called said, "Jay, I'd love to take on the case but I won't. I'm already overworked and my partners don't want to add people to the litigation section or to pitch in. If I take the case, I'll be even more overworked because I'll have to do everything myself." I ended up referring the case to a different firm.

Every partner in a firm should be producing some new business. If this is not the case, then make an analysis of why not, and take steps to correct the situation.

F-5
Does Your Compensation System or Workload Assignment Discourage Firm Members From Bringing in New Business?

I once offered a major, well-paying litigation case to another firm in town. I discussed the case in great detail with the head partner in the litigation section. He considered the case and said that he sincerely thanked me for the referral opportunity but declined the case.

I was shocked! This lawyer's firm could have earned a healthy high six or seven-figure fee on the case. In developing the conversation further he explained to me:

"Jay, it's a good case and a fantastic fee, but if we take it I'll have to do all the work. I'll have to work Saturdays and Sundays and my family won't see me for a year. The other partners won't take the responsibility for the case because they would have to give up their weekends. The firm doesn't want to "lateral hire" any senior level litigators so I'm afraid I'll have to turn the case down."

This firm lost an excellent fee simply because the workload assignments precluded anyone's helping in the supervision of the case and no one wanted to work any harder. Had an intelligent analysis been made, I believe the firm could have dumped some "dogs" (gotten rid of some bad cases and clients) and used the newly freed-up time to take on the big case.

The moral of this story is obvious. There's no point in seeking new business if there's no capacity to handle it.

Some firms do not recognize client development in terms of bonuses for client originators or compensation percentage points for new client originators. The attitude (conscious or subconscious) of the attorney is, "Why should I kill myself to get more business? There's nothing in it for me but more work, the same money, a pat on the back and a 'thank you.'"

Be sure you compensate directly or indirectly for new client originators.

F-6
Fee Allocation Formulas to Encourage Marketing

Every child knows the nursery rhyme, "Baa baa black sheep, have you any wool? Yes sir, yes sir, three bags full. One for the master and one for the Dame and one for the little boy who lives down the lane." This nursery rhyme had political origins and overtones and was in fact a complaint against a system of income allocation (taxation) that was perceived to be unfair.

Most formulas which allocate law firm fee income or net profits are deemed to be both political (keeping the old guard in power) and unfair (exploiting the working classes). They were usually tolerated because of the upward mobility goals of the young lawyers to move up from the exploited class (associate) and to become members of the exploiting class (partner) where they could get their just compensation.

While the system worked for many years it began falling apart when attorneys began doubting their ability to achieve status as an exploiter. The period of time to change classes kept extending from three years to five years to seven years to nine years to never (permanent associates). It has been said that as associates approach the goal line of partnership, the firm moves the goal line back ten yards farther.

Accordingly, younger attorneys began demanding and getting more money "up front," creating havoc in many firms not knowing how to adapt to the brand new world of the 21st Century.

Typically, a fee or profit allocation formulas compensates the following four classes:

1. Finders   The marketeers or rainmakers who bring in the clients.
2. Grinders   The production attorneys who do the work in a professional manner to provide the clients with their perceived legal needs and keep the client happy.
3. Minders   The attorneys who manage the practice, "run the store" and make it possible for both the Finders and Grinders to perform their tasks.
4. Binders   Although these attorneys never achieve prominence in Finding or Grinding or Minding, they somehow quietly and consistently provide the glue that holds the firm together. They provide the collegial atmosphere that sets the tone for the firm culture. They soothe the hurt egos and calm down the valued staff people who want to quit. They teach an associate without yelling or hollering.

The concept of the division of fees or income in some sort of predictable mathematical formula system (as opposed to an arbitrary tyrannical manner) is supposed to create harmony and fulfilled expectations.

The concept of a formula is most credited in its application to a Boston law firm called Hale & Dorr. Not surprisingly the concept is called the "Hale-Dorr" method, and most "experts" claim to be using a "modified Hale-Dorr" method. They could probably just as accurately be claiming to use a modified "Baa baa black sheep" method.

Some of the formulas are very simple, such as:

1/4th of Gross Fee to originating Partner as collected
1/4th of Fee to Production Partner as work done
1/2 of Fee to Firm "Pot" for expenses
       -or
1/2 of Fee to Originating Partner
20% to Production Partner
30% to the firm "Pot" for expenses
       -or
1/3rd to Originating Partner
1/3rd to Production Partner
1/3rd to "Pot"

Some of the formulas run two to three pages and require complex computer calculations. There are myriad variations on these themes.

I suggest that in adopting a formula a firm should consider the following criteria:

1. Every type of partner must receive some part of the fee (profits).
2. The amount of the fee should reflect the firm's current and projected year's needs.
    a.   Does the firm need clients and work?
    b.   Is the firm overworked and the problem is getting the work out?
    c.   Is there plenty of work coming in and plenty going out but no profit?
    d.   Is the firm so busy making money that no one is happy?
3. My suggestions are as follows:

    The originating partner should receive from 20 percent to 40 percent of the fee for the first five years.

    If the originating partner receives less than 20 percent there may be no incentive to bring in new clients. If the originating partner receives more than 40 percent he or she may spend all of his or her time being out of the office being a "bird dog" or commission salesperson and may lose professional competency or may lose the sense of being part of the firm.

4. The percentage should "self destruct" over a period of years, for example:

	Example A	*Example* B
Year 1	40%	40%
2	36	36
3	32	32
4	28	28
5	24	24
6	20	20
7	20	16
8	20	12
9	20	8
10	20	4
Thereafter	20	-0

In the Example A, the originating partner always has something coming which encourages the originating partner to stay with the firm and not be afraid to "turn over" the client to other partners to develop additional business from the client. This system has the disadvantage of the younger attorneys perceiving they are carrying dead wood.

In the second example, the younger lawyers will be happy to see the originating credit wither away, but the originating partner may simply leave the firm and take the client to another firm where there will be a higher originating partner percentage.

Both self-destructing formulas encourage the originating partners to keep bringing in clients.

In the first method the originating partner feels secure in that a backlog of residuals will always exist as long as the client is with the firm. In the second method the originating partner is forced to get more and more business just to maintain status quo (or alternately become a grinder or a minder).

5. The percentage should be reviewed every three to five years and changed if necessary to reflect the needs of the firm (lower the percentages when there is too much work; raise them when there is not enough work).

6. The percentage formula for a given client should not change with the needs of the firm after the client is a firm client. This could create destructive competition within the firm.

7. There must be a committee of final resort to reallocate fees or settle partner disputes as to who is or is not entitled to origination or production percentages. One of my partners once said to me "Jay, I don't care what system you use as long as I keep the books." He was right.

"Another partner once told me. Every system can be manipulated." He was right.

There must be a committee to make final binding decision.

No formula can be perfect. No formula can be forever. All formulas work well if the partners (and associates) perceive them to be fair. Accordingly, the job of the firm is not to compensate the marketers fairly in the abstract sense, but rather to compensate them in a system which addresses the needs of the firm and which the partners and associates perceive to be fair.

F-7
Getting Business From Associate Lawyers
Associates Can Be Taught

Associates often view the first one to five years after law school as a sort of paid internship program. They have expectations that they are going to be paid by the firm to spend part of their time learning how to practice law and part of their time actually practicing law. They often expect "the firm" to absorb the cost of their mistakes and inefficiency.

Partners, often feel they are overworked and that they don't have time to tend to the smaller cases and clients the associates tend to bring in. Accordingly, senior attorneys often discourage new associates from bringing business in. Additionally, the partners will loudly proclaim that the associates aren't producing enough billable hours in existing profitable cases as it is, so why is the associate wasting firm time on his or her low-level "small" cases that the firm really doesn't want.

The firm that doesn't let associates bring in their friends' and relatives' money-losing low-level cases is making a serious mistake. "Client getting" and keeping is not easy. The associate who shows an aptitude for and desire to bring in cases and clients can someday be a "rainmaker" for the firm. The instinct or talent or whatever it is that motivates an associate to bring in business can easily be stifled or crushed. When the partners "bad mouth" what the associate brings in, the associate will at some point simply stop trying. He or she will either refer the business to other firms, which makes the associate's firm look bad, or the associate doesn't refer the business anywhere.

Just as associates learn to try big cases by trying small cases, an associate learns to bring in big cases and big clients by starting off bringing in small cases and small clients. The firm should back up the associate with all its resources and guidance, whether it be a sole practitioner with one associate or a larger organization. Time records should be carefully kept. During the case and at the end of the case, the time expended by the associate and others should be reviewed by the associates. In this manner, the associate will get a clearer picture of how much the firm is investing in the associate. The associate will be grateful and will work those extra hours on weekends or at night on another paying matter to make up for the loss.

The art and skill of client getting is a delicate one which can easily be killed by rejection of what is brought in.

The associate who expects the firm *both* to absorb losses on the case and also compensate for the revenue by some sort of bonus is simply a pig. Associates can and should receive some form of compensation for profitable business brought in after the firm has recovered some of the time spent in helping the associate when the associate was bringing in money-losers.

Many of the profitable clients and cases an associate brings in will stay with the firm if the associate leaves the firm. These people will also refer other people to the firm.

In summary, support the associate's fledgling efforts at practice development because eventually it will be to benefit of the firm.

It is estimated that when a lawyer changes firms, the $2/3^{rds}$ of clients will follow that lawyer. $1/3^{rd}$ do not follow the lawyer, but rather stay with the firm after a period of time. There will be a large number of cases and clients who stay with the firm.

In summary, encouraging associates to bring in clients can have both short range and long range benefits to the firm.

F-8
Getting Clients From
Non-Lawyers In the Office

People who work in law offices often have friends who need lawyers. It's amazing how often a secretary or other non-lawyer will send a potential client to another law firm. Some non-lawyers actually believe there are ethical prohibitions against their firm representing their friends. Sometimes the employee is ashamed or embarrassed that their friends' legal matters are not large fee type cases. (The case might be a large fee case but the employee doesn't recognize it as such.) There often is a tremendous failure of communication between lawyers and non-lawyers in a law office. This is simply one example of failure to communicate.

You should announce in your personnel manual and by a periodic notice, perhaps once a year, the following:

"All employees are encouraged to refer the legal problems of their friends and relatives to the firm. Special attention will be given to their needs regardless of the size of the case. We consider the referral of a legal matter as a vote of confidence in the ability of the firm."

It would probably be prohibited fee splitting to offer the referring employee any compensation for referring a case (unless the referrer was a lawyer), but you should follow up with a thank-you note to the employee and a notation in the employee's personnel file for the referral.

I have written a list of more than 100 things a non lawyer can do to help the firm in its marketing activities. Copies of that list have appeared in many legal publications. A copy of the current listing can be obtained as an independent publication. Visit www.Foonberglaw.com for examples.

F-9
The Lawyer as a Notary to Attract Business

At one time I used to get a certain amount of new legal clients and work from clients who became aware of my capability to serve them as a lawyer when they came to me for notarial services. As I will explain later, I had to stop doing notarial work because of changes in the rules of the tax court. However, the amount of legal fees and business that came from my being a notary easily justified the time dedicated to it.

When I maintained a notary public's commission, I let it be known throughout the small office building where I practiced that I was available to notarize documents (technically acknowledge signatures). There was a CPA firm, a doctor and the office of a national liquor distributor in the building, as well as my law office. At first, secretaries would come in and ask me to notarize their bosses' signatures. I explained that I would be happy to notarize the signature for free, but I insisted on the signature's being acknowledged by the signer in my presence. Accordingly, the bosses of the various firms and the clients and principals of the CPA firm began coming to me for a notarization and I was able to meet these potential clients. I apologized for requesting the person to see me personally, but it was my *modus operandi* to do things right or not at all.

A small percentage of these people came back to me at a later time for legal work. There's no question that I first met these people when I did notarization work.

The rules of the tax court were subsequently amended to provide that a lawyer could not be the lawyer on a case where he or she originally was a notary on a document where the due execution of the document was in issue. I did not want to lose potential tax court work due to being a notary. I do recommend to others being a notary as a possible source of legal clients.

F-10
Having a Secretary as a Notary
As a Source of Clients and Cases

I have received some good paying legal work from previous clients and have gotten new clients by having a secretary as a notary public.

Existing clients know that my secretary is a notary and they call or come in to have their signatures acknowledged on various types of documents such as deeds. Sometimes when they call my secretary or drop in they will reason, "Well as long as I'm going there to get this document notarized, I might as well see Jay and get his opinion on the underlying transaction," or they may think, "I don't think I need a lawyer for this, but as long as I'll be there I'll ask Jay if I can do it myself or not."

When a person comes in for a notarization, the secretary doing the notarization should notify you that he is there. You should make a brief appearance to personally greet the existing client or to meet the person who is not now a client but who might become one in the future. When people come to your office, you have a golden opportunity to meet and impress them.

I have absolutely no hesitancy in offering my opinion as to the client's need of my legal services. Also I do not hesitate either to charge them (if I do work beyond the first quick review) or to send them a bill for consultation with "no charge" on it (if I don't do work beyond the initial quick review.) for the legal work done.

I see no problem with rendering legal services to people with whom I have a pre-existing relationship. The fact that their initial motivation in coming to see me might have been in connection with a notarial function does not seem to me to be "feeding." In some jurisdictions this might be a theoretical problem. I don't feel obligated to cross-examine my existing clients to ask them if they came to see me primarily because I'm a lawyer or primarily because we have a notary public in the office.

Additionally, it doesn't bother me to remind clients periodically in a firm newsletter that my secretary is a notary public. I personally am not comfortable about including notarial availability in a firm brochure and I have never seen it included in one, but I don't know of any reason why it couldn't be. I personally would not be comfortable reminding clients of available notarial services by means of a sign on the door or in the reception room or in a Yellow Pages display ad in the legal classified section. If you feel comfortable with this and it is in conformity with your local ethical rules, then by all means go ahead and do it.

I have gotten many new legal clients, including a very major fee, through my having a notary in the office. I had an office in a building where there were corporate offices of two or three small companies. From time to time one of the secretaries would come in and get some corporate document notarized. These secretaries often told their bosses that they were getting their documents notarized at "Mr. Foonberg's office" or at "the lawyer's office." The people in these offices realized that we were close by and immediately accessible.

You should be aware, however, that if you or a member of your firm acknowledges a document, and at a later time, the date or manner of execution of the document is an issue, you may be precluded from being the lawyer on the case because of your being a witness to a material fact.

Additionally, you should be aware of local rules, if any, on the subject of "feeding," and the rules, if any, on simultaneously practicing more than one business or profession. I don't think that my having my secretary be a notary in my law office constitutes a separate business or profession, but somebody else might.

If, in the course of notarizing something for a non-client or a client who already has a lawyer you notice that the person needs legal services, you should be cognizant of the ethical restrictions, if any, on whether or how you could suggest the use of a lawyer. You might want to or have to disqualify yourself.

Foreigners may also come to you as a notary because they may think they need a notary when, in fact, they need a lawyer. In many Civil Law countries, a notary does many of the things done by lawyers in the United States. They probably couldn't care less whether you function as a notary or as a lawyer so long as you get the job done.

In summary, having a notary public in the office is not a ticket to instant success or riches, and indeed you will have to exercise some caution and control over the way you handle (or don't handle) the new work from existing clients and new clients you meet. On the other hand, you will probably receive a new matter or a new client about once or twice a year as the result of your having an accessible notary. On balance, I recommend this technique to you for consideration in your own office. A sample letter to clients concerning availability of notarial services follows this chapter.

F-11
Sample Letter to Clients and Others
Re Availability of Notarial Service

The following letter probably tells people more than they care to know about notaries. You can modify it as you wish. The important thing is:

1. To communicate with clients;
2. To remind clients you do have a notarial service available for them and their referrals. Such a letter can also be used as the equivalent of a newsletter.

Dear Client:

Clients frequently call upon us for notarial services. Some of our clients are international businesses and individuals from countries where the role of a *notar* or *notario* is different from the role of a notary public here in the United States. Accordingly, we periodically send this letter out to our clients to remind them of what we can and cannot do to help them when they need a notary public.

We do have a non-lawyer notary public who can notarize signatures for our clients in our office. We will also do notarial work for a non-client who is recommended by you, a client, as a courtesy to you.

If we prepared the document involved, we will not charge for the notarial service, as such. If we did not prepare the document involved, or if the person is not a client, he may or may not be charged by the non-lawyer who does the notarial work, depending on the circumstances. Normally, the notary will not charge for personal signature notarizations, but might charge $10 to $20 for corporate notarizations. The fee does not go to the firm. It is donated to the City of Hope charity and, if you wish to, you can make out your check to the City of Hope and we'll forward it, and you will be acknowledged as being the donor (your name will go on the mailing list of donors).

We ordinarily do not allow lawyers to notarize documents because, at a later time. the *date* or circumstances of notarization may be in issue; a lawyer should not be in the position of being both a witness and a lawyer on a case. In some instances we will insist, for the client's own protection, that the person go to an outside notary (for example, when the mental or physical condition of the person may be at issue). Additionally, we cannot allow our people to leave the office to acknowledge the signature. The person must come into our office.

Please don't bring in a document signed by someone else and ask our notary to notarize it. He won't do it. There is a procedure where *you* can bring in a document *you* witnessed someone else sign and then *you* can sign before the notary that *you* saw the original signature.

In the U.S., a notary's principal role or function is that of an official witness to a signature to minimize the possibility of forgery of signatures and to have the person who is signing reaffirm that he/she is signing freely and swearing under penalty of perjury that he/she is the person signing.

In the United States legal system, private parties make their own contracts without the necessity of state or government approval to make the contract legal.

In many other legal systems, the state or government must be a party to all legal agreements and an agreement between private parties is not legal or enforceable until the state or government becomes part of the agreement. The addition of the state is usually done by registering the document or listing the document somewhere. For example, this is usually done at the offices of an official usually called *notar* or *notario,* depending on the country. Sometimes, when they are simple, *notar* or *notario* will prepare the forms or documents involved. For this reason, in some countries, the notary and the lawyer may be the same person. Because of the importance of the function of the *notar* or *notario* in other jurisdictions, people erroneously believe that a contract is not legal until I made official by a notary.

Please do not "drop in" for a notarization. The notary may be out of the office. Call first, and we'll do all we can to assist you.

Sincerely,

Chapter G
Getting Business from Others
Out of the Office

G-1
Your Present Good Clients and Referrers
Are Your Most Important Marketing Asset

From a cost and time-effective point of view, present good clients and referrers of clients are the best people to work with when marketing. You are already in contact with them and you are already doing work for them. You simply have to think about what you are already doing and then emphasize those things which encourage them to refer you more cases and clients and de-emphasize or eliminate those things which you are inadvertently doing to discourage them from referring more cases and clients.

If you are a lawyer with five or more years of practice, you will realize that everything in this chapter is self-evident or obvious. My purpose in writing this chapter is to remind you of what you already know and help you prioritize your efforts.

PRESENT CLIENTS. Present good clients are your single most important marketing asset. They are the ones who are paying fees *now*. They are the greatest single source of immediate referrers. They are the ones with whom you have ongoing contact. They are the ones who provide you with unlimited opportunities to expand your practice with more good clients. These are the ones you start immediately to work with.

Present clients should never be ignored in order to go after new clients. Remember that other firms are in fact going after your good clients, often on a very aggressive basis. No client can be taken for granted.

PRESENT REFERRERS OF GOOD CLIENTS. (This may include present clients, past clients and referrers who have never been clients.) These are probably your second most important marketing asset running a very close second behind present clients. These are people with a proven track record of sending you good clients. They are likely to lead to more cash flow in the immediate future. You know who and where they are and you simply have to continue doing those things which cause them to make referrals and de-emphasize those things which discourage referrals. Be sure to keep in mind whether those referrers have been sending you good clients and cases or bad ones.

FORMER CLIENTS AND REFERRERS OF GOOD CLIENTS. Former clients and referrers of clients are probably your third priority in terms of cost and time effectiveness. These are people with whom you have dealt in the past. You can most effectively find them, identify them and make contact with them. They can give you the information you may need to correct your errors. They can provide you with new business of their own and of others in the near future. You simply have to begin the process of contacting them.

PEOPLE WHO ARE NOT YET A CLIENT OR REFERRER OF CLIENTS. These people are a fourth priority. Without new clients, all business will eventually die. Your present and past clients and referrals of clients may not have the ability to send you as much as you want or need in the way of new clients or cases. New fields of law increase in importance and old traditional fields may decrease in importance as legislation and courts change the law and its interpretation. While new economic and social areas of our society come into being and old areas wither, you cannot ignore finding these people as yet unknown to you. If you ignore them, your practice may ultimately die. I only wish to point out that they are fourth priority in terms of new clients and business.

It is generally accepted that a lawyer's new files originate from the following sources. (Figures are approximate and will vary from practice to practice.)

1. Repeat business from former clients & present clients.   50%
2. Referrals from sources who are not clients, including
    other lawyers, CPAs, health care professionals,
    ministers, friends and relatives, lawyer referral services.   30%
3. All other services, media advertising, the internet,
    yellow pages, service and charity clubs and organizations.   <u>20%</u>

                                                    Total   <u>100%</u>

These statistics should remind you of the importance of present and past clients.

G-2
Will Marketing Result in Backlash On Existing Clients?

Some attorneys are afraid of "backlash." They are concerned that clients will equate active marketing efforts as an indication or admission that business is not good and that the firm is marketing because it needs clients and fees.

These attorneys are seeking some sort of guarantee or assurance that their marketing efforts won't result in the loss of an existing client.

I have asked thousands of lawyers at programs all over the United States whether they have suffered any "backlash" as a result of their marketing efforts. Not one attorney has ever related a single negative experience or loss of an existing client.

Anything is theoretically possible in this world. Perhaps some attorney lost a client because of marketing without knowing about it. Perhaps some attorney would not admit the truth. Perhaps the wrong people came to the seminars. I don't know if any of the foregoing could possibly have happened without my knowledge. I do know I have never encountered a single report of loss of an existing client through backlash.

I advise you not to be concerned about this remote possibility.

G-3
Getting Clients and Cases from Friends and Relatives

Friends and relatives are an extremely important source of clients and cases for every lawyer, but especially for a new lawyer. Typically, friends and relatives are the only "client base" a new lawyer has. After a lawyer has been in practice for a while, friends and relatives become less important, but they are still a good source.

They Want You to Succeed. Your friends and relatives want you to succeed. They will do everything they can to help you, whether it's to give you their own legal matters or to refer clients to you. They will never let you forget how they were one of your first clients or got you one of your first cases. They will send you business your entire professional life.

It's up to you whether they do or don't send you their cases and referrals. If you treat them right, they will be a good source for life. If you mistreat them, they'll stop trying to help you.

You have to communicate to friends and relatives that what they tell you is privileged. Often, they are concerned over your telling common friends and relatives about their legal problems. I've represented many people who had friends and relatives who were lawyers. These clients came to me because they were afraid that the other lawyer would discuss their cases with mutual acquaintances or relatives.

You took a course in Evidence; your friends and relatives did not, and accordingly, they don't know about the attorney-client privilege. Whenever a friend or relative approaches you for legal advice, you should somehow work into the conversation that when they seek legal advice from you, you are acting as an attorney and that the attorney-client privilege prohibits you from discussing any aspect of the case with others. This will reassure them.

Be careful NOT to discuss friends' and relatives' cases with other friends and relatives or in the presence of any of your own family members. I've seen situations where children blurted out things they heard their parents discussing, which can be quite awkward and embarrassing when the person whose matter they heard discussed finds out about it. If you violate the attorney-client privilege, you will lose the friend or relative forever as a source of clients and referrals.

Billing. When you discount a bill or fee for a friend or relative, be sure to communicate on the invoice or in a letter that you have given a discount. That person has to be informed by you that there has been a family discount. (See the chapter on "Family Discounts".) If you don't tell such clients about the discount, they won't know they received one.

Advice Sought at Social Events. When friends and relatives pull you aside at a wedding or other social event to ask you a legal question, you must react in a friendly yet firm manner. Hand them a card and simply say, "That's a very interesting question. Why don't you come to the office where I can get some more facts and where I have the facilities to check out the answer to be sure the law hasn't changed." If you are rude or hostile because they've invaded your personal life, they won't send you any business. You don't have to answer their questions at the social event if you don't want to. You simply have to accept these questions as part of the price you pay for the privilege of being a lawyer.

Remind your friends of your long-standing relationship with them. There must be 100 people who think they're one of my first clients. They love to be reminded of how they were one of my first clients "way back when...." They also love to remind me of the length of our relationship.

Announcements, Cards and Mailing Lists. Be sure to send friends and relatives all your announcements. When they ask for extra cards to give to their friends and acquaintances, give them the extra cards and say, "Thank you for thinking of me." Don't mumble some awkward statement about "You really shouldn't," because if you do, they won't. They don't want to get you into trouble so they won't give the cards to their friends if you tell them not to. If it makes you feel better to say, "Here, take some extras in case you lose or misplace one," then go ahead and say it, but don't tell your friends and relatives not to boost you.

Be sure you keep your friends and relatives on your mailing list for Christmas or season's greetings cards and client newsletters. If a relative referred you a client and the client got a greeting card or newsletter from you and the relative didn't, the relative may find out from the referred client and will be hurt or angry and may not refer any more clients.

When you send an email announcement to a client, you should add a "click here to forward to a friend."

G-4
The Spouse's Role in Practice Development

The tem "spouse" as used in this chapter is to include any person in the attorney's household. No legal or social implications are intended.

Does your spouse generate business for your practice? If not, why not? You might wish to photocopy this chapter and give it to your spouse to read.

Without realizing it, a spouse can have a positive or negative effect on practice growth and development or have no effect on it. Spouses work and have fellow employees and fellow social or athletic club members. The spouse and the attorney go together to many of the same social events at the same time. The spouse and the attorney can work either independently or as a team to develop clients and referrers of clients. A negative spouse can seriously hinder practice development.

PRIORITIES. I don't mean to suggest that a lawyer can only succeed with a supportive spouse or must fail with a non-supportive spouse. I simply wish to point out that the spouse can be a positive or negative or neutral factor and should not be overlooked as an integral part of the entire marketing effort. With the spouse's help, it's easier to get good clients; without it, it's harder. It can be something like the attorney's having one foot on the gas pedal and the spouse having one foot on the brake. A spouse can either take the foot off the brake or put it on the gas pedal, or at least keep it off the brake.

I'm not suggesting that every spouse become a "cheerleader" for the attorney spouse. I am suggesting that the financial and professional status of both can be improved if the non-attorney spouse actually assists the attorney spouse.

At the very least, the attorney and spouse should discuss what the role (or non-role) of the non-attorney spouse in practice development will or won't be. A spouse who resents the attorney's taking a prospective client to a basketball or football game or theater will cause marital strain if the problem is not identified and resolved. The attorney spouse and the non-attorney spouse must each be sensitive to the other in order to modify or adjust the client entertainment pattern to include, or at least not exclude, the other spouse for consideration.

As an example of a team effort, let me give you two examples of how my wife and I sometimes work together:

1. I have an excellent memory for faces and an excellent memory for names, but I don't always connect the two. Often, someone will walk up and start to talk to me and I simply don't know who the person is. If my wife is with me, she will bail me out of this

problem. She waits about 30 seconds, and if I haven't introduced her, she knows I'm stuck. She then introduces herself and the person, of course, introduces himself or herself. I then say something like, "I'm sorry. I thought you knew each other."

2. My wife helps me with professional cards. On rare occasions I don't have a card with me when an appropriate opportunity arises to give a card to someone. I will tell the person to whom I want to give the card, "I just gave out of my last card and I'll ask my wife if she has one." My wife will conveniently have "just one" in her wallet which she will hand me to give to the person.

Incidentally, you should never say you forgot your cards, or that you don't have cards. This is a subconscious "turn off" that may give the impression that you really don't want new business. You should say something like, "I just gave out my last card to someone who asked for it," indicating that you do ordinarily carry cards. This is a subconscious "turn on" that you are successful and in demand because people ask you for cards, and that this new person is indeed fortunate because you happen to have found one card for him or her.

A cooperative spouse can be a boost to practice development by cooperating in the entertainment of clients and prospective clients. I know of a lawyer who recently founded a new firm with several other lawyers. The lawyer had a buffet and a cocktail party at his home every Saturday night for six months for clients and prospective clients. He and his wife very successfully centered their work and social life around practice development for six solid months.

On the other hand, a spouse that absolutely refuses to help can actually be a detriment to practice development by creating feelings of guilt and conflict in the spouse trying to develop the practice.

Common sense must, of course, prevail. No one suggests bringing convicted rapists and murderers into your home. I, as do most lawyers, have clients whom I find personally disgusting and whom I would rather lose as clients than bring into my home.

If a spouse is aware that his or her efforts at practice development are valuable, then the spouse can and will produce good clients for the attorney. The spouse who doesn't create any practice just isn't trying.

Again, each couple must strike its own balance. As a general rule, my wife does not actively look for opportunities to suggest me as a lawyer to prospective clients. Once, at a convention of attorneys, she became friendly with another attorney's wife at poolside while I was at meetings. A few months later the wife of the other attorney suggested considering me for a referral in a tax fraud conflict situation. I was one of three attorneys suggested and the client chose me. I earned a very large fee on the case which enabled me to buy a new home. My wife had effectively communicated to the other wife that I did do tax fraud work instead of merely communicating without further elucidation that I was a lawyer.

I know of many people married to lawyers who are active In social and philanthropic groups and who are not at all embarrassed to suggest their own attorney-spouse when the group needs a luncheon speaker, or who somehow find a way of slipping into a conversation or speech that the spouse is a lawyer.

I must admit that in my experience I've often heard or seen wives boosting their lawyer-husbands, but I have never heard a husband boost his lawyer-wife. I know many successful female attorneys, and it seems to me that their husbands are not a factor in the practice development of their wives. The husbands seem to hang in the background. I have seen couples where both are attorneys and where the wife continually boosts the husband, but the husband does not boost the wife. I suppose my comments apply equally to unmarried couples as well as to married couples.

There are, many specific things a spouse can do or not do to aid in practice development.

1. The spouse should understand that marketing is a never-ending, 24-hours-a-day task. Good clients pay the bills, good clients pay for the family's housing, recreation, education, standard of living, retirement, etc. Good clients don't come easily and they don't stay easily. If you don't take good care of them, somebody else will. The attorney will not accrue clients solely through technical competency. Clients are not coconuts who randomly fall off trees waiting for someone randomly to pick them up. South Pacific natives know that if you want the good coconuts, you have to climb the tree after them and pick them before they fall.

2. When the spouse gives the attorney's card, he or she should always give only one. The spouse doesn't want to give the impression of being a one-person advance team drumming up business. The single card is sufficient for the person to whom it will be given. Even if the spouse is carrying 50 cards, he/she should say they have "one." If there are two or three people who want to get cards, then the spouse can say "I just happen to have two," or "I just happen to have three."

3. The spouse shouldn't complain about how hard the attorney is working or how the work load interferes with family or social life. This is a subconscious "turn off, II indicating that the potential client or referrer of clients would be adding to the spouse's distress by giving the attorney more clients and cases which would compete with family interests. The potential client won't want to exacerbate the domestic turmoil, and in fact, this could spread a negative factor in the marketplace that "Old Joe" or "Old Mary" is so overworked there are family problems and people should look for a different lawyer.

4. The spouse should be positive and supportive when the attorney occasionally misses a social event. Tell people, "Ordinarily Joe would not let his professional life interfere with our social life, but sometimes clients' cases, like medical emergencies, don't always happen 9 to 5, Monday through Friday. Joe is a good lawyer who cares

about his good clients and does whatever needs doing whenever and where ever it needs doing. I understand that and I support that. Joe didn't become a lawyer just to make money and live the good life, and we knew that when we got married (when he became a lawyer). If occasionally the practice interferes with our social or family routine, we'll make up for it by tacking on a couple of days to our next vacation with the kids."

While all of this may sound a little too Pollyannaish (especially if the spouse doesn't mean it), nonetheless, the spouse should reassure potential clients and referrers of clients by word and by conduct that he/she wants the spouse to have more and better clients and that more and better clients are a positive, not negative, factor in the family relationship.

5. The non-attorney spouse should always take the opportunity to tell people that the other spouse is an attorney, whenever it can be squeezed into the conversation. Something like, "My husband/wife is a very good attorney. He/she has a good practice with good clients." Remember that people want to ally themselves with winners rather than losers. Therefore, you want to identify that the attorney is good and has good clients. "He/she really likes to help people, and if you ever need a good attorney, you should give him/her a call. Here is his/her phone number. I happen to have a card with me."

What might appear to be "puffing" or "bragging" if said by the attorney is more acceptable if said by the spouse.

6. What kind of law does your husband/wife practice?

There's a whole chapter in this book on how to answer that question, and while I don't like referring from one part of the book to another, in this case I will do so to avoid lengthy repetition.

Oversimplified, the guidelines to answering this question are: a) if you know for a fact that the person specifically needs a tax or probate or litigation lawyer, you can say something like, "My husband/wife has a practice where I believe they handle cases like yours." Remember, there's an inference that the attorney doesn't want or can't handle cases outside of the fields stated in the answer. If you don't know for a fact exactly what kind of law the client needs or will need in the future, you should say something like, "My husband/wife practices with other lawyers who, among them, cover most areas of law. If my husband's/wife's group can't handle your case, they will help find an expert in the areas you need.

ATTORNEY-CLIENT PRIVILEGE. There is a very crucial point that every spouse should observe, even if he/she doesn't want to become actively involved in practice development. The attorney-client privilege is sacred to the basic confidential relationship between attorneys and clients. There is no exception for spouses. A spouse can do a lot of harm by blabbing about cases the lawyer is handling for clients. Potential clients will worry about *their* confidences if they hear spouses discussing the attorney's cases. On the other hand, your spouse can do a lot of good by stating, "My husband doesn't discuss client names or matters with me." (even if it isn't always 100 percent correct), in this way, people will feel assured that you keep client confidences sacred.

SUMMARY. A happy relationship and a happy home and family life, in my opinion, should be much more important than a successful professional career. Other people have other values and other priorities and these values and priorities can shift and change as circumstances shift and change. Spouses have to make or find their own value systems. So long as spouses understand that they can be a factor in the professional marketing picture, they can make their own decisions. I only suggest that it is an error not to consider this factor, and to reconsider it from time to time.

G-5
Bar Association Lawyer Referral Services
Are a Profitable Source of Clients and Fees

A lawyer should belong to as many Bar-sponsored referral services in as many categories of law as possible. They are a profitable source of new clients and good fees.

This chapter is based upon my own personal experiences in belonging to Bar-sponsored Lawyer Referral Services for more than three decades. Lawyers throughout the United States have reported experiences and successes similar to mine. Unfortunately, not all Lawyer Referral Services (LRS) function well. Accordingly, in this chapter I'll go into what the LRS has to do to ensure the success of the program and worthwhile economics to the attorney.

LRS VS. LRIS

LRS stands for Lawyer Referral Service. It was designed to bring together potential clients looking for a lawyer and lawyers willing to help.

Often the lawyer informed the potential client that the services of a lawyer were not necessary and the client could get help from a government or charitable agency or could handle their own matter without a lawyer. Many LRS became LRIS, Lawyer Referral and Information Services, with the service trying to reduce contacts with lawyers where the callers could get "information" without seeing a lawyer.

A properly run LRS can be a source of profit and professional and social satisfaction for the lawyer, the client and the Bar Association. An improperly run service will leave a bad taste for everyone involved.

To be successful for all, several events must come together in the proper sequence.

The attorney or attorneys must be made to understand, through Bar communications, that the LRS is profitable. I have done programs on practice development with Bar Associations all over the United States. Everywhere, the attorneys report LRS to be a good source of clients and profits.

The LRS must screen the "clients" to be sure that the clients are bona fide clients who need and can pay for a lawyer and not people looking for free legal advice. Some LRSs have reported to me that about 50 to 60 percent of all those who call don't really need a lawyer. These callers are often referred to various social welfare agencies, consumer agencies, appropriate law enforcement agencies or others. In other words, the people should be well screened by the LRS to be sure they need a private practice lawyer.

The potential clients must be willing to make a nominal financial commitment IN

ADVANCE of the interview so that they are qualified as being serious. (See my chapter on "cash up front" as being a commitment to the case by the client.)

The lawyers must be made to understand the following about the FEES:

1. A LRS is *not* legal aid. The clients are *not* indigents. They normally have money and can afford to pay private attorneys.
2. About 70 percent of the interviews will not lead to any fee for the lawyer (assuming the nominal cash up front goes to the LRS). They will be money loser for the lawyer. The lawyer will, however, have met a potential client who often will come back on another matter or refer someone else.
3. About 15-20 percent of the interviews will lead to small or moderate fees which make the particular matter profitable in and of itself.
4. About 10 or 15 percent of the interviews will lead to a very large fee. These few cases, on balance, will turn the LRS cases collectively into a profitable activity.

The lawyer must be made to understand that the CLIENTS who use LRS often:

1. Simply don't know any lawyer to call.
2. Have never used a lawyer in the past and don't know how to select one.
3. Are new to the community and have no local friends or relatives to recommend a lawyer to them. (Often they come from another state or country and want a new will which conforms to local law.) I have had several people who have come to me with no legal problems. They simply want to meet me so that they will know a local lawyer to call if and when they need one.
4. Have a local lawyer whom they have been trying to reach, but who is unavailable for a number of reasons.
5. Believe that the lawyer they previously used doesn't practice in the area of law they think they need.
6. Have been recommended to the LRS by a lawyer in another community or by a local lawyer who can't or won't handle their case.
7. Are looking for a "specialist" and believe that the LRS will find one for them. I have received many major corporate clients looking for a lawyer who practiced international law. Of the thousands of lawyers in our LRS system, only 2 of us were listed for international law. The large firms felt it was beneath their dignity and status to belong to an LRS or possibly never thought of it.
8. Are looking for an ethical lawyer and believe the LRS will find one for them.
9. Believe that the lawyers who are involved with Bar Association activities are "better" than the other ones who are not.
10. Sometimes cannot distinguish between "The Bar Association" and LRS. They sometimes believe the Bar Association, itself, is recommending a lawyer to them.

LAWYER RESPONSIBILITIES:

Treat the LRS client with the same dignity and courtesy as you would a new client recommended by your best client. Remember that the LRS client has already paid cash up front before seeing you. Most potential clients will not have demonstrated their seriousness before coming in.

Insist on the LRS cash being paid up front *before* you start the interview (unless the LRS has already collected it). Do not, under any circumstances, allow the interview to start until *after* the LRS fee has been collected. This is critical. People looking to pick your brain for free legal advice typically won't pay even the nominal LRS fee for half an hour for 30 minutes of your time.

You should give the amount of time required by the rules of your LRS to the initial interview. After that, treat the client the same as you would any other client.

You have no obligation to do more than what is required. (This is not normally legal aid.) You may, if you wish, do *pro bono* public work for the LRS client, but neither the client nor the LRS is expecting it.

Be immediately available when the LRS calls. Treat them as important referrers of clients. (Remember the 10-15 percent of the cases with the big fee.) The interviewer at LRS has to clear this case from their list and needs you to confirm that you will see the client. (I'm assuming you also would immediately be available for your important clients.)

Be as prompt as you can in reporting results to the LRS. It is often difficult to be prompt due to slow pay or no-show clients, but do the best you can.

After a while, you will gain a reputation with the LRS people for how you do or don't cooperate. If you do cooperate, they often will telephone you out of order when it's late in the afternoon and they've called four or five lawyers who are not available. Remember that you have to get a large volume of these people to get the 10 or 15 percent that makes the whole project profitable.

Don't see the clients when you obviously know nothing about the area of law involved. You'll simply be wasting everyone's time, including your own.

You must be patient. LRS may be a money loser for you for the first six months or year, but hang in there and eventually it will become profitable.

The people whom you don't serve past the interview stage will often become part of your client base and will refer you additional new clients in the future.

LRS OBLIGATIONS:

The LRS interviewing or screening is the key to success. They have to screen out the people who get active when the moon is full and those who simply have nothing else to do except talk all day.

The interviewer *must* emphasize and be sure that the client understands that he or she is not dealing with Legal Aid. They must prepare the client for the interview by collecting the LRS fee to separate the serious callers from the non-serious. The amount of the LRS fee may be small but it is adequate to keep out the non-serious clients. They must be informed that the lawyer is giving the first half-hour as *pro bono* public service to the community and that the client will have to pay for anything beyond that.

The LRS interviewer does not have to be able to distinguish between good and bad cases (it's helpful, but not necessary), but the interviewer must weed out the Legal Aid cases and the non-serious clients, as well as those client who simply don't need a lawyer to begin with. If the LRS sends Legal Aid cases. then soon the lawyer will stop receiving LRS clients.

A well-run LRS also leaves the client feeling good for the following reasons:

1. The LRS found them a lawyer who knows the area of law involved (assuming the lawyer is honest and doesn't take on cases he or she shouldn't).
2. They went to the right lawyer in a matter of hours or days because of the lawyer's giving priority to LRS referrals.
3. They feel good that they "have a lawyer" (they' II feel that way whether or not you go beyond the initial 30-minute interview).
4. They feel good because they have a lawyer who cares enough about people to volunteer the interview time.
5. They feel the American legal system works.

It is important that the LRS refer clients to lawyers on a non biased rotational system. If it seems that all the good big clients end up with the same lawyer(s) and the other lawyer(s) get the small matters, there may be a suspicion of corruption or paybacks and the lawyers who got only the small cases will drop out. The LRS may rationalize by saying the firm that gets the good cases will do a better job for the client or cooperates closely with LRS, seeing clients immediately or sending reports timely. These attributes given to the firm that gets the good cases may be accurate, but the LRS system may ultimately fail. If a non rotational system is going to be used all attorney participants should be made aware of the system which is in fact used.

CONCLUSION:

Each lawyer in the firm should belong to as many Bar sponsored LRSs as possible. Memberships are normally by lawyer and not by firm. Obviously in a three-lawyer firm you will have three times as many referrals and will get to the "good cases" three times as fast. Memberships in LRSs cost little, are profitable and increase both net profits and client base. Additionally. the lawyer is contributing some of his or her time to help serious clients. To be successful, the LRS has the responsibility of screening out the non-serious clients and the Legal Aid cases. Cooperation between the LRS and the lawyer benefits the lawyer, the sponsoring Bar Association and the client. Over the years I have gotten some very big fees and cases through LRS and, accordingly, recommend LRS as a very cost-effective source of fees and clients. Don't worry if the LRS doesn't make money for you the first or second year, or if many of the cases and clients are not meritorious. Eventually, the good cases more than make up for the bad ones-with lots to spare.

G-6
Non-Bar Sponsored Lawyer Referral Services As a Source of Clients and Fees

There are many non-Bar sponsored Lawyer Referral Services (LRS). While I generally am quick to recommend that lawyers join Bar-sponsored programs, I am not as enthusiastic about LRSs sponsored by non-lawyers. I'm not being negative or recommending against joining these groups, but I'm not being positive either.

These are probably many, many non-bar sponsored lawyer referral services that you never thought about. Typical examples of these organizations are unions, consumer and landlord groups, employer and employee associations, universities, etc. There are also language-oriented referral services, such as Spanish-speaking. In this chapter, I'll highlight the negative aspects that I've experienced as a member of a Spanish-language referral service which I joined as an experiment, and additional comments on similar services that I've received from lawyers throughout the United States.

Remember, I don't wish to condemn any particular LRS, but I do recommend that any lawyer who joins one of these organizations should have an escape clause to get out quickly if the lawyer isn't happy with the experience. The lawyer also should investigate the LRS before joining by talking to other members of the panel.

Some negative factors which lawyers have found in non-Bar sponsored LRS include:

1. There is high-pressure advertising which emphasizes the "free-ride" aspect ("No Fee Unless Recovery," etc.). Note that nothing is said about paying court costs and fees if the case is lost.
2. The interviewer who screens the cases is not a lawyer and not trained or supervised by a lawyer. Consequently, many non-meritorious interviewees come in and waste your time.
3. On those plans where there is a fixed per visit fee, such as in legal insurance or prepaid legal plans, there is pressure for you to use non-lawyers to screen and interview or to use extremely low-paid, inexperienced new lawyers or clerks who are waiting for bar results. Those interviewers often do not recognize the more sophisticated or subtle aspects or issues of the case. In some situations, the lawyer is required to use people with little experience to handle the case.
4. The interviewees often come in expecting unrealistic results. This is frequently the result of the LRS interviewer's making unrealistic promises of services.

I repeat, investigate carefully before you join and be sure you have an escape clause.

G-7
"Buying" a Law Practice

I have personally done extensive research on buying or selling a professional practice with emphasis on law practices and accounting practices. This research was done by surveying members of the American Association of Attorney-CPAs (lawyers who are also CPAs). To the best of my knowledge no other research has ever been done. The work was done in 2006. More information on this study can be found at the website www.FoonbergLaw.com.

I am suggesting the possibility of acquiring the law practice of another lawyer. I am not commenting on the ethics or current state of the law in your particular jurisdiction.

This is a newly developing area. Historically, solo practitioners could not "sell" their law practice because the law practice theoretically could not have good will. The older, larger firms could use the names of people long since dead and this type of interest in a practice could be bought and sold, but solo practitioners were supposed to leave their families memories rather than money. I predict that eventually solo practices will be commonly bought and sold with a figure for good will being about one year's gross fees collected.

Many of the mergers and lateral transfers are truly just buying and selling practices.

There are several ways one could "buy" or acquire a law practice, including the following:

1. Merging with another law firm and compensating the owner of the "acquired" practice based on client origination.
2. Making the owners of the "acquired" practice "of counsel" to your firm (or vice versa) with compensation based on client origination and retention.
3. Advertising for "retiring" lawyers to merge with your firm (to protect the value of their will and trust files and work in process for their estates).
4. Forming a "partnership" with the lawyer selling out. Then dissolve the partnership, paying for good will.

In buying the practice (where allowed), be sure that the clients will continue to use the acquired firm because of its legal abilities rather than the personality of the selling lawyer.

It is common to provide a contingency feature to the price to ensure the cooperation of the selling lawyers where possible.

If you set the price as a percentage of fees collected, you may or may not have to make some form of disclosure to the old clients.

A covenant not to compete with the selling lawyer may or may not be ethical in your jurisdiction.

You may or may not be required to notify the "acquired" clients of the sale and of their right to their files.

In terms of a new lawyer buying out an older lawyer, remember that good will may qualify for capital gains tax treatment to the seller and be non-deductible to the buyer. A new lawyer usually needs income, not deductions, and the older lawyer wants to pay less tax, so the government is in effect partially subsidizing the sales price.

Please note that these are a few general principles which must be observed:

1. Fee splitting with non-lawyers is never permissible.
2. Fee splitting and profit sharing with lawyers is permissible if the local rules are complied with.
3. Be sure of your malpractice insurance.

I predict that in the not-too-distant future, solo practitioners and small law firms will be able to buy and sell practices, including good will. Frankly, there is no longer any good reason not to allow these purchases and sales.

Again I refer you to the research I did on buying and selling a professional practice.

G-8
Naming Yourself or a Bank as Executor or Trustee, or Alternate Executor or Trustee, To Get Additional Legal and Non-Legal Income

I have been told, but have not independently verified that several mega size law firms have formed their own captive trust companies to serve as trustees/executors under the wills and trusts they write for clients. In this manner they can have 3 sources of income:

1. Trustees' fees which they set for themselves on a non competitive basis without court approval.
2. Legal fees for services to the trust at rate set by themselves by themselves as the trustees.
3. The value of the ownership interest in the trust company.

I personally have serious questions about conflicts and whether fiduciary beneficiary standards are met. I question how and when and how often or if the beneficiaries are informed of the relationship(s) between the lawyers, the law firms and the trust company and the potential for conflicts. I must stress that I have no independent information in this area but wish to point it out as an example of income production.

A. *SMALL AND MEDIUM-SIZED ESTATES.* It apparently is the custom in some parts of the country for a lawyer, when drafting a will, automatically to name himself/herself the trustee and/or executor in a will without even asking the client. This is particularly true in smaller and medium-sized estates where the surviving spouse doesn't have the experience or sophistication to do what is required of an executor or trustee. In these cases, the lawyer is going to have to do all the work and the executor or trustee simply signs where the lawyer says to sign. By having the lawyer serve as the trustee and/or executor, the estate or trust will be administered and managed correctly and legally and an unsophisticated person won't run the risk of mishandling the assets or being subject to a surcharge for negligent administration.

Having the lawyer serve as executor or trustee protects the assets of the estate and is simply a recognition of the reality that the lawyer is really going to do everything.

B. *LARGER ESTATES.* In larger estates, the lawyer names a bank or corporate trust company to serve as the executor or trustee. As a practical matter, the bank or trustee does all the work and the attorney is compensated as the attorney. A bank will almost always use the lawyer who drafted the will as the attorney for the estate. The law firm might own the trust company.

C. *COMPENSATION WHEN THE ATTORNEY IS NAMED* AS *AN EXECUTOR AND/OR TRUSTEE.* In some jurisdictions, an attorney who is the executor can also be the attorney for the estate and receive full compensation for each role. This is simply paying the person two fees to do two jobs.

In other jurisdictions, the attorney can do both jobs but can be compensated for only one unless the will or trust agreement expressly allows the dual compensation for doing dual work.

In some jurisdictions, the attorney individually can receive the executor's or trustees' fees and the attorney's law firm can receive the attorneys' fees, provided there is no sharing of the executor's fees. In these cases, I have heard of attorneys forming a partnership with another attorney for one probate case, so the partnership can be awarded the legal fee while the attorney gets paid the executor's fee individually.

The fee regulation can be imposed by state statutes, local rules of court or the whims of the local probate court. In those estates where there are state or federal death taxes, these fees are usually deductible and courts are more likely to award double fees for double work.

D. *NAMING YOURSELF AS EXECUTOR/TRUSTEE AND "TRADING" WITH OTHER ATTORNEYS.* In single fee jurisdictions, you can name yourself as executor/trustee and name another attorney as the attorney for the estate or trust. These other attorneys will also refer cases to you to be the attorney where he/she is the executor or trustee.

E. *NAMING YOURSELF AS EXECUTOR/TRUSTEE AND THEN RESIGNING IN FAVOR OF THE ALTERNATE EXECUTOR OR TRUSTEE.* In those communities where attorneys routinely name themselves as executor or trustee, they often name a bank as alternate or successor executor trustee. When the time comes to serve, the attorney confers with the bank to see if it will accept the executorship or trust. If the bank is willing to accept the estate or trust, the attorney declines to serve as executor and/or trustee and allows the bank to serve, and the attorney becomes the attorney for the estate or trust instead of being the executor or trustee. The attorney does not decline to serve if the estate is too small for the bank to accept. The attorney can decide whether he/she wants to accept the estate or trust. (See Chapter J-9 entitled "Holding Onto Minute Books, Wills and Other Client Records to Get Business.")

G-9
Send Thank-You Letters to Judges, Witnesses, Courtroom Personnel and Jurors

Over the years, I have received some good cases and clients through recommendations from judges and from witnesses who testified on behalf of my client, especially the employees of my clients who testified as part of their job duties.

I don't consider myself the reincarnation of Clarence Darrow. I can only attribute the referrals to my having on occasion sent thank-you notes to a judge after a trial. In order to avoid any criticism, I sent a copy to opposing counsel, as well, thereby complying with the rules concerning communications with the bench. (Although the trial was over, there was still time for appeals or motions and, of course, I didn't want to wait until the case and I-had become cold memories in the judge's mind.) Only in one such case did opposing counsel send a thank-you note as well, and his note was an obvious response to mine.

When a witness testifies on my side, I send a thank-you note to the witness. If the witness is an employee of my client, I send a copy of the letter to the employee's supervisor.

You must be very careful in these letters not to indicate that the judge or the witness "leaned" in favor of your client or did anything other than act impartially. Keep the letters short, simple and beyond reproach. Examples of sample letters follow.

I have never sent these letters to court clerks, sheriffs, etc. Nor have I ever sent them to jurors. (I don't think it would be proper until *after* the juror has been discharged from the jury pool.) Other lawyers tell me that they do send these letters to court employees, not so much to get referrals but to ensure a warm reception when they return to the courtroom the next time.

I leave it to your sense of comfort as to whom in the courtroom you send the letters, but I do recommend that you consider these people as possible referrers of business.

SAMPLE THANK-YOU LETTER TO JUDGE

Dear Judge Jones:

On behalf of my client, Last National Bank, and on behalf of myself,
I wish to thank you for the courtesy and judicial skills shown us and all other persons

by you and the courtroom personnel last week during the trial of Smith v. Jones.

(optional) While we were not totally pleased with the result, we nonetheless thank you for your hard work in reaching the result.

(optional) Even though you still have not rendered your decision, we nonetheless thank you for your hard work.

I am sending a copy of this letter to opposing counsel, Mr. Evil, whom I am sure would add his appreciation.

Very truly yours,

NOTE: Please be sure you read and know both your state and local rules before communicating with the court or the jurors. Possibly it would be improper in your jurisdiction to express the common courtesy of a thank you, especially if motions for reconsideration or other matters were still before the court.

SAMPLE THANK-YOU LETTER TO WITNESS

Mr. John Witness
c/o Last National Bank 123 Main Street
Los Angeles, CA

<u>VIA U.S. MAIL</u>

Re: Last National Bank vs. Smith, Case No. 987654

Dear John:

Thank you very much for your excellent presentation of evidence in the case of Last National Bank vs. Smith last week.

I believe that the sincerity of your testimony, coupled with the total preparation and knowledge of the facts which you demonstrated, were of great help in allowing Judge Jones to decide in favor of the bank. Your succinct testimony shortened the trial by several days, thus saving the Bank a lot in legal fees.

We are sending a copy of this letter to your Department Chief, Mr. Bucks, for his information and possible inclusion in your personnel file.

Sincerely,

G-10
Law Professors, Law Schools, and Other Experts As a Source of Clients

Professors can be good sources of referrals for a variety of reasons, such as:

1. They often are unlicensed, not having passed the local bar;
2. Their law school employment contract may prohibit outside trial work;
3. They simply don't have the secretarial facilities or the time to meet with clients and handle cases; and
4. They don't have malpractice insurance.

Some law schools maintain their own formal or informal referral service giving big preference to those firms who in turn support the school financially.

Many lawyers report law professors as a good source of worthwhile clients and cases. I, frankly, have no personal experience in this area but pass it on to you for your consideration. Although I taught for a year as an adjunct professor of law at Southwestern University Law School in Los Angeles, I never really became friends with the other professors at Southwestern; nor did I have a chance to be friendly with my law professors at UCLA Law School as I was married and had to work full time at nights and on weekends while in law school.

When you have a heavy problem in an area which is a law school type subject, use the professor as a research aide. Hire the professor to do research and give his or her opinion of the case. Let the professor know you are doing work (or want to do work) in the area of the professor's expertise. After the professor knows you can (or you want to) handle this type of case, you hopefully will be contacted when the professor can't or doesn't want to handle the case as a lead lawyer and would rather be compensated for assisting you in the case.

I've been told that law professors are continually on the lookout for attorneys to hire and to whom to refer matters. Again, I have no personal experience in this area as a source of work but pass it on to you.

G-11
Getting Work from Big Firms

A recent trend has come to my attention. Big firms are increasingly referring work to non-competitive, smaller firms. In the past, large firms tended to refer work and clients only to larger "known" firms. It seems that in recent years there is more open, increased competition among the big firms for the same clients. This has resulted in "client stealing" (or perceived client stealing) among the big firms when cases are referred.

Historically, large firm "A" would refer work to large firm "B." Large firm "B" had an unwritten (and sometimes written) obligation not to "steal" clients from firm "A." After firm "B" did the referred work, they were obligated not to accept additional or new work from firm "A's" client. During the last few years, this "gentlemen's honor system" has often collapsed due to the increasing competition for clients.

In recent times, some large firms have begun to look for smaller, non competing firms to refer work to:

1.) When there is a conflict of interests; and
2.) When the work is not within the competence (scope) of the larger firm.

Your marketing problem, of course, is to make known to the larger firms that you are available to accept their referrals. You must, of course, emphasize that you are big enough to handle the specific matter, but not big enough to handle all the client's work and are, therefore, no threat.

I would suggest that the initial contact(s) must identify who in the law firm actually decides *to whom* the cases are referred. There are many possibilities including, but not limited to:

1.) The individual lawyer facing the client makes the decision;
2.) 2) The managing partner decides;
3.) A managing committee decides;
4.) The department head decides; and
5.) Others.

G-12
Getting Work from Law School Classmates

There are several instances where your law school classmates or anyone you knew in law school can refer you legal matters or recommend you to their clients. Some examples are:

1. When you practice in a different city.

This is especially true if you practice in a smaller community or in a community where you are likely to be the only class member in that area. There are many places where lawyers frequently have to send legal work in addition to the normal occasional need for a lawyer in another city. Resort areas and some winter places where snowbirds go are examples, as well as the principal state and federal administrative offices. I have received matters from classmates solely because of my location in Beverly Hills, California.

2. When you are recognized as highly competent in certain specialty areas of practice.

I personally have received many referrals from classmates (and others) because of my specific practice areas in the area of law, even though I am not board certified as a specialist.

A. International transactions (particularly Brazil, Argentina, Colombia and The Peoples Republic of China).

B. Criminal Tax Fraud (particularly in the investigation stages which, in my opinion, is the most important level for killing an investigation).

C. Matters which require a financial type of background, because of my background as a CPA.

Every lawyer, including yourself, has one or more areas of law which he/ she likes and does especially well in, whether it is an offbeat or a recognized specialty.

You can and should keep some form of contact with your classmates on an annual or other basis. A special letter to them would be good, reminding them of where you practice and what you or your firm does.

Communicating with your classmates to keep them informed of what you are doing is relatively easy. You can keep your mailing list current by working with your law school alumni affairs office or simply going to the internet.

1. Automatically include them on your mailing lists for announcements.

2. Keep the law school alumni magazine or newspaper informed with occasional letters of what you and your firm are doing. Depending on the interests of the particular editor or the need for news or your status as a donor of money to the school, you may find yourself constantly featured in the publication.

3. Look for former classmates at state and local and other Bar functions. Spend a few minutes visiting with them.

4. Attend the law school reunions.

5. Give money to the law school or alumni association. This will guarantee your inclusion in at least one issue of the magazine.

G-13
Getting and Increasing Referrals
(Foonberg's Rule: Network the Networkers)

A networker, in my terminology is a person or institution that has the ability to send you one of their clients or patients or members. A single networker may have hundreds or even thousands of contacts whom may need legal services.

You do not spend time and resources on another attorney or law firm because you want them for a client. You want their clients to become your referral clients. The other attorney or law firm is the networker you are seeking as a source of referrals.

In most law practices, as much as $1/3^{rd}$ of your new files will come from referrals from others who have never been your client. In some practices all of the new matters are from referrals.

In order to get more referrals of work, you must analyze where your clients already come from and what legal services you can or cannot competently handle economically to both you and the client.

Review the following list to see if you recognize where your referred clients already come from and for ideas of new referral sources worth developing. Some of the most common sources of referrals are:

1. Friends and Relatives.

They can be a great source of clients. You must be friendly and polite and respectful when they want to send you something, even if you know it will probably be a waste of time. Tell the person referred that you give special attention and immediate service to anyone referred by the friend or relative (if true). This will get back to the referrer who will then feel very important and refer more matters.

2. Other lawyers.

Over the years, other lawyers will probably be the best source of referrals. They will understand the client's legal problems to be sure you can handle it and they will try to screen out the bad clients and cases. You must alert your receptionist to get you on the phone when they call. If they have a client sitting across the desk and can't get hold of you, they may call lawyer no. 2 on their list. Meet all the lawyers you can at Bar Association meetings and send them a letter or email or take them to lunch or get them a drink at the convention or association meeting to find out what you can send them and what they can send you. Never charge another lawyer for helping that lawyer with information.

3. CPAs.

There is no limit on the kind of matters a CPA can send you. They have continuing contact with clients who have a huge variety of legal problems ranging from a complex corporate problem to wills to a child facing a drugs charge.

4. Health Care Professionals.

Health care professionals will be especially interested in sending you matters where they won't get paid unless you can pay them out of the client's recovery. Many will dislike or even hate lawyers for a variety of reasons, real or imagined. Their dislike might soften when they learn that you can get them paid for otherwise uncollectible fees.

5. Personal Financial Planners.

As America ages and the Baby Boomers achieve 60, 70, and 80 years of age there is a big need for financial planning. You may need to take courses to be licensed or skilled in this new area.

This is a new and expanding source of referrals, especially for those planning retirement or in retirement.

6. Clergy.

People with serious problems often turn to the clergy for help. Clergy may be able to send you many clients if the needs of the client can meet with your abilities.

7. Other Sources.

The type of referral sources is limited only by your imagination. The starting point is to analyze what you already have and decide if you want more of the same or something different.

Some Tips and Techniques:

1. When referring a client to another source, give the client the names of 3 lawyers (or CPA's or whatever). Tell the client to contact each one and make his or her own decision as to which he or she would like to work with. In most, if not almost all cases, the client will only meet with one. You want to protect yourself, should the client not work well with the one chosen by the client. Sometimes the chemistry is just not there. If the client did not meet with all 3, then it is the client's fault for not having chosen after meeting with all 3 of the recommended professionals.

2. Send each of the 3 a fax and an email to accompany a telephone call as follows:

To: Arthur Smith, Esq.
Smith and Smith

Re: Ms. Jones

Dear Arthur, We have recommended Ms. Jones who has a sophisticated tax problem which is beyond our ability to handle as we primarily handle business litigation (or PI, or whatever). Please take her call if she calls. Ms Jones appears to have the ability to pay for the needed services (optional). Let us know if there is anything you my need from us.

Sincerely,

Mary Goodguy

The reason for sending three such telephone calls, Emails and faxes are to let 3 law firms know you are trying to refer them work. Hopefully there will be three law firms trying to refer you work in your identified area.

3. Referral fees. This is a matter of local rules and local custom. Be sure you know what is and what is not permissible.

4. Gifts. If you are going to give a gift, I recommend "continuing gifts." Find out the referrer's hobbies or interests. Buy 2 magazine subscriptions to magazines in that interest area, and send one to the home and one to the office. The referrer will then be able to think of you 24 times a year. You can do this with other items such as fruits or candy of the month.

5. Thank you notes. Ask the client if you have permission to send a thank you note and phone call. If the answer is "yes" immediately thank the referrer both by phone and in writing.

6. You may wish to do parties, dinners, seminars, or other forms of saying "Thank you" to a large number of people. Invite all the referrers to the party.

7. Keep written records of "Referrals In" and "Referrals Out". You want to refer matters to firms which have the same level of confidence in you as you do in them. If you are not receiving referrals from those to whom you send matters, call and find out "Why Not"?

8. Do some "Due Diligence" on the referred to firm. In some jurisdictions, a lawyer can be liable for negligent referrals.

No lawyer can be all things to all people. Lawyers must be able to seek and get help for their clients from other lawyers who may have greater expertise in a matter.

G-14
Sample Thank-You Letter For a Referral

Here is a sample thank you letter that can be used with clients (or others) who refer potential new clients to you:

To: John Client
123 Main Street
Any town , USA

VIA U.S. MAIL

Re: Referral of Arthur Smith

Dear John,

Thank you very much for recommending Arthur Smith to us. We are most appreciative of your expression of confidence in us. Client recommendation is a very important source of new clients to us. We are grateful for your recommendation and are doing our best to give them excellent care.

I am sure that you appreciate that the ethics of the legal profession forbid us from letting you know anything about the legal matter involved or even whether or not Mr. Smith used our firm. However, whether or not Mr. Smith uses our firm, we are truly appreciative of your thinking of us. Mr. Smith has given us permission to send this thank you note.

Again, thank you for thinking of us. We shall do our best to justify your recommendation.
Sincerely,

Alternatively, you can use a preprinted card, such as the one shown below:

Thank You

FOR REFERRING: _____

TO ME FOR PROFESSIONAL SERVICES.
YOUR EXPRESSION OF CONFIDENCE IS SINCERELY APPRECIATED.

_____
MARY L. JONES
9461 CHARLEVILLE BLVD., #416
BEVERLY HILLS, CA. 90212
_____

(310) 652-5010
Email@Lawyer.com
WWW.LAWYER.COM

Be sure to ask the client if it is okay to send the card. It might otherwise be a violation of the attorney client relationship to disclose that the client even came to see you.

G-15
Buying or Selling Cases for Referral Fees

After 40 years of practice I personally am totally in favor of referral fees provided 3 requirements are met:

1. The client is referred to a lawyer or firm competent to handle the mater.
2. The fee to the client is not increased to cover the referral fee paid.
3. The client knows at the inception there is or may be a fee division and gives informed consent.

To begin with, you never want to tell a client that you're referring the client "out" to another attorney. This connotes abandonment of the case and client and lack of interest. It's better to say you are "bringing a specialist in" to assist. No one objects to paying for a needed specialist.

The "buying and selling" of cases for referral fees from any place other than Bar Association Lawyer Referral Services is an area with many pros and cons for both the short term and the long term. I do not wish to debate whether referral fees lead to a higher or lower level of case attention for the client.

The ethics and legalities of referral fees are usually covered by the rules dealing with fee splitting or division of fees, and you are most strongly advised to read carefully your local rules before doing anything in this area.

There are some general rules:

1. Fee splitting with non-lawyers is never permissible. This cannot be gotten around by the subterfuge(s) of percentage rents, management fees, consultation fees, etc. In some jurisdictions, a lawyer who is not licensed to practice in that particular jurisdiction is considered a non-lawyer, even though the lawyer *is* a lawyer in the jurisdiction from which the case originated.

2. The client must be informed in writing of the fee splitting (division).

3. The client cannot be made directly or indirectly to pay a higher fee because of the fee splitting.

There are several situations in which fee splitting is or is not permissible. The principal circumstances under which fee splitting *is* allowed are:

1. There is sharing of both work *and* responsibility in the case. There must usually be some relationship between the amount of the fee sharing and the amount of the work and the responsibility. (Note that there would then be two legal malpractice insurance carriers on the hook.)

2. There must be sharing of the work *or* the responsibility on the case. It would seem to me that if I say, "Oh, we'll share responsibility, but you do all the work," that this would satisfy the rules. (Note that there are still two malpractice insurance carriers on the hook.)

3. There must be a referral of a case and the fee is clearly a forwarding fee without any sharing of work or responsibility. This is becoming the new wave of referrals simply because there is only one malpractice insurance carrier on the hook.

Short term effect of referrals. In the short run, referring clients out (bringing experts and specialists in) is a quick-fix for cash for the referring attorney. The hourly rate is fantastic because the lawyer may have only an hour of interview time and a few minutes of finding the right specialist.

Long-term effect. Referrals out (bringing specialists in) can, and often do, hurt a law firm's long-term growth. Sometimes the client feels that he/ she should stay with the referred lawyer because the client is familiar with that lawyer who can better serve the client's legal needs.

For alternatives to referrals, see the chapter on "How to Keep a Client When You Can't Do the Work."

(Note that when firms give client origination fees to a lawyer in a firm for sending work to another lawyer in the firm, there does not seem to be a problem. When a lawyer gets a referral fee from a lawyer outside the firm, there is a concern that the referring lawyer is simply a commission sales person.

Again, I have no problem with referral fees from lawyers outside the firm if the conditions are met.)

G-16
Client Secretaries and Assistants
as A Source of Business

You are a fool if you ignore your client's secretary or assistant (particularly the secretaries and assistants to your good clients). She may have much more effect over the client's decision as to what lawyer to use than you'll ever have. Many times in my career, the client's secretary, not the client, decided to call ME rather than another lawyer when the client said, "Call the lawyer."

There are several things you can do to be on good grounds with your client's secretary.

1. Learn her name and use it.
2. If she screens calls, greet her with, "How are you?"
3. Make small talk with her when you are waiting to talk to your client.
   Be genuinely interested in anything you can find out about her.
4. Send her a birthday card if you can find out the date.
5. Send her flowers on National Secretaries Day. (Don't ignore your own secretary!)
6. Send her a big box of candy for Christmas. Send it to the office and let her decide whether or not to pass it around the office.
7. Send her a Christmas or season's greeting card.
8. If the secretary or assistant is male, you may wish to modify the above.

G-17
How To Increase Your Income From Referrals

I do a one hour presentation at Bar Association conferences on "How to Increase Your Income from Referrals." The presentation may be available from www.FoonbergLaw.com.

1. Understand that as much as 1/3 of your fees (a national average) may come from referred matters.
2. Understand and ask why people do or don't refer legal work to you or others.
3. Chose your referrals out based on lawyer competency to handle the matter and on whether they refer matters to you.
4. When you do refer a client, refer the client to 3 law firms, notifying each of the referrals so that you may have 3 law firms referring you work.
5. Chose appropriate ways of saying "thank you" to insure more future referrals.

Chapter H
Ethics: Using Ethics to Create
New Opportunities to Get Clients

H-1
Communicating Ethics As a Factor In Getting Clients

Clients want attorneys who are ethical. A client or potential client should be assured or reassured from time to time that you and your firm are ethical.

There are several ways to communicate your ethical concerns and standards.

1. During the initial interview, simply state: "We are an ethical law firm. We have a reputation for a high level of ethical practice and are committed to high ethical standards." You can reassert this from time to time.
2. In your initial fee letter, add some comments about the ethics involved in the situation. This is easy to do where you have multiple parties with potential conflicts of interests. You can use part of the "Standard Instruction Letter" which follows this chapter.
3. Include a few comments about ethics in your newsletter. You can simply restate your high standards and commitments or you can excerpt and modify parts of the "Standard Ethics Letter" which follows this chapter.
4. Reproduce or modify the "Standard Ethics Letter" which follows this chapter and:
   a. Distribute it to all personnel in the firm so they can reassure clients or potential clients where appropriate;
   b. Distribute it to all clients or the entire mailing list (I don't recommend this);
   c. Leave a copy in the reception room; or
   d. In your client newsletter, inform clients that the "Standard Ethics Letter" is available to them upon request. (I do recommend this. Even if they don't request it, they know you have it.)
   e. Put it on your website

H-2
Office Confidentiality as a Marketing Tool

This chapter will give you specific marketing techniques which can both increase your practice and improve your confidentiality procedures.

Violating attorney-client confidences is not only unethical, it's harmful to practice growth and client relations.

Clients want an ethical lawyer. The American Bar Association's study, the Legal Needs of the American Public, proves conclusively that ethics are high on the list of factors which result in being recommended to other clients. If a client or potential client believes that you violate attorney-client confidences they'll leave you or won't recommend others to you.

Lawyers don't normally intentionally violate the confidentiality of the attorney-client relationship. The result of violating confidences or allowing staff personnel to violate confidences could be disbarment, loss of the client whose confidences are violated and loss of referrals from clients and others who perceive you to be unethical.

The practice of law includes a T & C Factor. T & C stands for Trust and Confidence. Clients bring you their darkest secrets. They tell you things they can't confide to their spouse. They admit embarrassing and even heinous acts. They admit to doing what they shouldn't have done. They trust you not to reveal their confidences.

Clients do not normally want the public to know that they are about to file bankruptcy or that they intend to get a divorce or that they have been charged with a crime. Often a breach of the confidential relationship is not only prejudicial to their position in the community but is also prejudicial to their legal case.

Some law offices are unknowingly riddled with breaches in protecting the confidential relationship. This chapter is designed to help you find and plug and prevent the leaks in your own office.

Rather than repeat the common mistakes lawyers make, a check list type of self administered test may help reveal some of your deficiencies. As a lawyer you should answer correctly all of the 58 questions. You do not need a key to score this test. You'll instinctively know whether you've answered correctly.

The results of this test can be used to both plug existing leaks and to prevent future leaks of information. After you have improved your office management procedures, you can use the improved procedures as a tool to help market the practice. Every person in the firm should affirmatively tell clients and potential clients of the strict procedures the firm uses to protect the confidences of a client. This will enhance the firm's reputation for ethics and improve the firm image and reputation in the community. As firm personnel do (or refrain from doing) these procedures in the presence of a client or potential client, you should expressly communicate to the client what you are doing to protect their confidence. For example, when you bring a client into your office and close the door behind you, you could say something like: "Let me close the door. Now we'll have some privacy and no one can accidentally overhear what you say or even know that you're here."

1. Do you have a written statement of the attorney client privilege and the protection of client confidences in your office manual or which you give to all attorneys and all non-attorneys in the firm at time of hiring?   _____

2. Do you have a written acknowledgement of receipt of the previous statement in which the attorneys and staff acknowledge that violation of client confidence is cause for discharge?   _____

3. Does your receptionist repeat who's calling and why they are calling in the oral or visual presence of clients or strangers who are within hearing range?   _____

4. Does your secretary repeat who's calling and why they are calling in the presence of clients or others within hearing range?   _____

5. Does your receptionist open mail, do "light typing," word processing, or filing in an area where clients can see other clients' names?   _____

6. Does your receptionist affirmatively cover up client papers in the presence of clients so that clients know that you protect attorney-client confidences?   _____

7. When your client goes from reception area to your office do they pass secretarial, paralegal, or word processing work stations where they can see file folders or screens or items with client names?   _____

8. When the client goes from the reception area to your office passing secretaries, paralegals, word processors, screens, etc., do the staff people cover up client papers in the presence of the client, so that clients know you protect confidences?   _____

9. When someone in your firm is assembling a complex pleading or contract and has papers, exhibits, and information spread all over the conference table or library, do they cover up the papers before going to lunch or out on a break, or home for the evening?   _____

10. When you bring your client into your office or conference room do you close the door to give the client the feeling of privacy and protection of the confidential nature of the attorney-client relationship?   _____

11. Do you allow clients to go unescorted from the reception area to your office or conference room allowing them to look at computer screens, file cabinets and files on desks with client names and matters?

           _____

12. Do you escort the client to and from the reception area to be sure that the client doesn't wander into an area where there are confidential matters which can be seen or heard?

           _____

13. Is (are) your conference room(s) near the front of the office so visitors can be met without their passing through firm work areas?

           _____

14. Do you use only numbers or codes instead of client names on file covers and documents to protect confidentiality?

           _____

15. Do your secretaries, word processors, paralegals, etc., cover their documents or close file folders when they go to lunch or on break so that a client passing by won't see any client names?

           _____

16. When you see clients in your personal office do you remove or cover up all documents with clients' names or at least close all files which the client could see?

           _____

17. Do you restrict access to the files and file area to only those who have a need to know the contents of the files?

           _____

18. Have you considered meeting clients in your conference room instead of your private office, explaining to them that you meet clients in the conference room instead of your office because you have a lot of client files and papers in your office and you want to preserve attorney-client confidences for all clients including the client you are seeing?

           _____

19. Does your support staff (paralegals, secretaries, clerks, etc.) have a place where they can interview or work with vendors in privacy out of the presence of other office staff?

           _____

20. Do you or others in your office use speaker phones in offices with open doors where clients passing by or in another office can hear the receptionist or your secretary telling you who's calling and why they're calling or can hear your conversation with a client?

           _____

21. Are your word processing or billing equipment screens facing the client areas where the clients passing by can see what's on the screen?

           _____

22. When you get an emergency client call, when you are in conference with another client, do you tell the caller, "I'm in a conference with another client and I can't discuss a client's confidential matters in the presence of another client. I'll call you back in 30 minutes." Or alternatively, do you say, "I'm in conference with another client, please hold on while I go to another room so I can discuss your case." Alternatively, do you leave the room to take the call? _____

23. Do you really know what happens to the papers you put in the waste basket? Have you ever stayed or had someone stay and observe the process of waste paper removal to see the access points where a stranger or adverse party or private investigator or competitor or police officer could go through the trash looking for information which could prejudice your client's case? _____

24. Do you have a paper shredder for destruction of files with very sensitive client information? _____

25. Do you have telephone procedures for handling telephone information requests? For example, when a voice over the phone asks for a client's address or phone number, do you tell the caller, "I'm sorry, but we don't give out any client information over the phone, please send us a letter asking for the information, and *if* the person is a client, we'll forward your letter onto them and they can respond." Or if the caller says it's an emergency, do you inform the caller that you can't reveal whether or not the person is a client, but *if* the person is, you'll try to pass the message on for the person to call the caller? _____

26. When a client tells you that they believe their telephones may be "bugged" in some manner by a spouse or competitor or government authority, do you classify them as paranoids undeserving of your legal talent or do you take reasonable steps to avoid telephone conversations which, if the phones really are bugged, could be damaging to the client? _____

27. Is your receptionist instructed not to allow unidentified maintenance and repair people into the office unless escorted by someone from the firm? _____

28. When someone shows up at your office with a tool kit or a tool belt claiming they are there to "fix the phone" or some piece of equipment, do you ask for identification? _____

29. Do you assign someone to watch repair and maintenance people while they are working to be sure they do not look at files?

_____

30. When you receive a call from a person who claims that they are a lawyer and that your client wants their file sent to the lawyer do you insist, when feasible, on a letter signed by the client authorizing the release of the file and the information in it to a specific person, and another from the recipient acknowledging they will accept the file from you?

_____

31. Does your administrator have a private area to interview vendors or job applicants where they cannot overhear office discussion or see client files?

_____

32. When attorneys and staff discuss client matters do they do so behind closed doors where other clients or office personnel not involved in the case cannot overhear the conversation?

_____

33. When you send a bill which contains great detail as to the work done, do you mark it "personal and confidential" or similar notation, or address it to an individual to prevent unauthorized access to its confidential information by the wrong person accidentally opening it at the client's home or business?

_____

34. Are your attorneys and staff prohibited, in writing in the staff manuals or otherwise, from discussing client matters in public places such as restrooms, elevators, hallways and restaurants?

_____

35. Do you and your attorneys and staff violate attorney-client confidences by telling third parties who your clients are or were, and what legal matters you were or are handling for them, without first getting client permission?

_____

36. Would you tell Client "A" how you helped or got a good result for Client "B" without masking the identity of Client "B"?

_____

37. Do you keep telephone messages in a location where others can see who called and why they called?

_____

38. Do you have signs stating "Respect Client Confidences" in your elevators, rest rooms and common areas?

_____

39. Do you have a separate exit for people who want to enter or leave your office without meeting people in the reception room who might recognize them?

_____

40. Do you tell your clients that you have a separate exit for the foregoing reason and that you will be happy to escort them in and out of this exit?

41. Have you ever suggested meeting a client out of your office so that other clients won't accidentally see them or recognize them?

42. Do you have security procedures to prevent unauthorized people from accessing your computer information?

43. Do you have a security system to prevent unauthorized access to your computer files?

44. Does your telephone system have a privacy system to prevent others from listening in to the conversation?

45. Do you have an agreement in writing with your landlord that they will take reasonable steps to instruct their employees and the contract cleaning personnel that all information in your office including the Information In waste baskets is to be considered confidential and is not to be given to third parties who ask for it?

46. Do you discuss client names and cases at home with your spouse at the breakfast or dinner table in front of your children so they can tell their friends who can tell their parents so it can get back to the client?

47. Do you discuss client legal problems on the telephone at home in front of your spouse and children?

48. Have you and each person in the office instructed their children and other household members not to repeat any office information they accidentally (or intentionally) overhear or see?

49. When the case is over and you put the client's file into a public warehouse, do you get an agreement with the warehouse that they acknowledge that the contents of the files are confidential and that they won't allow access to the files to anyone unless that person is designated by you in writing?

50. When you get mail to sign, is the letter accompanied by the mailing envelope or mailing label as a double check against sending your client's mail to another client?

51. Does your secretary or mail room have a procedure to double check that copies of mail and email are matched to envelopes or mailing labels to prevent sending copies to the wrong people?

52. Does your mail room or bookkeeping section match invoices against envelopes or mailing labels to prevent sending the bills to the wrong clients, thus revealing both the identity of the client but also the nature of the work being done? _____

53. Did this test bring some of your deficiencies to light? _____

54. Do you intend, as the result of this test to put a special section in your personnel manual? _____

55. Would you consider photocopying this list and using it as the basis for an addition to your office manual? _____

56. Would you consider modifying the questions in this test to become part of your personnel testing and screening? _____

57. Do you have a DVD or tape on the subject of "confidentiality" that can be shown to all new hires as part of their indoctrination program? _____

58. Do you have a paragraph for emails and faxes indicating that the information contained is confidential with procedures to prevent accidental dissemination of information? _____

Almost all of the foregoing questions are rhetorical in that the correct answers to the questions are suggested in the questions themselves. Score three points for every correct answer giving you a possible 174 points. A score of 100 would be barely passing.

Remember, protecting client confidences is an easily observable representation of your ethical concerns. Clients and others are likely to recommend you to others and use you for repeat business if they perceive that you go to great lengths to preserve their confidences. Failure to protect confidences is easily observable and will cost you clients and repeat business.

H-3
Using Ethics As a Tool In Prompting
a Potential Client To Change Lawyers

I have very successfully "stolen" a client or potential client from other lawyers using ethics as a tool. I have no shame over what I've done and highly recommend the technique.

A client or potential client may say something along the following lines to me:

"We're using or thinking of using the firm of Dewey, Cheatem and Howe. One of the partners there told me that they represent Mr. A., Mr. B. and the Last National Bank and that they just got $1 million for Mrs. Smith in a case similar to mine."

At this point, I may say, "Are you sure you heard all this? In our firm, we consider it unethical to blab our clients' names in public or to others. We are concerned that our clients don't want the whole world to know they have legal problems. I suppose it's possible that the clients gave the lawyers permission to seek publicity using their names, but we don't do that. If you ask us for some of our representative clients, we would recommend you to the Martindale Hubbell Law Directory, which is an ethically approved client reference source. We are also concerned that when people start blabbing about who their clients are and what kinds of cases they have, that they'll also blab information about the case which could be harmful if the other side found out about it. Many of our clients will tell people we are their lawyer and refer people to us, but we don't publicly blab about our clients or their legal matters. We consider that unethical."

The client or potential client rarely responds at that point, but subsequently I'll sometimes receive a telephone call wherein the potential client decides not to use the firm who did the blabbing.

I also make comments such as this when I am with a client or potential client in an elevator, restaurant, or even in a washroom in an office building when I hear attorneys discussing their clients' cases with others. I'll ask the potential client if he or she would like the client's own case discussed in restrooms or other public places where the information could leak back to the other side.

I highly recommend using this technique.

H-4
How to Avoid Losing Clients And Fees
When You Have Conflicts of Interest

It's easier and cheaper to stay out of trouble than to get out of trouble.

This is a book on how to get clients and cases ethically. It would be a counter-productive effort to get the clients and cases into your office and then have to give up or lose the client and have to disgorge the fee because you mishandled the situation. This chapter and the suggested form letters that accompany it can help you ethically keep both the client and the fee.

Newer lawyers have difficulty recognizing the conflicts problem and even experienced lawyers sometimes don't know "how to handle it" even if they recognize it.

Most of this chapter originated with my book, *How to Start and Build* a *Law Practice*. I am repeating much of it here because it is worth the extra few minutes required for any lawyer to review the basics of recognizing the problem, and worth any lawyer's time to consider my solutions to the problem.

Recognizing the existence of a conflict. A lawyer is a fiduciary and a client is a beneficiary. The duty of loyalty owed to the client by the lawyer is absolute and total. Anything which does or might impair that duty of total loyalty is a conflict and must be dealt with.

All lawyers, especially new lawyers, are prone to problems involving conflicts of interest for the following reasons:

1. They don't recognize the problem when they see it.
2. They don't know how to handle this problem when they recognize it.
3. They are afraid to broach this subject for fear of frightening the client away and losing a fee.
4. They don't realize they can still do the work and gain a fee if the conflict problem is handled properly.

I. *The importance of recognizing and solving conflicts of interest at the beginning:*
   A. *To You* as *the Lawyer:* If you don't recognize and solve the problem:

   1. You may have to withdraw from the case.
   2. You may not be able to collect any fees due you.
   3. You may have to refund any fees previously paid you.
   4. Depending on the extent of the problem, you may be disciplined-or disbarred for your stupidity.

   B. *To the Client:* The client will have to obtain a new lawyer and waste a lot of time and energy locating and educating the new lawyer. This delay might even prejudice the case.

II. *How to Recognize the Conflict Problem:*

    A. *Simple Conflicts.* These are conflicts between you and the client. To the extent that lawyers are compensated by clients and clients compensate them, there is always a theoretical conflict between the client and the lawyer. This theoretical conflict comes close to being actual when the lawyer is compensated by "a piece of the action" or other economic interests beyond an earned fee. This problem, however, is normally treated by Bar associations under the category of unreasonable or excessive fees rather than conflict of interest.

These simple conflicts also can arise when you have two clients unrelated to each other, such as:

1. Client A wants you to collect $5,000 from X and Client B wants to collect $8,000 from the same X. X only has, or is ever likely to have, $2,000. Who would get it? Client A or Client B or both A and B in some ratio?
2. Client A wants you to argue as a lawyer for a debtor that involuntary repossessions are unconstitutional; Client B wants you to argue to in the same or a different court in a different matter that involuntary repossessions are constitutional. Do you take both cases on the theory that the court makes the law and not the lawyer?

    B. *Complex Conflicts:* These are the more common situations and arise out of the fact that multiple parties want to use only one lawyer, typically to save fees. The most common situations are:

1. *Partnerships:* Each partner and the partnership are independent entities and there are conflicts and potential conflicts in the situation.
2. *Corporations:* Each incorporator, each director, each officer, each employee and the corporation are independent and/or could have conflicting interests, depending on the capacity in which they will be acting
3. *Divorce:* Husband and wife have conflicting interests. In theory, the court represents the children. In some jurisdictions, another lawyer is appointed to represent the children.
4. *Multiple defendants* or potential defendants in criminal cases. The defendants may later wish to turn on one another or try to get immunity or other favorable treatment in exchange for testimony.
5. *Auto Accident* Cases:
   (a.) Insufficient insurance or assets. There may not be sufficient insurance or assets to cover all the injured parties. For example, suppose that the defendant has a $25,000-$50,000 policy and there are four seriously injured parties in your client's car. Suppose that the claims of each are reasonably worth $30,000 or more. Suppose further that the defendant is an indigent who can successfully go bankrupt on a personal injury judgment debt. Suppose further that the insurance company is willing to pay the entire $50,000. If you take all

four cases, how do you divide up the insurance money? Can you take all four cases? Which client(s) do you keep or reject? If you advise one or more people to get independent counsel (probably the lesser-value cases), should you explain why? Would an explanation be a conflict with the clients you keep?

(b.) Passenger or driver. Can you represent both the driver and the passengers? Is there a possibility of suing the driver/owner for negligent operation or maintenance of the vehicle, or under a guest statue?

(c.) Hidden Conflicts. A lawyer is a fiduciary and a client is a beneficiary. The lawyer has a duty of total loyalty to a client. Anything which could affect 100% loyalty is a conflict whether it is a financial or personal relationship with a client or a financial or personal relationship with a non-client or former client.

6. *Other Conflict of Interest Situations:* Obviously, there is an infinite number of possible conflict of interest situations. Anytime you have, or may have, more than one client in a matter you should ask yourself, "Do I have a conflict of interest situation here?" If you are not sure, call another lawyer and get that person's opinion or call the local Bar Association and get the name of a member of the ethics committee. Some ethics committees will answer only requests of the Bar Association itself, as opposed to individual members of the Bar Association. Some ethics committee members will respond only to written questions for fear of misunderstanding of the facts.

You should get another lawyer's opinion for the protection of both yourself and the client. The opinion of another experienced lawyer can help you decide whether you have a conflict. The fact that you were sufficiently concerned over the possibility of a conflict that you took steps to get another opinion(s) would probably be of help to you in the event of a subsequent problem.

III. *How to handle the problem.* Be honest, be forthright and put everything in writing!

The Code of Professional Responsibility does *not* totally prohibit your representing clients when there is, or might be, a conflict of interest. The lawyer may represent more than one party provided the client understands the conflict and waives it. If you can't solve the conflict problem, you're better off losing the client before you do the work than after you do the work and end up not getting paid.

All ethics questions are fact specific and are subject to local ethics rules. There is no substitute for periodically reading and re-reading the local rules.

Form Letters. Following this chapter is a chapter containing form letters you may wish to use or adopt to solve conflict problems.

IV. *Periodically read and re-read the local rules and cases.*

The increased size of law firms has caused many changes in the rules. As firms grow in size there will be more changes.

H-5
Form Letters for Fee Agreements
to Cover Conflict of Interest Problems

The accompanying set of form letters, or applicable modifications, depending on local rules, can be used when you have a conflict of interest situation and don't want to give up the client or fee. Please note that the letters emphasize "repeating in writing" what you previously said in the office about the fact that you are an ethical, forthright lawyer who raised the problem as soon as it became apparent.

Note that the general format is to set forth the problem of the conflict and to point out the client's right to have independent counsel, and then to show the client how to continue to use you if he or she wishes.

A waiver of conflicts or any waiver by a client must be a knowing waiver. The lawyer must explain what is being waived.

Not all states require waivers of rights by clients to be in writing, but it is the best practice to do so.

In addition to obtaining a waiver from the client it may also be advisable to obtain "a consent to representation" wherein the signer consults to the representation by you of the other person.

(SAMPLE LETTER, USE YOUR LETTERHEAD)

Name of Client Address,
Etc.

Re: Matter involved

Dear _____:

I am writing to you to repeat in writing what I told you earlier in the office. I cannot commence work on your case until you (each of you) have returned the enclosed copy of this letter indicating your preference.

As I explained to you in the office, a lawyer cannot be on both sides of a fence, nor can a lawyer ethically represent people who may have conflicting interests unless the parties understand they may have conflicting interests and understand they can each use a different lawyer if they wish to. You can continue to use our office to do all the work by waiving the conflicts.

Partnerships, Corporations, Business Ventures:

Each of you is a legal entity, and in the eyes of the law the partnership is a legal entity. Theoretically, each of the three of you should have a different lawyer to protect your respective interests.

I can draft your partnership agreement to conform to what you have agreed to and can raise additional problems which have to be solved by you, but I cannot take sides.

(Alternative 1):

In the event of a dispute among you, I shall have the right to withdraw from the case and not take either side.

The file shall be the joint file of all of you and will remain in the custody of the firm. It may be copied by any of you at your own expense during ordinary business hours with a prior appointment.

(Alternative 2):

In the event of a dispute between "A" and you, you must understand that I would have to represent "A" since "A" is actually my client.

(Alternative 3):

In the event of a dispute between you, you have agreed that my client will be the partnership and you understand that I would not represent either of you personally.

(Alternative 4):

In the event of a dispute between you, I will choose a client between you.

I would not intentionally favor one of you over the other, but you may feel more comfortable with a lawyer who is actively representing your individual personal interest.

Divorces:

(**Note:** Some states allow a lawyer to represent both the husband and wife under special circumstances, but this should be avoided to prevent future problems.)

You asked me to represent both of you in order to save legal fees and costs.

You told me how you wanted the assets and liabilities handled and the amounts you have agreed on for alimony and child support. I explained to you that if you wished to fight in court, a judge might give either of you more or less assets or more or less alimony. I explained that the issue of child support cannot be bargained solely between you and that the court keeps jurisdiction to decide child support and custody regardless of what you have agreed to. I have also cautioned you on the necessity of making full disclosure of all assets, liabilities, income, expenses, etc., and that the intentional or negligent omission of important facts might cause a court to overturn the whole agreement in future years.

I also explained to you that in later years, it may be relevant who was the plaintiff and who was the defendant in the divorce action and that it was possible for each of you to sue the other for divorce.

You indicated that notwithstanding your rights you wished to proceed with the divorce as a default proceeding and to honor the provisions you have agreed upon.

Multiple Defendants:

A. *In a Criminal Proceeding:* You have indicated that you wish to be represented together and I indicated to you that you are each entitled to individual separate counsel, and that if you can't pay for separate counsel, a public defender may be available. I also informed you that you may wish to "finger point" at each other, or that one of you may be able to receive immunity from prosecution or other favorable treatment for testifying against the other.

B. *Auto Accident Cases:* I explained to you that there may not be enough insurance or assets for all of you to recover what you are entitled to, and you indicated that if this should happen you would divide the total proceeds between yourselves as you will agree, and that if you can't agree that the funds will be held in my trust account while you arbitrate between yourselves the share that each of you is entitled to. I would not represent either of you in any such arbitration, which would be at additional expense to each of you.

Waivers:

Most conflicts can be waived by the client provided the waiver is a knowing waiver. (The client must understand what is being waived.)

Consents to Representation:

In addition to a waiver of conflicts, it may be necessary to get consents to representation whereby each client consents to your representation of the other(s).

Waivers and consents may or may not be required to be in writing depending on local rules.

Multiple Plaintiffs:

You have agreed that Ms. Plaintiff One will give us instructions and that we may follow her instructions when discussions must be made including settlement discussions. You understand that you have been advised that you may seek independent legal advice from a lawyer of your own choosing before agreeing to the terms of your representation.

H-6
Materials for Standard Ethics Letter to Clients and Potential Clients (To Be Excerpted from as Appropriate)

1. Our confidential relationship. Everything a lawyer (or any member of the law firm) learns about a client during the representation of the client is confidential. Our lawyers are not allowed to discuss your case or legal matters with anyone outside the firm. Our lawyers and employees are strictly prohibited from breaking the sanctity of the attorney-client relationship.

What you tell your lawyer is similar to what you tell your priest or doctor. We can't be effective in helping you unless we know all of the facts, including all of the unpleasant and embarrassing facts. To encourage full disclosure by you, we are prohibited by ethics and by law from discussing anything about your case with anyone. The mere fact that you need a lawyer can sometimes be a matter you don't wish to disclose. For this reason, we do not allow our people even to disclose the names of our clients unless we have their permission.

Lawyers are forbidden to discuss these confidences with their spouses or family members, or to discuss a client or case in a public place where they might be overheard.

If a lawyer brags to you about the names and legal matters of a client, you should be concerned about the ethics of this lawyer and the firm, and whether you can expect your name and the details of your legal matter to be broadcast to people who might use the information against you.

In truth and in fact, lawyers sometimes do discuss their cases with other lawyers or with their spouses, particularly the unusual and bizarre cases. Normally the discussion would be in such a way that the identity of the client could not be determined. Any lawyer who discusses a client or client's case out of the office runs the risk of being unethical and being disciplined by the State Bar.

2. Contacting adverse party represented by counsel. Contacting an adverse person represented by an attorney is unethical. A lawyer cannot ethically contact someone on the other side of the case, if that person is represented by an attorney.

Therefore, if you have a dispute with Mr. A, Mr. A's lawyer cannot communicate with you orally, in writing or through a third party, and I cannot communicate with Mr. A. Mr. A's lawyer can communicate with me or I can communicate with him. You should not talk to Mr. A unless we have told you to do so. You could inadvertently say or do something prejudicial to your case. There is no ethical restriction on the adverse parties talking to each other, but you shouldn't talk to your adversary without first getting the approval of your lawyer.

The most common violation of this rule by unethical or ignorant lawyers is for a lawyer to send a letter to his own client with a copy to the adverse party, or for the lawyer to send a letter to the other lawyer with a copy to the other lawyer's client. If this happens to you, please report it to us immediately.

3. Trust accounts. Mishandling your trust money is unethical and illegal. Lawyers are required to have trust accounts for client funds; they may not mix a client's funds with personal or other client's funds and may not borrow funds from the client funds. Under my own state law, interest on a trust accounts goes to an agency called IOLTA. Special arrangements can be made with a bank for the client to receive the interest on the funds.

4. Fee problems. Fee problems also can be ethics problems in certain cases, such as where a fee amount might be excessive in view of the facts involved. Most local Bar Associations have a procedure for arbitrating or deciding fee problems between lawyers and clients. Our firm is always willing to discuss fee problems and, recognizing there can be honest differences of opinion over fees, we are always willing, at the inception of the fee dispute, to let the Bar Association arbitrator arbitrate a fee problem. The Bar Association fee arbitration committees usually bends over backwards to protect the client. Normally, fee problems are not ethics problems but on some rare occasions they are.

5. Conflicts of interest. A lawyer cannot ethically represent both sides where there is a dispute, or a potential dispute, unless all parties agree. A lawyer must ethically do his or her best for the client. A lawyer is not a judge deciding what is "fair and reasonable." A lawyer normally is an advocate, out to protect his or her client at the expense of the other party, if necessary. For this reason, a lawyer cannot represent both a husband and wife in a divorce, or represent every shareholder and also represent the corporation, or represent each partner and also represent the partnership. The lawyer must steer clear of even potential conflicts of interest, such as two people in a criminal case where one may have to testify against the other at a later time. Representing multiple people against the same defendant in an accident or collection case may be unethical where the defendant won't have the ability to pay everybody and a decision concerning who gets what must be made.

On the other hand, we must be practical. The American public can't afford to go out and hire a lawyer for every person on every nickel-and-dime deal. Therefore it is normal and customary in some situations for a lawyer to, in effect, represent multiple people with actual or potential conflicts of interests in order to save legal fees and to expedite the delivery of the work. For example, we might prepare all of the corporate documents affecting the rights of the 10 shareholders instead of having 11 lawyers (one for each shareholder and another for the corporation) involved in the start-up of a small business. In these situations of potential conflicts, each person will be advised as follows:

A. That each person has a right to select his or her own lawyer.
B. To whom the firm is looking for payment of legal fees.
C. That the firm will raise questions and suggest commonly used solutions which the parties may wish to accept, reject or modify.
D. Who, if anybody, the firm would represent if there were an actual dispute at a later date.
E. That each person understands there could be a conflict of interest between that person and the other parties and that he or she is waiving the conflict and consenting to the representation of the others.
F. That the person can, at some point, consult his or her own independent lawyer to be sure the legal position is understood before signing the final agreement or document.
G. Access to, and control of the case files in the event of a dispute.

All of the above should be explained to all of the parties involved and preferably in writing and acknowledged in writing by the client.

Failure to recognize properly and explain conflicts of interest is a serious ethical violation.

A lawyer normally will not buy something from a client or sell something to a client without sending that client to another lawyer to get independent legal advice or at the minimum of the right of that client to get independent legal advice from another lawyer before signing such an agreement. Failure to do this is a serious ethical violation.

6. Self dealing with clients. The relationship between a client and a lawyer is a fiduciary one.

7. Failure to communicate with a client. Generally speaking, it is *not* unethical for a lawyer not to keep a client informed of what's happening on the case or not to return telephone calls promptly. These practices may be bad client relations, bad business or just plain stupid, but they're not unethical in most cases. There are a few situations where not communicating with a client could be unethical, but these situations usually involve the attorney's hiding something from the client or not responding to a reasonable request for information within a reasonable time. As a fiduciary, a lawyer must respond to reasonable requests for information within a reasonable time. A lawyer must act as a fiduciary toward a client and cannot lie to, or hide things from, the client. In these rare situations, failure to communicate could be unethical.

8. Extortion. Occasionally the other party in a dispute has committed a criminal act, either before, during or after the act in dispute between the parties. (Employee embezzlement is common, but other examples are income tax evasion or violation of some licensing law.) The client wants to use the lawyer to threaten to expose the person to authorities or police unless the person does what the client wants (typically to make restitution or sign documents.)

If the lawyer did what the client wanted done it might be unethical in some states, but it would be a crime in most states. The crime would be the crime of extortion. (Generally, extortion is the threat of criminal prosecution *unless* the other side pays the consideration of doing what the client wants done.)

Usually, a good lawyer will skillfully handle the situation by saying something like, "My client (we) will pursue all legal remedies," or "My client (we) will take all steps available under the law, but our lawyers will not knowingly write a letter in such a way as to commit extortion."

9. Pretending to have special influence over a judge or government official. It is usually unethical for a lawyer to state expressly or to hint that he or she has a special influence over a judge or other official. The lawyer is implying that the results will be determined by who the lawyer is rather than the merits of the case.

Be careful of a lawyer who expresses the ability "fix" a case or cites some form of a special influence. This lawyer is giving you open notice of being unethical. This lawyer might not be able to help you if legal skills are required to win your case.

It would be questionably ethical for a lawyer to tell you expressly how he or she and the judge play tennis or golf together or are socially close or go to the same church. (Remember also that if the judge could be influenced by these factors, the other lawyer representing the other side may play more golf or tennis together or be closer socially or be more important in the church.)

It would be proper for the lawyer to state that he or she has appeared before that judge and is familiar with the kind of evidence the judge looks for, or that he or she is familiar with some of the judge's idiosyncrasies or prejudices in the courtroom.

The above are obviously not all of the possible ethical situations that could arise during a legal matter, but are some of the more common ones.

We, as lawyers, will never practice law unethically. We believe that, in the long run, you, the client, will best be served by ethical lawyers. We will be aggressive when it advances your case. We will give common courtesies to opposing counsel if that will not harm your case. We will never knowingly be unethical and trust that you understand that this is in *your* best interest.

H-7
Sample Ethics Pamphlet
(To Be Given to a Client When
Another Lawyer Has Been Unethical)

The previous chapter deals with letters you can send to a client emphasizing *your* ethics where you have an ethics problem you wish to overcome in order to keep a client or case. This chapter is a form pamphlet you can use as a marketing tool when another lawyer is or may be unethical and you want the client to change lawyers. You can highlight the applicable unethical conduct of the other lawyer.

Consider putting this on your website. Many potential clients actually seek ethical lawyers.

1. Our Confidential Relationship. Everything a lawyer (or any member of the law firm) learns about a client during the representation of a client is confidential. Our lawyers are not allowed to discuss your case or legal matters with anyone outside the firm. Our lawyers and non-lawyers are strictly prohibited from breaking the sanctity of the attorney-client relationship.

What you tell your lawyer is similar to what you tell your priest or doctor. We can't be effective in helping you unless we know all of the facts, including all of the unpleasant and embarrassing facts. To encourage full disclosure, we are prohibited by ethics and by law from discussing anything about your case with anyone. The mere fact that you need a lawyer can sometimes be something you don't wish to disclose. For this reason we do not allow our people even to disclose the names of our clients unless we have their permission.

Our lawyers and non-lawyers are forbidden even to discuss these confidences with their spouses, or other family members, or in a public place where they might be overheard.

If a lawyer brags to you about the name and legal matters of a client, you should be concerned about the ethics of this lawyer and whether you can expect your name and the facts of your case to be broadcast to people who could use the information against you.

In truth and in fact, lawyers do sometimes discuss their cases, particularly the unusual and bizarre case, with other lawyers or with their spouses. Normally, the discussion would be in such a way that the identity of the client could not be identified. Any lawyer who discusses a client or client's case out of the office runs the risk of being unethical.

2. Contact with a person represented by an attorney. A lawyer *cannot* ethically contact anyone on the other side of the case if that person is represented by an attorney. Therefore, if you have a dispute with Mr. A, Mr. A's lawyer cannot communicate with you either verbally, in writing or through a third party. I cannot communicate with Mr. A. Mr. A's lawyer can communicate with me or I can communicate with him. You should not talk to Mr. A unless I have told you to do so. You could inadvertently say or do something prejudicial to your case. There is no ethical restriction on the adverse parties

talking to each other, but you shouldn't talk to your adversary unless your lawyer approves first.

The most common violation of this rule by unethical or ignorant lawyers is for a lawyer to send a letter to his client, with a copy to the adverse party, or for the lawyer to send a letter to the other lawyer with a copy to the other lawyer's client. If this happens to you, report it to us immediately for possible discipline.

3. Trust Accounts. Lawyers are required to have trust accounts for client funds and may not mix client funds with personal funds and may not borrow funds from the client. All deposits and withdrawals for your funds in the trust account must be reported to you as rapidly as is reasonable.

4. Fee problems. Fee problems can become ethics problems in certain cases, such as when a fee charged might be very large in view of the facts involved. Most local Bar Associations have a procedure for arbitrating or deciding fee problems between lawyers and clients. Our firm is always willing to discuss fee problems and, recognizing that there can be honest differences of opinion over fees, we are normally willing to let the Bar Association arbitrate a fee problem. The Bar Association's fee arbitration committee usually bends over backward to protect the client. Normally, fee problems are not ethics problems but, on rare occasions, they can be if failure to refund unearned fees is an issue.

5. Conflicts of interest. A lawyer cannot ethically represent both sides in a dispute. A lawyer must ethically do the best possible for his or her client. A lawyer is not a judge deciding what is "fair and reasonable." A lawyer normally is an advocate, out to protect his client at the expense of the other party, if necessary. For this reason, a lawyer cannot represent both a husband and wife in a divorce, or represent each shareholder and also the corporation, or each partner and also the partnership, or even conflicts of interest such as two people in a criminal case in which one may have to testify against the other at a later time. Representing multiple people against the same defendant in an accident case or collection case may be unethical where the defendant won't have the ability to pay everybody. A lawyer may not represent a client if representation of that client and total loyalty to that client could be impaired by the lawyers relationship with another person or client.

On the other hand, the world must be practical. The American public can't afford to go out and hire a lawyer for every person on every small transaction or deal. Therefore, it is normal and customary in some situations for a lawyer to, in effect, represent multiple people with actual or potential conflicts of interest in order to save legal fees and expedite the delivery of the work. For example, we might prepare all of the corporate documents affecting the rights of the 10 shareholders instead of having 11 lawyers involved in the start-up of a small business. In this situation each person should be advised as follows:

A. That each person has a right to select his or her lawyer and, indeed, do so if he or she wishes.
B. To whom the firm is looking for payment of legal fees.
C. That the firm will raise questions and suggest commonly used solutions which the client may wish to accept, reject, modify or regulate.
D. Who, if anybody, the firm would represent if there were a dispute at a later date.
E. That each person understands there could be a conflict of interest between that person and the other parties and that he or she is waiving the conflict.

F. That the person may, at any point, consult an independent lawyer to be sure his or her legal position is understood before signing the final agreement or document.

G. Access to, and control of, the case files in the event of dispute.

All of the above should be explained to all of the parties involved, preferably in writing.

Failure to recognize and explain properly conflicts of interest is a serious ethical violation.

A lawyer should not buy something from a client or sell something to a client without advising that client of the client's right to get independent legal advice from another lawyer. Failure to do this is a serious ethical violation.

6. Self dealing with clients. The relationship between a client and a lawyer is a fiduciary one.

7. Failure to communicate with a client. Generally speaking, it is not unethical for a lawyer not to keep a client informed of what's happening on the case or not to return telephone calls promptly. These practices may be bad client relations, bad business or just plain stupid, but they're not unethical in most cases. There are a few situations where not communicating with a client as the status of a matter could be unethical, but these situations usually involve the attorney's hiding something from the client. A lawyer must act as a fiduciary toward a client and cannot lie to, or hide things from, the client. In these rare situations, failure to communicate could be unethical.

8. Extortion. Occasionally, the other party in a dispute has committed a criminal act either before, during or after the act in dispute between the parties. (Employee embezzlement is common, but other examples are income tax evasion or violation of some licensing law.) The client wants to use the lawyer to threaten to expose the person to authorities or police unless the person does what the client wants (typically, to make restitution or sign documents.)

If the lawyer did what the client wanted done, it might be unethical in some states, but it would be a crime in most states. The crime would be the crime of extortion. (Generally, extortion is the threat of criminal prosecution, unless the other side pays the consideration of doing what the client wants done.) Usually, a good lawyer will skillfully handle the situation by saying something like, "My client will pursue all legal remedies," or "My client will take all steps available under the law," but the lawyer will not, or a least should not, write a letter in such a way as to commit extortion.

9. Pretending to have "special influence" over a judge or government official. It is usually unethical for a lawyer to state expressly or to hint that he or she has special influence over a judge or other official. The lawyer is implying that the results will be determined by who the lawyer is rather than the merits of the case.

Be careful of a lawyer who expresses the ability to "fix" a case or cites has some form of special influence. This lawyer is giving you open notice of being unethical. This lawyer might not be able to help you if legal skills are required to win your case.

It would be questionably ethical for a lawyer to tell you expressly how he or she and the judge play tennis or golf together or are socially close or go to the same church. (Remember also that if the judge could be influenced by these factors, the other lawyer representing the other side may play more golf or tennis with the judge or be closer socially or be more important in the church.)

It would be proper for the lawyer to state that he or she has .appeared before the judge and is familiar with the kind of evidence that the judge looks for, or that he or she is familiar with some of the judge's idiosyncrasies or prejudices in the courtroom.

The above are obviously not all of the possible ethical situations that could arise during a legal matter, but are some of the more common ones.

We, as lawyers, will never practice law unethically. We believe that, in the long run, you, the client, will best be served by ethical lawyers. We will be aggressive when it advances your case. We will give common courtesies to opposing counsel if that will not harm your case. We will never knowingly be unethical and trust that you understand that this is in *your* best interest.

H-8
Conforming to Ethical Requirements For Mailings

Before you do any postal mailings, or faxing, or emailing to strangers, you should carefully check out your local ethical rules to determine what is or is not permissible. If there are existing guidelines or rules, you should know what they are BEFORE you spend time and money designing your campaign and your materials.

If your mailing campaign is successful, you can expect one or more lawyers to complain to the Bar when they lose a client to you or a client shows your letter to them.

One way to protect yourself is to send a copy of the proposed mailing (before it is distributed) to the appropriate Board of Governors or Ethics Committee of your Bar. This may afford you some standing at a later time when you are able to say to a complainant, "Before I sent this out, I sent a copy to the Bar and they raised no objection," or 'They approved it," or whatever. Your particular Bar may simply not respond to your notification or they may approve or comment, depending on their predilection to "get involved."

I predict the day will come when all direct mail, fax, and email solicitations will become permissible as long as the contents of the mailings are truthful. This, however, is not yet the state of the law and you should be sure you are not going to waste both your time and money and have problems with the Bar.

Chapter I
Getting Work From Large
or Publicly Held Companies

I-1
Some Differences Between Getting Business From Publicly Held Businesses and Closely Held Businesses

There are many differences between the real and perceived legal needs of publicly held companies and those of closely held companies. There are many similarities, and also differences, in their criteria for choosing and using lawyers. In this chapter, I wish to point out some factors for you to keep in mind. When you meet with prospective clients, you'll have to be subtle about finding out what the prospective client needs or thinks he needs.

1. Whose money is being spent?

A. In the closely held company, legal fees are out of the pocket of the owner(s). Even though there may be tax benefits available, the net legal fees are still out of the pocket of the small business owner. Accordingly, you may have to convince the owner of a small firm that the money being spent on legal fees is either:

1) An unavoidable necessary evil;
2) A good investment of funds.

In a small company, the owner has to decide whether money being spent on legal fees is simply throwing good money after bad. The owner may think the money would be better spent building inventory, repaying indebtedness, etc. In other words, the owner of a small, closely held business often has to be convinced of the necessity of incurring legal fees. Often the owner will elect to forego legal rights and remedies because there is a better, higher use for the funds. You must communicate to the owner that you understand the alternative uses of the money and that you will keep the business' best interests in mind.

B. In the publicly held company, the person deciding on the expenditure of legal fees is not spending his or her money. The money being spent is "company money" or shareholder money. The money does not come out of the pockets of the decision-maker. Therefore, when you meet with this person you can relate orally how you understand that the company has alternative uses for the funds. The person will appreciate hearing this and may repeat your statement to his or her superior as an indication of your integrity and care for your clients. Realistically, however, alternative uses for the money normally is not a factor in publicly held companies.

2. Where is the cash to pay legal fees going to come *from?*

A small company has to obtain the cash to pay you from savings or from current or future earnings. Small companies must be "out of debt" to their banks periodically. Accordingly, major litigation may not be feasible for a small company unless the lawyer "finances" it by sacrificing getting paid for a given period. No banker is knowingly going to provide funds to finance litigation or legal fees. Larger corporations, on the other hand, don't have the problem of having to be "out of debt" to the bank. They can stay in debt 365 days a year and they can issue debentures and other long-term evidence of indebtedness.

The lawyer when dealing with the smaller company can use that difference as a marketing technique by offering to work with the smaller company. The lawyer can say something along the following:

"Look, I know that from time to time you may have a cash flow problem when you must use your cash to get out of debt to your bank. I'll work with you. Normally, I must be paid currently because I have to pay my own bills currently, but when you have to get out of debt to the bank, tell me in advance and I'll try to schedule the work to have as low a bill as possible during the period of cash flow problems. Just be sure to let me know in advance, not after you've received the bill"

Even larger publicly held companies have cash flow problems from time to time. Your indication of being willing to work with them if necessary will be appreciated even if not needed.

The offer to work with the client shows you understand the problems of, and have compassion for, the client. It is a good technique.

I-2
Recognize that Job Protection May Be a Factor for the Person Who Chooses Outside Counsel for A Large Corporation

In a large company, the ultimate bottom-line factor in the mind of the person(s) who decides which lawyer to use is the job protection of the person doing the deciding.

"Quid est in re mihi" is a fine old Latin expression meaning "What's in it for me?" In a larger company, the person who hires you may have absolutely no concern over what the shareholders or the board of directors will think of your being used as a lawyer. That person is only considering his or her own personal situation or, in some cases, the department in which the person works.

There is a lingering fear in the selector that if you are chosen and do well, you'll get the credit, and if the case or matter turns out badly, he or she will get the blame. It's a lose-lose situation for the person doing the hiring. You have to address this concern.

If you are selected and the case is lost the person who chose you may be blamed for choosing the wrong lawyer for the case. On the other hand if the largest firm in town is chosen and the case is lost, the person who chose you will not be blamed for choosing the wrong firm.

I anticipate and address this factor directly and honestly as soon as I'm sure I'm dealing with a decision-maker. I may say something like: "Look, I know you want to be sure that using my firm will work to your benefit, or at least not work to your harm. You won't have to worry about any problems. "

While this statement may be vague and possibly not reassuring, it's better than leaving the question unanswered or unaddressed.

I-3
Getting Work from Large Corporations

I have rewritten this chapter about 20 times in the last two decades. It has become increasingly difficult for the small firm (five or fewer lawyers) to get work from big corporations and the difficulty is becoming more intense by the day. At one time, getting work from big companies was no harder than getting work 'from small clients; it simply required slightly different marketing techniques. It was enough to emphasize that you had a super subspecialty or were very good in what you did; and that being a small firm, you could be more responsive to the needs of a big client, be more appreciative of their work and give them a faster turn-around time. Today that's not good enough.

In this section, I'll give you those techniques which I believe are most likely to be successful, but you should not expect a high rate of success if you are a small firm. The techniques that work for the small clients also work for the large client, but they aren't enough. You must understand the mentality that drives people who make decisions for large companies. Not everything in this chapter will work for every large client, but you will get some help, nevertheless.

Preliminary Information You Need Before You Can Hard Sell:

Get as much of this information as you can *prior to* your first meeting(s) and as much of the remaining data as you can *during* the first meeting(s).

1. Identify the decision-maker often referred to as the "COI," center of influence. There is no point in spending a lot of time and effort talking to the wrong person. You may have to convince many different people. The decision as to which lawyers to use or not to use may emanate from:
   a.) The head of the department which will utilize your services;
   b.) The head of the activity, whether departmental, regional or other, which has to write your check or approve your fees;
   c.) The actual department which will be charged for the legal fees on its profit and loss accountability;
   d.) The administrative vice-president in charge of coordinating all legal outside work;
   e.) The chief of the law division or other internal legal section;
   f.) The internal general counsel;
   g.) The outside law firm which acts as general counsel (see special section in this chapter on trying to avoid contact with outside general counsel);
   h.) Business development personnel at various levels. Some companies assign out legal work in return for patronage referred or in hopes of getting business back from the lawyers (banks are among the best examples);
   i.) Some combination of the above; and
   j.) None of the above (possibly the president makes the decision).

2. Try to learn what their criteria are for selecting and/or using outside law firms. There may be a well-defined set of criteria set down in writing or the decision may depend upon subconscious or "gut" reactions.

3. Try to determine those areas of legal work for which the company already uses outside law firms. In those areas, the decision has already been made to use outside counsel. It's a matter of getting some of that type of work from the company.

4. Try to determine whether there are areas in which the firm is considering changing from in-house to outside legal counsel. You may want to encourage the use of outside counsel, generally, and you, specifically.

5. Try to determine if there is some new area of legal work developing that will be given to outside counsel and decide if you can prepare for it.

6. Learn everything you can about what the company is doing by accessing search engine data banks to get information from newspapers, trade journals, publications and securities exchange information. Know who the corporate officers and directors are. When the potential client expresses amazement at how much you know about the company or the people in the company, you can tell the client you believe the better-prepared lawyer often wins a borderline case because of preparation. Potential clients want to hear how much you know about them.

I-4
Establishing Contact with the
Targeted Large Potential Client

There are at least two good ways of taking your first step toward your targeted client:

A. Find someone you already know in the organization or "accidentally" meet someone in the organization. Try to determine if there is anyone you already know within the company; your "old boy" network is a good entree. Tell that person frankly that you're interested in doing some legal work for the company. See if your contact will identify the proper decision-makers to contact, help you by setting up the first meeting or a golfing date or at least allow you to use his or her name as the door opener. This insider can possibly get you the preliminary information about the company that you should have.

If you don't already have a contact in the targeted company, you can "accidentally" meet one by going to Continuing Legal Education courses where people from that company are likely to go, or to service club meetings where one of the principals from the company will be speaking. Tell that person frankly that you're interested in doing some legal work "with" the company ("with the company" sounds better than "for the company"). The worst that can happen is that the person won't meet with you. You might be able to reach the person you want through their favorite charity.

B. Find a third party to introduce you. There are many third party sources you could go through for an introduction to a key person in the company. Your book sellers may service their law library. Accountants, bankers, insurance agents, travel agents and many others can make the introduction for you if you ask for their help. Your banker may not be able to make the actual contact but may be able to establish a contact through the bank.

I-5
Be Sure You Understand and Address the Client's Philosophy Toward the Use of Outside Counsel

Try to determine what the client expects from outside counsel. Then decide if you are willing and able to deliver what the client wants. Answer the following questions concerning potential clients:

1. Do they want to "turn over" the case to counsel and then go back to other things, leaving you to function independently?
2. Do they expect to *control* every aspect of the case with your firm being the "front" for them, executing their orders, etc.?
3. Are they interested in solution of disputes purely as a commercial decision, weighing the cost of attorneys fees against the price of a settlement?
4. Are they "righteous" people who will fight for principles regardless of the costs?
5. Do they look upon litigation and other legal expenses simply as a cost of doing business, or do they perceive these expenses as "stealing" from their net profit?
6. Who will decide how much legal work should or should not be done in each situation: the client or the lawyer?
7. Will the client control the cases to the point of having to approve all pleadings, documents, etc.? If so, are you willing to work under these limitations on your professional judgment?
8. Do the clients look upon adversaries and the adversaries' lawyers as being dishonest people being represented by dishonest or marginally ethical lawyers?
9. Do they simply want cost controls because their stock is selling for seven times legal fees?

By finding out exactly what clients want, you may be able to get them by promising to deliver (and delivering) what they want.

I-6
Anticipating House Counsel as Being Either a Friend or an Obstacle to Using You

Most major companies have some sort of in-house legal staff, ranging from hundreds of lawyers world-wide to a part-time lawyer who does routine matters such as corporate minutes, defending and dragging out smaller litigation until outside counsel takes it to trial, or handling routine collection cases.

You must be prepared to answer the following question, which may be open or subconscious: "Why should I hire your firm instead of hiring a part-time or full-time lawyer in-house?" Some possible answers are as follows:

1. There's more to a law firm than just the lawyer. Other resources such as secretaries, legal assistants, libraries, equipment, telephone, rent and other occupancy expenses will also be present.
2. You can't "turn on and turn off" the need for house counsel. A substantial investment in training and organization must be made. During periods of lesser activity, there is the problem of excess capacity, which is difficult or expensive to reduce (unemployment claims, etc.) and very expensive and time-consuming to reinstitute again when needed.
3. The in-house lawyer may not get the diversity of experience needed when he or she represents only one client. An outside lawyer with many clients is more exposed to fresh and new dangers and trends.
4. The in-house lawyer or staff may not be ambitious enough, or willing, to work weekends, evenings and holidays. Overtime costs for such work may more than offset any savings.
5. The company will find house counsel normally is a current legal fee expense which is difficult or impossible to defer (see chapter on accounting for legal fees).

You can compare using outside counsel versus in-house counsel to the decision between owning equipment and renting equipment when you need it. It often seems more expensive to rent, but an analysis of all of the costs may prove that renting is much cheaper than owning. And just as you're always assured of the latest technology available when renting, you're assured of the and best people available (on demand, as needed) when a client uses outside counsel.

I-7
Anticipating Outside General Counsel as Being Either A Friend or an Obstacle to Using You

A. Anticipate the Reaction of the Outside General Counsel.

Find out who the existing outside general counsel are and then avoid them. This is a calculated risk. If existing outside general counsel recommends you, then you have an extremely good chance of success. On the other hand, you have to be realistic. Existing outside counsel in all likelihood may simply regard you as competition and do everything they can to cut your feet off before you can set a foot in the door. I can tell you from first-hand experience some of the low, rotten things outside general counsel have done to try to freeze me out. These are firms where all the partners wear only gray suits, white shirts and thick-soled shoes with laces. The lawyers often graduated from the prestigious national law schools and were prominent in all the right organizations, including bar activities. Those firms will fight to protect what they perceive to be their vested interests and exclusive domain with all of the ferocity of a mother wolf protecting her den and cubs.

I don't mean to imply that all outside general counsel react this way, but in general, it is extremely difficult to make a breakthrough in today's competitive atmosphere.

B. Anticipate the Potential Client's "Protecting" the Existing Outside Counsel.

The decision maker may ask openly or subtly, "Why should I use you instead of my existing general counsel?" Hopefully, you will have learned something about the potential client's unhappiness with existing counsel to give an answer that responds to this inquiry.

Hopefully, you also will have learned who their counsel is, by reading Martindale-Hubbell, the potential client's financial statements or court filings, or having made a database internet search. You can use techniques such as, "Catchem, Holdem and Skinem is a fine firm, but no firm is any better or worse than the specific lawyer doing the work. Are you receiving ongoing attention from the same lawyer or do you find you're running a training school for their young associates at your expense? In our firm, you'll be working with only one or two people, primarily me." Will you have the right to veto any lawyer assigned to your case, to prevent a bait and switch, or will you be giving them a blank check?

You can say something such as, "Dewey, Cheatham and Howe is an excellent firm, however, I believe in competition. If we did some of your work, even if just a little, they wouldn't take you for granted and would realize they have to continue to give you good service." I found this technique to be very successful where the client felt their long term client lawyers were taking them for granted and not giving good service.

In some companies, outside counsel sit on every major committee and attend every departmental meeting, ostensibly to "protect" those present from committing illegal acts; in actuality, they are there to protect their firm from possible competition.

On balance, I think you'll do better staying away from the outside general counsel's attention for as long as possible or until you are well entrenched.

I-8
A Method of Accounting for Legal Fee Expenditures By Capitalizing Your Legal Fees to Maximize Profit

Typically, smaller closely held companies are more interested in reducing profits for income tax purposes than increasing profits for creditor or shareholder purposes. This is because they may have to pay a significant percent of their profits for income taxes but only 10 percent to 15 percent of the money involved for interest, and cash flow may be more important than profit and loss. (See chapter on tax deductibility of your bill.)

Larger or publicly held companies, on the other hand, don't have the cash flow problem and are more concerned in maximizing profits for shareholders. A one-cent increase in their profits per share may increase the price of the stock 10 or 20 times the increase in profits.

Higher profits per share for the corporation equals higher values to the share price. . . which equals happy shareholders. . . which equals greater compensation for the corporate officers and employees.

A given department of the company or its manager may be concerned with the legal fee expenses for that department, even if the company as an entity is not concerned. Accordingly, in your discussions with a potential larger client, you should discuss the possibility of capitalizing your legal fees in order to prevent the lowering of per share profits.

Capitalizing legal fees is simply a process of not deducting the fees for profit and loss purposes until the particular case or matter is over. In effect, the fees expended are carried as an asset until the case is over; accordingly, there is no effect on profit and loss until the case is over. When the case is over, the accumulated capitalized legal fees are then recognized for profit and loss purposes. If the case is successful, the amount of legal fees charged to the case will be deducted from the client's recovery or added to the client's loss and, thus, brought into the profit and loss picture. The legal fees, by being offset against the case recovery or loss, may never show up in the financial statement of the company or of the department as a "line item" legal expense.

This technique of capitalizing the legal fees can also "hide" the legal fees from shareholders or superiors in the company for as long as the case lasts. Thus, even on a loser or a terrible result, the loss can be kept off the profit and loss until profits increase generally, or until the corporate employee can get a new job within or outside of the company. Banks often use this technique with problem loans.

This technique of deferring recognition of the legal fee expense until the case is over can also be used to defer recognition of the underlying legal problem. The department can "bury" its problems for a few years by giving the case to you and simply telling upper management that the matter is "in the hands of the lawyers" and a report will issue when the case is over. The company's outside accountants mayor may not ask you for a legal opinion at a later time.

I have, in fact, used the above approach successfully to get major companies listed on the New York Stock Exchange as clients. Obviously, my legal fees would not impact the earnings of the entire corporation, but they would have impacted the earnings of the particular department involved. The department head discussed the procedure with the company accounting department, which gave them an account number for legal fees as a deferred charge. When the department head found he could spend money on legal fees without impacting current earnings, he gave me a big backlog of cases where he was deferring legal action because of the short-term impact of the legal fees on earnings. Had the firm's general counsel suggested this accounting technique to the department head, there would not have been any backlog for me to pick up. This technique got my foot in the door and got me a good client.

Even if the potential client doesn't care to use the technique of capitalizing legal fees, or wouldn't be allowed to by the company's accounting policies, this is still a good technique to discuss with a client or potential client because it demonstrates that you understand the profit and loss responsibility and that you are trying to help the client by suggesting creative accounting treatment of your legal fees.

Please don't misunderstand what I am saying here. I am not suggesting that you become part of a system of hiding department mistakes from shareholders or corporate management or creating false earnings reports or hiding the existence of litigation. In fact, it would not be possible to hide mistakes in companies where there are good internal and outside accounting, auditing and management controls and procedures to find the problems. In most cases, however, even if the purpose of the department head, unknown to you, was to defer or bury the problem for some period of time, the amount of legal fees involved would not likely have a significant effect on company earnings. The auditors would regard the practice of capitalizing your legal fees as being 'TSTA" (Too Small to Adjust), even though the fees are considered big by you.

You may wish to ask your CPA to explain this to you more thoroughly or even to give you a written current set of the accounting rules for accounting for deferred charges or capitalizing expenses. You could then use that written opinion in dealing with the potential client. Fortunately for me, I am a CPA and, accordingly, was able to explain the theory to the potential client.

Don't try to use this technique until you understand it. Alternatively, photocopy this chapter and give it to the potential client (with appropriate copyright credit, of course).

I-9
Keeping Legal Fees at Less than Court Awarded Interest Plus Court-Awarded Attorney's Fees As an Incentive for a Large Corporation to Use You

In representing a bank, I once calculated that in almost all cases of debt collection I could budget the legal fees on the case as being less than all accrued and earned interest plus the amount of court-awarded attorney's fees. Often there would be two to three years' interest accrued prior to the cases coming to me, and another year or two of interest until judgment could be obtained. The court also made an award of attorney's fees.

Thus, if the debt was ultimately collectible, the client would recover the principal intact and the attorney's fees would be covered by the interest and court-awarded fees; the client would get a "free ride."

By expensing legal fees in this manner, I encouraged some new clients to use me for the first time. They liked my analysis as applied to a large corporation's profit and loss situation. Additionally, capitalizing fees paid, there was no legal fee expense on the case if there was a recovery.

I-10
Be Prepared to Emphasize Use of
Non-Lawyers and Technology in Your Office,
and Have Your Rate Schedule Available if Necessary

If your new client is going to give you an opportunity to show what you can do, one of the considerations will be cost.

The client is not looking for a cheap lawyer and is willing to pay prevailing legal rates. The client normally will be very interested in knowing who will take the lead 'in litigation, how many paralegals are on the staff, and what their cost per hour will be.

Sophisticated buyers of legal services know that very little of the work in a law office has to be done by senior partner level lawyers. Computers and lower-priced legal assistants working under a lawyer's supervision can do much of what lawyers used to do.

Point out that larger firms will use new lawyers at $200 to $300 per hour to get legal experience on routine matters at the client's expense. Emphasize how you can use paralegals and computer technology to do the same routine work at a fraction of the large firm's price. Show that routine work done by expensive lawyers can be done as well by lower-paid staff in your firm. Be sure you have a rate schedule with you.

Don't emphasize your being cheap or low priced. Emphasize how you use technology and paralegals to do work normally done by expensive lawyers in other firms (or done by younger lawyers who "get experience" at the client's expense).

In the world of good management, this is known as giving people the tools they need to do the job properly and then assigning the work to the least compensated person competent to do the work.

I-11
Be Realistic When You Market for Big Companies

In general, institutions prefer to deal with institutions. They want the assurance of dealing with the "biggest firm in town." No one can be criticized when a case was lost using the biggest firm in town. On the other hand, the company stands to be criticized if the same case is lost by a small firm.

When the potential client asks you how you are going to handle effectively a case that will require the full-time efforts of three lawyers for a three-month trial, you have to be honest and say that you wouldn't undertake any case you couldn't properly handle.

A large company may have a subconscious fear that when a small firm breaks up due to death or otherwise, the company will have to start over again with another firm. The more names the large company client sees on the law firm's letterhead, the more comfortable the client becomes.

You have to emphasize your experience in the legal area concerned, your desire to represent that client, or your availability.

In some companies you have no chance of breaking in, regardless. Accept that and go to other potential clients. Don't' waste your time "beating a dead horse."

Chapter J
The Office and Office Procedures as a Factor in Keeping Clients

J-1
Your Street Address, Your Post Office, Your Building and Public Transportation Facilities as Factors In Attracting Business

A. Your street address as a factor. Your street address is very important, unless your firm is well established or unless you practice primarily over the internet. Existing clients will, within limits, follow you wherever you practice and will recommend clients to you wherever you practice. Newer firms (or any firm in the earlier stages of growth or where growth is not primarily by client recommendation) do need an address and building consistent with the kind of clients they want to attract.

Every community has one or two streets that are well known locally as being the "success" streets in the area. These streets will be recognizable in the community, the city and possibly even throughout the world.

I've practiced most of my career on Wilshire Boulevard, Beverly Hills, California. Wilshire Boulevard is the main financial and business artery of greater Los Angeles County. Wilshire Boulevard runs approximately 12 miles from downtown Los Angeles through Beverly Hills and Santa Monica to the Ocean Pacific. The street name is well known and recognized. Mail from Asia addressed to Wheel Chair Boulevard arrived.

On the other hand, I practiced two years on Century Park East in Century City. Outside of Southern California, very few people have even heard of Century City, much less know that it borders Beverly Hills. Century Park East, like most of the streets in Century City, is only about five blocks long, and it took 10 minutes to explain to clients how to find the street and the parking lot. Clients and others came to meetings late and in an agitated state of mind because they or others were late.

All things being equal, you should give serious consideration to the street on which you will locate your office. Streets like Wilshire Boulevard and Park Avenue are world famous. If people have never heard of your street, they may think less of you as a potential lawyer than if your street is well known. I'm not suggesting that your street address will necessarily mean success or failure to your firm, but I am suggesting that it can have some beneficial or detrimental effect on your practice and, as such, should be considered.

B. Your post office as a factor. Beverly Hills, where I live and practice, is world famous for the movie stars' houses, luxury shopping and luxury hotels. I was in the first group of American tourists allowed in The People's Republic of China since 1947. The interpreter in Shanghai saw my luggage tags and asked me about the movie stars in Beverly Hills although there hadn't been an American movie shown in China in 30 years. My zip code 90210 is also recognized throughout the world.

There are some hilly areas adjoining Beverly Hills which are technically in the city of Los Angeles but which are served by the Beverly Hills Post Office and therefore have a Beverly Hills mailing address. People pay $400,000 to $600,000 extra for these houses which are called "B.H.P.O." meaning Beverly Hills Post Office. Whether or not the Beverly Hills mailing address is worth more or less than this amount is not within the scope of this book. The fact is that people are post office conscious. There are many communities where lawyers rent mailing addresses to give the appearance of being where they are not. Some examples are: Cambridge, MA; Princeton, NJ; Newport, CA, etc.

If you are in a suburb of a major city, you should consider indicating the city somewhere on your letterhead or card. Examples which come to mind are:

Bloomfield (Detroit), Michigan
Greenville (Dallas), Texas

C. Your building as a factor. Business clients are accustomed to parking their cars in a parking structure which charges a ridiculous price and then taking an elevator to get to your office. They might feel "awkward" or "out of place" if you practice in a ground-level, store-front office in a shopping center. The reverse might be true for workers' compensation and family law clients.

D. Public transportation as a factor. The elderly, injured and poor often need public transportation to get to a lawyer's office. If they can't get there in this manner, they won't go there. I know of one lawyer who bought out the lease of a cleaners located near a bus stop at a major transfer point for bus riders. The store was also across the street from a telephone operator installation. He built up a good practice from commuters who came to see him between bus transfers. He also received a good amount of business from telephone company operators. The lesson should be obvious. Public transportation access can be a factor, depending on the clients you're seeking.

J-2
Firm Name as a Factor in Practice Development

For the sole practitioner and the small law firm, firm name may not be as important as it is for the large firm. I'm not saying that firm name is unimportant. I'm simply saying that firm name may be more important to larger firms that want to sell their image as a permanent and ongoing institution.

I also believe that we as lawyers place more emphasis on firm name than do our clients or potential clients. Again, I am not saying that clients and potential clients don't recognize and appreciate "brand name" firms. I'm saying that we as lawyers tend to overemphasize the importance of a firm name as a factor in client development. Many of the largest and oldest law firms in America have merged into other firms and firms many that were "Brand Names" have simply disappeared apparently with no harm to the survivor.

I was recently at a luncheon where a lawyer was introduced to the group. The introducer couldn't remember, or didn't know, the name of the lawyer's firm. The introducer said, "I want to introduce Mr. John Smith, an attorney with the firm of Somebody, Somebody and Somebody. All lawyers are either with Somebody and Somebody, or else they are with Somebody, Somebody and Somebody." The non-lawyer audience laughed and applauded. I believe this demonstrates that people seem accustomed to firms with names two, three or more words long. When you have too many names or words, it becomes awkward both to the person answering the telephone and to those identifying the firm. The person or device answering the phone frequently mumbles the names or says them so rapidly, the caller cannot clearly hear the names. Consequently, people in and out of the firm tend to shorten the name to the first two or three. Long names can create problems for e-mail addresses and URLS (web addresses).

In some firms, the firm name is similar to a TV laugh track. Often when making a TV program, a laugh sound track is added. The master recording of the sound track can be 30 or 40 years old. All of the people who did the laughing could have long since died and been buried, but their voices are still being used as props for background laughter "on cue." Similarly, many of the persons whose names make up the firm name could now be dead and buried, but their names are still being used as "props" in advertising.

Most experts in "brand name" advertising, and many lawyers, advocate not using more than two or three names for a firm. I agree.

I personally have changed firm name three or four times in my career, and very few clients have commented on the changes. Name partners and non-name partners regularly change firms, taking "their" clients with them without any significant loss of business.

I've also noticed a tendency among clients and former clients to criticize the entire firm when they are displeased with services received, but to praise the individual attorney in the firm when they are happy with services.

It is difficult when a small firm or sole practitioner has to compete with a big firm. People who buy their jeans by brand name probably will be prone to buy their legal services by brand name. There is very little one can do about this. If you are a "Brand X" firm, you have to work with what you've got.

Fictitious Names. Many jurisdictions now allow lawyers to use fictitious names in addition to the fictitious name firms where one or more of the "names" in the firm name is not active in the firm. Many firms use names that describe their practice area. A name that is used in Southern California is "Four Bitches From Hell." I leave to your imagination what the firm does. A sale practitioner told me he uses a fictitious name, which is practice area related, so that potential clients wont immediately recognize from the name that he is a solo practitioner.

Some "one liners" are often effective when someone indicates they are considering using a "brand name" firm instead of you.

The client or prospective client may say, "What do you know about the firm of 'Dewey, Cheatham and Howe'?" Your response could be, "They are a well-known large firm, but you know, in any firm, the firm is only as good as the individual lawyers handling the case. It's something like a hospital. The hospital is only as good as the doctor treating you. You should find out which lawyer will be handling your case(s) and whether your case(s) will be shuttled from lawyer to lawyer over the years as a teaching device for new lawyers." (You are aware that the "brand name" firm is unlikely to guarantee which lawyer will be handling the case in future years.)

On the other hand, the lawyer from the larger firm can emphasize the firm name by saying, "Our firm is well known. We are something like a highly respected hospital. We take great efforts to screen our attorneys and non-attorney staff carefully to be sure we have only the best people practicing under our name. The best hospitals get the best residents and the best interns. You will get a lot of attention from as many attorneys as needed, working under the specialist in charge of your case."

I personally would try to avoid totally ethnic names such as, "Schwartz, Greenberg and Goldberg" or "Chin, Wong and Fong" or "Sanchez, Gomez and Rodriguez" unless it is your desire to be identified as an ethnic firm. This is a matter of personal choice.

I would also try to avoid answering a telephone with "Jones, Smith, Grisberg, Ananofsky, Patterson, La Fontaine and Xanadopholies." The operator will probably mumble the name and the caller will lose patience.

Again, firm name is a factor in client development, and it is hard to compete with well-established firm names. But in the final analysis, the reputation of the individual lawyer is normally more important than firm name with clients. Studies done by an international CPA firm indicate that 65% of the clients will go with the lawyer when "their" lawyer changes firms.

J-3
The Periodicals in Your Reception Room

I was surprised when a client said to me, "I didn't know you did a lot of divorce work for wives." I told him that family law was no longer one of my practice areas and I was curious about why he had that idea.

He told me that the only publication in the reception room for clients to read was "Ladies Home Journal" with back issues extending over the period of a year. He was right. I had abdicated the selection of the reception room periodicals to the office manager. She was simply ordering what she wanted to read, then taking the magazines home to read when they arrived. She would bring them back to the office after they were two or three months old and she was through with them. I was oblivious to what was in my own reception room.

The message here is clear. Your client or prospective client can get an impression of what kind of work you do, or don't do, based on the publications in your reception room. I have kept the following (and changed them for a specific expected person):

"The Wall Street Journal." (People with high incomes read this newspaper).

"Rental Equipment Register." (This is the trade publication of the equipment rental industry; I do a lot of work in this industry, particularly in the buy-sell area.)

"Manchete." This is a Brazilian color photo magazine similar to "Life Magazine." Clients ask me why the magazine is in the reception room and this is my entree to tell them that we can handle their international business problems. It also allows me to convey our foreign language abilities.

"Journal of Taxation." This conveys to accountants, insurance agents, other attorneys, etc., our tax capacity.

"Flying" to indicate our firm's involvement in aviation law.

The local daily newspaper, general news magazines, "National Geographic", Sports Illustrated", "USA Today", etc., are all excellent periodicals which would be interesting for our clients or potential clients to read, but they do little or nothing to convey a message to your clients as to the kind of legal work you can do for them.

You want to communicate to clients and potential clients that you can competently handle legal work in those areas of law where you want more work. Sample kinds of publications for you to consider for your reception area could include the following:

1. The "Wall Street Journal", if you want business clients;
2. Industry trade publications in those areas where you want more (or some) work. If you represent a lot of clients (or want to) in a given industry, you should determine the leading publications in that industry and then subscribe to one or more of them.
3. Technical legal journals and publications for lawyers in specialized areas of law. Many of these journals can be obtained inexpensively from the appropriate

section of the American Bar Association or from your state or local Bar Association. Examples are "Trust Journal", "Tax Journal", "Family Law", etc.

4. Firm brochure or client newsletter which clearly explains what your firm can do (see chapter on firm brochures).
5. Various Bar Association pamphlets on wills, buying and selling a house, etc.
6. Reprints of published articles written by firm members.

Avoid publications that deal with travel, tennis, golf, skiing or boating. When your client can't get hold of you in an emergency, he or she will think you are on the golf course or tennis court and may become frustrated and angry.

Your clients shouldn't be in the reception room long enough actually to read the publications, so don't be concerned that they won't be able to understand them. These publications are simply props to communicate what you can do.

You can change them to suit what a specific client or potential client may be interested in.

A magazine rack is preferable to allowing magazines and newspapers to clutter a coffee table. Be sure that a person (usually the receptionist) has a specific job description responsibility for keeping periodicals current and for trashing or circulating back issues.

If your periodicals get to your office after being read at home, be sure to remove mailing labels from the periodical before you put it out in the reception room (unless you want clients knowing where you live).

J-4
Introduce Your Staff to the Client
(Part of Office Tour)

It is important that your client meet face to face at the earliest possible opportunity with the people who will be or may be helping with his or her legal matters. Make it a point to introduce the new client to your secretary and to the receptionist or whomever will have telephone contact with the new client. You should always introduce your new client to the other lawyers and non-lawyers in your firm who are likely to work with or have contact with the client. It takes only a few minutes to do it at the end of an office meeting with the client.

1. Introduce your secretary or administrative assistant.

I take the new client to my secretary and say, "This is Kay, my secretary. We have been working together for many years. She knows me better than I know myself. She tells me where I'm supposed to be and when. Kay makes all my appointments for me. I used to make my own, but it's easier to let Kay make them. Also, sometimes Kay can get information for you more quickly than I can."

Allow a few moments for your secretary to accept the compliment, smile and offer to shake hands with the new client. If your secretary truly resents doing this, then you have a problem. If the secretary does not enjoy working with and meeting clients, then he or she will convey that resentment, subtly or openly, in communication with the client. This will cause the client to avoid your secretary, and eventually, possibly avoid your legal office as well.

2. Introduce your receptionist.

Be sure to introduce your client to your receptionist or to whomever answers the telephone. A receptionist will react more favorably by telephone and in person when he or she has met the client face to face. (I have covered the entire subject of telephone answering in more detail elsewhere in this book, but am reinforcing here the value of having your new client meet the receptionist face to face). The receptionist should acknowledge the new client and say something like, "I am looking forward to helping you." Don't forget to have the receptionist ask the client if he or she is spelling and pronouncing the client's name and/or company name correctly. People love to hear their name pronounced properly and to see it written out.

3. Introduce other lawyers in the firm.

Introduce your new client to at least one other lawyer in your firm (or suite, if you are solo but sharing offices). Tell the client something like, "This is Mary Smith, my (associate or partner, etc). If for any reason you can't get hold of me or you need a lawyer immediately, ask for Mary. If she can help you, she will; if not, she will find somebody who can help you. You won't be without legal help when you need it. There will always be somebody to help you."

4. Cross market other lawyers in the firm.

Go down the hall, stopping at open doors and say to the client, "This is John, his area of specialty is anti trust" (or litigation, or whatever). Emphasize you can meet many clients' needs.

5. Introduce your information technology person, librarian or photocopy machine operator, etc., if you have them.

You can say something like, "This is John, our word processing operator and IT. specialist. When you need a document in a hurry, or we have a computer crash, John is the person who gets the job done. This is Jane, our photocopy machine operator. She makes sure that you get all of your copies in clear, readable form and that all are in correct page order and right side up. This is Joan, our librarian and electronic information specialist. She helps keep us up to date with the latest journals and legal works. She tells us what is new and available that we might be interested in. She also knows what materials are available from other sources on microfilm or computer. Sometimes she gets materials for your case from the Library of Congress or the law school library." She also gets information off the internet and is very good with search engines. June is an expert in finding information and even some legal research for attorneys. She helps keep your bill down."

6. Introduce your paralegal (legal assistant).

It is most important that your new client meet the paralegals as soon as possible. I personally prefer to introduce them to the client as "legal assistants." I will usually say something like, "This is May, my legal assistant. She is not a lawyer, but she is professionally trained to help me work on your case. She does not make the decisions. I make the decisions; however, she helps me implement the decision by doing some of the routine paperwork and fact gathering in order to help keep your legal fees as low as possible. (The clients love that part.) You may have a little or a lot of contact with May, depending on how your particular case develops."

7. Introduce anyone in the office, who is likely to show up on the bill, by name and function.

You can also combine the series of introductions with a tour of the office facilities, if you wish. (See Chapter on "Office Tour.")

The client is usually impressed by meeting the people who will be helping the client. To reinforce this good impression, you should say something like, "It takes a team of quality people to turn out a quality product and to give you quality legal services. I wanted you to meet the people on your team."

Often the client will say something like, "Now I know why you charge so much per hour for your time. You also have to charge for all of the people who are necessary to turn out a quality product."

After the introductions, which may take place from a few moments to a half hour or so, your new client or potential client will feel important as a part of the team.

This investment of time pays for itself many-many times over in terms of a good, happy, healthy relationship between your staff and your client.

Introducing the client to staff and other lawyers may prevent the anger clients may feel when they review bills with unknown names rendering service.

J-5
The Importance of Your Telephone Number
In Getting and Keeping Clients

Your telephone number is an extremely valuable asset. Try never to abandon or lose it.

When you change locations, try to keep your old telephone number(s). If you have to change phone numbers, try to get one incoming line with the old number. If you cannot hold on to the old number, have the telephone company forward or refer your calls from the old number to the new number for as long as possible.

If your area code changes, consider getting your number for both the new and old area codes with call forwarding from the old to the new. A change in area codes is a good excuse for sending an announcement to clients.

Clients put your number in their PDA's, their Palm Pilots, address books and various other databases. They retain your card in their wallets and purses. Your old telephone number is on public pleadings and documents. If the client calls you at the old number and gets a "Joe's Body Shop" or "This number is no longer in service" answer or recording, they may go to another lawyer whose number they have readily available. They may not want to spend the money to call information or wait for an operator to answer when they call information. They may be calling from a public telephone and not have the change to call information. They may not want to pay $1.00 or more to call information from a cell phone.

I learned about the value of a telephone number from a client. The client called me to tell me that his competitor was going under and, in desperation, the competitor was selling his telephone number on the last day of business for $3,000 cash. My client needed legal advice on how to purchase the number. Subsequently, the client told me that he had received $225,000 in new business on the purchased phone number the first year and $150,000 the second year. This gave me a bright idea. I checked on a former number I hadn't used in six years. It was by then being–used by someone else. I requested the number from the phone company and, when it became available, the phone company assigned it to me. It is only for incoming calls. I have about one call a week from people who haven't called me in years. Many of these people didn't know I had twice moved my offices and changed firms. I have earned tens of thousands of dollars from callers on the old number. I'll never know how many called me on the old number when it was no longer mine and then called someone else when they couldn't reach me. In any event, 15 years later I still have the old number and people still call on it.

I've never had the courage to seek out the old telephone numbers of law firms who have changed phone numbers after moving. I know of one lawyer who told me he had done so after reading an earlier edition of this book. He told me that the other lawyer's phone number was in advertising and phone books & produced a lot of profit over a period of many years. I suspect that by doing so I could pick up some new business intended for another lawyer. However, I am concerned about interference with the attorney-client relationship between the caller and the lawyer whom the call was intended.

The actual telephone number can be clever. For awhile, I used 1-800-4-CAL-LAW for my statewide calls, but frankly, people complained that the number was hard to remember. Possibly 1-800-366-6529 (FOONLAW) would have been easier to dial.

If you share a phone number with others, be sure that you have an agreement as to the use of the phone number when you split up. If you can't agree, then get a call referral service or system to answer the old number and share the cost.

Be sure that your telephone number including area code is in large, easy-to-read type on your stationery and professional card. If your number is a direct dial, be sure your line switches over to the office system or receptionist when the caller wants to dial "0" to reach a live person.

If you hope to get calls from foreign clients and lawyers, be sure to add the international code for the United States before the area code. The code for the US is currently 01 + 1 + area code, however, you should check to be sure to be current.

J-6
How to Handle Telephone Calls
From Potential or New Clients

Probably 99 percent of all new work starts with a telephone call (e-mail & fax are treated in another chapter). If you or someone in your office is not reasonably available to new clients or potential clients or lawyer referrals, then the potential client will simply call another lawyer. Most people know of at least two or three potential lawyers they could use on a new matter.

A former client or an existing client probably will be more lenient about waiting to contact you than a new client will be. Even an existing client will eventually go somewhere else if he or she can't get hold of you in what they consider to be a reasonable time.

I once saw a sign that read:

1. I needed a lawyer
2. I couldn't reach you
3. I reached another lawyer
4. I don't need you any more.

Lawyers sometimes hide from prospective clients' calls and then are surprised when the client goes to another lawyer who was immediately available.

When a client chooses a lawyer there are several factors that the client considers. A joint survey done by the American Academy of Advertising and the American Bar Association revealed what clients consider to be important in "choosing" a lawyer. (The factors for recommending a lawyer are somewhat different.)

(In order of importance)

1. Availability
2. Reputation
3. Experience
4. Specialty
5. Fee

It is an old maxim of marketing that a customer is not going to buy a box of soap under a bushel basket in the basement of the store. The customer will buy the box of soap on display in the front of the store. The analogy is obvious. Vendors to supermarkets pay "rent" or display charges" to supermarkets to place products on supermarket shelves. A lawyer must be available if the lawyer expects to be hired.

You must systematize your telephone answering in your office to avoid losing out when the new client calls.

When the caller says, "it's a new case," or "I've been recommended by Mr. Smith," or any other words that suggest the client is calling with a new matter, all alarms should go off and the call should receive priority treatment.

If the lawyer can be called at another number and connected to the new client by patch this should be done.

If the lawyer requested is not reachable, another lawyer should take the call. If there is no other lawyer to take the call, then the marketing director or a secretary or someone else should take the call, starting out the conversation with:

"This is Mr. Jones. Mr. Foonberg isn't in the office. May I help you until Mr. Foonberg can get back to you?"

If the lawyer is in a client consultation and receives an emergency call, he or she should take the call long enough to say:

"Mr. Jones, this is Mr. Smith. I'm in a meeting right now but I took your call because it's an emergency. I don't want to discuss your affairs in front of other people. Give me the number you're at and I'll call you back in minutes." Then turn to the client in the office and say, "I apologize for the interruption. The secretary put it through because it was an emergency that couldn't wait 45 minutes. Don't worry, you won't be billed for the time on that call.

You can have the same privilege. If you have an emergency situation that won't wait 45 minutes tell my secretary and my meeting with another client may get interrupted.

I generally don't like interrupting a meeting for a call, but doctors and dentists do it and it doesn't seem to affect their business. I interrupt conferences only for bona fide emergencies and new clients."

Alternatively, you may wish to step outside of your office to take an emergency call so that another client cannot overhear the conversation.

In addition to telephone availability, availability by e-mail and fax can be important to major clients and foreign clients. Putting these numbers and addresses on your stationery and professional card is a form of advertising your availability to potential clients. Be sure to include the international code for the United States before your area code. The international code for the US is currently 01. Thus your fax number might be 01-1-310-652-5019.

J-6A
How Do You Sound on the Telephone?

Have you ever heard your own voice on the telephone? You may be in for a surprise!

You may wish to try this technique if you are in a jurisdiction where it is legal to record your incoming telephone calls.

The Internal Revenue Service, as do may other agencies & companies, routinely records every incoming telephone call after announcing to the caller that the call "may be monitored for quality control purposes."

The IRS trainers then play the recordings to check on the accuracy of information being given to callers to determine if the IRS employee required further training in any given area. The called employee was allowed to listen to the recorded call simultaneously with the trainer.

As an unintended benefit of this procedure many of the employees said they were surprised at how badly they came across on the telephone in terms of rudeness, arrogance, interrupting the callers, impatient and a host of other deficiencies. Many of the IRS employees were so shocked by their own demeanor they attended classes on how to answer a telephone call.

You or a staff member might be pleasantly surprised or shocked at how you sound to a caller.

A Checklist for Increasing Your Profitability and Client Satisfaction by Training Your Staff to Properly Handle Incoming Telephone Calls and Emails

I believe 99% of all legal matters begin with a phone call from an existing client or referrers of clients. The way the incoming emails and telephone calls are handled can assure you a client for life or that the caller will never become a client or set the stage for an unhappy relationship after the call or email.

I have created a rather simple checklist for increasing profitability and client satisfaction.

1. A telephone call or email from a client or potential client can never be ignored. It must be processed as rapidly as humanly possible. Response time must be measure in hours not days.

2. No person should be allowed to answer a telephone or email unless and until they are trained to do so. Some telephone companies provide trainers or materials. There are also various State Bar CLE videos on answering phones.

3. Whenever possible, the lawyer should respond. The caller or writer will be very favorably impressed to receive a response from the professional.

4. If the professional cannot respond within a few hours, someone else must do so instead of the professional. Speed in returning or accepting the call or email is more important than the status of the person returning the calls.

5. If no one can return the call or email due to the office being closed, an email response can automatically inform the sender that the office is currently closed, and that it is office policy to respond to emails within one business day of receipt during regular office hours whenever possible.

6. A telephone caller should always be given the option of pressing "0" during office hours for a live operator. Clients usually feel the need to talk to a human.

7. Receptionists or others who answer incoming phone calls should be given a list of the clients who call the most with a guideline for how to pronounce and spell their names.

8. Telephones should be answered with self identification of the party answering the call ("This is John Smith, how can I help you?). When the person answering knows they are identified, they will tend to be friendlier than when they are anonymous.

9. All people in the office, especially those who respond to phones & emails, should be informed of marketing efforts. It is embarrassingly awkward and a sign of incompetency when the person answering a phone doesn't know that the firm is making a marketing effort to which the caller is responding.

10. Lawyers & others who receive direct dial calls and direct email must have a "back up" "follow up" system to respond to prevent client dissatisfaction and malpractice claims.

11. Screening of calls. Many offices receive calls originating in Yellow Pages. A separate number for Yellow Page ads is recommended. I have been told, but have not verified that about 10% of those who call in response to Yellow Page ads potentially have legal matters requiring attention.

    This 10% should be directed to an attorney. Ultimately one third of the 10% will have meritorious matters party. In other words 96% of all calls should be screened to assume that the prospective clients receive immediate attention and to avoid wasted attorney time.

When screening a call, always be polite and friendly. The caller who does not currently have a meritorious matter requiring a lawyer may have one at a later time or may be able to refer a client.

J-7
Avoid Losing a Prospective Client Through Bad Telephone Techniques When You're Not In

Ask your receptionist how frequently the following scenario occurs each week in your office.

A. You are not in;
B. The caller asks for you;
C. The caller is asked, "Who's Calling?";
D. The caller identifies himself/herself with an unfamiliar name;
E. The caller is told you are not in;
F. The caller says, "No message, I'll call later";
G. There is no message or call back instruction. (Sometimes the message is merely "Mr. Smith called, left no number, will call back");
H. The caller doesn't call back.

That caller was probably a potential client or referrer of a client. You weren't available. The caller simply called the next lawyer on the list.

Imagine that you are in your office with a client across the desk whom you want to refer to another lawyer. If the first lawyer you call is not in, would you keep the client in your office until you get a return call? Obviously not. You would simply go to the next attorney and the next until you reached one.

HOW TO AVOID THE "NO MESSAGE" SYNDROME.

The caller should be told "Mr. Foonberg is not in right now. I expect to hear from him shortly. Is there a number you can be reached at?" or, "This is his assistant (secretary), Joan Smith. May I help you?" or when applicable, "Can another person in the office help you?" or "Can another lawyer in the firm help you or would you prefer his voicemail?"

The critical thing is not to abandon the caller or to have the caller think they must wait indefinitely for a return call (which may or may not be coming.) The caller will simply go to another lawyer.

By giving the caller a range of choices you are most likely to make the caller comfortable by giving the caller control over what he or she prefers.

Listen in when someone calls for you when you are not in the office. You may be shocked!

J-8
Exploit Your Closed Files
Closed Files Can Be a Gold Mine of Future Work
Mine Your Inactive Files; Set Up 20-Year Calendar

Your open and closed files contain a lot of future legal work your clients will need. When you periodically remind them of their need for this work, four things happen:

1. You demonstrate to your clients that you care about them and are watching their legal matters.
2. You protect yourself from malpractice liability.
3. You protect the client's legal interests.
4. You get legal work.

To set up a 20-year calendar, you need only a blank book or calendar system with 240 pages (one for each month), a tickler system or a computer calendar system.
Examples follow:

1. *Corporation Formation and Records Maintenance.*
Almost every state requires an annual meeting of shareholders and/or directors. Suppose you form the Decennial Corporation for a client in the month of March with a fiscal year end of March 31. Calendar ahead, for about 10 years, to send the following letter every January. Copies may be sent to the corporation's CPA or insurance advisor as well as to each director and officer. By sending these copies, you may reach potential new clients or referrers of clients.

To Board of Directors   January 10, 20XX
Decennial Corporation
123 Main Street
Anytown, USA

Attention: John Doe, President

Re: Annual Minutes

Dear John:

As you know, Decennial Corporation has its fiscal year end on March 31. Under the laws of this state, every corporation is required to have an annual meeting of directors and an annual meeting of shareholders. These meetings and their proper documentation are important for many reasons, including:

1. Protecting the officers, directors and shareholders from personal liability to past, present and future creditors and tax agencies.
2. Preparing for income tax audits.   Auditors may need corporate documentation of certain activities and deductions relative to such areas as:
   A. Officer compensation and expenses.
   B. Pension or profit-sharing plan contributions.
   C. Bad debt treatment of certain items.
   D. Officer or shareholder transactions with the corporation.
   E. Various elections.

These meetings are important, even if only routine elections of officers and directors occur.

The minutes of these meetings should be as contemporaneous as possible.

Waiting until problems arise and then back dating minutes of prior meetings can cause problems and should be avoided.

Please let us know if you require any help in preparing these minutes or preparing for a meeting.

Sincerely,

Jay G Foonberg

cc: John Doe, CPA
cc: Mary Smith, insurance agency
cc: All Directors
cc: All Officers

If you don't receive a response by March 31 (the fiscal year end), send a follow-up photocopy of the letter with a rubber stamp notation "For Your Information." Don't do more or the clients will think you're soliciting business.

2. *Lease Renewals and Other Contracts with Renewal or Cancellation Clauses.*

Suppose you drafted a five-year lease with an effective date of April 1, 2005, with three renewal periods of five years each, requiring that written notice of exercise of option to renew be sent at least six months prior to the expiration date of March 31.

You should calendar ahead to about 90 days prior to the option exercise date(s) in the months of July 2009, 2014 and 2019 to send the following letter:

To Mary Doe, President   July___, 20XX
Smith Company
123 Main Street
Anytown, USA

Re: Lease for 123 Main Street

Dear Mary:

As you know, your lease for the property located at 123 Main Street contains a clause in Paragraph 8 on page 10 which gives you an option to renew the lease for another five-year period. The lease terms require that the option be exercised in writing on or before October 1, 2009, 2014 or 2019.

Please let us know if you want or need our help in preparing a legally effective notice of exercise of option to renew.

Sincerely,

Jay G Foonberg

cc: John Doe, CPA
cc: Mary Smith, insurance agency

Obviously this type of reminder can be used for any contract which contains a renewal or a cancellation date.

If you receive no response after 30 days, send a photocopy of the letter with a rubber stamp notation, "Reminder."

The copies can go to the CPA and to the insurance agency because the CPA has ongoing periodic contact with the client and because often the lease or contract contains certain insurance requirements.

3. *Children Reaching Majority.*

When you prepare a will for a client, find out the birth dates of the minor children and include them in your 20-year calendar. About 30 days prior to the child's reaching majority, send a letter along the following lines:

To John Doe
123 Main Street
Anytown, USA

Re: Mary Reaching Age of Majority

Dear John:

According to our records, Mary was born June 1, 1988. According to the laws of our state, she legally became an adult on June 1, 2006. In your will prepared in 1995, you provided for your wife to be Mary's guardian. The provision will no longer be valid.

May we suggest that you re-examine your financial affairs in view of Mary's new status as an adult.

May we also suggest that Mary may need her own will to cover disposition of any property she may receive by inheritance from you. We would be honored to prepare the will and thus serve the second generation of your family.

Sincerely,

Jay G Foonberg

cc: Mary Doe

Your sending a copy of the letter to the client will reinforce to the child that you are the family attorney.

Do not send a reminder or follow up. Many people do not like thinking of aging or death.

4. *Client or Client's Parent Reaches Age 65.*

I have devoted an entire separate chapter to this area and to which I refer you. Briefly, I'm suggesting that when a client or client's parent reaches age 65, based on the facts in your will file or other file you should consider sending one or both of two letters.

A. A letter suggesting allowable dividing up and giving away assets to children in order to qualify for MediCal, Medicaid or a similar program and to prevent using up the life's savings for a prolonged illness such as Alzheimer's disease or stroke. This is sometimes called a "spend down" and may be heavily requested or even prohibited or ineffective in some jurisdictions.

B. A letter suggesting a Living Will to allow death with dignity. I mention these two subjects here because the information to trigger the sending of the letters should lie in your files.

C. A letter suggesting a Durable Power of Attorney or designation of conservator or guardian.

5. *Judgment Renewals.*

When you get a judgment entered for a client, calendar ahead about six months before the judgment expires to remind the client about renewing the judgment.

6. *Conviction and Arrest Expungements.*

Calendar ahead to the earliest possible date that a convicted client or a client who was arrested can apply for expungement.

7. *Closing Files.*

Every time you close a file, ask yourself the question, "Is there something to be done in the future?" If the answer is "yes," then include that information in the 20-year calendar.

J-9
Holding on to Minute Books, Wills and Other Client Records to Get Business

It is customary for attorneys to hold on to client records such as wills, minute books, corporate seals and deeds after they are recorded. This is an excellent way to get repeat and new business.

A. *WILLS.*

Holding on to client wills to get the probate is a long-established way for attorneys to get business. Traditionally, a big will file was considered a lawyer's Social Security supplement.

When I was a law student, my professor in Wills advised us to write all the wills we could "for free or for a dollar each" in order to get the probate estate as a client. At that time in California, attorneys earned reasonable fees in probate matters and probate business was worthwhile. Since that time, the California legislature and courts have so cut attorney's fees in probate that probate work is not worthwhile except in the large estate. Accordingly, you should not go after probate business unless you know you can properly handle it for the prevailing fee.

I have developed a standard "explanation" that I give to clients after they sign a will, and I believe that I will want to be the lawyer for the estate. My explanation goes along the following lines:

"Look, this will belongs to you. You've paid for it and you can take it with you if you wish. I recommend however, that you leave it with me for safekeeping, for several reasons. I have a special safe deposit box in a nearby bank where I keep client wills. Anytime you want the will you can have it. Just ask for it. The box is fireproof and damageproof.

"Most important, no one can steal or destroy the will or attempt to cut themselves in with a forgery or alteration. Someone who is not happy with your will provisions could steal it and claim that you revoked it by destruction if they could inherit more through a prior will or through intestacy. It's very difficult to give effect to a missing will.

"I think it makes more sense for you to leave the original with me and to take the photocopy with you. In this way, you'll always have a copy and no one can destroy the original. There is no charge for this service. Also you're less likely to attempt to do your own codicil or modification if you don't have the original. People have caused a great deal of unnecessary confusion and expense by attempting "do-it-yourself" changes to their original wills.

"Only one or two clients have ever declined my offer to hold the original wills."

I normally staple my card onto the original will and to the copy which I give the client. I also enclose a form letter on letterhead stationery with the copy which says:

The original of this Will is kept in a Safe Deposit Box at the Crocker National Bank, Wilshire and La Cienega, Beverly Hills, California. Please contact our offices should the original be needed.

Very truly yours,

Jay G Foonberg

B. *HAVING A BANK HOLD ONTO THE ORIGINAL WILL.*

A variation of the lawyer's holding onto the original will is to have the bank which is named as executor and/or trustee hold on to the will for safekeeping. The bank will often do this for free if it is named as the trustee, executor or co trustee. If it accepts the position after the death of the testator it will usually name the lawyer who drafted the will to serve as the attorney for the estate. (See the chapter on "Naming Yourself or a Bank as Executor or Trustee . . .") There is a danger that if you move or change offices or telephone number that the bank will give the estate to another attorney on their list, claiming they couldn't get hold of you.

C. *CORPORATE MINUTE BOOKS.*

Many lawyers hold onto their clients' corporate minute books and corporate seals to keep a contact with the client. This gives the lawyer an additional reason to send clients an annual reminder as to the necessity of annual meetings of shareholders and directors. By keeping the minute book and seal, clients will not lose track of you and will come to you from time to time whether or not you send annual reminders of their need to update the minute books.

D. *OTHER DOCUMENTS.*

Leases with renewal clauses, deeds, mortgages, stock certificates, etc., are typical of various client records which you can safeguard for a client and which can result in the client's calling you from time to time, thereby keeping you in mind. Some clients want you to keep records for them to relieve them of the burden. Other clients are embarrassed or intimidated about asking you for their records for fear you might be offended.

Be sure that you obtain adequate insurance coverage to cover those items in your possession which are not your property.

At some point in your practice you may find yourself with old files for former clients. Disposal of the files can be a problem, especially if there are originals of wills, etc. Some lawyers prefer to scan everything and send all files to the client to avoid this problem. I have written on the subject of file destruction on other publications.

J-10
The Importance of On-Time Completion of Work

SETTING A TARGET DATE FOR COMPLETION

Double your time estimate. Lawyers consistently under estimate how much time they will require to accomplish a task. To be safe, double the time estimate and discuss the target date with the client. If the target date is not a good one, the client will tell you so. A client will never be upset if you finish early. Clients will be very upset if you are late. Remember you set the target date.

We live in an age of instant gratification. People want things NOW! People want one-day service at laundries and dry cleaners for clothes that will hang in the closet for weeks. People want (and are getting) walk-in medical care at hospitals and clinics. The trend toward wanting everything immediately is not yet as bad in most law offices as in other service enterprises, but the trend is there. Clients want you to file a lawsuit "immediately", even though the matter has been on their desks for two years and will be in court for another five years after filing. Clients send an e-mail with a 20 page document attached and call you by telephone 30 minutes later asking for your opinion.

The heyday of that mythical law firm of Bungle, Bungle, Stall & Delay is past.

Most clients will accept less than immediate service, but you should give them a time schedule and then stick to it.

Clients are upset when you don't deliver what you promised or scheduled. They equate inability to deliver work as promised with inability to do the work competently. When "you" set the deadline and then "you" don't deliver as promised, clients aren't charitable about accepting excuses for your delay. They may equate your failure to deliver either to your inability to estimate or to your not understanding the legal issues or work required. They may also equate your failure to deliver on time with your own inefficiency or the inefficiency of your "back office" to deliver the work.

You can do several things when you know you can't deliver as promised. You have to take an assessment of the best way for a particular client. Some suggestions are:

1. Ignore the problem. Deliver the work late and don't say anything at all. If you're lucky, the client won't even realize the work was late. If the client says anything, apologize for the delay and explain that there were "emergencies" which disrupted your work schedule (if true).

2. Call the client as soon as you realize you're going to be late. Tell the client you are having a problem meeting the promised date due to some unexpected emergency (if true). Ask the client if the deadline is important enough for you to work nights and weekends. Most if not all clients will be sympathetic and cooperative to this approach. You must be willing to make good your promise, however, if the client says that the time deadline "is" important. You may expend some money on overtime wages, but you'll have a satisfied client.

3. Blame the other people in the office (if true). This is a questionable technique, however. If you are dealing with a supervisory person, the client may be sympathetic. Often, a client will not sympathize and may get upset that you are passing the blame off on your people instead of standing behind them.

4. Have another person, such as a secretary, paralegal or associate, call the client accepting all of the blame (if true). The client ordinarily is not upset with non-lawyers.

You may have other solutions that work well for you. The important thing is to make a concerted effort to stick to the time frame stated and deliver as you promised.

According to a recent survey done for the American Bar Association, timely completion of work is an extremely important factor in the attorney - client relationship. 83% of satisfied clients perceived that their lawyers or firm promptly did the work. Only 41 % of dissatisfied clients perceived their lawyer or firm promptly did the work.

On the other hand, don't allow yourself to be pressured into answering a legal question you are not prepared to answer. You may need time to consider the question before giving answer (s).

I often say to the client "Look I can give you a gut answer which is probably correct or I can get you the right answer if you can wait a few days. I cannot accept professional responsibility for a gut answer, as the law often changes rapidly. Which do you want, the gut answer or the right answer?"

J-11
Getting the Kind of Business You Want by Offering "Same-Day" and "Next-Day" Service For Routine Matters

I built a very substantial, multi-million dollar bank collection and litigation practice by providing and delivering next business day service on all routine matters when properly documented with a system I created. Before the firm breakup, I had 19 major banks and financial institutions as clients within a period of a decade. I had gone from solo practice to a multi city large firm in multiple locations using one day service to get and keep the clients into the firm. Later, I expanded with the same clients giving other non routine services without one day service; but it was the reputation for one day service that brought the clients in and established my credibility in the area of bank litigation.

I was able to grow rapidly, handling profitable business for major clients by giving the clients one day service on their routine litigation matters. Often a loan had been in default within the bank for a year or two before the bank brought it to me. The case might be enmeshed in the courts for another one to three years or more, yet the clients loved and paid for one day service. Other law firms just didn't see any urgency to the case (from a case result point of view, they were correct). The clients, however, wanted fast service and gave us an ever-increasing share of their legal work.

I had to invest a lot of my time, my money and my energy to invest in systems which made it possible to assemble a case from an instruction form and allow legal assistants to prepare all the litigation documents for the court, etc., in a few hours.

If there is a type of practice area you have (where you're familiar with the processing and legal problems) and which you want to increase, you should devise systems to give same day and next day service. Be sure your existing client(s) know you are giving same-day or next-day service and you'll get a large increase in that kind of legal work.

When the firm broke up, I sold out at a very handsome profit and signed a covenant not to-compete for the bank business. If I go back into litigation work, I expect to be able to provide "same day" instead of "next day" service using digital forms and communication.

A copy of the "litigation transmittal" forms I developed follows this chapter.

This type of information could have been transmitted by fax or email or intra net but I felt it was important for me to personally review the underlying original documents before filing the case in court. The client didn't care who prepared the case at lower fees so long as I personally reviewed what was happening.

GENERAL LITIGATION TRANSMITTAL AND INSTRUCTIONS

This PINK FORM is to be used for all litigation, including Claim & Delivery actions. Use separate PINK for each cause of action, i.e. if 2 Notes, use 2 Pinks. Additional forms will be required for (1) Auto Deficiency Suits (Yellow); (2) Cash Reserve/Balance-Plus Suits (Buff); (3) Master Charge Suits (Blue); (4) Objections to Discharge in Bankruptcy proceedings (Green).

PLEASE TYPE YOUR NAME (ADJUSTOR), NAME OF CONCERN, ADDRESS, ZIP CODE, TELEPHONE NO. & TODAY'S DATE

Name: _____ Concern: _____ Address: _____
Title: _____ Phone: ( ) _____ Date: _____

A. Name of Debtors to be sued. Include all known aliases, aka's dba's and wife.
   1. _____
   2. _____
   3. _____

B. Addresses (Home and Business) of Debtors to be sued. INDICATE IF RESIDENCE R/A OR BUSINESS B/A.
   1. _____
   2. _____
   3. _____

C. IF DEBTOR IS A CORPORATION, PARTNERSHIP, ETC., SPECIFY: _____

D. PROMISSORY NOTE or CONTRACT BEING SUED UPON:
   1. Date & Original Amount of Notes: _____
   2. Date & Amount of scheduled first payment: _____
   3. Amount Debtors have paid to date, exclusive of late charges: $ _____
   4. Late Charges paid to date: $ _____ ; Other Charges, specify: $ _____
   5. Date and Amount of LAST PAYMENT MADE: amount: $ _____ Date: _____
   6. Name and Address of Seller (Dealer): _____
   7. Date of Assignment to you from Dealer: _____
   8. DUE DATE OF DELINQUENT PAYMENT: _____
   9. If due date (#8) different from Agreement please indicate reason for change: _____
   10. Date interest paid through (if interest included through maturity of Note and/or Contract, please so state): _____
   11. GROSS UNPAID BALANCE NOW DUE, exclusive of late and other charges: $ _____
   12. Please specify if V.S.I. or Lienholder's Single Interest Insurance included in Gross Unpaid Balance; if so, amounts: Premium: $ _____ +Fin. Chg:$ _____ =$ _____
   13. NET PAY-OFF AMOUNT, exclusive of late charges: $ _____
   14. Date Pay-Off Amount good through (DATE OF REBATE): _____
   15. SPECIFY AMOUNT REBATED: _____
   16. Late Charge Now Due: $ _____

E. EXECUTIONS:

	#1	#2
1. Banks, Savings & Loans &/or Credit Unions		
Names on account as reflected on Signature Cards:		
Bank Name & Address:		
Account Number		
2. Automobile		
Year, Make, Model:		
License & I.D. No.:		
Registered Owner/s as reflected per DMV:		
Location of Automobile:		
3. Salaries and Commissions:		
Debtors being executed upon:		
Employer's Name:		
Address of Employer:		
Debtor's Soc. Sec. No.:		
Employee's Position:		
Employee No.:		

   4. Real Property (Attach Lot Book Report):
   Street Address: _____
   Legal Description: _____
   Record Owners (exact names) and their addresses _____

   Is Property Homesteaded? _____
   Does you want tenant's (occupants) rent garnished: YES _____ NO _____
   If available, please give tenants' names and apartment number _____

   5. OTHER EXECUTIONS (Personal Property, Escrows, Keepers, etc.): _____

   6. OTHER INFORMATION (Foreclosed Security, etc. If security valueless, give specific reasons why, etc.?): _____

G. DOCUMENTS REQUIRED FOR COMMENCEMENT OF SUIT:
   1. Original Notice and/or Contract, plus 1 clear copy.
   2. Original Guaranty, plus 1 clear copy (front and back).
   3. Original of Security Agreement/Chattel Mortgage, plus 1 clear copy.
   4. Description of Property to be claim and Delivered, i.e. Certificate of Ownership, plus 1 clear copy.
   5. Credit and/or Loan Application.
   6. Copies of all Financial Statements.
   7. Assignment, if separate form Contract.
   8. V.S.I. Policies and/or Declaration Pages.

FOONBERG & FRANDZEL, A Law Corporation
8530 Wilshire Blvd., Fourth Floor
Beverly Hills, California 90211
Telephone No.: (213) 659-2611

San Francisco Office
433 California Street, Ninth Floor
San Francisco, California 94104
Telephone No.: (415) 421-0726

J-12
Practicing in a Law Suite to Get
Clients and Cases by Referral From Other Lawyers

A law suite may be a good way for the solo practitioner or small firm (up to five or six attorneys) simultaneously to get legal work and to reduce occupancy costs.

By definition, a law suite is a large office where many attorneys practice. These attorneys may be sole practitioners or they may be small firms, but they are not the tenants of the owner of the building. They are subtenants or licensees of the prime tenant and they share the cost of reception, conference rooms, library and common areas through their rent charges.

Often, as many as 50 lawyers practice in a single law suite. There are many advantages to practicing law in this arrangement from an administrative point of view. (If you are interested in the cost savings aspect of practicing in a law suite, I recommend that you read the chapter entitled "Practicing in a Law Suite" in my book "How to Start and Build a Law Practice", published by the American Bar Association.)

I shall concentrate here on the client or case getting aspects of practicing in a law suite.

A. *Referrals in Legal Specialty or Niche Areas Where You Have Expertise or Want to Acquire Expertise.*

Before moving into (or not moving into) a law suite, try to meet as many of the tenants as possible. Ask them what kind of law they practice and tell them what kind(s) of law you practice. Ask them frankly to whom they now refer work of the type you are practicing. Ask them if they would consider referring any of that type of work to you if you moved into the suite. Ask them how long they have been in the suite and how long they expect to remain.

You may find you have a specialty or niche area of law that no one in the suite has and that you could get a lot of work from the other lawyers in the suite. You might even decide to acquire new expertise to be able to get the referral work from the other lawyers in the suite.

Referrals are also based on work overflow. You may find that your areas of legal expertise are not at all unique vis-à-vis the lawyers in the particular suite, but that the lawyers (or some of them) are very busy and would like someone nearby to handle the overflow work from time to time.

B. *Cash Fees.*

If you are a new lawyer or a lawyer with a serious cash flow problem, you may be able to pick up some quick cash by doing hourly work for the other lawyers in the suite. Typical examples are attending depositions, making routine court appearances, doing research, writing trial and appellate briefs, etc.

C. *Referral Fees.*

If you are the kind of person who can generate a lot of legal work, but don't want to (or can't) handle all of it yourself, a law suite may give you the opportunity to refer the clients and cases to the "specialists" in the law suite with you and to receive a referral fee from them. Not only will you receive fees but also the client will be well served. You'll be able to easily drop in on the referred lawyer without prior appointments to get updates, status reports, etc., and be conversant with the client as to the status of the case should you continue to have social or professional contact with him or her. You, of course, should understand and carefully follow your jurisdiction's rules on referral fees. One law suite operator told me that the suite had received an ethics opinion stating that the lawyers in the suite could hold themselves out as partners or as "of counsel" to one another on referred cases and could therefore ethically share the fee without the necessity of informing the client in writing of the fee division. Since everyone in the suite had the same address, it was simply a matter of printing up the appropriate stationery and complying with the laws and rules applicable (including malpractice insurance requirements). Be sure to check local rules before doing this.

D. *Back-up Expertise in New Legal Areas.*

Often you are exposed to a situation where a case appears to be an excellent one from all aspects, but you are a little uncertain about your ability to undertake it for fear that, as the case develops, you won't have enough expertise. Having the backup available to you in the form of another lawyer(s) in the suite with expertise (one either associated into the case or merely available) gives you the capacity to accept the case. The back-up lawyer(s) can either be associated into the case, be a consultant, be of counsel or be partner(s) for the one specific matter, in accordance with your local rules.

E. *Vacation Coverage.*

A semi-retired lawyer once told me that he picks up extra money by agreeing to cover for other lawyers in his suite when they took vacations by handling their emergency calls. He told me that he charged a basic weekly rate plus a nominal hourly rate when he handled the other lawyers' incoming calls and emergencies. The vacationing lawyers left with a free mind knowing that client emergencies would be covered and that new cases would not go to other lawyers through their absence. The covering lawyer made good, quick money and everyone benefited.

There are some disadvantages of this arrangement from a client relations point of view which should be considered.

Disadvantages to Practicing in a Suite.

Inconsistent Practices. Although other lawyers in the suite having different types of practices will be good for you, their clients may adversely affect your practice. If you have conservatively dressed, higher-income clients, they may not feel comfortable in the same reception room with workers' compensation or personal injury clients who are dressed in their work clothes and who drag along their children because they can't afford babysitters. Your clients, not realizing that these are the clients of a different lawyer, may question the type of practice you have. (The reverse may be true in that your personal injury or workers' compensation client may not feel comfortable in a room with conservatively dressed tax and business clients.) The solution to this problem obviously is not to allow your appointments to linger in the reception area. Get them into your office or a conference room as soon as possible.

Reception Room Periodicals. There is another chapter in this book about the effect of reception room periodicals on your clients. Reception room periodicals should be reflective of the kind of practice you have or want clients to think you have rather than the practice of other lawyers.

Receptionist Indifference. The receptionist in a busy law suite won't be able to leave her (his) post and won't be able to bring soft drinks or coffee to your clients. Often there is no telephone available for another attorney or your client to use to make an outside call while waiting to see you. The receptionist may refer clients to the public phone at a gas station down the street. (This actually happened to me and soured me for many years on law suites.)

Malpractice Insurance. Ideally every lawyer or firm in the suite should indicate in their client retainer agreements that the other lawyers in the suite are not professionally responsible for the client's matter. This clause in retainer letters should be mandated as part of the master lease between the suite operator and each of the attorneys.

Evening and Weekend Access. Office access for the attorney's personnel to work or for seeing clients may be a problem due to lack of security or the lack of lighting or air conditioning. This is a problem with all law offices and not just suites.

Paul Fegen (pronounced, "FEE JIN") is the pioneer in the concept of the law suite. It is to his credit that the law suite is also known as the Fegen Suite. Paul and I are contemporaries. I have known him since he first began his concept in Beverly Hills, California, where his headquarters are now located. His company, and others, now rent to thousands of attorneys throughout the United States. I would recommend that any attorney considering the opening or the relocation of offices contact Paul before making a move. If Paul has nothing in your city, he'll recommend someone else. By visiting Fegen Suites, you'll have a rough idea of how low your occupancy cost per attorney can be and what kind of cases, clients and fees may become available to you.

J-13
Photocopying Settlement Checks and Judgments

Paul Luvera of Washington State is an excellent trial lawyer for whom I have the highest professional and personal regard. I visited his office and saw enlarged photocopies of many million dollar and over settlement checks framed on his walls. I thought this was remarkable, since a million dollars was a lot of money at that time. I was favorably impressed. Since that time, I've heard of other attorneys who regularly send copies of settlement checks and verdicts and judgments to clients, other attorneys and others. Some attorneys display these blown-up copies on the walls of their reception rooms, conference rooms and personal offices. Some attorneys make scrap books of them and leave them in the reception areas. Some attorneys include these items in their newsletters and firm brochures.

I personally have no experience or feedback on the effectiveness of this technique. My own personal objection to this technique is that the attorneys who do it use their clients' names in the ads. Obviously, this is permissible if the client fully gives permission. Without the permission of the client, this seems to be an improper violation of the attorney-client privilege. If I remember correctly, Paul had a note from the client next to the photocopy, indicating that the client not only gave permission but was extremely pleased with the hard work done by Paul on the case, thus recommending both Paul's professional skills and professional ethics.

J-14
Simplified General Description of
Marketing Committee or Marketing Director

Every law firm has to have someone in charge of the marketing effort. Solo practitioners are in charge of their own marketing, whether or not they want to be. In a small firm, one of the partners should be in charge. In a larger law firm there can be (and often is) a marketing committee. Some firms hire non-lawyers to be in charge of marketing.

Although there are many ways to describe what has to be done in marketing, it usually includes the following "basics":

1. Identify the services the firm can provide.
2. Identify additional services the firm wants to provide (include new or expanding areas such as hi-tech law or elder law or health care law) as well as traditional areas not yet provided by the firm.
3. Identify the general market for those services.
4. Identify the specific potential clients for those services (qualified leads) .
5. Teach marketing skills and procedures to everyone in the firm and reinforce them.
6. Stimulate referrals from existing clients and non-clients who refer clients.
7. Make initial contact with the potential clients.
8. Make a presentation (subtle or direct) to the potential clients.
9. Negotiate how and at what prices these professional services can be provided.
10. Close the deal (get the first work from the new client).
11. Manage the relationship at all times to ensure additional new work and additional new referrals.

The above represents *what* the persons in charge of marketing have to do. This book can help those people by offering specific techniques for doing it.

J-15
Consider Relocating to Get Clients

A few years ago, I did some research for the State Bar of California in my capacity as Chair of the New Lawyers in Practice Committee.

I accidentally discovered that there are states which don't have enough local law school graduates to fill the legal needs of the community and which, therefore, must "import" lawyers.

These states were:

Alaska	Nevada
Arizona	Nebraska
Colorado	New Hampshire
Delaware	New Jersey
Hawaii	North Carolina
Idaho	North Dakota
Indiana	Oregon
Louisiana	Rhode Island
Maine	Wisconsin
Mississippi	

These (or other) states may be worth looking into as a possible place in which to relocate.

Professor Rick Rogers in his North Carolina Start Your Own Law Firm (NCSYOLF) course at Campbell University helped new lawyers and young alumni successfully start law practices in under several communities by analyzing the economic activity of a county per lawyer rather than the population per lawyer. He analyzed sales, bank deposits, real estate values, real estate sales, payroll, etc. to determine which locations were best for a lawyer to begin a practice. The same system on a larger scale can be used by larger firms.

J-16
Small Town and Rural Practice Development

Although I theoretically live in a "small town," (Beverly Hills population 32,000) my small town is in a megalopolis of several million people (Los Angeles). The Beverly Hills Bar Association has more than 4,000 lawyers so, theoretically, we have about one attorney for every eight people.

Not having practiced in a true small town myself, I can only repeat here what I've heard other lawyers suggest as successful practice development techniques and problems.

A. Shop and buy in your local community. If you go to the big city to buy your new car or stationery, don't be surprised when the car dealer or the printer go to the big city for a lawyer.

B. Accept the fact that you live in a fishbowl. Everything you see and do will be observed by someone you know or who recognizes you. Your social relations will be observed.

C. Don't be arrogant. If you're originally from that town or if you're the only lawyer, people will go out of their way to help you to succeed. They want you to "make it." Everyone in town is your potential client. Be respectful and grateful and appreciative even though they bring you small cases and cases you really don't want. If you are rude or arrogant or haughty toward them or their cases, they'll spread word of it throughout the entire community.

D. Be involved in local politics, civic organizations etc. As a lawyer, this role is expected of you. If you don't participate, people will think you're haughty or aloof.

E. Be very careful about preserving client confidences (this includes your spouse as well).

F. Develop your skills at turning conversations at social events into paying office visits. (See Chapter M-23 on this subject.)

G. Be tolerant of "drop-in" and "walk-in" clients who don't bother to make appointments. This is more common in smaller communities than in larger ones.

H. Be prepared to barter your services for other goods and services. (See Chapter M-19 on Barter.)

I repeat that these are tips passed on to me by small town lawyers.

J-17
Choosing or Changing Your Firm Name

There are many reasons why one might want to change firm name.

Many of the largest corporations in the world change their name.

It is my recommendation that your firm name(s) should either reflect what you do or who you are. Note that I said names the plural not name the singular.

Many states allow fictitious names and/or professional corporation or LLP names. Thus an individual lawyer (Mary Smith) could be on the firm letterhead of AB&C as Mary Smith, LLP. This allows the individual lawyer to get and use their own individual web site, e-mail address, URL, etc. Mary Smith can simultaneously market both her firm and herself. Accordingly, if Mary Smith leaves the firm, whether by her choice or the firm's choice, she will have her own book of clients within the firm. The extent of her book of clients of course may be a factor in her decision or the firm's decision to part company or not part company.

There can be valid reasons for wanting to change a firm's name.

A fictitious name describing your practice: Delaware Lawyer, Divorce Lawyer, Accident Lawyer, Aviation Lawyer, etc., may be preferable to using your name (John Jones, etc.) for any number of reasons.

If you are over the age of 50 or at any age where you might someday wish to sell or "cash out" you probably can maximize the price you get with a fictitious name. The clients will be used to dealing with the fictitious name even though a different lawyer may be delivering services.

You may wish to not publicize that you are a sole practitioner or small firm by not using lawyer's names in the firm name.

If someone in your firm has been disbarred or you wish to disassociate yourself from that person, or persons, a new name may be just what you need.

My favorite law firm name is "4 Bitches From Hell." That's really the firm name. I can only imagine the law they practice.

You of course must check out what is permissible under local rules and may have to comply with the same fictitious name laws as any other enterprise using a fictitious name.

J-18
Historical and Ethical Prohibitions
Against Marketing of Legal Services

There are many different theories which try to explain the historical prohibitions against marketing. To some degree all of the theories are probably correct depending on the time and place of the prohibition.

In America prohibition against advertising and marketing were imposed by Bar Associations on systems which previously allowed advertising.

A few minutes of history will be beneficial. The Roman Empire included most of what is now Western Europe. In the Roman legal systems what we would now call the practice of law was divided between advocates who went to court and notaries who processed many transactions including real estate, companies, wills, etc. Today we would say "trial lawyers" use the court system and office lawyers do the work that does not involve litigation. This system still exists in some civil law countries. The word "advocate" signified "being called." The advocate who went to court had to be called by the client or by a notary. The advocate could not go out and seek work. The word advocate stems from the Latin, advocare – to call out for help.

In English legal practice, the advocate became known as the barrister and the notary became known as the Solicitor. Again, as in Roman Law, the Barrister who only went to court had to be "called" by a solicitor. The Barrister could not accept clients directly (called direct access), but had to accept clients and cases only from Solicitors. This system still exists in some degree in Commonwealth Countries (formally called the British Empire). This system also protected the trial practices of the Barristers who typically were from wealthy families.

When the United States revolted against England, most of the lawyers were loyalists and left the United States. The new nation desperately needed lawyers to write the laws and to do the legal work of a rapidly expanding nation and economy. The new American Lawyers did both court work and transactional work and they advertised in newspapers to inform new markets of immigrants and other new arrivals of their availability. Abraham Lincoln and other lawyers advertised.

Before and immediately after the US Civil War, lawyers became lawyers without going to law school. They "read the law." Abraham Lincoln did not attend high school, college or law school. He "read the law."

Bar associations began being formed in the late 1800's. Most if not all were elitist. They excluded women lawyers, lawyers of color, lawyers who were not from wealthy or influential families and lawyers who had not attended "approved" law schools.

Whether Bar Associations were simply trying to protect their turf or upgrade the profession can be debated indefinitely.

The original American Bar Association canons of ethics did not prohibit either advertising or solicitation. These prohibitions were added by the American Bar Association and other Bar Associations in the early 1900's. Again, one can debate whether they were trying to protect turf or upgrade the profession. The Bar Associations were able to get their rules adopted by courts and legislators in order to punish those who broke rules. It is an interesting phenomenon that the Bar Associations were able to govern the conduct of lawyers who were denied membership in the Bar Associations. Advertising and solicitation were even declared to be criminal conduct as Barratry and Champerty. Lawyers were criminally prosecuted and convicted for advertising and soliciting.

In the landmark Supreme Court case of Bates adv. State Bar of Arizona in 1977, the rules against advertising and soliciting were struck down.

Currently, a few bar groups still regulate advertising and solicitations.

I have long predicted that all forms of advertising will be permitted and should be permitted so long as they are truthful. Many years ago I predicted that the restrictions on lawyer advertising, lawyer marketing, or lawyer availability were unnecessary restrictions on the public's right to know of the availability of legal services. Subsequent decisions of the United States Supreme Court and of various state courts have vindicated my position.

From professional calling cards, to television commercials, to the internet, advertising is simply a matter of degree. The old line conservative firms that used to cream "Ambulance Chaser" at every new marketing development now spend millions of dollars on internal sales staffs, media advertising and promotion, consultants, and all the staff, institutions, and methods one would find in the marketing of beer or cigarettes or used cars. Some law firms are reported to spend as much as 10% and more of receipts on marketing.

There will always be debate on whether a method of advertising is "tasteful" but the prohibitions against marketing and advertising are now essentially ancient history.

J-19
Never Let the Sun Set on a Non Returned Phone Call

Returning phone calls promptly gets you happy clients and more business. Failure to promptly return phone calls is a major source of client dissatisfaction and client complaints to bar ethics committees.

An ABA research project found that 83% of satisfied clients said their lawyer returned telephone calls promptly. Only 42% of dissatisfied clients said their lawyer returned phone calls promptly.

"Promptly" to a client means 2 hours. They expect a return call within 2 hours. The call can be from anyone in the office. The receptionist or a secretary or assistant can return the call to the client. He or she can explain that you are still out of the office and can ask the client, "Is this an emergency?" "Can I help you?" "Can anyone in the office help you?" The client will be happy that someone returned the call even if it wasn't you.

The person returning the call can make a "telephone appointment" with the client., setting up a time for you to call or be called and a telephone number for the call. The person returning the call can offer or get an e-mail address if the client is agreeable to e-mail contact when it is more efficient than telephone contact.

Often the office person can offer "Mr. Foonberg does check his voice mails if you would prefer to leave a voice mail."

The Office person can then call you on your cellular phone if you are available and you can sometimes return the call from your cell phone.

Lawyers generally have a bad reputation for returning telephone calls. I know of one law firm whose yellow page ad and professional cards carried the slogan "We return telephone calls promptly." They said this got them work from clients who were unhappy with their current lawyers.

It is important that your policy and system on returning telephone calls be explained to the client at the first meeting or first opportunity so that they don't have unreasonable expectations. Sometimes I jokingly tell a client "I first promptly return calls of the clients who promptly pay their bills." Clients get the point.

J-20
Voice Mail System

Voice mail systems can be a valuable asset in satisfying clients and keeping them happy. They can also result in anger, frustration and looking or a new lawyer.

Voice mails have replaced the old fashioned answering machine. A major difference is that the old answering machines were only used when the office was closed. During office hours a caller got a live person to help. Many older clients (including executives in major businesses) expect a human voice when they call during regular office hours.

I personally know of one company that gave out millions of dollars in legal work that changed lawyers because the first law firm stupidly insisted on the voice mail system being used. The company was a multi million dollars in fees client. The new law firm, as part of the engagement, gave the Vice President, Legal a special number, just for him that was answered via a live human being. The telephone line probably cost them $15/month, an investment that resulted in millions of dollars of legal fees.

A voice mail can never replace a live person when the client needs a lawyer immediately or when the subject matter of the call is personal or embarrassing.

Many lawyers hide behind voice mails, not accepting any calls. These people are easily identifiable because they call back a few moments after you leave your name and number and message.

Poor voice mail systems may save you pennies on receptionists and cost you dollars in lost business when the potential client calls another law office where they can get a human to help them.

I personally highly recommend a live person answering incoming calls. Alternatively I like a system which answers "You have reached the law office of Jones and Smith. You may speak with an operator at any time simply by dialing "0".

Voice mails should be cleared by you or someone else before going to lunch and before going home for the day.

I know of one horror story where the voice mail of a lawyer continued to take messages for 3 weeks after the lawyer was dead and buried. No one was checking his voice mails.

I personally like voice mails that recite the day and when the person will return calls with an option to dial another number if immediate help is required. This alleviates the concern of the caller that the attorney is out of the office on vacations for two weeks.

Call yourself from outside the office and listen to what other people hear when they call you.

A good voice mail system keeps clients happy. A poor system will drive the client or potential client to another lawyer or firm out of frustration with your system.

J-21
Get A Star Receptionist And Give Him Or Her The Tools To Do A Super Job

Your receptionist is your ambassador to the whole world. He or she is often a client or potential client's first impression of you or your firm. A good receptionist makes callers feel welcome and that they have chosen the right law firm. A poor receptionist can and does alienate and anger clients and potential clients to the point they go elsewhere.

Lawyers who hire a receptionist based on cheap and then give the receptionist time wasting tasks like stuffing or addressing envelopes are making a serious mistake.

Call your own firm and listen to the receptionist. Do they mumble the firm name incoherently and "brush off" the caller? Do they leave people on hold so long they fall asleep holding on and wondering when, if ever, someone will talk to them?

Give your receptionist a list of the clients who often call and how they spell and pronounce their names. People like to hear their names pronounced correctly and get angry when their names are is pronounced. Clients expect the people to know how to spell their names no matter how complicated the name might be. They get upset when they are cross examined repeatedly on the correct spelling of their name. Tell your receptionist its better to spell out a client's name phonetically on a message than to cross examine the client. On the other hand the receptionist should not hesitate to ask for a telephone number and repeat it back to the client. The receptionist can say "I'm sure Mrs. Jones has your number but if you'll give it to me gain, I'll put in on the message and she can get back to you more easily.

A receptionist who sounds bored, tired, non caring or who actually alienates a client should be counseled and if necessary replaced.

No lawyer or firm can afford the hiring or keeping of a poor receptionist. I would not allow the receptionist to have a cell phone, internet access or a TV. I have seen many instances of law firms' receptionists ignoring incoming calls to finish their personal cell phone conversations or surf the net or switch TV channels.

Chapter K
Bombarding Your Clients With Paper

K-1
Always Have Professional Cards With You

Always carry a professional card with you. Not having a professional card is a "turn off." Not having a card is a message to other people that you really don't want them to contact you with their legal problems. Always keep one card with your driver's license. Rarely do you not have your driver's license with you. This "emergency card" will bail you out when you forget your card case.

If you really don't have one with you, you can make light of the neglect (you must attack the perception that you don't care) by saying something like, "A professional card is like an umbrella: when you need one, you don't have one. And when you do have one, you don't need it." Offer to write out your information on the back of their card. People have given me the address portion of an unused check. Offer to send them one of your cards at a later date and then DO it.

My wife always has one of my cards in her purse. When appropriate, she recommends me to people she meets or knows. If I truly don't have a card with me, I often say, "I've given out the last card I had with me (you didn't say when you gave it out, which might have been months previous), Lois, (my wife) do you have one with you?" and she always does.

I was amazed when I asked a touring barrister from Barbados for his card. He informed me that barristers don't have professional cards because barristers would be considered advertising or soliciting if they had a card. Some time later, I needed some legal help in Barbados and couldn't remember his name. I ended up with a different lawyer from the one whom I had met and whom I would have preferred. The message should be obvious. Don't be surprised if you don't get called by the person to whom you didn't give a card.

K-2
The $55,000 Bar Association Handshake
(More Than $100,000 in 2007 Dollars)

In 1988 I did a marketing seminar for the Montgomery County Maryland Bar Association at Rockville, Maryland.

A lawyer came over to me at the intermission and related the following story:

"Mr. Foonberg, I heard you speak in Washington D.C. at Georgetown University in 1976. You told us that whenever we go to a bar association meeting or service club meeting or any professional meeting we should turn to the person on our left and shake hands and give them a professional card and then turn to the person on our right and shake hands and give them a card. I immediately started doing this and I shook hands and gave my card to a woman lawyer from Alexandria, Virginia at a meeting of the D.C. Bar about 30 days after your program. Six months later the phone rang and it was the attorney from Alexandria. She needed an attorney in Maryland and my card was the only card she had readily available from any Maryland attorney. I got the case. I earned a $55,000 fee on that case and I've gotten several referrals over the years by giving my card and shaking hands with the professional on my left and the professional on my right any time I go to a professional meeting. Thank you for your suggestion."

This attorney then told me that he had come to hear me speak several times over the past 12 years at American Bar Association meetings. I then asked him why he waited so long to tell me about his success when he'd had so many opportunities. His answer was, "I was afraid you'd ask for a referral fee."

Other lawyers have related similar results from introducing themselves and giving a card to the person on the immediate left and on the immediate right and shaking hands. No other attorney mentioned any specific fee figure, but the time and effort are slight and the returns good for the little investment of a card and a few moments.

I highly recommend this technique to you. The object of this story should be obvious. People can't use you if they don't know you or know of you and where to find you.

PRESS THE FLESH and give them a card!

Additionally, ask for one of theirs and put the information from their card into your database.

K-3
What Should Be on Your Professional Card?

A. Basic Information to Put on Calling Card.

There are four things that should be obvious and prominent on your calling card:

1. Your Name. Spencerian Script or Gothic Lettering may be beautiful, but may be difficult or impossible for an older person or a foreigner to read. Use block letters for your name or else repeat it elsewhere on the card in block letters. You do want people to be able to call you or write you by name.

2. Your Legal Profession. People may keep your card because you're a lawyer, even though they forget your name. When they periodically discard old cards, they may still keep yours, remembering absolutely nothing about you but keeping your card because it's a lawyer's card. Accordingly, I personally don't care for descriptions such as "counselor" or "counselor at law" or "advocate." I have had people ask me the difference between being a lawyer and being an attorney. I personally recommend that the words "Lawyer" or "Law Office" appear prominently on your card, even though you personally prefer and want to list some other title such as "attorney" or "counselor." If you are incorporated, I recommend not using the abbreviation "P.A." (Professional Association), as people may believe that stands for "Public Accountant." If you are a "P.A." spell it out. The use of "Inc." or spelling out "Professional Association" is better, and I personally think that the term "A Law Corporation" or LLC or LLP is best.

3. Your Phone and Fax Numbers and Email Address. Your phone and fax number, including domestic and international area codes, should be prominent as people are likely to contact you initially by telephone when they need a lawyer. Many doctors and lawyers put their telephone numbers in extremely large type that is easily read by their nearsighted, middle-aged and older clients. You may wish to have a client usage cell phone number as well.

You'd be amazed how many lawyers omit their area code. If you have a direct dial or extension, use it to help people access your voice mail.

4. Your Address. This should include city and state. I have seen many cards with no city or no state indicated. I frankly can't understand why any lawyer would omit the complete address where one could write to his or her offices, but I've seen many lawyers who seem to assume that "the whole world knows where Main Street is," and that a city or state is not necessary. Add your email address and web site URL. The purpose of a card is to give people a way to contact you when they need you.

B. Mechanical Production of Professional Cards

1. Never lose sight of the fact that the best use of your calling card is its being kept in someone else's wallet or desk, or on a bulletin board for the convenience of people who might need your services. The information may also be entered into their database. I recommend cards engraved on a thin, high-quality stock. Thick cards are simply too bulky to be kept in a wallet, and people just toss them out. The card definitely should fit

in your wallet. If it doesn't fit in your wallet, it probably won't fit in anyone else's wallet either, and will be discarded. Accordingly, thick cards, oversized cards and irregularly shaped cards (square or circular or in the outline of a courthouse) may be artistically clever but don't accomplish the purpose intended, which is to serve as a constant reminder of your availability and to be retained by your client or potential client. I have seen cards printed on plastic, wood, fiberglass, metal and various other materials. These cards may or may not cause the recipient to remember you, but I don't think the more sophisticated consumers of legal services are "ready" for this avant garde form of professional card, but more importantly, people don't put such cards in their wallets or keep them where they are readily available.

2. Printing. As indicated, I am a strong supporter of engraved cards. Avoid flat press (it looks like you can't afford better) and avoid the type of raised printing where the letters can be scratched off with your fingernail. This kind of process creates a fear in people that the ink might dissolve and ruin other papers in their wallet. Accordingly, the card gets thrown away rather than getting placed in their wallet.

3. Artistic Designs on Cards. I have seen many "artistic" designs on cards, such as scales of justice, a courthouse, a judge on the bench, a gavel (a retired judge I know serves as an arbitrator and has printed on his card "Have Gavel; Will Travel"), law books and even a face behind bars. I have seen several cards with a photo or sketch of the law building where the lawyers practice or even of the lawyer. I personally don't recommend these designs on cards because I believe they detract from the information you want to convey, that is, name, address and phone number, and the fact that you are a lawyer. On the other hand, the lawyers who use artistic cards tell me that clients, potential clients and others comment favorably on the designs because it makes the cards stand out by being different. The lawyers tell me that potential clients call them long after getting the card and say, "I kept your card because I liked the picture on it. It was different. I need a lawyer." I can only suggest that you might experiment with a few "cutesy" cards of various designs and see what kind of reaction you get from clients or potential clients. If you are afraid this kind of card will alienate or offend existing clients, then give them only to non-clients. If you offend a non-client, you won't lose much.

C. Foreign Languages.

In California where I practice, it is not uncommon for cards to have both sides printed. One side is in English and the reverse side is in a foreign language, typically Spanish, Japanese, Chinese or Korean. I once had cards printed in Hong Kong with all the information on one side in Chinese. I depleted the cards. Years later, people still refer to me as the lawyer with the Chinese cards. They were very impressed and obviously kept the card and remembered me. I stopped using Spanish language cards because of the wide variations in the terminology, depending on whether the person was American Hispanic, Mexican, Argentine, etc. Try a few and see what the reaction is.

D. Other Things You Could Put on Your Cards.
1. Web Sites

2. Fax. If you have a fax number, you can show it. We have one but it is rarely used. While the fax number looks good on the card, we find that overnight express services and email attachments do the job just as well in almost all cases.

3. E-mail address. Put your e-mail address on your card to show your efficient way of doing things and to allow 7/24 written communication.

4. Calendar. I have seen attorneys put out calendar cards like stationery stores give out. For obvious reasons, a new card is sent every year.

5. Miranda Warnings. I have seen criminal lawyers' cards with Miranda Warnings printed on them along with instructions on what to do if arrested.

6. Other local or international office affiliations.

7. Fees for routine cases. I've seen cards where the lawyers advertise their fees for specific routine cases such as traffic offense, divorce and accident cases.

8. Professional designations and degrees (in the name line). An example would be:
   JOHN DOE, AB, JD, CLV, CPA, MAIA, etc.
   ATTORNEY AT LAW.

9. Lawyer's photo. (Don't ask me why or if they are successful. I just know that some lawyers have them on their cards.) They tell me clients like being able to connect a name and a face. Some use it because people can associate a name with a face.

10. Legal holidays.

11. Specialty areas of practice.

12. Map on how to find the office.

13. Instructions on what to do if in an accident.

14. Specialty areas of law or areas of law in which you want cases. (Be aware that you may be "turning off" a client who thinks that you or your firm only practice that indicated area of law.)

E. Substitutes for Cards.

I've seen lawyers use other substitutes such as note pads with the lawyer's name and address, and index card-sized cardboard note cards with the lawyer's name and address. I'm not in favor of these substitutes because, typically, the client or potential client can't fit them into the wallet.

F. Consider using more than one card.

I have used two different professional cards and several other cards. One card indicated I was a board certified specialist in taxation and I used this one for people who want or need a tax lawyer. My other professional card omits reference to my tax specialty to avoid the connotation that my firm only does tax work. I also have other cards which indicate my affiliation with various trade associations in which I am involved. I use these at trade shows and meetings of the association and when appropriate.

G. Future Trends.

I predict that in the near future a lawyer will be able to put anything he or she wants to put on a card, so long as it's truthful.

K-4
Use Your Card to Communicate that You're a Lawyer

People can't use you as a lawyer or refer legal work to you if they don't know you're a lawyer. They also can't use you as a lawyer or refer legal work to you if they can't remember your name.

Your card is in many cases the best way to quickly tell people you're a lawyer and also to have your name remembered as a lawyer.

Your giving out professional cards is similar to the legendary Johnny Appleseed's planting apple trees. Only a few of the trees survived, but those that did gave good results. On occasion, people will use you years later when they come across your card.

Use your calling card as a form of scratch paper in the following situations:

A. When someone asks you for directions, make a map on the back of your card and give it to them.
B. When someone asks for a phone number give it to them on the back of your card.
C. When someone asks how to spell something, write it on the back of your card and give it to them.
D. Give one to someone else to use for scratch paper.

You don't have to say you're a lawyer: our card will say it for you and you will have communicated it in a proper way.

As one lawyer told me, "If you don't want to be called on don't raise your hand." Giving a card is one way of raising your hand to be called on.

K-5
How to Start a Conversation and Present Your Card Without Appearing Pushy

Whenever you travel or meet people, you should make an attempt to start a conversation. It doesn't cost anything. Depending on the circumstances, conversation may be a welcome respite from an otherwise monotonous passage of time. Make it a point to mention that you are a lawyer. Somewhere in the conversation the person may ask your name. Complain that noise is a problem and show the person your name on your professional card. Alternatively, you can simply say it and hold out your card to the person, who will probably stick it in the shirt pocket or purse.

The chances are 99 in 100 that the person will never contact you. However, that once in a hundred opportunity does happen, and sooner or later you will probably get some legal business from somebody who took your card. I've gotten some minor legal work in this manner.

From the point of view of time invested and dollars received, it probably is not a worthwhile activity deliberately to engage in conversation to get clients. However, if you are otherwise an outgoing person, you should somehow work into the conversation that you are a lawyer and get your card to an available position where the other person can take it if he or she wishes Always present your card with two hands and receive other cards with two hands to comply with common courtesy practice world wide.

If you don't know how to start a conversation, a good way is to comment on an article of clothing or jewelry the other person is wearing. "That's an interesting tie (or purse or ring, or what ever) you have." The other person will almost always want to tell you about it.

K-6
What to Do With The Professional Cards You Receive

It is more important to collect cards than to give out professional cards. These cards can be part of your marketing database. If you can do so unobtrusively, you should jot down on the card the date and place you collected the card. (Or else do so after you've been separated from the card's presenter.) These cards can be filed together in various types of available card files and they can be entered in your database, added to your mailing list and used for a follow-up letter. In time, you'll get some business out of one of these cards you've collected.

Immediately after collecting a card write when and where & the name of the event where you obtained the card. Doing so will eliminate finding cards in your wallet or purse which cannot be identified.

A sample letter I received from the partner in charge of the Los Angeles office of a large international CPA firm is as follows:

Dear Jay:

It was a pleasure meeting you and Mrs. Foonberg at the home of the Consul General last week. I would be pleased to get together with you for lunch to discuss how we might work together to our mutual profit.

If you would like to get together, please ask your secretary to contact mine so that we can clear a date.

My best to Mrs. Foonberg.

Sincerely,

You can also send a firm brochure or a letter describing the kinds of legal services your firm provides.

A sample letter could be as follows:

Dear Mary:

It was a pleasure meeting you
-at the Bar Meeting
-at the trade show
-at the Jones' party
-on the flight from Chicago
-at the reception

I am enclosing a
-firm brochure
-firm letter

which we use primarily for our recruiting and for our existing clientele. You may find it interesting. You may also wish to visit our website at www.Lawyer.com.

If you would like to get together, please ask your secretary to contact mine so we can clear a date.

If we can be of any help to you here in the Los Angeles area, please let me know.

Sincerely,

Jay G Foonberg

Enclosure: Firm Brochure

You must send the letter within a few days of meeting the person or they will forget who you are.

These letters are "long shots," but they are cost and time effective because your secretary can do everything without your doing anything more than giving the card to her when you return to the office.

Alternative letter after receiving a card:

Dear Mary,

I enjoyed meeting you at the Bar Association Luncheon (or whatever) last week. I have added your name to our VIP mailing list and from time to time we will be sending you information which you may find useful.

I am enclosing some information about our firm. If I can be of help to you or your clients please let me know.

Sincerely,

Jay G Foonberg

I recommend sending a letter rather than an email. Emails often are filtered out or deleted.

K-7
Why Clients Like to Get Letters and Information From Lawyers

In another chapter, I have greatly expounded the importance of "bombarding your client with paper." In this chapter I want to give some examples of what clients have told me:

I sometimes jog in the mornings at a local track. One of the men whom I met while jogging is the president of a multi-million dollar oil company. He told me about a litigation matter for which he is spending $75,000 per month in lawyers' fees (2007 Dollars). His conversation with me ran along the following lines:

"Jay, I really like my lawyer. He sends me copies of all memorandums of telephone calls and all correspondence in and out. He sends me a letter once a week outlining what he has done during the preceding week. I am a very busy man and I am often out of town. My schedule is so busy that I have very little time to talk to him by telephone and even less time to meet with him. I accumulate his letters to me and I read them on a plane or whenever I have a few free moments. His letters and memos allow me to keep abreast at my convenience of what is happening on my case. I do not always understand the specific details but I get enough information. As a matter of fact, I don't even know whether he is doing a good job as a lawyer, but I am happy."

A few days later, I was buying gas and the station owner and I got into a conversation. When he found out I was a lawyer he started telling me about his big case involving the lease to his gas station. He told me why he liked his lawyer. His conversation went something like this:

"I really like my lawyer because he sends me letters telling me all the things he is doing for me. Jay, I'm not too educated, but I'm not stupid. Sometimes when there is a meeting, I'm too embarrassed to tell him that I really don't understand what he is talking about. When he sends me a letter, I take it home and I study it in my den. I can read it and re-read it slowly until I understand it. The technical language goes by me too quickly on the telephone. When I read his letter in the privacy of my home, I can write down the things I still don't understand and then ask him about them. I don't know if he is good or not but he was highly recommended by some mutual friends and I like his letters."

Both of these businessmen liked the lawyers' letters because they were given an opportunity to read them carefully "at their own convenience" and to keep abreast of the case. Your clients may also need your letters to allow them to keep current at their own pace and their own convenience.

A widow once related to me, "Jay, since my husband died, I don't sleep well. I often get up in the middle of the night. I take your letters to the den and read them and re-read them and understand them."

Many clients have told me they don't always read the letters I send them, but the letters reassure them that their matter is not languishing or has not fallen into the cracks.

Even if you send your clients email, there's no harm in sending them a copy of the email by U.S. Mail. Emails do get filtered out, lost and misdirected and the client will normally appreciate the follow up. (Provided you don't charge them for the postage or delivery charges.

The moral of this chapter should be obvious. Send your clients lots of letters, lots of information which they can read and re-read at their own convenience. These letters can be recorded and billed as "status reports," and they are guaranteed to make your clients happy.

K-8
Tell Your Old Clients About
Your New Services and New Personnel

There is no such thing as too much communication with your current and former clients. "Every time you communicate with them, you are telling them you care about them".

When you add someone to your staff who has expertise in a new area of law, or when you have handled enough of a certain type of case to feel especially competent in the area, you can send a letter to your client list informing them of your new area of law or new staff person.

These letters are generally good from a client relations point of view and may even result in the referral of new work in the new area(s) described in your letter.

An example follows:

Dear Clients and Colleagues:

1.   I am very pleased to announce the association of Attorney Mary Smith to our practice. Ms. Smith is a graduate of Harvard University and of UCLA Law School. Prior to her association with us, she did extensive work in the area of personal injury litigation from both the defense and the plaintiff's side. Ms. Smith's abilities and experience enable us to expand our services to you in the litigation field.

2.   We have recently done equipment leases for several clients who are buying equipment in their own name and then leasing the equipment to their corporations. This technique allows the individuals to take the tax advantages of the investment credit and the depreciation on their personal returns. In view of the apparent new interest in this type of transaction, we thought you might be interested in knowing of this technique. These leases are very technical and require very special drafting to comply with the tax laws. Please let us know if you are interested in these equipment leases.

3.   We have recently done several divisions of community property for married clients, including a transfer of ownership in the family home. These new steps are now possibly desirable due to a new law. In this manner, it is not necessary to use up all the community property or sell the family home when there are, or may be, large nursing home bills.

Please let us know if you are interested in this new area of estate conservation.

4.   We have recently assisted several clients with the purchase of fractional jet ownership and aircraft ownership. If you would like to know more about this expanding area of aircraft ownership, you may wish to visit our website at: www.fractionaljetownership.com.

5.   We are pleased to announce that Ms. Mary Jones has joined us as a legal secretary/assistant. Her knowledge, along with our new computer systems, make it possible for us to provide more rapid production of legal documents to give our clients faster, more accurate documents. Ms. Jones comes to us with 12 years' experience. We are pleased to have her with us.

6.   A change in zip code or area code or email address is a good excuse for making a communication to a client. I suspect some lawyers change an email address at least once a year to create a client communication.

Very truly yours,

Jay Foonberg

LAW OFFICES
OF
JAY G. FOONBERG
8500 WILSHIRE BOULEVARD
PENTHOUSE
BEVERLY HILLS, CALIFORNIA 90211

TELEPHONE (213) 555-5050
TELEX 91-4855 (CAL USA LAW)
TELECOPIER (213) 657-5078
CABLE ADDRESS: CAL USA LAW
MAIN (800) 4CAL LAW
456-NET 466

December,

To Our Clients and Colleagues:

A law firm is more than just lawyers. It is a team of people each of whom is vital and important. The days of one lawyer with one secretary, a typewriter and a few books delivering legal services is about gone. To deliver superior legal services in a cost and time efficient manner requires technical equipment and skilled people. The traditional typewriter and secretary have been replaced with word processing equipment and people. Our team includes good people skilled in word processing, communications, operations, receptionists, archivists, librarians, accountants, and a myriad of other specialities necessary to deliver high quality cost efficient legal services.

This year we are departing a bit from tradition and recognizing these people who are so important by name on our annual Seasons Greetings card. We hope that you appreciate the gesture.

In any organization, a client may only know some of the people in the organization. Over the years, many of you have not had the opportunity to get to know some of the lawyers in the firm. Therefore, we are taking this occasion to tell you a little bit about each lawyer on our team.

The firm, as you may know, is rated "a v" by Martindale-Hubbell Law Directory. This is the highest possible rating for legal ability and reputation by other lawyers. We are sometimes known as "lawyers' lawyers" because of the high recommendation we get from other lawyers.

As most of you know, we are a full service firm, emphasizing business and tax law and business litigation and other litigation. If you need a super-specialist in any area, we will help find the right one for your case.

As some of you may already know, I went to UCLA undergraduate and graduated from UCLA Law School in 1964. I

---

am licensed both as CPA and as an attorney and am certified as a specialist in taxation. The bulk of my own activity is devoted to business law, tax law, business litigation and tax litigation, and also some areas of international law. My particular hobbies are jogging and scuba diving, with an occasional ski trip. I can communicate in Spanish and Portuguese, when necessary, to help our clients with problems in Latin America.

Sheri ___ is a native of Denver, Colorado, and has been with the firm for three years. She graduated from Pitzer College of the Claremont Colleges undergraduate and Southwestern Law School in Los Angeles. The work which she does with the firm is primarily corporate and business and she does much of the document and agreement drafting and review. Sheri's hobbies are writing and aerobics. Sheri and her husband Marc are expecting their first child momentarily.

Mark ___ is a graduate of the University of California at San Diego and of California Western School of Law in San Diego and has been with the firm for two years. Mark's areas of concentration are litigation and international law. He is fluent in French, having lived and worked in Paris for two years, and he has served as an Assistant Legal Adviser with the International Energy Agency (O.E.C.D.). Mark's hobbies are racquetball, music, and the study of political science.

Shahen ___ has been with the firm for one year. He speaks Armenian fluently and is a graduate of the Armenian Mesrobian School in Pico Rivera. He received his law and MBA degrees from DePaul University in Chicago, and previously was with the international and tax departments of Laventhol & Horvath's Los Angeles office. Shahen is very actively involved in the tax and business practice of the firm. Shahen's hobbies include writing and racquetball.

Jay ___ is of counsel to the firm. This means that he works only on particular cases. At present, he is spending much of his time in a major litigation matter involving Indian Law which is now before the Claims Court of the United States and ultimately the Supreme Court of the United States. Jay is also an expert on Travel Law and the author of a soon-to-be-published book in this area.

Jay is a graduate of the SUNY at Stony Brook, New York, and has his MBA and JD degrees from UCLA. Jay's hobbies include skiing, sky diving, and karate.

Les Chayo has left the firm for solo practice in Los Angeles. We sincerely wish him success in his first experience as a solo practitioner.

The firm remains unwaveringly committed to its policy of the highest possible quality of legal practice for the business and general community. We will continue to expand our areas of practice and personnel as necessary to serve the needs of our clients.

All of us wish to thank you for your continued trust and confidence. We thank you for the new clients you recommend to us and we thank you for allowing us to help you with your legal needs.

We wish for all of you a healthy and happy New Year.

Sincerely,

Jay G. Foonberg

JGF:kc

K-9
Press Releases

I have never personally used press releases. Over the years, newspaper and TV publicity to the general public has not yielded me any worthwhile clients. Most of the people who have contacted me as a result of newspaper or TV publicity have been the kinds of people who seem to come out when the moon is full or people who want free legal advice by telephone. Accordingly, I have not gone out of my way to attract more of these people.

On the other hand, it is possible that for some lawyers and some law practices, press releases can serve a useful means of image building and client getting. Certainly they don't cost much and they can reach a lot of potential clients if published in the right places.

The writing of a press release requires some journalistic skill, whether already possessed or to be acquired. I am told that the two magic phrases to appear on a press release are:

1. "Press Release"; or
2. "For Immediate Release" (although I've never seen anything in a press release that couldn't wait a few days).

Some lawyers post on their website and send to clients copies of "Press Releases" which were prepared by the lawyer but which were never in fact sent to or published by any newspaper. They feel the client will be impressed by the fact that the lawyer sends press releases. Perhaps the client believes someone is printing the press release, thereby establishing the lawyer as being an expert or as being newsworthy.

I don't pretend to be an expert on this subject. My personal preference has been to avoid the cost in time and money of putting one or a series of them together. I have had a few lawyers tell me that the money and energy spent on press releases were of little, if any, measurable value. No lawyer has ever mentioned to me getting good clients through press releases. I am sure that some lawyer, somewhere, has benefited from press releases, but I have never heard from that lawyer.

If you wish to try press releases, I encourage you to get the help of a competent professional public relations firm in preparing and distributing the release. I would also appreciate hearing from you about your experiences, good or bad.

Samples are shown on the next pages.

The Los Angeles Daily Journal

Wednesday, December 23.

Profile

Who was that masked man?

Well, if you've just come from a seminar on how to start your own law practice, the answer may be Jay Foonberg, a 46-year-old Beverly Hills attorney and accountant who has written one of the few books extant on establishing law practices.

Foonberg has this penchant for dressing up — but not exactly in a tie and tails. He's been known to show up at bar association-sponsored seminars all around the country dressed as an Arab, a Chinaman, or an English barrister complete with wig and robe.

"It's kind of hard not to notice me," Foonberg said in an interview last week. "It's very effective."

Also effective are the stories Foonberg, who admits to trying to entertain his seminar listeners, tells to illustrate his points.

Stories like the one about the pioneer attorney who traveled west to find the best place to establish his practice but ended up dying defending the Alamo. (Moral: "There's more to this world than just making money.")

Or the one, repeated in his book, "How to

FROM THE DESK OF

Jay G. Foonberg

Dear Clients & Colleagues,

Being featured in this column is a special honor, and I thought you might be interested.

Jay

Jay Foonberg

Start a Build a Law Practice," about how he and his wife were the only ones at a baby shower not bearing a gift. The reason was that Foonberg had arranged for the baby's adoption.

"I stated that I couldn't say anything about the new baby because I couldn't disclose a client's confidence," Foonberg wrote. "Over the years, I've gotten a lot of business and a lot of referrals from the people at that party and that couple. If my friends had doubts about my professionalism before this episode, the doubts were over afterward."

When he tells the story on the seminar circuit, Foonberg adds a punch line: "And I saved the cost of a baby gift."

"This is something I learned by doing 150 (or) 200 programs," Foonberg said last week. "I have heard very bright men who are more intelligent than I, maybe men who are more intelligent than I, maybe men who are more knowledgeable than I, get up and give a very informative talk. Nobody remembers the first thing they said.

"I find that by being somewhat of an entertainer — by giving emphasis, by use of props, costumes — that people will remember what I say."

A Large Crowd

The people who remember Foonberg are becoming an increasingly large crowd.

Foonberg estimates he delivers two or three free lectures — he asks seminar sponsors only for the cost of his trip — each month or 30 to 40 each year for the last 13 years. A spokesman for the American Bar Association, which distributes Foonberg's book and keeps all the proceeds for two of his sections, estimated some 14,000 copies have been sold — with sales particularly brisk just after his seminars.

The seminars have taken Foonberg to some 45 states. He has a wall full of plaques and letters of appreciation in his cluttered office to prove it. His practice — primarily business and international law — also takes him away from his office, and he lists the government of Brazil among his clients.

Foonberg had just returned from the Bahamas where he represented one of the promoters of the Muhammed Ali-Trevor Berbick boxing match ("The Drama in Bahama") the day before the interview last week. And he was set for a trip to Las Vegas the next day.

Although Foonberg travels throughout the world and lives in a Beverly Hills manse previously owned by the likes of Betty Grable, Harry James, and Edgar Rice Burroughs, his life hasn't always been this way.

Horatio Lawyer?

In fact, to hear Foonberg tell it, his life has been a sort of Horatio Alger, attorney-at-law, story.

His father was a bankrupt immigrant Jewish butcher and his mother a secretary, and the family was very poor.

How poor were they?

Well, they were so poor that while Foonberg studied accounting at UCLA in the early 1960s, he had to spend part of each Monday, Wednesday, and Friday and all day Saturday working as a clerk in a Mexican delicatessen in Grand Central Market in downtown Los Angeles because there was a lot of Spanish and German-speaking people, he said.

And it also led him to play cricket — because he had to find a sport he could practice on Sunday.

The end result, he explained, was a healthy interest in things international.

Foonberg said he majored in business ("by default") because counselors told him that "at least you can get a job" in that field.

He spent about four years working as an accountant, "and then one day I realized I didn't like accounting.

Thought Lawyers 'Not Competent'

Foonberg did some of his accounting work for the state Board of Equalization and often came into contact with attorneys.

"Very frankly I felt that lawyers then were not competent in the tax area," Foonberg said. So, thinking he could do better than the attorneys he met, Foonberg entered UCLA law school.

After he passed the California bar exam, Foonberg said he was offered a good job with an established law firm but turned down the offer to start his own practice.

His experience in successfully developing his own firm, which broke up about three years ago, provided part of the material for his book, written and first published in 1976. Most of the rest of the material came as a result of questions and suggestions offered during the many seminars he began speaking from 1968 on.

Foonberg at first could not find a publisher and had 1,000 copies printed at his own expense. Once he made back his approximate $2,000 investment in book sales, Foonberg was able to persuade the ABA to take over distribution.

The first seminars were offered by the California Association of Attorneys-CPA's (certified public accountants) organization. In 1968, Foonberg said, "it was a new organization, and we were thinking about what we could do for the organized bar and a group of us said, 'Why don't we put on a program on how to start and build a law practice?'"

Subsequently, in 1972, Foonberg noted, the American Bar Association formed its economics of law practice section. (The section and the ABA's law student division are the beneficiaries of the proceeds of Foonberg's office management section, and Foonberg was the first full-term chairman. He has also been chairman of the ABA's new lawyers committee for about 10 years.)

'Creative,' 'Dynamic'

Lawyers familiar with Foonberg give generally favorable comments, describing his work and his lectures as "creative" and "dynamic."

"I don't think there's any doubt about the worth of the book," said an ABA official.

One law office, a management expert criticized the book as a series of "truisms," but another had high praise for Foonberg.

"I have cited it along with other books for students to take a look at," he said. "Some people might say that he's an egomaniac," the lawyer said, but "I think he did that book in a sincere effort" to help new attorneys.

The same lawyer also praised Foonberg for devoting "an awful lot of time and attention to trying to help young lawyers" in his seminar appearances.

Another attorney praised Foonberg as an innovator, noting he was one of the first to install and design a computer system in his firm.

Foonberg said he did not feel he was an egomaniac but admitted "there's a very fine line between self-confidence and arrogance. . . . I try to be self-confident."

The Breakup

The amount of time Foonberg has devoted to his seminars may have led to the breakup of his law firm, Foonberg & Frandzel, some three years ago.

"I paid a very high price" for spending so much time out of the office, he said. Since then, Foonberg spent some time with a Century City firm and then moved on to a new law school.

Foonberg's role in the firm is what he calls "the very highest form of law — "issue-spotting" — and then leaves it to associates to do what is necessary to solve the problems.

And he continues his trips away from his office — trips that have helped him become "a walking encyclopedia of information that nobody else has" by being able to listen both to questions and fellow lecturers.

Foonberg doesn't claim to have invented everything in his book, and there are a few other books on law office management. One of the others, published in 1976, is also by a local attorney, Gerald Singer. The books contain similar information and were published the same year, leading some observers to wonder whether either author derived material from the other. There are, however, some significant differences between the two books.

Hardcover Book

The Singer book, "How to Go Directly Into Sole Practice (Without Missing a Meal)," is published in hardcover by a national law book distributor and is formally divided into sections similar to a book of statutes.

Foonberg's book is nothing but reprints of a typed manuscript with illustration in advanced slick figure style. The writing is much more informal.

And while Singer advocates such things as appealing weak cases in order to earn interest, and telling clients that attorneys can force a settlement on them, Foonberg's book regularly points up ethical considerations.

"The lawyer and client stand in a fiduciary relationship," Foonberg said. "I think it's extremely important to be an ethical lawyer."

Foonberg also believes there has been a decline in the general level of competence of lawyers, partly attributable to what he agrees is a glut of new attorneys. He adds that even lawyers who have been in practice, for example, for five years may only really have two or three years of experience because they have been underemployed, he said.

Foonberg is currently considering publishing a new book on marketing lawyers. He also may be updating the law practice book, including the addition of new chapters on advertising.

Advice to Students

And what would an expert on making money practicing law tell students considering a legal career?

"I would tell them a law degree is no guarantee of a job," Foonberg said. Only those from name law schools or those ranking very high in their classes will have an easy time, he added.

In fact, in a preface to the book, Foonberg tells new lawyers that if they look upon their license to practice law simply as "a ticket to making money," they are not likely to succeed.

"To succeed in the long run, the practice of law requires a deep and sincere dedication to helping people. With proper management, the economic rewards will follow the rendering of high quality legal services," Foonberg wrote.

"There are more lawyers than we need," he said. But for "the lawyer who cares about human beings . . . it's a wonderful, wonderful profession. You get self satisfaction out of it . . . and you can also make money at the same time."

For Foonberg, apparently, the rewards have been great. "Everything I have I owe to the fact that I am a lawyer," he said.

And the time spent on the book and lectures are "my way of putting some of it back" into the profession.

—MILT POLICZER

LAW OFFICES OF
FOONBERG & CHAYO
PENTHOUSE

TELEPHONE (213) 652-5010
TELEX: 67-4253
TELECOPIER (213) 652-5019

8500 WILSHIRE BOULEVARD

BEVERLY HILLS, CALIFORNIA 90211

CABLE ADDRESS: CALUSALAW
WATS (800) 4-CALLAW
ABA NET 1428

September 11,

Dear Clients and Colleagues:

RE: Decoration from Brazilian Government

I am honored to relate to you that on September 7 of this year, the Brazilian National Day, the decoration known as the "Order of Rio Branco" (Ordem De Rio Branco) was delivered to me by the Brazilian Consul General to Los Angeles, Ambassador Joao Paulo do Rio Branco.

This award is normally given primarily to Brazilians. Only fourteen were given to foreigners, including myself. This is a rare recognition. The award was given for my services to the Brazilian Diplomatic Corps and my services as the President of the Brazil-California Trade Association and as the organizer of many seminars on doing business with Brazil.

I am most proud of this award which comes twelve years after the award of the "Order of the Southern Cross" which is the highest award Brazil can give to foreigners. I believe I have the rare distinction of being one of the few people if not the only person in the United States to be so twice decorated.

I wish to thank all of those colleagues, clients and other individuals who have worked so hard over the previous 15 years in increasing the flow of trade, technology, tourism and good will between Brazil and the West Coast of the United States.

Sincerely,

FOONBERG & CHAYO

Jay G. Foonberg

JGF:dh

K-10
How to Create Business and Keep Clients Happy When You Read Advance Sheets and Technical Journals

I spend about an hour a day reading advance sheets and journals for the following reasons:

1. To be a good lawyer by keeping current on the law.
2. To make money.
3. To impress clients that I care about them and their legal matters.

I read the journals with a red pen or felt-tip in hand. When I find an article or new case that affects or may affect a case in the office, I circle it and write the case name and client name on the face of the journal, as well as the page number where the materials can be found. I then prepare a letter. (You can do it the next day at the office; or, if like me, you read advance sheets at home, on airplanes or during commuting, you can use a portable machine to dictate the letter immediately.) I also enter the letter on my time records. I normally bill for the letter when I bill for other work and rarely get a complaint. Usually the client is happy to pay, knowing that I am continually aware of his or her case or problem.

A sample letter follows.

K-11
Sample Letter With Advance Sheets

Ms. Mary Jones
123 Main Street
Hometown, USA

Re: Jones vs. USA USDC Case
        Smith vs. USA decided May 15, 20XX

Dear Ms. Jones:

I am enclosing a copy of the decision of the Second Circuit Court of Appeals in the case of "Smith v. U.S.A." This case was decided on May 15 and was just reported in the May 25th issue of the Daily Journal. A copy of the case is enclosed for your files.

The facts and legal issues of the Smith case may have an effect upon your case. The case was decided by the Second Circuit Court of Appeals in New York. We are in the Ninth Circuit here in Los Angeles, but nonetheless the Department of Justice (the trial lawyers for the government) will be aware of the case and it may affect the Judge's decision in your case.

You will note that one of the principal issues in the Smith case is the principal issue in your case (e.g., deduction of travel expenses for spouses).

No response on your part is necessary. We thought you would appreciate receiving this information.

Very truly yours,

I do not separately send a bill for this letter, but I do record the letter in my time records and do put a copy of the case in the client file. When I bill for other work. I will also bill for the letter.

K-12
Sending Copies of Clients' Mailings and Correspondence to Potential Clients and Potential Recommenders of Clients

A. *MASS MAILINGS:*

When I send a mailing to clients, I often include an extra copy for them to forward on to another person.

For example, when I send a tax newsletter in November of each year, I often send two newsletters with the following statement:

"We are enclosing an extra copy of this newsletter for you to pass on to your accountant or tax advisor."

Sometimes I get a call from a CPA along the following lines: "Old Joe is a client of mine and sent me a copy of your newsletter. I've got another client who has a problem which you've covered in your newsletter and I'm recommending him (her) to you."

Sometimes the client will pass the extra copy on to a friend or business associate or competitor, who will subsequently call you for legal work because the competition or friend recognizes your expertise or ability in the field.

In addition to tax letters, we sometimes send out letters relative to new case decisions or laws concerning insurance or tort liability. In this case we will state:

"We are enclosing an extra copy of this letter for you to pass on to your insurance advisor for his (her) opinion as to whether any charges are necessary in your insurance coverage or your contract forms."

Of course you can expand the fact situation as you wish as to which "advisor" you wish to include a copy for.

By suggesting that the client send a copy to an advisor, you accomplish the following:

1. The client may consider that you are the appropriate advisor in the legal area and contact you for legal work.
2. The advisor will be grateful (if he/she gets a copy or sees a copy) that you are not trying to shortcut or "end play" the advisor.
3. The client will not react to the letter as an attempt to solicit work.
4. The client may pass the copy on to yet another person or business who may contact you.
5. The client's advisor may recommend a client to you.

Mass Mailings should be "faxable, xeroxable, and scanable," for easy copying by a recipient who wants to send a copy to someone unknown to you.

B. *CLIENTS' CORRESPONDENCE:*

When applicable, it is a good technique to send copies of correspondence to your client's advisors. By doing so, you are communicating your ability to do work in a given area. This communication can serve the dual purpose of advising your client's advisor as to your client's activities and getting referrals from the advisor. You will also be able to ethically add the client's advisor to your mailing list for newsletters, sessions laws, etc. Maintaining these mailing lists is not difficult and is especially easy using client relations or contact databases.

Sample advisors are: accountants, bankers, insurance agents and brokers, stockbrokers, trust officers, real estate brokers or agents, pension plan administrators, physicians, etc. The list is endless, depending on the kind of legal work you're doing. Always keep in mind that the client's advisors are potential clients and potential referrers of clients.

C. *WILLS:*

When you do a will for a client, you should ask the client if it's all right to notify the beneficiaries and executors of the fact that their names appear in the client's will without being specific as to amount of inheritance.

If the client gives you permission to do so, your letter of notification becomes, in effect, a recommendation from the client to use you for wills and estate planning.

Each of the above three areas is simply a way to expand your client base using your existing clients' correspondence as the "door opener."

D. *E-MAILS:*

I normally have some hesitancy about routinely sending copies of correspondence concerning legal matters by e-mail unless the client first assures dissemination of the information is not a problem.

When written correspondence is mailed "personal and confidential" there is a reasonable expectation that only the client addressee will open it and either keep it or destroy it. Email is accessible to many people and almost impossible to easily completely destroy or delete. On the other hand, it is easy to send an email with a "click here" to forward a copy to another person unknown to you.

LAW OFFICES

FOONBERG, JAMPOL & GARDNER

A PARTNERSHIP INCLUDING PROFESSIONAL CORPORATIONS

JAY G FOONBERG*
ALAN R. JAMPOL*
DAVID B. GARDNER**
LESLIE E. CHAYO
NOLAN F. KING
CHRISTOPHER POLK
*A PROFESSIONAL CORPORATION
**LICENSED AS A SOLICITOR IN ENGLAND

8500 WILSHIRE BOULEVARD
SUITE 900
BEVERLY HILLS, CALIFORNIA 90211
TELEPHONE (213) 652-5010
FAX (213) 652-5019

LONDON ADDRESS
14-15 FITZHARDINGE STREET
MANCHESTER SQUARE
LONDON, W.I. ENGLAND
TELEPHONE 01-936-3651

To: Clients and Colleagues

Re: New Tax Law

The new tax law could have more effect on the net profits and the taxes and the cash flow of small businesses than any law passed by Congress in the last 25 years.

On August 12, the President signed the new Income Tax Law. This law creates major changes for owners and managers of small businesses. Every small business owner or manager should be familiar with the new provisions that apply to them in their business or personal life.

We suggest that you read the materials and circle the parts you don't understand and ask your tax advisor how they affect you. You should consider sending a copy of this letter and the materials to your accountant, your CPA, your attorney or whoever you use as your tax advisor. It has been squeezed in to save space for printing.

We have written these very technical materials in plain English whenever possible which creates the risk of over simplification and possible misinterpretation. Accordingly, you should check with your tax advisor before taking action especially with respect to the effective dates of the particular sections you are concerned about. The numbers and dates which are in the materials are for the benefit of your advisors so that they can find the law.

Please feel free to call or have your tax advisor call if you have any questions. Mary Jones helped me prepare parts of the material and can also help with your questions.

Again we wish to stress that these materials should be read immediately while you still have time to decide between this year and next year.

Sincerely,

FOONBERG, JAMPOL & GARDNER

Jay Foonberg

LAW OFFICES
FOONBERG, JAMPOL & GARDNER
A PARTNERSHIP INCLUDING PROFESSIONAL CORPORATIONS

8500 WILSHIRE BOULEVARD

SUITE 900

BEVERLY HILLS, CALIFORNIA 90211

TELEPHONE (213) 652-5010

JAY G. FOONBERG*
ALAN R. JAMPOL*
DAVID B. GARDNER**
LESLIE E. CHAYO
NOLAN F. KING
CHRISTOPHER POLK

*A PROFESSIONAL CORPORATION
**LICENSED AS A SOLICITOR IN ENGLAND

LONDON ADDRESS
14-15 FITZHARDINGE STREET
MANCHESTER SQUARE
LONDON, W.I. ENGLAND
TELEPHONE 01-936-3651

NEW TAX LAWS THAT AFFECT
THE EQUIPMENT RENTAL INDUSTRY AND
OTHER BUSINESSES AND INDIVIDUALS

A. Outline Format

    This outline is in 5 sections.

    1.   New tax laws that specially affect the equipment rental industry. (Pages 4 through 10.)

    2.   New tax laws that affect businesses generally. (Pages 11 through 17.)

    3.   New tax laws that affect individuals in their personal (non business) income taxes. (Pages 18 through 20.)

    4.   New tax laws that affect estate and gift taxes for individuals. (Pages 21 through 24.)

    5.   New tax laws that affect sales (and purchases) of rental centers. (Pages 25 through 26.)

    B.   Action Required.   You should read the entire outline. I've simply organized the materials in this manner for presentation.

    C.   Outline Date.   This outline was prepared for the California Rental Associations Annual Convention in Sacramento on October 20,   and the materials are believed to be current as of that date. As with any new law it will take several years until all regulations and interpretations are issued. I have omitted most technical references to make the materials more readable.

    D.   Authors Qualifications.   Attorney at Law, California admitted to U.S. Supreme Court, (1968) ; Tax Court and Supreme Court of California (1964). Certified Public Accountant, California (1962); Board Certified Specialist, Taxation, California Board of Legal Specialization 1975, recertified 1980; Legal Counsel to California Rental Association since 1964. Rated "AV" by Martindale Hubble (highest possible rating for an attorney) 1975.

Page 2

LAW OFFICES
FOONBERG, JAMPOL & GARDNER
A PARTNERSHIP INCLUDING PROFESSIONAL CORPORATIONS

JAY G FOONBERG*
ALAN R. JAMPOL*
DAVID B. GARDNER**
LESLIE E. CHAYO
NOLAN F. KING
CHRISTOPHER POLK
*A PROFESSIONAL CORPORATION
**LICENSED AS A SOLICITOR IN ENGLAND

8500 WILSHIRE BOULEVARD
SUITE 900
BEVERLY HILLS, CALIFORNIA 90211
TELEPHONE (213) 652-5010
FAX (213) 652-5019

LONDON ADDRESS
14-15 FITZHARDINGE STREET
MANCHESTER SQUARE
LONDON, W.I. ENGLAND
TELEPHONE 01-936-3651

January 6,

To: All Clients and Colleagues

Re: 1. New Tax Law
        2. London Seminar
        3. Your Will
        4. Special Enclosure

Our office has prepared an analysis of the new Tax Law including an analysis of the Estate and Gift Taxes as well as the Income Tax changes. If you wish a copy of the analysis, please return the stub at the end of this letter.

Your Will may be obsolete as of next January 1, due to new estate tax laws. We most strongly recommend that you contact your tax adviser concerning a new Will. The Will should take into account the new tax laws and your current situation.

There are also significant areas in the estate and gift tax laws. You should be aware of the following:

1.   Spousal Gifts and Bequests - There is no tax on gifts or bequests to a spouse.

2.   QTIP Trusts (Qualified Terminable Interest Trust) – You can leave property to a trust with your spouse getting the income during his/her lifetime and others receiving it at their death. There is no estate tax on the death of the first spouse.

3.   Tax Free Gifts - You can give $12,000.00 per donee, per donor, per year with no tax consequences.

4.   Gifts and Bequests to Non-Spouses (After the $12,000.00 annual exclusion) - The unified credit is being increased over a period of years so that eventually a $1,000,000.00 on estate could pass tax free to non-spousal beneficiaries.

5.   Tax Rates - Are being decreased over a period of years.

NOTE: This letter has been modified to eliminate references to specific dates and amounts.

LAW OFFICES
FOONBERG, JAMPOL & GARDNER
A PARTNERSHIP INCLUDING PROFESSIONAL CORPORATIONS

January 6
Page Two

The above are simply highlights of estate and gift changes in the New Tax Law. If you and your spouse have a net worth of $500,000.00 or more (including your residence and life insurance) then you probably need a new Will.

P.S. We are proud to enclose an article printed on December 23, Los Angeles Daily Journal concerning the public interest work of Mr. Foonberg. We are also enclosing an article concerning the activities of our firm in a tax and investment seminar in London in February.

For those of you who missed our seminar of October 19, at the Beverly Wilshire Hotel, we have prepared the transcripts on the sections concerning doing business in Latin America and new techniques in real estate financing as well as professional corporations and Indian title claims.

If you or your tax advisor have any questions, please feel free to contact Mary Smith or Jay Foonberg.

Sincerely,

FOONBERG, JAMPOL & GARDNER

JGF:yo

- -

Foonberg, Jampol & Gardner
8500 Wilshire Boulevard, Suite 900
Beverly Hills, California 90212
U.S.A.

_____ Please send me your analysis of the new tax laws which went into effect January 1.

_____ Please send me the transcript of the seminar on new laws held on October 19, at the Beverly Wilshire Hotel.

_____

Name

_____
_____

Address

www.Foonberglaw.com

LAW OFFICES
OF
JAY G. FOONBERG
& ASSOCIATES
8500 WILSHIRE BOULEVARD
PENTHOUSE
BEVERLY HILLS, CALIFORNIA 90211

JAY G. FOONBERG
MARK E. FINGERMAN
SHAHEN HAIRAPETIAN
SHERI J. RAPAPORT

JAY A. ZVORIST
OF COUNSEL

TELEPHONE (213) 652-5010

March 4,

TO: All Members of BCTA

RE: Visit of Mayor Tom Bradley to Brazil

        I had hoped to deliver this report to you at the meeting
of the BCTA on the 1st, but the meeting schedule didn't work
out and accordingly I am writing to you. Unfortunately, I
shall be meeting in Florida with the President of the American
Bar Association as a member of the new Inter American Affairs
Commission of the American Bar Association on the 15th of
March, the new meeting date.

        I recently had the honor and privilege of accompanying
the Honorable Thomas Bradley, Mayor of the City of Los Angeles,
on his Trade Mission to Brazil. The purpose of the Trade
Mission was to stimulate trade between and through the Port of
Los Angeles and Brazil. The Mayor, two Port Commissioners,
and two of the Port Executives went at City expense, and I
travelled at my own expense in order to assist in the Trade
discussions.

        Although Mayor Bradley's purpose for the Trade Mission
was to stimulate trade, there were some political aspects in
view of Mayor Bradley possibly becoming a future Governor of
the most powerful state of the United States. Several
Brazilian authorities also felt that Mayor Bradley could
possibly be a future Vice Presidential candidate.

        This was Mayor Bradley's first visit to Brazil and
accordingly, I was able to assist at various times during the
Trade Mission. Although technically I was accompanying the
Trade Mission in my capacity of Advisor for Latin America for
Dr. March Fong Eu, the California Secretary of State, I did my
best to also represent BCTA at every function as the Vice
President for Special Projects.

www.Foonberglaw.com

LAW OFFICES

OF

JAY G. FOONBERG

& ASSOCIATES

BCTA
February 25,
Page 8

and California and trilateral trade between Brazil, California
and Asia.

If any of you have any questions, please don't hesitate
to call me or write.

Sincerely,

Jay. G. Foonberg
Vice President
Special Projects

JGF/gdl

Enclosures:
1. Photos at Itamarity, Brasilia
2. Photo at Federation of Industry at State of Sao Paulo (FIESP)
3. Photo at Portobras, Brasilia
4. Photo at American Chamber of Commerce Special Luncheon Meeting,
   Sao Paulo
5. Photo at Varig Lounge at LAX
6. Estado de Sao Paulo, p. 25, October 5,

Mayor Bradley at Itamarity in Brasilia with Port Commissioner Heim, Ambassador Paulo Tarso da Flecha Lima and Jay G. Foonberg, B.C.T.A.

Mayor Bradley in Sao Paulo at FIESP

Meeting at Portobras, Brasilia

Meeting at White Hose with Presidents of Brazil & United States and Their Cabinets

Table of Contents

Readers are invited to submit original articles of a technical nature on legal subjects, as
well as to draw our attention to material published elsewhere that would tend to serve our
readership.

www.Foonberglaw.com

How to Advise Your Client Who Wants To Do Business With the Peoples Republic of China

By Jay G Foonberg *

I am going to speak this morning on how to advise your client who wishes to do business with the Peoples Republic of China. This address is based upon my experiences in three trips to the Peoples Republic of China during the last year, as well as discussions I have had with people now doing business there.

As many of you know, my principal area of international trade has long been with Brazil, and to a lesser degree, some of the Pacific Basin countries such as Hong Kong and Australia. The opportunity arose last year to be among the first group of American tourists ever to be allowed into the Peoples Republic of China. I seized upon the opportunity to visit the most recently opened of the Pacific Basin trading area countries. At the same time I was asked to give some assistance to the Brazilian government personnel in Peking who were themselves constructing a guide and doing business with China.

I shall in this speech try to give you a forty to forty-five minute overview of the situation you can expect to find. Obviously, I cannot in that time condense and distill the approximately five thousand pages of material I went through and

the hundreds of hours I spent.

I wish to caution you that developments are occurring on a daily basis and some of the information I will give you can change rapidly based on new political or economic decisions reached in Washington or Peking.

Chinese Names

If you or your client are going to do business with the Chinese people, you should learn something about Chinese names. What we would call the first name is actually the last name or family name. For example. Chairman Mao Tse-tung has the family name of Mao and not the family name of tung. Dr. Sun-yet-sen is Dr. Sun and not Dr. Sen.

It is also common to hear or be referred to as "Comrade". You may find yourself referred to as Comrade Smith rather than Mr. Smith. You properly should call the person with whom you deal by the first title of "Comrade", whether they are male-or female.

You should talk to your interpreters, guides, translators, and business counterparts as "Comrade Wong" or "Comrade Cheng". This will show your respect for them and their system. If however, you want to call them Mr. and Mrs., it will be acceptable to them.

Non-Statisticals

I am not going to bore you with statistics of how many metric tons of soy beans or cubic feet of some commodity or other were imported or exported during the fiscal year. I don't think you are really interested in or care about general statistics on general trade, nor do I think you will remember the numbers.

---

* *Principal, Slavitt, King & Foonberg, Beverly Hills, APC, California. The text is from a speech given by Mr. Foonberg before the California Society of Certified Public Accountants, the American Association of Attorney / CPAs and the French / American Chamber of Commerce, lastly on November 8, 1978. Since that date, President Carter has announced the recognition of the Peoples Republic of China and the intended opening of an Embassy in Peking on March 1, 1979. In addition, some of the matters predicted herein, such as the Boeing 747 transaction referred to, have recently occurred.*

4

K-13
"For-Your-Information" Letters, Emails and Faxes As "Products"

As I will continue to emphasize, clients love to receive paper mail, faxes, and email from lawyers. They will save everything they get. You should encourage them to maintain a duplicate file on their case. Every time you communicate with clients, you are telling them you care about them.

The communications they receive from you is to them a PRODUCT; the "thing" you sell, the tangible personal property they can identify with. Every time you send them a piece of mail or any form of communication you are communicating that you care about them and their legal matter. When they get your bill, they will know that you have been working hard on their matter because they will have received lots of mail from you.

Sometimes your communication to the client doesn't justify in your mind a formal letter, or you may not want to charge for a cover letter what you would charge for a formal letter. In those cases, you can use a "for your information" letter. A typical situation is a letter with fewer than 25 words one or enclosed with another document.

"For your information" letters are cheap to print up in advance or as needed and you can charge for them as "correspondence to client" with a standard charge equal to your minimum time segment of 1/6 or ¼ hour, depending on how you record time.

The exact format of your letter will depend on your practice. You can start off with a form like the one I've designed and then revise it after a couple of months. You can have them printed very inexpensively at a local instant printing or office copy shop or you can do it in-house.

You can set them up in your fax program and your email program. You can send the letters as email attachments in addition to making a copy. (The copy is to provide the client with something tangible to touch.)

Remember to note the sending of the letter on your time records, both to create evidence of your having notified the client and also to have a record for billing purposes. If you feel awkward about including this on your time record, then have your secretary keep a record for malpractice and billing purposes. If you prefer to charge a standard fee such as $15 or $25 per email or letter rather than a time unit, then you could do so.

If you wish, you could also use the for your information form letter as the basis of instructions to the word processor to send out a formal letter on formal office stationery to impress the client.

The important thing is to use the emails, faxes and letters on a routine basis to communicate with your clients.

A sample form follows with numbered comments for your consideration.

(1)

LAW OFFICES OF
JAY G FOONBERG
8500 Wilshire Blvd, Beverly Hills, California
(310) 652-5010
Jay@Foonberglaw.com

TO: _____

_____

_____

ATTN: _____

FOR YOUR INFORMATION

(2) Date _____

File Name _____ File # _____

(3) Enclosed is a copy of

_____ Correspondence from _____ Dated _____

concerning _____

_____ Correspondence to _____ Dated _____

concerning _____

_____ New case on law which may concern your case

_____ Interrogatories sent to us, please review

_____ Complaint we intend to file for you

_____ Answer we intend to file for you

_____ Answer filed by _____

_____ Cross-complaint filed by _____

_____ Copy of legal research

_____ Copy of article from _____ Date _____

concerning_____

_____ Copy of proposed Will

_____ Copy of proposed complaint

_____ Copy of memo of telephone conference with _____

_____ Information you asked for_____

(4) ACTION REQUIRED BY YOU:

_____ No action required on your part--for your information only

_____ Please read and look for errors or corrections

_____ Please call _____ with corrections

_____ Please call _____ for appointment to review with

www.Foonberglaw.com

_____
____ Please obtain information described on enclosure

(5) TELEPHONE CONVERSATION
    ____ You called on_____. We have tried several times to
    return your call at _____ without success. Please call
    again and ask for _____ or _____ or please drop
    us a note.
    ____ We have been trying to reach you by telephone at _____
    without success. Please confirm your current telephone number.

    Thank you.

    (Dated)

(6) White copy to client
    Green copy to client file
    Yellow copy to originating person
    Pink copy to billing

(7) E-mail copy to above persons _____

(8) Fax to above persons _____

Comments on "For Your Information Letter"
1. Show your postal mailing and e-mail address and phone and fax numbers so the client can call you or write you or reply to your e-mail without looking up your address or phone number.
2. Identify the type of communication and the date and the file where the copy goes.
3. Identify the document you have enclosed.
4. Indicate what action you are expecting the client to take, if any.
5. This is a good way to communicate to clients after you have tried unsuccessfully to return their calls.
6. This is a subtle way to remind you not to forget to charge for the communication.

"FOR YOUR INFORMATION"

TO: DATE:

RE:

FILE NO.:

COURT:

CASE NO.:

_____ REPLY NOT NECESSARY

_____ PLEASE REPLY IN WRITING

_____ PER YOUR WRITTEN/TELEPHONE INSTRUCTIONS

_____ 1.   This will hereby acknowledge receipt of the following original documents: _____
_____

_____ 2.   Suit has been filed and papers are out for service.

_____ 3.   Execution to be levied at/on _____

_____ 4.   Execution levied at_____ on _____ states: _____
_____

_____ 5.   Defendant(s)_____ served on _____
_____. If no answer filed by _____ or extension granted, Defendant(s) default
will be taken on_____

_____ 6.   Defendant(s) Default will be filed today. Please estimate 3-4 weeks for Judgment entry. If we are not
_____. If no answer filed by_____ or extension granted, Defendant(s)
presently knowledgeable of assets to levy upon after judgement, please check for assets to execute upon and
advise this office of information asap.

_____ 7.   Do you wish a judgment debtor examination conducted for possible asset information?

_____ 8.   Defendant(s)_____ not served. Reason: _____
_____

_____ 9.   For your files, information and review, enclosed please find: _____
_____

_____ 10.   Enclosed is_____ County Sheriff/_____ Warrant Check # _____
Dated _____ in sum of $_____ representing_____

_____ 11.   Judgment entered on _____ against Defendant(s)_____
_____

	FOR:		
		PRINCIPAL	$
		ATTORNEYS' FEES	$
		INTEREST	$
		COSTS	$ _____
		TOTAL JUDGMENT	$ _____

_____ 12.   Abstract of Judgment will be recorded in the following counties:

____ SANTA CLARA	____ MARIN	____ LOS ANGELES	____ VENTURA
____ SAN MATEO	____ ALAMEDA	____ ORANGE	____ RIVERSIDE
____ SAN FRANCISCO	____ CONTRA COSTA	____ SAN BERNARDINO	____ OTHER: ____

_____ 13.   Please advise if you wish Abstract of Judgment recorded in any other county: _____

_____ 14.   Money in the form of a county warrant will be forwarded to you in 2-6 weeks. Delay is due to processing
required by the County Auditor.

_____ 15.   _____
_____
_____

THANK YOU.   BY _____

....

PLEASE PROCEED AS FOLLOWS RE FILE NO._____ RE DEFENDANT _____
_____
_____

DATE:_____ COMPANY:_____ SIGNATURE:_____

K-14
Session Laws and "Client Alerts"

Most state legislatures meet in sessions. Typically, the legislature passes new set of laws every session. Typically, but not always, all or most of these laws go into effect at the same time. You should go through these laws just after they are passed and before they go into effect to determine the laws which affect your clients or those people whom you would like as clients.

Many states, either through a legislator or through the office of the Secretary of State, will give you a free email and internet link to a summary of the new laws and legislation. After selecting these new laws, you should prepare and send out a "client alert" with wording to the following effect:

To all clients and colleagues:

ALERT: New laws that could affect you.
A few days ago, on September 29, our Governor signed about 300 new laws, most of which will go into effect on January 1.

Attached to this letter is a list of approximately 100 new laws which might affect you or your business. Each law is identified by Bill Number and a very brief description of the effect of the new law. If you need a copy of the law or if you wish to discuss it with us, please call us or return the enclosed stub of this letter or contact us by e-mail to receive the new laws by email. You can also find summaries and links to the law on our website.

If you have any questions, please don't hesitate to call.

Sincerely,

Your Law Firm

Your Signature

TO: Your name
Your address
Your city, state, zip code

Dear _____:

Please send me a copy of _____

Name _____

Address _____

_____

January 10,

Table of Contents

**Legislation Digest: A Summary of Changes in the
Major Practice Codes
Legislative Session
By Judge Brian D. Crahan and Allyn M. Sullivan**

Page

Digest of Changes in the Major Practice Codes Made by the 2000 California State Legislature

By Judge Brian D. Crahan, Los Angeles Municipal Court, and Allyn M. Sullivan, Staff Attorney, Planning and Research Unit Municipal Courts of Los Angeles County

The following analysis of 2000 legislation has been prepared exclusively for The Los Angeles Daily Journal. The laws, unless otherwise specified, became effective on Jan. 1, 2001.

INTRODUCTION

During the first year of the 99-2000 legislative session, the Legislature introduced, as usual, approximately 4000 bills. Of the influx of legislation, approximately 1600 of those bills were chaptered. This digest includes only the changes made with respect to the Civil Code, the Code of Civil Procedure, important areas of the Penal Code, Vehicle Code, Evidence Code and Probate Code.

In addition we are including, as we have in the past, a penalty chart for violations of driving under the influence and driving with a suspended or revoked license.

If you have any questions or comments about this annual Legislative Digest, please feel free to write us at the Los Angeles Municipal Court, 110 North Grand Avenue, Los Angeles, California 90012.

We are, as usual, indebted to the entire staff of the Los Angeles County Municipal Courts Planning and Research Unit and the committee of judges that oversees this Unit. We want to particularly thank Joyce G. Cook, the Directing Attorney, as well as Staff Attorneys Dragutin M. Ilich, Kiyoko Tatsui and Leslie Admire, for their invaluable assistance.

BRIAN D. CRAHAN
ALLYN M. SULLIVAN

Civil Code

TORTS—IMMUNITIES

Section 43.92 is added to the Civil Code to provide that psychotherapists are immune from lawsuits arising out of a failure to warn of and protect from, or predict and warn or protect from, a patient's threatened violent behavior, except where the patient has expressly communicated to the psychotherapist a serious threat of violence against a reasonably identifiable victim.

AB 1133; Chapter 737.

IMMUNITY OF PROPERTY OWNERS FOR TORTS INJURING FELONS

Section 847 is added and provides that any property owner, including a public entity, having an interest in real property shall not be liable for injury or death that occurs upon that property during the course of, or after the commission of a specified felony, or an attempt to commit a felony, by the injured party if the injured person's felonious conduct was the proximate cause of the injury.

An owner of public or private property is still liable for torts based upon malicious or willful failure to guard or warn against dangerous conditions or activities on such property.

AB 200; Chapter 1541.

TORT INDEMNIFICATION IN CONSTRUCTION CONTRACTS

Section 2782 is amended and §2782.2 is added to the Civil Code to allow plants and firms worth more than $10 million to indemnify their engineers, agents and employees against liability exceeding $250,000 for negligence committed by them.

SB 638; Chapter 567.

CIVIL RIGHTS

Civil Code §51.7 is amended to provide that the prohibition against discrimination is not

K-15
Sample Letter to Clients Telling Them
You Have Nothing to Report
("No Action" Letter)

Mary T. Client
123 Main Street
Anytown, USA

Re: Client v. U.S.A.

Dear Mary:

We have not communicated with you for 60 days. The purpose of this letter is to reassure you that this lack of activity on your case is normal and you should not be concerned.

We are waiting for a trial date notification from the court. We will contact you again when we have meaningful information.

If you have any questions, please don't hesitate to contact us.

Sincerely,

YOUR LAW FIRM NAME
Your signature

Via: U.S. Mail _____
        E-mail _____
        Fax _____

K-16
Do-It-Yourself Manuals for Clients and Potential Clients

Legal manuals and checklists for existing clients are excellent tools to get more business from existing clients and referrals of new clients. The manual can be as short as a one-page checklist or as long as an extensive booklet. Often you can simply take a procedures manual or checklist already in use in your own office and, with minimal or no additional work, convert it to a client-oriented document.

Manuals or checklists will assure the client that you have expertise and really know what you are doing in the particular area of law covered by the manual. On the negative side, it may also have the undesired effect of misleading the client into thinking this is the only area of law you practice.

The manual or checklist will, in all probability, be kept on or in the client's desk, where it can be a constant reminder of your firm. Additionally, the client's employees will take the manual with them when they change jobs and show it to their new employer, giving you an inside line to the new employer. (This has happened to me several times.)

These manuals are more likely to be cost effective in business situations where a client has many similar cases rather than on a personal basis where a client is likely to only have one or two accidents or divorces during a lifetime. On the other hand, as long as you've already done the internal office work of developing a checklist or manual, you might as well give a manual or checklist to individual clients who may use it or may show it to friends who need a lawyer in the area covered by the manual.

Typical areas of law where instruction manuals could be useful (you can add others, depending on your clients' ongoing needs):

1. How to present your case in small claims court.
2. How to evict a tenant.
3. How to contest an unemployment claim.
4. Permissible and non-permissible collection procedures.
5. How to repossess merchandise.
6. How to foreclose on mortgages or trust deeds.
7. How to handle mechanics lien procedures.
8. How to prosecute a freight damage claim.
9. How to file a probate claim.
10. How to file a bankruptcy claim.
11. Accident reporting procedures.
12. How to conduct yourself pending a divorce (dissolution) proceeding.
13. How to conduct yourself as a witness or as a client during a specific type of case- accident, worker's compensation, etc.
14. How to present documentary evidence to a court to avoid personal appearances.

Mechanical aspects of the manual
The manual should:

1. Contain your letterhead in several places and your name and e-mail address on each page so that the client will be able to call or contact you without looking up your telephone number.
2. Be bound (preferably with a clear plastic cover) so that no one can remove your letterhead.
3. Be dated on each page so that you and the client can know the client has the latest information.
4. Be easily copyable by fax, photocopy or email so that it may be forwarded on to others by the recipient.

Contents of the manual: The manual can range from a one- or two-page letter of instructions to cover the simplest procedures to a small book. The manuals could contain:

1. Preface.
2. Sample form letters.
3. Sample legal forms to be filled in, where to obtain them, and procedures to be used such as using registered or certified mail with return receipts.
4. Addresses, telephone numbers and web sites of the various governmental agencies involved.
5. Instructions on employees' conduct or demeanor in court or when dealing with adverse parties.
6. Instructions on how to build the evidentiary case from the records and files of the client.
7. Litigation checklists and transmission forms.
8. A list of situations where the client should call an attorney or supervisory person for help before going further.

One purpose of the manual should be to convince the client that you do not want the client's personnel or user to incur unnecessary or unauthorized legal expenses and that the client should do whatever can do to reduce, minimize or eliminate legal expense by the client doing those things which don't have to be done by a lawyer. By listing procedures necessary prior to using a lawyer, the client can be sure that he or she won't start legal action that can't be finished economically; thus, the client won't be wasting legal fees.

Accordingly, the manual should contain:

1. An introduction on your letterhead warning that the manual contains general advise, current as of a certain date, and that often general advice does not apply to specific situations. Furthermore, it should advise the client that laws and procedures are always being revised and changed and that the user should call for help when there is a specific question.

2. A description of how to recognize when a specific legal problem may be present, given different factual situations.
3. Specific instructions on what to do, or not to do, when a particular legal problem arises. Include form letters to be sent and procedures such as registered mail. Be sure to educate the client as to things they are not allowed to say or do?? Which could negatively affect the client's legal rights.
4. A caution that prior to starting litigation, certain economic consideration should be given to such things as:
   A. The amount of money or property to be gained or lost.
   B. Timetables for enforcement of legal rights.
   C. Out-of-pocket costs to prepare the matter for legal action.
5. A statement as to whose approval the client or organization is required to obtain to utilize outside counsel.
6. An offer on your part to be available to respond to specific questions.

Over the years, I have developed a lot of new legal business from clients using these manuals. Clients often call for an updated manual, and potential clients who have seen a manual sometimes telephone for a meeting to discuss hiring me when they are thinking of changing lawyers.

THE PREFACE TO THE MANUAL

The manual's preface is extremely important for protecting the client and protecting yourself. It is really a form of disclaimer on your part. It should be on your legal stationery and should be dated (actually, each page of the manual should be dated), and should contain language to the following effect:

This manual was written to assist you in handling routine legal matters without incurring unnecessary attorney's fees. Laws are constantly changing with new court decisions, new statutes and new administrative decisions being promulgated daily. Accordingly, you should check with legal counsel when a matter is not routine or when you are concerned that you need more current information. This manual contains general information for routine, common situations and cannot possibly apply to every factual situation. If you have any questions or comments about the use of the manual, please feel free to call me.

Very truly yours,

Jay G Foonberg, Esq.

I have appended this chapter with some sample formats which you may wish to use as examples.

FOONBERG & FRANDZEL
A LAW CORPORATION

We have prepared this Small Claims Court Manual to provide guidelines for maximizing recovery of small balances owed to our clients.

When reading this Manual, it is important to keep in mind that each Judge operates under a different set of rules procedures. Thus, be prepared to make adjustments according the desires and inclinations of each particular Judge.

Remember, too, that your demeanor is important in every Court. Therefore, whenever possible, bend over backwards to be courteous to the Judge, even if that Judge should rule against you.

We hope that this Manual answers any questions you might have regarding Small Claims Court procedures.

Very truly yours,

RDF/hem
Enclosure

SMALL CLAIMS COURT MANUAL

TABLE OF CONTENTS

APPENDIX TO SMALL CLAIMS COURT MANUAL:

K-17
Expand Your Practice Using Research Memoranda and Published Articles by "Using Ink" (The Rubber Airplane Technique)

In the aircraft industry, a tremendous amount of money is spent on the basic design of an aircraft. Often the manufacturer will offer several different versions of an airplane, such as long-range, short-range, all-cargo, extended-range. high-density seating, mixed cargo-passenger, etc. The manufacturer may also have a variety of military versions in addition to the civilian versions. In all cases, the basic aircraft is unchanged. Only minor modifications are made to the basic aircraft body.

You can do the same thing with your research memos to expand your practice in a given area(s). The basic concept is to rewrite your research memorandum for distribution directly or indirectly to targeted markets. The same memo can be rewritten and republished and distributed in multiple written and non-written forms. The writer can expand or contract the memorandum and make it more, or less, technical for the intended publication on market.

When the article is published, you have established yourself as an expert.

Sample publications include:

1. Law reviews (this may require additional work).
2. Law journals.
3. Legal newspapers.
4. Trade association journals (this may require simplifying the article/ memo).
5. Local newspapers (this may also require simplifying the article).
6. The publications of various professional and social organizations to which you belong.
7. Multiple combinations of the above. Many writers do not realize that most publications will republish articles previously published else where.

It has been said "the value of ink is not the ink, but rather what you do with the ink."

The publication of the article(s) itself (the ink) may produce a small amount of business from the people who read it, but this is not the principal usage to be made of the article (what you do with the ink).

The purpose of getting the article printed is to establish yourself as an expert on the subject of the article or in the field of activity where the publication is published. Publication of an article by you validates you as an expert in the subject of the article.

For example, when I had an article on corporate retirement plans published in various versions in the *National Law Journal*, the *Rental Equipment Register*, the *Los Angeles County Medical News*, the *Medical Equipment Rental Industry Guide* and *The Estate*

Planners Guide, I simultaneously became known as an "expert" in all of the following fields of law:

1. Corporate Income Taxation
2. Personal Income Taxation
3. Estate Taxation
4. Deferred Compensation Taxation
5. Taxation of Closely Held Businesses, and
6. Structuring and Taxation of Sales and Purchases of Businesses.

Due to the nature of the publications and their distribution, rather than to the article itself, I became established as an "expert" in the following areas of business activities:

1. The equipment rental industry
2. The health care industry
3. Tax and financial planning for doctors
4. Tax and financial planning for lawyers
5. Tax and financial planning for corporate executives
6. Buying and selling closely held businesses

Thus, you can see that by modifying an article or the title of the article, you can get it published in multiple publications, each of which can establish you as an "expert" in a different field of law or different field of commercial activity. The basic article can be merely a rewrite of a research memo.

After the article is published, you can usually arrange with the publisher to print reprints for you at little or no cost, or you can reprint the article yourself, using the cover of the issue of the publication in which the article appeared. (You may wish to leave off the date so that the article doesn't appear to be obsolete when circulated years later).

The reprints are the real ammunition in your marketing campaign. As indicated, you can get a certain amount of business from the people who have read the article, but the real value is in how you can use the reprints and the credits you have received. For example:

1. For existing clients. Send the reprint to existing clients. Clients like to brag how their lawyer is a big "expert." The reprint you send will depend on the particular client. I sent the *Rental Equipment* article reprint to one group of clients and the *Estate Planners Guide* reprint to another group.
2. For the reception room. Leave some reprints in your reception room where existing clients can see that you're an "expert."
3. As qualification to speak to a particular group. I used the reprint from each of the publications as my "qualification" to speak when I asked the various groups to be a featured speaker at their meetings. (Remember that the group is boosting you to their members when they publicize the talk.)
4. For professionals who can refer you new clients in a particular industry. I sent the reprints from the *Estate Planning Journal* to CPA's. (You could include CPA's

with whom you already have clients in common as well as CPA's with whom there has been no prior contact.)

5. For friends and relatives. They will put the article on their coffee table or mantelpiece and show it to anybody who will sit still long enough. They will brag about your skills to the same extent as your existing clients, if not more so.

6. For a select mailing list that you have developed or which you purchase. The printed articles will establish you as the instant expert on the subject. I've never done this, but other lawyer tell me these lists are a good investment of money.

7. As the subject of a press release.

Don't forget that in establishing your "credentials" by listing your publications, you can list each of the publications where the article appeared, even though each was only a modified or re-titled version of the original research or article.

All of these benefits from a research memo are, of course, in addition to your sending a copy to the original client for whom the research was done.

You can also put the reprinted article(s) on your website, using a different page for each article. By email link to the targeted group, you can publicize the article to a huge number of people at extremely low cost.

K-18
Why You Should Send Christmas or Season's Greetings Cards

Season's greetings or Christmas cards are a very good, cost-effective method of good client relations and a good, immediate source of business. They don't require much technology, professional assistance or outlay of money, and they produce both long- and short-range results.

When you send any kind of greeting card to a client, you are communicating to that client that you care about him or her. The client also knows that it is a form of saying "thank you" for the professional relationship.

When you send a card to a former client or inactive client, you are reminding that person that your firm still exists and is available for more work.

When you send a card to a referrer or potential referrer of clients, you are also reminding that person that your firm still exists and that you are saying "thank you" for the work they have previously referred to you.

Each year when I send cards, I immediately get more than enough work to pay for the cost of the cards and mailing. Some typical responses have been:

"Jay, I just got your Christmas card and it reminded me that I have to update my will because I have a new grandchild."

"Jay, your card reminded me that my brother-in-law and I need some sort of legal document. We bought a condominium together in Palm Springs and we need something in case one of us dies or we have a disagreement over whether or not to sell it."

"Jay, your card reminded me that I have to update our corporate buy-sell agreement."

"Your card reminded me that my cousin needs a lawyer for her accident case. Can you handle it?"

"Your card reminded me that I want to discuss some tax planning before year-end."

The examples are endless.

I am not an expert on the root causes of divorce. Family law experts tell me that when couples are about to split up, they usually stay together for one last Christmas "for the kids' sake." They tend to split up right after Christmas. Accordingly, your Christmas card is reaching two potential clients, the husband and the wife. If they are going to sell the house, you'll get even more legal work in those states where lawyers still take part in "closings."

1.   The Card Itself: The fact that you send the card is probably more important than the exact wording on the card. I personally avoid cards that are deeply religious unless I truly have a close relationship with the recipient. I send "Season's Greetings" rather than "Christmas" cards for several reasons. "Season's Greetings," encompasses New Years, Kwanza, Chanukkah, and possibly other holidays. You may innocently offend a non-religious or non-Christian client or potential client. I have many non-Christian clients, including Buddhists, Jews, Moslems, etc. Some clients may resent the commercialization of Christmas and dislike religious cards in a commercial context. Others feel that the commercialization of the holiday season of Christmas and New Years should place more emphasis of Christmas and religion. Some of my Armenian clients are Greek (Eastern) Orthodox and the deeply religious ones tell me that there is a debate among religious scholars as to the holiness of Christmas. Mixing religion into your practice relations should be a "no-no," unless you truly know well the person who will get the card.

2.   Humor: I opt for a humorous card. Many of my clients collect and save my Christmas (Season's Greetings) cards. One year I failed to send cards. Several people called me to find out why they hadn't received one. They enjoyed the cards and looked forward to receiving them.

3.   Your Name on the Card: Check the local rules. Some Bar Associations have a rule that if you send a card with your firm name you are advertising, but if you list the names of individual lawyers you are not advertising, even if you list 100 lawyers. In my opinion, rules such as these don't make much sense, but they may exist in your jurisdiction. At one Bar program I did in Connecticut in 1976, the Chairman of the Ethics Committee of the local Bar stood up in the middle of my program and loudly proclaimed that he would start a disciplinary proceeding against any lawyer who sent a Christmas card to a client, as there was a specific rule against lawyers' sending Christmas cards. I'm sure this rule has been changed by now, but you should be aware of any local rules on how you sign a Christmas card.

4.   Enclosures: For 20 years, I never even thought of putting enclosures of any sort in with Christmas cards. First, department stores, and then doctors, dentists and others began putting season's greetings cards in with their regular December monthly bills and advertising. Then I began receiving bill inserts from other lawyers in the form of a photocopied letter explaining what they and various members of their family had been doing during the previous year. Finally, I began receiving practice update newsletters with the cards.

In 1984, for the first time, I put an information letter into Christmas cards as a test. I truthfully felt a bit odd doing it. The reaction was negative, so I won't do it again. If the reaction had been positive, I would have done it again. I suggest that you do the same and experiment. Try an insert and see what happens.

You might include information on one or more of the following subjects:

A.   New personnel

B.   New areas of law

C.   Honors received

D.   Bar Association activities

    E. Civic activities

    F. Family news of staff members

You might also enclose a Rolodex card or professional card or photo.

5. Late Arrivals: A Christmas card really has to arrive before December 25 or it is late. A season's greetings card, however, can arrive anytime before January 1 and still be timely. The problem of late delivery of Christmas mail is a factor in favor of season's greetings cards.

6. Signing Christmas Cards: As firms get larger, the pen and ink signing of a card becomes more and more complex.

There are some questions that get debated every year ad nauseam.

    1. Is the printed firm name enough?

    2. Should the principal or partner responsible for the lawyer sign it?

    3. Should all lawyers who do work on the clients matter sign it?

    4. Should every lawyer in the office sign it?

    5. Should staff sign it?

7. Email Cards. I personally prefer receiving an email card to receiving no card. I like the music and animation. Others feel that sending an email card degrades the event for which the card is sent and the sender. Email cards can be sent easily and cheaply to anywhere in the world. You can create your own cards, but may have copyright problems over the music used. If you are debating between an email card and no card, send the email. If you are debating between an email card and a paper card, then treat each recipient on a case by case basis.

In some firms, the signing of Christmas cards is so burdensome that people start signing the cards in October and November. So many cards get sent that signing cards becomes an interference with billable hours, especially if wording in addition to signatures is added.

I personally feel that multiple signatures is an unnecessary interference with billable time and is not timely.

A few (I emphasize few) words written on a card for a client with whom you are personally close adds a nice personal touch. Simple phrases like "Have a great New Year – Jay" or "I wish you Health and Happiness – Jay" or "Thank you for being a good friend – Jay" are more than adequate.

"It's another battery case. . . . they weren't included!"

SEASON'S GREETINGS
and best wishes for a Happy New Year!

JAY G FOONBERG	**MARK E. FINGERMAN**
SHAHEN HAIRAPETIAN	**SHERI J. RAPAPORT**
JAY A. ZVORIST	**MICHAEL D. MANDELL**
MICHAEL WINKLER	**DEBORAH HOWARD**
KIMBERLY CHRISTENSEN	**ANGELA M. ROSSI**
GAIL THAMES	**DECI DENNEY**
NAOMI NAKAGAWA	**CARMITA YOUNG**

and NENA ALLEN

K-19
Christmas Cards in July

I attended a course in International Comparative Advocacy at Cambridge University, England. I became friendly with one the Dons (Professors) of the law faculty. He told me that he belonged to the International Law Section of the American Bar Association and the International Bar Association and that he went to the conventions of both and knows hundreds of American lawyers.

He then asked me if I knew a particular lawyer in California, whom I didn't know.

I asked the Don why he asked me about this particular lawyer when he had explained to me that he knew hundreds of American lawyers.

His answer surprised me. It was, "Oh he's the one who sends me his Christmas card in July." I was confused and thought I had misunderstood.

The Don explained to me that this particular lawyer sent his Christmas cards in July along with a personal note. He was sending the cards in July to emphasize that he was sincere in his holiday greetings. The note indicated that if the card was sent and received in December it would get lost with all the other cards being sent and received at that time of year.

The note related that a Christmas card sent and received in July would receive special attention.

The Cambridge Don certainly remembered the lawyer who sent the Christmas cards in July.

I personally would not be comfortable sending a Christmas card in July, but I receive other types of cards from attorneys whom I remember for sending the cards. Typical unusual cards I receive every year include my Birthday card, Thanksgiving cards, Rosh Hashanah cards, Halloween cards and St. Patrick's Day cards—all from lawyers.

Because of the large volume of computer label Christmas cards every client receives I try to personalize the cards for the more important clients and insert a short handwritten comment such as "Have a Good Year- Jay" or "Best for Next Year - Jay." Obviously you can't send a long handwritten note to distinguish your card from other cards but you should try to do something distinctive to make your card stand out. You might want to send it in November to be among the first cards received.

In some law firms they start signing the cards in October (right after the Thanksgiving cards have gone out).

K-20
Send Your Christmas Card to as Many People as You Can

I recently heard of some self-styled expert on lawyer marketing who advocated sending as few Christmas cards as possible on the basis that sending a large number of cards was in some manner "insincere." I totally disagree with this advice and I'd love to meet this "expert" who ever he or she is to debate the point. Obviously, the recipient of one of your cards has no way of knowing how many other cards you've sent.

In 1988 I participated in a marketing seminar at Austin, Texas for the Young Lawyers Association. A woman lawyer (whom I'll call Ms. Jones) told the group that she had heard me speak in the early 80's at a convention and remembered my advice to send a Christmas card every year both to remind your clients of your availability and to update mailing lists. This attorney had included in her mailing a little old lady for whom she'd drafted a will some years earlier, but with whom she had no contact for several years.

The client had given up her apartment and had moved into an expensive retirement home. The client called the attorney and said something to the following effect:

"Ms. Jones, since you drafted my will a few years ago almost all the people named in the will and most of the people I knew have died. Your Christmas card was the only Christmas card I received. I was thinking of doing away with myself. Now I don't feel alone and forgotten. God Bless you and thank you."

The client then set up a meeting to update her estate plan and the client recommended Ms. Jones to three more residents of the retirement home for estate planning as well.

The attorney, Ms. Jones told me: "Mr. Foonberg if I had never gotten a fee ever from sending Christmas cards, that one call made it all worthwhile. As it turned out I had four excellent fees from that one card but the fees were minor compared to the good feelings I got when the client told me that mine was the only card she'd received and that she decided not to do away with herself. It made me feel good to make another human being happy."

I don't know if this motivates you to send more cards but I hope that it does.

K-21
Survey Your Clients for Feedback

I personally have never done this, but several lawyers have reported client feedback surveys as being very helpful in practice development for analyzing weaknesses and strengths and acting on the information obtained.

One lawyer consulted a book put out by an advertising specialist on how to prepare a client survey, and another simply collected brochures from six or seven hotels and synthesized his own questionnaire from the hotel questionnaires. Other lawyers have consulted with experts for theirs.

The lawyers who used these feedback questionnaires found them very helpful in identifying and correcting weaknesses and in identifying and emphasizing strengths.

When I asked if the sending of these questionnaires in and of themselves produced more work, the attorneys using them could not specifically identify new business obtained as a result of the questionnaires, but they all felt that the sending of them was a form of client contact and, more importantly, a *caring* client contact. They felt that the contact was in itself very valuable. As proof of the effectiveness of the feedback questionnaires, the attorneys report that as many as 40 percent of their clients returned the questionnaires.

You can survey your clients and former clients verbally or in writing. I've heard of firms where the lawyers personally do the surveying by telephone or over lunch. I've also heard of law firms which hire professional telephone interviewers to do the information gathering.

I've also heard of law firms which routinely contact targeted non-clients "by accident" or as part of a "survey." (See the chapter on Phony Surveys to Get New Clients.)

The written survey form may be more effective than verbal surveys in that people can answer anonymously if they wish. In verbal interviews, people often tell you what they think you want to hear to avoid unpleasant reactions.

Surveys done by third parties might be more critical and point out more deficiencies. Surveys done by professionals can phrase and twist questions so as to always get favorable answers (note that an airline never asks about leg room in coach). Surveys can also be done by interactive email.

Following this chapter is a sample Client Survey Form. This form is a compilation of several different forms. I specifically wish to acknowledge that the form of Allen E. Kaye, an immigration lawyer from New York City, was exceptionally well done. It specifically met the needs of an immigration lawyer with a large "office visit" type of practice.

The form I have put together is a general purpose form. You could design a different form for different kinds of clients and cases and use the appropriate form for each situation.

To repeat, I personally have not formally surveyed clients and former clients, but the lawyers who *have done* so tell me it's very worthwhile and has no "backlash."

Please note that my form is an affirmative sales effort as well as a questionnaire. Whether or not the client fills it out, you have shown the client that you care. The questions asked are sensitive to the areas that do or do not lead to more legal work and to the concerns of the client.

K-22
Sample Questionnaire
To Survey Your Client For Feedback

(ON FIRM LETTERHEAD)

Re: Client Questionnaire

Dear Client:

We very much care about our clients. We realize that we are not perfect. Like any other human, we are capable of upsetting our clients. Sometimes a client can be upset over how they are treated, even though they receive superior legal services from us.

We value your opinion and your suggestions. We ask you please to take a few minutes to answer the enclosed questionnaire and return it to us in the enclosed self-addressed, stamped envelope.

Thank you,

Jay G Foonberg

CLIENT QUESTIONNAIRE

1. How did you first hear of our firm? (You may check more than one)
    __Recommended by a then current client_____
    __Recommended by a former client_____
    __Recommended by a friend or relative_____
    __Recommended by the Bar Association_____
    __Knew an attorney in the firm_____
    __Knew a non-attorney in the firm_____
    __Yellow Page listing_____
    __Found you on the internet after a search_____
    __Other (please explain)_____
    _____

2. When you made your first call to us, were you satisfied with the way your call was handled?_____
    _____
    Was anything said or done on the first call that pleased or displeased you?
    *(Yes / No)*_____. If yes, please describe:_____

3. How long did it take for a lawyer to contact you after the first call?
Immediately?_____. Other:_____

4. In what kind of case did we represent you?_____
_____

5. How long was the case from first contact with us to its conclusion?_____

6. Do you feel we moved the case along as expeditiously as reasonably possible?_____

7. Were you always treated courteously on the telephone when you called?_____
Were you ever put "on hold" for too long?_____
Were you ever cut off while "on hold"?_____
Did you ever hang up while holding?_____
If you were ever treated discourteously, we would appreciate your identifying the person who was discourteous so we can see that it doesn't happen again._

8. Were your telephone calls, voicemails and email returned promptly?_____
If not, who didn't return your calls or voice mails or emails quickly enough?_____

9. On your in-person visits to our office, were you treated courteously by our receptionist?_____
Was the reception room clean, comfortable and well lit with sufficient reading material?_____
Do you feel that you were seen quickly enough by the person you came to see?_____
Were you offered coffee or something to drink?_____
Were there any publications or periodicals that were not there, that you would have wanted to read?_____
Did you feel you were ignored while you waited?_____

10. Is our office location convenient for you?_____
Did we offer to validate your parking?_____
Did you have any difficulty finding parking?_____
If you came by public transportation, was our office convenient to get to?_____

11. Do you prefer to come to our office or do you prefer telephone or email contact?_____

12. Were you shown our computers, communications equipment, electronic library and other facilities?_____

13. Did the attorney(s) who worked on your case:
Keep you informed as to what was happening?_____
Treat you courteously?_____
Answer your questions?_____
Explain to you as soon as possible, the nature and extent of the work your case required?_____
Demonstrate that we really cared about you and your legal matters?_____
Do the work promptly as promised?_____

14. Were you informed at the beginning of the case how fees would be charged?_____ Verbally?_____ In writing?_____

15. Were you satisfied with the efforts of the firm? If not, please explain why not._____

16. Were you satisfied with the results of your case?_____
_____

17. Do you feel our fees were reasonable and fair based on the nature of your case and the extent and amount of work involved?_____

18. If you feel the fee was not reasonable and fair, please tell us why._____

19. Is there any person(s) you wish to single out as being:
    a. Courteous and helpful?_____
    b. Discourteous or not helpful?_____

20. Would you use our firm again if you had another legal problem? Please give us your comments._____

21. Would you recommend our firm to a friend, relative or business associate who needed a lawyer? Please comment if you wish._____

22. Have you been receiving our season's greetings cards?
Do you appreciate receiving them?_____
Do you receive our client newsletters?_____
Do you appreciate receiving them?_____

23. Is there anything you feel we should have done for you that we did not do?_____

24. Is there anything you feel we can still do for you?_____
_____

25. Please rate your perception of the overall quality of legal service you received.
    Superior_____; Excellent_____; Good_____;
    Adequate_____; Fair_____; Poor_____

26. Please rate your overall perception of how you were treated as a client.
    Superior_____; Excellent_____; Good_____;
    Adequate_____; Fair_____; Poor_____

27. Is there anything you feel we forgot to ask you, or anything you wish to tell us?_____

28. Would you like to discuss any of these matters by telephone?
    *(Yes / No)*_____. If yes, best day & time to call:_____

29. (OPTIONAL)
    Your Name_____
    Address_____
    _____
    Telephone Number_____

Please place this questionnaire in the self-addressed, stamped envelope we have provided for your convenience and return it to us.

Thank you for your time and help.

THE LAW OFFICES OF JAY G FOONBERG

Chapter L
Your Invoice - A Factor In
Satisfying or Angering Clients

L-1
Your Invoice as a Marketing Tool

Whether you realize it or not, your invoice is a marketing tool. Some invoices anger or annoy clients. Some clients like or don't like receiving certain types of invoices. In this chapter, I'll try to suggest several different approaches to how you should word and send an invoice. There is no single type of invoice which will please all clients.

I have been surprised at some clients' reactions to invoices and other lawyers have reported similar problems in their practices.

Just as a menu in a restaurant lists different kinds of food prepared in different manners, you may wish to send different kinds of invoices to different clients. No hard and fast rule says you cannot vary your invoices to suit your client's needs or wishes.

It never hurts to discuss with clients and prospective clients what kinds of invoices they want. It also never hurts to ask from time to time if the current invoices you are sending meet their information and accounting needs. There is also no harm in checking periodically to see whether they're basically satisfied with your invoicing or whether there is something they wish to change. In this chapter, I'll make some generalizations about different types of invoices and leave it to you to discuss with your clients which kind(s) they like or which they do not.

1. "SERVICES RENDERED $_____" without details. In the past, most lawyers billed for "services rendered" and gave no details. In general, most clients do not want a bill without a description of the services rendered. Some typical situation where a "services rendered" invoice is appropriate include the following:

A. Supine clients. They just don't care what anything costs and are happy to pay bills without being informed or reminded of the services they are paying for.

B. When a business is paying and work is being done for the owner or employee which is not a tax-deductible expense for the corporation (an adoption or criminal matter, for example), in which case the attorney may be told either, "Bill the company" or "Send the bill to me at the company address."

It is no concern of yours if the company pays someone's personal expenses and then makes a journal entry or other correcting entry on the books of the company and the information returns filed with the IRS.

C. When the bill contains information which could be prejudicial to the company. For example, the bill might be for work done in connection with a potential liability. Depending upon the circumstances, the details on the bill may or may not be later obtainable by discovery or other legal process.

D. When the bill contains information which could be prejudicial to the company if known by the people in accounts payable or mailroom who routinely have access to or see legal bills in their processing. For example, a client wouldn't want employees to know about a pending sale of the company, lie detector or drug tests, extremely high profits, possible criminal conduct by the company, violation of industrial safety orders, etc.

E. When the client just doesn't want to know the details. Some clients get very upset seeing their legal problems set forth in a legal bill and demand that the bill not contain these details. If a client doesn't want or like or need detailed descriptions of the work done, there's no reason to provide them. Indeed, as is pointed out, there are times when a detailed description of the work done can be prejudicial to the attorney.

You may wish to send a "Services Rendered" bill with no details accompanied by a non discoverable "Status Report" on which is written, "Privileged and Confidential." This method will allow the recipient to keep the letter and forward the bill on for paying.

2. BILLS SHOWING GREAT DETAIL AS TO EVERY LAWYER WHO WORKED ON THE MATTER AND THE AMOUNT OF TIME THEY DEVOTED. Sophisticated buyers of legal services such as insurance companies and large corporations want information with this great detail. You may have no choice but to give it to them as a condition of doing their work.

Unsophisticated clients get confused and angry at this type of bill. They simply can't understand a lawyer's charging $350 an hour when they earn only $700 a week gross before taxes. These people also don't really understand exactly what you're doing and why it takes so long. In my opinion, you should never send an unsophisticated person this type of bill.

3. BILLING PERIODS.

A. Billing on completion of matter. Many years ago, lawyers billed once a year or at the conclusion of the case. This system met its death when inflation hit the law office. In some types of work such as personal injury and probates, you have no choice (see chapter on "Contingency Cases"), but to send a "bill" at the end of the case. You should detail it so that the client understands the difference between fees and costs.

B. Monthly billing. Most business demand monthly billings so they are able to match income and expenses. You should also insist on monthly billings and payments for two reasons:

1) To facilitate paying your own bills; and

2) To spot a problem client before he or she becomes too far behind in payments.

C. Advance billing. Use this technique with new clients and criminal cases and cases which will cost a lot of money over a long period of time.

Getting cash in advance by advance billing or advance deposit in your trust account may be your best bet (see chapter on "Cash Up Front").

4. BILLING STATIONERY. Most lawyers use note-sized letterhead paper of stationery quality. Many lawyers are using computer printouts generated bills that people don't object to. I personally dictate my bills and have them typed (actually word processed) onto computer paper stock. Thus, the bill appears to be computer generated. People are so used to accepting what a computer "says" that they seem less likely to question bills which come from a computer as often as bills which were typed on stationery. Eight- by five-inch stationery for billing allows you to squeeze a lot of words onto a single piece of paper, thereby permitting you to project how hard you work for the client. Some clients want the bill by email which eliminates this problem.

5. BILLING WORDING. I personally emphasize the *documents* which I prepared, since the client has already received a copy of them. (See the chapter on "Bombarding Your Client with Paper".) Every letter, sent or received; every pleading and supporting or accompanying document (I would detail the answer, and the verification and the proof of service by mail, and the nature of the motion, affidavit of client in support of motion, points and authorities in support of motion, proof of mailing, etc.); every memo to file regarding telephone conversations; every research memo, including principal cases and statutes cited (the client should have received a copy of them). If the client has been kept informed properly by being bombarded with paper, the bill simply reminds him or her of everything you've already done, and you have projected efforts. Other lawyers emphasize action verbs-drafting of, appearing before, meeting with, analysis of, preparing for, etc.- to show the client they have been doing something. Try to avoid "telephone call" in the singular, and use "telephone conferences" to lump multiple telephone conferences together where possible. When you charge for photocopying, try to avoid charging for "photocopying," *per se.* Signs in shop windows everywhere advertise photocopies for 5 cents. The client forgets that at 5 cents, they provided their own labor and bookkeeping. Use words such as "document reproduction" for photocopying costs. Billing for photocopy may anger a client who expects email attachments for free.

I next emphasize meetings with the clients (the clients will remember them). Then I next emphasize court appearances and meetings not involving the client. Again, I want to remind the client how hard I worked for the client.

6. WHERE TO SEND THE BILL. Always ask the client and the clients accounting or accounts payable person where to send the bill and who must approve it. Some clients don't want their families to know they are using a lawyer. Some clients don't want their employees to know what's happening. I've had clients who didn't want the bill going to either place; they picked up the bill and their mail from my office. Some clients open a P.O. Box for legal correspondence.

7. ADDRESSING THE BILL. Always send the bill with some person's name on it, even if it is only to that person's attention. People don't like seeing their name on an unpaid bill and will try to get it paid more quickly then if the bill is addressed only to a business.

8. WHEN TO SEND THE BILL. Try to send the bill to arrive between the first and fifth of the month. Many businesses (and individuals) pay bills once a month (typically on the 10th) or twice a month (typically on the 10th and 25th). Ask the client when would be the best time to send the bill.

9. ENCLOSURES WITH THE BILL. Some lawyers always send a cover letter with the bill. The cover letter is usually a status report. It may also personalize a large bill to lessen its shock. Some lawyers use the cover letter to protect privilege which might not apply to an invoice. Most lawyers don't send anything with the bill for fear it will be diverted out of the bill-paying procedures to someone's personal desk where it will languish awaiting payment. Some lawyers send a monthly newsletter with the bill. Whether or not you send something with the bill is up to you. But you should consider the opportunity to communicate with the client. You should always enclose a colored (preferably powder blue), postage-paid return envelope with the bill. This avoids the delay of your check sitting on your client's desk for lack of an envelope or stamp, and also allows you to identify immediately the checks in the incoming mail.

In summary, try to take a few minutes on occasion to discuss the format of your invoice with the client, both before you send your first invoice and from time to time thereafter. The client will appreciate the fact you asked.

10. OTHER BILLING CONSIDERATIONS. Courts & Administrative Agencies, individual courts & judges often have their own special rules on how a bill must be worded & submitted. If your bill might require court approval for any reason, be sure you get & read the rules. These rules often are not on the internet, but available only on paper in the courtroom. Family law, probate matters and bankruptcy are common examples.

11. OTHER PUBLICATIONS. I have co authored a book with J. Harris Morgan entitled, "How to Draft Bills Clients Rush to Pay." Harris wrote the parts dealing with wording & I wrote the parts on the mechanics of getting paid.

L-2
Ten Ways to Antagonize and Lose Clients With Bad Billing Practices

This is a short chapter on things you can do with your invoices that can alienate a client to the point of leaving you.

The client's bill is a very sensitive document. A client may have real or imagined problems with you on the case. The bill may simply be the thing he complains about when, in reality, it's just a convenient excuse to demonstrate other dissatisfaction.

Alternatively, a bill can truly upset a client to the point that he or she complains not about the bill but rather the way you are handling the case.

The client will equate your lack of efficiency in the preparation and handling of the bill with general all-around inefficiency.

The important thing is not that you have a bill you can defend in a fight with the client (no one ever "won" a fight with a client). The important thing is that insofar as possible, the bill itself does not become a stimulus for a fight. The following are billing practices that are sure to infuriate the client:

1. *Send the bill to the wrong place or the wrong person.*
Bills for legal services often refer to sensitive matters, such as a divorce or criminal matter or purchase or sale of a business. The information can cause anxiety or fears or concerns or unnecessary curiosity as to what is happening.

2. *Continue to send the bill to the wrong place after the client has called you to correct the bill.*
This will truly convince the client of your firm's over-all incompetency.

3. *Send the bill three months after the work was done.*
The client may have little or no memory of any of the work for which the client is being charged. This also creates dissatisfaction when the client realizes there are three more months of charges coming. (See chapter entitled "Clients Curve of Gratitude").

4. *Blindly charge the client for all time devoted to the case, even if the bill preparer makes a mistake.*
A good example is your charging a client for the time you spent on the telephone explaining that there was an error in the bill.

5. *Charge for "research."*
Some clients don't like to pay for research. They think you learned the law when you went to law school. They can't understand why you don't "know" the law. After all, you said you were experienced and competent. So why are you charging for "research"?

It is probably safer to refer to the this time as "analysis of applicability of facts to law."

6. *Charge for photocopies & Messenger Services.*

Clients see copy centers in every office building where photocopies can be had for a few cents per page. When you charge 5 to 10 times that price, they sometimes get upset. They may ask you why you did the work "in house" instead of sending it to a commercial source. It is probably better to call this "Document Reproduction Services".

Clients will also ask why you don't email documents to them instead of photocopying or messenger services.

7. *Provide great detail in those unusual situations where the client wanted no detail at all.*

When the client wants only "legal services rendered", listed on the bill, don't, for example, go into great detail to explain that the client is using company funds to pay for his son's criminal defense. The client, the client's accountant and the IRS will all be pleased when your invoice is used to disallow a deduction.

8. *Charge for "telephone calls."*

Clients hate to pay for telephone calls. They fly into a rage when you bill for telephone conversations and nothing else, especially if the telephone call is from or to them. When the only service rendered on the case is telephone calls, it is better to defer the telephone calls until you can combine them with something else at a later date. It is also better to describe them as "telephone conferences." Don't ever charge for or describe the time spent in discussing the bill itself.

9. *Send* a *bill when the client is totally unaware of anything you've done on the case.*

Clients get upset when the only piece of paper they've received since the last bill is the present bill. The situation can sometimes be alleviated by sending a letter with the bill explaining what was done and why the client hadn't been notified. In some cases, it may be best to defer sending the bill until you've informed the client of what you've been doing. This problem is also obviated by keeping the client informed. (See chapter entitled "Bombard Your Clients with Paper.")

10. *Neglect to Have* a *responsible lawyer review the bill just before it goes out.*

Many, if not most, of the client-antagonizing things on a bill can be caught by a lawyer familiar with the case who reviews the bill before it goes out. Billing clerks, office managers and computers can prepare the bill, but a lawyer has to review it before it goes to the client.

L-3
Discount Billing for Friends and Relatives

It is important when billing a friend or relative who is going to pay less than fair market value that the client know the true value of the services received. Clients do not know the value of the services they receive. You have to tell them. Unless you tell them the value of what they have received, they don't know.

Consider for example the following invoice:

Re: Professional Services Rendered in Connection with Client vs Insurance Company

Office conference with client to obtain facts of case and to review documentary evidence; analysis of law relative to "bad faith for failure to settle"; preparation of complaint against Insurance Company in Municipal Court; prepare cover letter to Insurance Company re: filing complaints with Insurance Commissioner and with court re: claim "not adjusted fairly"; preparation of release form and instructions re: negotiation of insurance draft.

Services Rendered:
January 3, 4, 8, 9,10, 20XX	$1,950
Less: Family Discount (50%)	(975)
TOTAL NOW DUE AND PAYABLE	$975

THANK YOU

If you had simply billed "Services Rendered $975," the client would have had no way of knowing whether the fair market value of the work you did was $250, $500, $950 or $1950.

People like to feel they're receiving special consideration. The discount shows them that you consider them to be special people.

One attorney from New York told me that he had an old-time friend who always complained about lawyers fees both to the attorney and to their mutual friends. Anticipating a fee problem, this attorney calculated that he wanted a fee of $5,000 for the work done, even though it was worth $7,500. He was sure that if he presented a bill for $5,000 the client would complain and delay payment. Accordingly, he presented the following bill:

Re: Professional Services Rendered	$7,500
Less Family Discount	(2,500)
BALANCE NOW DUE AND PAYABLE	$5,000

On receipt of the bill, the client called the lawyer to ask if there had been a mistake since he was not a member of the attorney's family. The attorney responded that he had known the client so long and so well that he considered the client to be in the same category as family.

The client said that he was honored and flattered to receive a "Family Discount," paid the $5,000 bill in full the day of receipt and then loudly bragged about his great lawyer who charged $7500.

The science of retailing continually uses advertisements showing a recommended list price or "value" with the price "X"-ed out and a discounted price shown instead.

You should not indiscriminately use this method and you should not artificially inflate your price before showing the discount. Subject to your following these admonitions and subject to your feeling comfortable with them, I highly recommend "discount billing" for friends and relatives, where appropriate, as an efficient client pleaser resulting in good client relations, good cash flow and good future referrals.

Referral Considerations

Some clients are "show offs" who like to brag. They brag about how their lawyer "charged" $7,500. They don't say they "paid" $7,500. They often add "expensive but worth it." You want $7,500 referrals not $5,000 referrals.

L-4
The "No-Bill" Bill

A variation on the "discount bill" is the "no bill" bill.

For one reason or another, you may wish to do legal work for free-in whole or in part. This, of course, is your option. You should capitalize and get maximum mileage out of the fact that you are giving your client a price break.

Two recommended methods are:

A.

Re: Professional services rendered in
connection with research issue of
recision and preparation of Letter of
Notice of Recision .... N/C
N/C = No Charge

B.

Re: Professional services rendered in
connection with research issue of
recision and preparation of Letter of
Notice of Recision $350

Less courtesy discount   (<u>$350</u>)

TOTAL NOW DUE AND PAYABLE   <u>-0-</u>

The purpose of the "no bill" is obviously not to raise cash. Its main purpose is to show the clients what you are doing for them and the value of what you are doing for free. It also to prevent the possibility of the client's thinking you "forgot to bill," or worse, forgot to do the work.

When you do work for free and neglect to send a "no bill," the client may think you forgot to bill and may go to another lawyer for the next legal matter for fear that if the client calls you, you will discover the "forgotten" bill. The "no bill" bill eliminates this possibility and keeps the client happy and close to you.

Some clients, in gratitude, will refer you matters whenever they can.

L-5
Discount Billing for Professionals
Who Can or Do Refer Work to You

It is good for practice development to get work through referrals from certain professionals (doctors, CPAs, other lawyers, etc.). You want these recommenders of clients indebted to you for a favor but often don't want to do the work for them free either because they can well afford to pay or, because even when you consider the clients they send you, you don't earn enough from these clients to do the professional work for free. If you charge them a fee in such a situation, you should seriously consider the discount bill. Discount bills for professionals and referrers of business are similar to discount bills for family members.

The main goal of the professional discount is to show the professional the true value of the services rendered and the fact that you have discounted the bill.

Additionally, when a business client has some non-tax deductible personal work along with deductible work, you may wish to discount that nondeductible fee, giving recognition to the fact that deductible legal fees are more appreciated than non-deductible fees.

An example of a professional discount bill follows.:

Re: Professional Services Rendered in Connection with Formation of Sub Chapter S Holding Co.:

Office conference to discuss advantages of holding title to Blackacre as a Subchapter S corporation under new tax laws; Formation of corporation including Articles of Incorporation; preparation of Minutes for Meeting of Incorporation; Minutes of Meeting of Shareholders; preparation of Minutes of 1st Meeting of Directors; preparation of Ratification of Share Issuance; preparation of Share Certificates; preparation of various documentation for Internal Revenue Service.

Services rendered:

January 3, 4, 8, 9, 10 20XX	$1,950
Less professional discount (50%)	(975)
Total now due and payable	$975

THANK YOU

As with discount billing for friends and relatives, you should not artificially inflate the bill before applying the discount, and you should be somewhat sparing in deciding which people you will do this for.

L-6
Tell Clients and Potential Clients
When The Bill is or May Be Tax Deductible

"IT'S DEDUCTIBLE." With these two magic words, charities raise millions of dollars every year from people who otherwise might not be willing to give money for a worthy cause.

There will be times when the deductibility or partial deductibility of your legal fee will determine whether or not the client is willing or able to spend the money on your legal fees.

If you practice a given type of law, it behooves you to learn what determines whether your legal fee is, or is not, tax deductible to the client.

If you practice business or tax law, most of your fees are either deductible to the client under Internal Revenue Code Section 162 or Internal Revenue Code Section 212 or some other section of the code.

Internal Revenue Code Section 212 deals with expenses deductible by individuals and allows deduction of ordinary and necessary legal fees paid (for cash basis taxpayers).

1. For the production of, or collection of, income;
2. For management, conservation or maintenance of property held for the production of income; or
3. In connection with the determination, collection or refund of any tax.

It is not possible to list the myriad possibilities where your legal fee is (or is not) in whole (or in part) deductible. A reading of Regulation 1.2121 would be helpful to you as a start.

Internal Revenue Code Section 162 allows a taxpayer to deduct ordinary and necessary legal fees in connection with a trade or business. Here again, it is not possible to list all the possibilities of legal fees which are partially or totally deductible.

You should attempt to analyze the most common legal fees charged by you to determine which fees are , or might be, deductible to your clients.

Incidentally, you must be careful when a client asks you to bill an obviously non-deductible legal fee "to the business." Be careful! At best, you can send an invoice to

Mr. John Doe
ABC Industries
123 Main Street Anytown, U.S.A.

As far as you are concerned, ABC Industries is the mailing address where the bill is sent. If the company pays the bill with a company check, charging the payment to Mr. Doe, or subsequently makes a journal entry reclassification of the expenditure, that is their business, not yours. No one requires you to be an IRS auditor for the government.

You can also remind your clients in November of each year that they must actually pay you before December 31 to get a tax deduction for the year if they are cash basis taxpayers.

Occasionally your bill is fully deductible or fully non-deductible or capitalizable or a combination of all of the above or entitled to some special treatment. It's worth the effort for you to analyze your legal services and prepare and allocate your bill to get the maximum possible tax benefits for the client.

The client will appreciate the fact you care enough to allocate at least a small portion of the bill as a tax-deductible item.

L-7
Create a Sense of Urgency on Your Bill

A client once told me the following:

"You lawyers are at fault for all of your uncollected bills. You don't create a sense of urgency on your bill. You give the impression that all lawyers are rich and don't need the money. Your bill looks like you don't care when or if you ever get paid. You should give your bill a sense of urgency so that clients will know they're expected to pay it immediately."

I asked her how she thought a bill should be drafted to create a "sense of urgency." She responded, "It's simple. Put a certain date on the bill."

Look at all the bills you receive. They all have a payment date such as:

Due and payable by March 13th
Delinquent if not paid by March 13th
Pay by March 13th to avoid late charges
Pay by March 13th to avoid penalties
This bill is now due and payable

"You lawyers don't create any sense of urgency on the bill so we clients just take our time about paying them. Then when we don't pay them right away, you get mad at us even though it's not our fault."

I thought about what she said and think that she may have been right. I began putting "Now Due and Payable" on my invoices and began dating back amounts due so that my bills now read:

Unpaid balance due and payable for services rendered in October	$XXX
Unpaid balance due and payable for services rendered in November	$YYY
Total amount now overdue	$X+Y
Due for services rendered the month of December	$ZZZ
Total amount now due and payable	$X+Y+Z

I don't know for sure if this format makes clients pay any faster, but this format sure makes me call sooner when a client is delinquent. Since I review the bills *before* they go out, I'm often on the phone to the client before the bill leaves my office rather than waiting for an accounts receivable aging report after the bills have gone out. I also quickly stop working on a case when I see the delinquency and can't get a satisfactory payment arrangement by calling the client.

I can't bring myself to put a date certain on the bill. I think it is too commercial, but I recommend that you try it or at least do something to give your bill a sense of urgency.

Chapter M
Getting Paid for What You Do

M-1
What is a "Good" Client?

A Good Client is:

"A Client Who Pays His Bills to Me So I Can Pay My Office and Personal Bills"

This is not my definition. It is *your* definition.

I have asked lawyers all over America (and, indeed, outside of America) to answer the following question:

"If you could have any kind of clients and cases you wanted to have, which would you choose?"

The answer is always, "A client who pays his bills to me so I can pay my office and personal bills."

Lawyers from every size firm, from sole practitioner to mega firm, answer the question the same way. Lawyers with rural practices, urban practices, corporate practices, criminal law practices, tax practices, high-tech practices, etc., all answer that question the same way. Male lawyers and female lawyers answer that question the same way. Lawyers at every level of experience from first year of practice to more than 50 years of practice answer that question the same way. Lawyers who are struggling and lawyers who are very profitable answer that question the same way. Lawyers in every region of the country answer that question the same way.

I'll never forget the African American female lawyer practicing in a poor ghetto area who said to me, "Mr. Foonberg, I didn't become a lawyer to make money. I became a lawyer to help my people. I've turned down partnership and job offers in fancy, high-income law firms in fancy, high-income neighborhoods. I'm happy using my skills to help my people. But, Mr. Foonberg, I've also learned that somebody has to pay me or I can't pay my own bills. I have to have some clients who pay their bills or I won't be in practice to help anybody because I won't be able to pay my bills."

Abraham Lincoln is reputed to have advised a young lawyer, "Get at least one railroad as a client. Then you'll be able to pay your bills with the fees from the railroad while you do work for clients who can't pay your bill." I don't know whether the story attributed to Lincoln is true, but it might well be.

Abraham Lincoln and the African American female lawyer are no different from the rest of the lawyers and professionals in America (or at least the ones who are reading this book).

I recognize that money is not necessarily a prime motivation in a person's becoming a lawyer or remaining a lawyer. There are many non-monetary reasons for becoming and remaining a lawyer. Nobody would accuse either Abraham Lincoln or the African American female lawyer of being "money hungry" or "greedy." Yet each recognized the need to have fee-paying clients so they could pay their own bills and stay in practice to help the poorer clients.

I ask you to believe me when I tell you that if you became a lawyer because you want to help people, you will be a happy person enjoying your professional and personal life and making money will follow. Law will be your profession and you will feel a calling to it as much as a priest or physician feels a calling to help others. (The word Advocate is from the Latin Advocare – to call out for help.)

If you became a lawyer only to make money, then you will never make enough to be happy. Your professional life and home life will not be as happy as they could be. Law will not be a profession to you – just a business where one measures success by the amount of dollars extracted from the public. You will leave the profession for some other economic activity where you will not have ethical requirements.

Getting paid is critical to survival, but don't let it become the only reason for practicing law.

M-2
Put Your Fee Agreement in Writing

This material covers the necessity of fee agreements from a client relations point of view rather than from the point of view of creating rights and liabilities.

Putting your fee agreement in writing will not in and of itself get you any good clients, but it will help you avoid taking on some bad ones. Written fee agreements will help you break off from, or substitute out of, representing some bad clients before they become absolute disasters from an economical or professional point of view. The written fee agreement will also help protect your fee if the client dies, loses interest in the case or wants to change lawyers.

In 1968, I publicly advocated written fee agreements signed by the client as a pre-condition to doing significant legal work. I was called "unethical" and "unprofessional" by some lawyers and Bar Associations. In 1976, I published a model fee agreement in the first edition of my book, *How to Start and Build a Law Practice*, now in its 5th edition. The book was considered "controversial." In 1985, the American Bar Association published a monograph with sample written fee agreements and several states now make written fee agreements mandatory and, indeed, would make failure to get a signed written fee agreement grounds for disciplinary action.

I relate this four-decade earlier history of my connection to written fee agreements to make two points:

1. Plenty of written materials now exist covering the wording of fee agreements.

2. We live in a rapidly changing world relative to client relations. What was considered unethical to do in the 1960s is considered unethical not to do in the 21st Century. You must be flexible and aware of what is currently acceptable. I recommend a personalized fee agreement for each client rather than a preprinted agreement, for two reasons:

A) The client can't claim he or she was given a form to sign and didn't understand the terms (Contract of Adhesion); and

B) It offers proof you reached a fee agreement with the client *after* discussing the specific case.

I also recommend using the word "agreement" instead of "contract" because it is less formidable. The word "contract" can scare off some clients.

In this chapter, I simply wish to list some of the points your fee agreement could cover and why it's important from the point of view of getting and keeping good clients. I'll leave it to you to fit the wording to your particular kinds of cases. This list is taken essentially from *How to Start and Build a Law Practice* (5th edition.)

1. DETERMINE THE MATTER INVOLVED. Your client may have several different legal matters. There must be a clear description of what cases you are accepting responsibility for to avoid confusion at a later point. This also demonstrates to your potential client that you have a wide breadth of legal knowledge because you can describe what cases you are not handling (if you know them). If you are aware of other actual or potential legal matters of the client for which you are not accepting responsibility, list them.

2. ESTABLISH YOUR CREDIBILITY. When you dictate the fee agreement in front of the client, you can impress the client as to your ability to do work promptly. When the client gets the letter in the same or next day's mail or email, or alternatively, when you tell the client the letter will be sent on a certain date, you can establish your credibility for on-time, as promised delivery of legal services. Additionally, you need to protect yourself in the event the Statute of Limitations had run out before the client came to see you.

3. DECIDE A LAWYER IS REQUIRED. You want to demonstrate to your client that you wouldn't want a client to spend money on legal fees unnecessarily if there is a more economical alternative. Also, you protect yourself if the client subsequently claims you told him or her that no lawyer was necessary when, in fact, you urged the client to get a lawyer.

4. SUGGEST OTHER LAWYERS. Let the client know that you are not desperate for the particular case. People want to use lawyers who are successful. By your being a little bit distant Just a little bit, not a lot), the client will feel that you have mutually chosen each other. Additionally, emphasize that you're not accepting professional responsibility for the matter until the fee agreement is signed and returned with the retainer check.

5. DESCRIBE THE BASIC FEE. This establishes preliminarily your minimum fee and lets the client know whether he or she can afford to retain you, and you know whether you can accept the matter at that price.

6. DESCRIBE THE WORK THE BASIC FEE WILL COVER. This lets the potential client know the effort you will have to put forth in the case for the basic fee. This way the client knows there is no overcharging in the fee and you are earning the entire fee.

7. DESCRIBE WORK THE BASIC FEE WILL NOT COVER. This establishes your legal skill in handling the matter as it demonstrates your knowledge of what may have to be done as additional work.

8. DESCRIBE METHOD FOR PRICING ADDITIONAL WORK. The client should understand clearly your *method* for charging for work over and above the basic work (by time, by stage, such as depositions, conferences, etc.).

9. EXPLAIN THE MINIMUM FEE. The client must understand the minimum amount of money he or she would need to pay.

10. EXPLAIN THE MAXIMUM FEE. If you can judge or estimate the maximum fee, you should do so. No one wants to go into bankruptcy just to make lawyers rich. If necessary, tell the client you will review the potential maximum fee periodically. You don't want a client who can't, or won't, pay for what they need. An honest client won't spend money to start something he or she can't finish.

11. EXPLAIN OUT-OF-POCKET COSTS. Be sure to explain potential out-of-pocket costs. Point out that the costs are in addition to basic fees, and not part of, the basic fee. By listing these items (such as court filing fees, recording fees, corporate seals and books, bond costs, expert witnesses, etc.) you are demonstrating your competence and expertise in handling the case. You also avoid any misunderstanding as to what the total of fees and costs could be.

12. THE AGREED UPON CASH FLOW SCHEDULE. You each must have a clear understanding of *when* you expect to be paid; in advance or on receipt of invoices monthly, at conclusion of case or some combination of these. Running up huge unpaid bills will quickly sour the relationship between a lawyer and a client.

13. YOUR MUTUAL RIGHT TO TERMINATE SERVICES. This makes clear to the client that if certain things occur or do not occur – non-cooperation by the client, case becomes non-meritorious, non-payment by client - you can terminate your services. This communicates that you wouldn't knowingly prosecute a non-meritorious position which would of course waste the client's money. This also communicates that your retention of the case is conditioned upon the client doing what is expected of him. You and the client will each understand your relation to each other in terms of undone work and fees for work done in the event the client wishes to change lawyers. Naturally, you are going to be subject to certain limitations in criminal work, divorce work or any situation where the client's rights would be unnecessarily prejudiced.

14. YOUR OPINION OF THE CASE. The client wants to know the probability of success or failure. You can demonstrate your competence and experience by giving an opinion of the case based on the facts known at that point. The client must understand there is a risk that any case can be lost due to factors beyond the lawyer's control-new laws, new administrative or judicial rulings, jury findings, etc. If the case is, in fact, lost, or doesn't come up to the client's expectation, the client won't be surprised and won't refuse to pay the final bill.

15. TELL THE CLIENT HOW TO MAKE THE RETAINER CHECK PAYABLE. This establishes early on in the relationship that the client is expected to write checks as required by the agreement. It also establishes the bona fides of the client. (See the chapter on "Cash Up Front.")

16. SET AN OUTSIDE LIMIT FOR RETURN OF THE LETTER AND CHECK. This lets the client know that, in legal work, things move according to a schedule beyond his or her control. Also it establishes that the client must cooperate with you and be timely if you accept the case. This also establishes that you will not accept professional responsibility unless and until the fee agreement is returned with the client's retainer check.

17. BE SURE THE CLIENT SIGNS THE LETTER, PREFERABLY ON EACH PAGE. I've had two or three situations where the client returned the letter unsigned along with the retainer check. Later the client claimed the agreement was different from what the letter stated. Refusal to sign the fee agreement is normally a sign of a problem client, one you'd be better off without.

The importance of the written fee agreement, especially for first-time clients or new matters for old clients, cannot be overemphasized. As indicated, you should tailor the agreement to suit your needs and that of the particular case or client.

M-3
How Your Lifestyle Changes
When You Have Good Clients

1. You have more free time for your family.
2. You have more time for yourself.
3. Your cash flow improves and you don't wake up at 3:30 in the morning worrying about how you are going to meet your payroll or your child's educational expenses, or your retirement.
4. You have more free time for continuing education to update your skills as a lawyer.
5. You have more time for spectator sports and participant sports.
6. You have more time for traveling, for writing the great American novel or for just doing nothing.
7. You have more freedom to select voluntarily the clients and cases you want to handle for free.
8. Your staff and you feel you are helping clients who deserve to be helped.
9. Non meritorious ethics complaints and malpractice complaints from unhappy clients are eliminated.

M-4
Foonberg's Rule of Cash Up Front

For more than 40 years I have been preaching "Foonberg's Rule" (also known as, 'The Rule in Foonberg's Case"). Foonberg's Rule is similar to "Shelley's Rule" (also known as "The Rule in Shelley's Case"), because each deals with "fees." Fees simple in Shelley's Rule and simple fees in Foonberg's Rule.

Foonberg's Rule can be stated in three words and restated in three explanations.

Foonberg's Rule (in three words) is: CASH UP FRONT.

The concept of cash up front is a critical one for two reasons:

1. The case selection process for all lawyers new and experienced.
2. Economic survival for new lawyers.

As indicated, Foonberg's Rule can be stated in three alternative ways:

1. Clients who can't, or won't, pay you cash up front at the beginning of the case are the same clients who can't, or won't, pay you cash during the case, and are the same clients who can't, or won't, pay you cash at the end of the case.
2. If you can choose between doing the legal work and not getting paid or not doing the legal work and not getting paid, you are better off not doing the work and not getting paid.
3. Bona fide clients who seriously care about their cases will give you a cash advance for costs, and/or fees, to the best of their ability. Flakey clients, or those who hold back on telling you everything, will not advance cash because they know things either about the case or themselves that would affect your accepting or rejecting the case. (There are some exceptions in criminal cases.)

Abraham Lincoln is reported to have advised a new lawyer to always get some part of his fee in advance from the client. That way, the lawyer knows he has a client and the client knows he has a lawyer.

Foonberg's Rule is just an adaptation of Abraham Lincoln's advice to a new lawyer.

M-5
People are More Willing to Pay
For What They Need and Don't Have
Than To Pay For What They Already Have

This is another way of saying, "cash up front." People make decisions about which bills to pay. They have their own scale of priorities. When it comes to bill paying, different people have different ethics and standards about paying their bills.

Some reasons people pay their legal fees include one or more of the following:

1. It's the moral thing to do.
2. They owe the money for services they received.
3. They don't want to damage their credit rating.
4. They don't want to be sued.
5. They have no choice. They must pay before they can receive the services they want or need.

I've seen people deeply in debt for legal fees spend money for cruises, new cars, jewelry or vacation condos.

Unfortunately for lawyers, legal fees don't rate very high on the payment priority list AFTER the legal services are rendered. Legal fee payments often fall behind department store bills, credit card bills, rent, parent or child support, car payments, mortgage payments, student loan payments, taxes, telephone bills, utility bills, etc. People need these goods and services on an ongoing basis to maintain their standard of living. Their standard of living won't suffer if they don't pay a legal fee.

Accordingly, you simply must recognize that legal fees don't rate very high on the priority of payment scale, and that this is especially true when people have' already received what they want or need from you. When people perceive they need you, or will need you, you will be high on their priority of payment list. That is the time for you to get paid. People somehow are simply more willing and able to pay you when they need you rather than when they no longer need you.

M-6
Rate Your Clients According to
Cash Flow - Prioritize Your Work

You should rate your clients and cases and prioritize your services and attention accordingly.

Not every client or case has the same value insofar as your cash flow is concerned. Clients and cases with good cash flow contribute to your sense of well being and satisfaction, and enjoyment of your professional and personal life. Bad cash flow can cause you to wake up at 3:30 a.m. worrying about how to pay your bills and meet payroll. Bad cash flow causes you to question your career decision of becoming or remaining a lawyer. Bad cash flow spills over into a general dissatisfaction which makes it impossible to enjoy your personal life. This dissatisfaction caused by bad cash flow can lead to alcoholism and divorce.

You should rate every client and case in the office and give corresponding priority or service.

My simple system is as follows:

A. "A" Clients and Cases:

"A" clients and cases are those matters for which you are paid in advance or for which the client pays the bill the moment received. "A" clients and cases get instantaneous legal service the moment they approach you with the problem because your bill is paid the moment they get the bill. I've had "A" clients call me up and say the following:

"Jay, I got your bill today, but I've got some questions. I've instructed the bookkeeper to pay your bill in full so I keep my "A" rating with you. Please call me back later and we'll discuss the bill." I then credit the next bill, if necessary. I don't mind working nights or weekends for these people because I'll receive immediate reward for my labor. I return their calls and emails first (subject to urgencies in other matters), often in minutes.

B. "B" Clients and Cases:

"B" clients and cases are those where I get paid in the ordinary course of business after they receive the bill. I do their work in the ordinary course of business after I get the work. I'll work a night or a weekend only if it's truly important to the case. I work on "B" clients' cases after I work on "A" clients' cases. I return their telephone calls and emails next.

C. "C" Clients and Cases:

"C" clients and cases are slow-pay ones. Most contingencies and probates are in this category. There is very little you can do to move these cases along toward getting your cash flow. Judicial and administrative calendars are such that no matter how hard you push, there is little or nothing you can do to speed up the conclusion of the case or the payment of your fee. Whether the client is a slow-pay one because of inability to pay faster or unwillingness to pay faster is immaterial. The end result is that you don't get paid. Since "C" clients and cases are slow-pay 'ones, I am slow to work. I take care of the "C" clients' cases *after* taking care of the "A" and "B" clients' cases. Again, I return their telephone calls and emails after the "A" and "B" clients, often the next day.

D. "D" Clients and Cases:

"D" clients and cases are no-pay ones. They force me to become a no-work attorney. When I recognize a client or case as being a "D," I recognize that it is time to stop working. These clients and cases not only don't increase your cash flow, they reduce it because of the overhead and salaries it costs you to do business. Naturally, every lawyer has some no-pay clients and cases. There is nothing wrong in doing some "D" work if you want to. You must be careful, however, not to take care of the "D" clients' cases until after you have taken care of the "A," "B," and "C" clients' cases, in that order.

Obviously, you cannot prejudice your client's case and you must perform all necessary work in a timely fashion, but there is nothing to prevent your prioritizing your work. Additionally, I explain the system to the client at the first meeting; if the system is not acceptable to them, I don't take the case.

When I review the status of all the cases in the office periodically, I review the "A" cases, then the "B" cases, then the "C's" and finally the "D's." Without "A's" and "B's," it would be difficult to do the "C's" and even more difficult to handle the "D's".

I have no problem explaining this "A" client system to clients. I emphasize their case would not be prejudiced nor delayed in result based on this system, but I must use it to be sure the staff, rent and insurance get paid. Clients don't seem to mind and I had a client tell my receptionist, "I am an "A" client, be sure he gets my message."

I must stress that in no event is any client or matter prejudiced in terms of result or needs. Additionally, you must always factor in your like or dislike of the client type of work involved.

The message here is quite simple, improve your cash flow by prioritizing your work in accordance with cash flow.

M-7
Ten Kinds of Bad News Clients to be Avoided

This is a book on how to get and keep *good* clients. By definition, then, there are bad cases or clients which you don't want.

Not all clients are sources of professional or financial satisfaction. Some clients are classic "no pays." Some will cause you aggravation no matter how lucrative the case. Some will eventually get you in trouble with the State Bar or worse. Some will be the cause of your marital or family discord.

Some lawyers will accept these clients only at an "A" Rate, the "Aggravation Rate," which is usually 1 to 2 times the normal rate. Every lawyer has his or her own list of "bad news" clients. In this chapter I will simply relate to you my own personal list of 10 "indicia" which to me warn, "Watch out, trouble ahead." I'm sure you can add from your own experiences. Don't take these clients unless you are well paid (at the Aggravation rate) in advance. Even then, think carefully about taking the cases.

1. CLIENTS WHO BAD MOUTH THEIR PREVIOUS ATTORNEY(S). It's just a matter of time until you will be included in their list.

2. CLIENTS WHO WANT TO RECORD YOUR MEETING. Often these people are only trying to get a free lesson in the law of their case. They'll ask you myriad questions about how and when you do everything on the case. You will rarely see these people a second time and it will be even rarer that they pay.

3. CLIENTS WHO TAKE EXTENSIVE, PAGE AFTER PAGE NOTES. Same as No. 2 above. Be doubly careful if they are using yellow legal pads.

4. CLIENTS WHO WANT TO USE YOUR OFFICE STAFF AS THEIR OWN. They want you to type letters for them on their stationery, make photocopies for them, etc. They want to use your phone and email system for incoming and outgoing messages. They may also want to use your mailing address. These people expect the whole world to be obsequious even though they rarely are willing to pay for any of this.

5. CLIENTS WHO WANT TO USE YOUR TRUST ACCOUNT AS A BANKING SERVICE. These clients may want to use the respectability of your office to "launder" money or obscure fraud.

6. CLIENTS WHOSE FIRST CONCERN IS THEIR PARKING VALIDATION. I don't know why but these clients almost always turn out to be flakes. The good clients never ask you to validate their parking tickets. You have to ask them if they have a ticket to be validated. The bad clients will ask you for a validation before they even meet you. They don't mind wasting your time, but wouldn't waste their money for parking. Clients who are preoccupied with free parking are almost always problem clients. Be careful.

7. CLIENTS WHO ASK FOR A LOAN OF MONEY AGAINST THE CASE. When a client threatens to go to another lawyer unless you lend him or her some money, let the client go. Sometimes the client's case is non-existent and the "client" is simply a "bunko" artist. These "clients" often describe a fantastically great contingency case which never really existed.

8. CLIENTS WHO SAY, "IT'S THE PRINCIPLE, NOT THE MONEY. YOU CAN HAVE ALL THE MONEY." This type of client simply wants to use you for personal revenge. After the case is started, the client often loses interest in the case and becomes uncooperative. Don't touch these cases unless you are well paid in advance for whatever you do.

9. RELIGIOUS FANATICS. When a client says, "God sent me to you and God will see to it that you make lots of money," I cringe. These people are sincere in their belief. Unfortunately, something usually gets lost in the communication between them and God, and you get stuck on a bad case for a non-paying and often non-cooperative client who leaves the details of getting evidence to "you and God." I recommend doing church service instead of doing work for these clients if God's approval is what you want.

10. CLIENTS WHO REFUSE TO COME INTO THE OFFICE. These people want free legal advice by telephone. They don't want to waste their time coming to your office because they don't intend to pay you.

I'm sure you can easily expand this list with some of your own favorites.

M-8
Cases That Should Be Turned Down

Abraham Lincoln reputedly advised a new lawyer upon passing the Bar, "Young man, it's more important to know what cases not to take than it is to know the law."

There are some types of cases that will turn out to be financial disasters no matter how skillful you are as a lawyer and no matter how aggrieved the client is. If you want to take these cases on and spend time and money that could have gone to your family, it's certainly your privilege to do so. Don't blame anyone but yourself when you've spent a lot of time and money, received a financially disastrous result for a client, and the' client, in turn, thinks you're a bad lawyer because you didn't do better.

The following are examples of cases which should be turned down:

1. *Cases in which you are the second or third lawyer on the case.*

It is theoretically possible that the client and the previous lawyer just didn't get along, but this is not normally the case. Check with the previous lawyer to see if that lawyer claims some sort of lien on the case. Normally you fill find that the problem is:

    a.) A non-meritorious case; b) An uncooperative client; c) A non-paying client.

2. *Hurt Feelings Cases.*

In this type of case, there is often wrongful conduct on the part of the defendant, but no special damages or only nominal damages provable by your client. Recovery and your compensation will depend on punitive damages which often are non-obtainable or non-collectible. Examples of these cases are:

    a.) Libel and slander;
    b.) Bar room brawls;
    c.) Most assault & battery cases.

3. *Landlord-Tenant Cases.* (Unless you are paid in advance)

These cases are often more bitter than divorce cases. It makes no difference whether you represent the landlord or the tenant, your client will hate you and resent paying your fees by the time the case is over. The landlord is infuriated at having to pay you money to evict a tenant who hasn't paid the rent. It's double loss for the landlord. The tenant is stalling for time, using court delay to get rent free occupancy until the landlord gets the uncollectible judgment and the Writ of Possession. Often the tenant can't leave because he hasn't got the first and last month's rent for another place. He may want some money to move out. Landlord-tenant cases are often hate matches and both sides want to use the lawyer for free.

Suggest legal aid to the tenant and suggest the Apartment Rental Association to the landlord. (These associations often have "house counsel" who do routine eviction cases on a mass production basis at a low price for landlords. Another suggestion is to tell the landlord you'll charge your regular fees, but that you'll teach him or her how to bring the process *in propria persona* without a lawyer. In this way, you may keep the client in the future.)

4. *Divorce (dissolution) cases in which people are heavily in debt (unless you are paid in advance).*

Financial insecurity is often part of the background in a divorce. At the inception of the divorce, the parties still have liquid and non-liquid assets and credit cards. They may have a borrowable equity in real estate or other assets. They will soon dissipate their assets as they learn that it's much more expensive to live apart than it was to live together.

In accepting a divorce case, you must be firm about being paid in advance since the initial retainer fee may be the only fee you'll ever see. The whole world of divorce law is changing. As women gain increased earning capacity and increased property rights, there is an increasing ability of people to afford and pay for lawyers. This is a trend which should continue. The present reality, however, is that there is not enough money to compensate the attorneys adequately. Don't blame anyone but yourself if you take cases that legal aid would have taken.

5. *Criminal cases in which you are not totally paid in advance.*

You can't collect a fee from a client in jail who earns only cigarette money. Once you are in the case, it is difficult, if not impossible, to get out. You are in a system where only the defense lawyer is expected to work for free. The judge won't work for free when there is an indigent defendant. The prosecutor won't work for free for the indigent defendant. The court reporter, bailiff, clerk, etc., all expect to get paid even though the accused is indigent. It is only the private practice defense lawyer who will be expected to work without compensation. Don't take cases that should be handled by a paid public defender.

6. *Bankruptcy (unless you are paid in advance).*

I was the laughing stock of the courtroom when my client pointed to me from the witness chair in bankruptcy court and amended his schedules of unpaid debts to include the fees due me.

7. *Cases in which the client is proceeding on the basis that the other side will settle right away because it can't afford the publicity of litigation.*

People who say this normally believe what they are saying. Unfortunately, the reality is that it never happens that way. The reality is that the other side will begin to talk settlement AFTER the United States Supreme Court denies *certiorari*. Before accepting this type of client, you must gently convince this client that you should be paid hourly in advance and not on a contingency basis since a contingency fee would be unfair to the client if the case settles as the client predicts it will.

8. *Cases totally without legal merit.*

Don't take cases totally without merit, hoping for a quick nuisance settlement or for experience. Not only can these cases cost you a tremendous amount of uncompensated time, they can also lead to sanctions against you and the client as well as disciplinary proceedings against you.

9. *Slip-falls (unless there are large damages).*

Insurance companies will talk settlement right after the United States Supreme Court denies *certiorari*. Even the most meritorious cases are difficult to settle on a reasonable basis. Some lawyers claim to be experts on handling these cases. Refer the case to them.

10. *Vengeance* cases *totally without merit.*

Don't accept vengeance cases that are totally without merit. Clients often want lawyers to prosecute or defend non-meritorious cases just to stall for time or to use the lawyer for personal vengeance. These cases not only lower your reputation with opposing counsel and the court, but often are not economical because the client can't, or won't, pay you. Let some other lawyer go broke on dubious cases.

11. *Cases that belong in small claims court.*

The economics of these cases rarely, if ever, justify using a lawyer. If the client is adamant, be sure you are paid in full in advance.

M-9
Client Costs as a Factor in Accepting or Rejecting a Case

The subject of cost advancement is subject to debate and disagreement in many jurisdictions. The purpose of this chapter is not to take any position but to caution that the lawyer can go broke advancing costs. Costs should always be considered and handled from a cash flow point of view, keeping in mind your economic survival from a profit or loss point of view and also from a case acceptance or rejection point of view.

Never be afraid to ask an experienced lawyer what out-of-pocket costs and fees should be anticipated in a given type of case and at what stage of the proceeding they will have to be paid.

If at all possible, you should not finance client costs. You are not a bank or financial company. You should *always* ask the client for estimated costs *in advance* and place the money in your trust account to be used as needed and replenished as used. You should ask for costs in advance even in contingency fee cases.

The reality of life however, is that you will finance client costs for a number of reasons, such as:

1. Indigent client with a meritorious case that has a recovery.
2. Convenience. You expend the money for the client because it is more convenient, especially with smaller amounts such as long distance telephone calls, court fees, etc.
3. The competition. Other lawyers in your community don't ask for, or receive costs up front and you're afraid of losing the client if you insist.

Even though you *should* ask the client for costs up front, in certain cases you could indicate to the client that, if necessary or convenient, you can make an advance subject to monthly reimbursement or reimbursement at the end of the case (for meritorious accident cases, corporate formation, fee, etc.).

In some cases you shouldn't take the case unless the client pays all the costs including expert witnesses up front (slip falls, doubtful recovery cases, etc.).

Sometimes the amount of costs required on a meritorious case is so large that neither you nor the client can afford the costs, in which case you should associate a well-financed law firm that can advance the costs. Examples of such cases are those that require large amounts of investigation or outside experts (antitrust, medical malpractice, etc.), and cases where the pre-trial the trial and the appeals will take years.

There are a few groups of lawyers that will invest funds in a big case with big recoveries. This concept is a new one. I know the groups exist, but I never have had to use them.

M-10
Cash Up Front for Client Costs
On Contingency Cases

Asking for cost money the moment the client comes to you for the initial interview.

You are at the client's mercy with respect to his or her version of what happened. Sometimes, in order to induce you to take the case on a contingency basis, the client won't give you all the facts or will color the facts. The client is hoping you will start the case in order to gain "revenge" on the other side.

Additionally, all factors of our existing economy tend toward making cost advancement by the lawyer foolish. Inflation lowers the value of the account receivable for costs you have advanced. Interest paid by the attorney for bank financing increases the cost the advance as time goes by. Increasingly, jammed court calendars increase the time of carrying of the advance as a receivable. In the final analysis, we should also remember that a certain number of these cases will be lost due to client's death, client's moving away, client's lack of interest in their case, and just plain adverse verdicts and judgments and insolvent adverse parties.

By asking a client for cost money up front, you will reduce your economic costs of doing business and increase your profits and cash flow.

Clients who truly believe in the merits of their case will advance cost money, if they can raise it.

Clients who don't truly believe in the merits of the case, or have been turned down by several previous lawyers, will not put up their money in advance to cover costs.

If clients have a meritorious case but truly can't put up the money for costs, then the lawyer simply has to decide whether to take the case on the traditional contingency basis.

How to get money up front for costs.

You should simply say to your client, "I really believe in your case. I believe in your case to the point that I will invest my time in handling it. On the other hand, I cannot be your banker. I'll expect you to pay all out-of-pocket costs such as court filing fees etc., and I'll ask you for a check for a trust account. I'll put your money in the account and if we need more I'll ask for it. Also, if I don't use all of it I will give you a refund."

TYPICAL CLIENT COSTS

If you are handling a certain type of case for the first time, or are not quite sure yourself, ask an attorney experienced in the area of law for help in estimating the kinds of costs to" anticipate. Listed below are some of the typical or "classic" costs you are likely to encounter in any given type of case.

1. *Litigation.*

Police reports, court reporter, minimum appearance fee, transcript costs, deposition appearance fees or transcript costs, medical examinations, medical opinions and reports, medical testimony, investigations, photocopy costs, record copying costs (employer and hospital), expert opinion and testimony costs in addition to non-medical, including accountants, actuaries, engineers, etc., sheriff's fees or other process fees and travel expenses. Inability to pay expert witness' fees in advance causes many clients to abandon meritorious cases.

2. *Business Formation and Business Generally.*

Advance payment of franchise or income taxes, filing fees for Secretary of State or for County Clerk, permit fees for stock issuance, transfer taxes, certified copies, recording costs, newspaper notices and advertising, stock certificates, corporate seals and books, notarial fees, travel costs, long distance telephone calls and communication costs, title searches and reports, and out-of-state attorneys.

Again, these are only sample costs to be considered.

ESTIMATING CLIENT COSTS ON CONTINGENCY CASES

Often, when a client discusses engaging you, he or she will want to know what the *total* fees and costs will be. If you misquote costs, you could find yourself turning a profitable case into a losing case.

If you are handling a certain type of case for the first time or are not quite sure of yourself, ask an experienced attorney in that area of law for help in estimating the kinds of costs to be anticipated.

M-11
Be Careful Which, If Any,
Contingency Cases You Accept or Keep

Lawyers have gone bankrupt handling good contingency cases. A good contingency case can involve thousands of hours of your time with its attendant costs of overhead and out-of-pocket expenses.

It may be years until a case is settled or litigated to a final judgment. There can also be appeals before you begin to try to turn a judgment into cash.

Obviously, I have presented a rather harsh scenario. In truth, most contingency cases settle in a reasonable amount of time (nine months to one year) with reasonable fees for the attorney. This is particularly true when you are dealing with an insurance carrier or a large, responsible opponent. Private individuals and smaller businesses often don't like to pay any settlement, reasonable or not, because they equate payment of a settlement with an admission of guilt or fault of some nature. Insurance carriers normally are in the impersonal business of closing cases. Unfortunately insurance carriers and their attorneys sometimes decide to occasionally oppose all matters, even the most meritorious, to "teach" claimants and their lawyers a lesson. Responsible companies look at a payment for a claimant's clients simply as a cost of doing business.

An attorney can - make good fees and indeed "hit the proverbial home run" on a contingency fee practice or a practice that includes contingency cases. I recommend budgeting a minimum percentage of your office time for contingency cases, unless you do predominately contingency work and are adequately financed.

You should do several things in order to upgrade your fee income from contingency cases.

Case Selection.

Obviously, the secret is to be sure you take the right cases or, more accurately, turn down the wrong cases. You should develop some sort of an evaluation formula or system in the acceptance process.

Ask yourself at least the following questions:

a.) Do I really know the law?

b.) What is my best guess of when the case might first settle (in months or years)?

c.) If the case doesn't settle within the estimated period, when is it likely to be tried or heard?

d.) How much time do I have to dedicate to the case to get it ready for a settlement or to get it ready for trial?

e.) How much is the case likely to settle for or what is a reasonable judgment amount?

f.) Multiply your time estimates by 1.5 or even double it, to get a more accurate picture of the economics involved. (Lawyers are not good at estimating time and they tend to minimize the time required when they do budgets.)

g.) What are my fees likely to be if the case settles or goes to trial?

h.) How much per hour will I have earned on the case?

i.) How much will I have to advance in cost money for:
Preliminary investigation?
Doctor's or experts examinations and reports?
Depositions and copies?
Service fees?
Other costs or expenses?

If after making the above analysis you want to take the case, then by all means take it. However, don't make the mistake of blindly accepting contingency cases without making this kind of analysis.

From time to time, re-analyze the cost in time and dollars to see if your opinion of the case changes, based on the true numbers and facts becoming known.

If you find you have a loser, then get rid of it immediately. Don't get a bear by the tail. Cases which are economically bad always seem to get worse, not better. It is better to bleed a little than to hemorrhage.

The best way to get out of a bad contingency case is to be honest with the client and to stress that the case is not economically meritorious. No Bar Association will fault you for refusing to prosecute a non-meritorious case.

M-12
Sample Letter to Drop a Bad Contingency Case

Mr. Bad Case
123 Main Street Anytown, USA
Dear Mr. Bad Case:

After a great deal of soul searching, I have concluded that our firm can no longer handle your case on a contingency basis. When we began the case, we believed in the merits of the case. The case, as it has developed, however, does not appear to be economically meritorious.

There is no fee for our services. We would, however, appreciate being reimbursed for our out-of-pocket costs. We will be pleased to cooperate with your new attorneys. You should proceed to choose a new attorney as rapidly as possible as there is still plenty of time for a new attorney to accept the case. There will be no prejudice to your attorney or to your case if you act promptly in obtaining new counsel. If you delay, you may be prejudicing your case.

We wish to emphasize that, in our opinion, it is not meritorious to proceed with the case. Another lawyer or law firm might have a contrary opinion and be eager to accept the case. We recommend that you consult with as many attorneys as possible. We would be happy to assist you in finding a young lawyer with a lower overhead who might be interested in taking the case on. The County Bar Association maintains a lawyer referral service to assist you.

Please contact us on receipt of this letter to discuss your options. If we do not hear from you, we shall have to make a motion in court to be substituted out as your attorneys. Such a motion would be based on this letter to you and would put into the court record our opinion that the case is not meritorious. This opinion in the court record could be harmful to your case if read by the opposing side.

If you have any questions, please don't hesitate to contact us.

Very truly yours,

The foregoing letter can be Exhibit A in your motion to be relieved as counsel. You have suggested seeking other counsel who might disagree with your opinion so that you are not subsequently sued for malpractice for your opinion that the case doesn't warrant prosecution. You have indicated that there will be no prejudice to the case if the client acts readily, but there might be if the client waits. By expressing your opinion that the case is not meritorious, no Bar Association or Ethics Committee will fault you for refusing to congest the court system with a non-meritorious case. By your selecting the next attorney, you may be able to salvage a forwarding fee in addition to recovering costs expended.

Naturally, you'll have to modify the letter to suit your particular situation.

M-13
Upgrading Your Practice by Getting Rid of Losers, Using the 100 Percent Refund
(Dump the Dogs)

Over the years I have received many unsolicited thank you letters from lawyers for passing this concept on to them.

At least once a year, review all of the cases in your office to see which you want to get rid of in order to free yourself for the cases and clients you enjoy handling, and which are financially and professionally satisfying.

You should ask yourself a series of questions about the case, the client and the economics of the case. If you wish to assign some sort of point value to each of the factors, you can do so, or you can simply rely on a "gut" feeling for which cases to get rid of.

Some typical questions you can ask follow:

The Case:
1. Do I enjoy this area of law?
2. Am I competent in this area of law?
3. Is this case a case which enhances my professional satisfaction?
4. Am I handling the case well?
5. Would the client be prejudiced if I substituted out?

The Client:
1. Is this client cooperative when cooperation is needed?
2. Are the client's requests or demands for attention reasonable or unreasonable?
3. If the client's demands are unreasonable, can the client be educated to be reasonable?
4. Does the client have other matters in the office?
5. What was the source of the client?
6. Will the source of the client be affected if I don't continue representation of the client?
7. Is the client appreciative of what is being done by the firm on the case?

The Financial Aspects:
1. Is this case a profitable case for
   a.) the firm?
   b.) the client?
2. Would either the client or the firm or both be better off financially if another firm with more expertise in this type of case or client were to handle the matter?

3. What cash flow (or deficit) is this case likely to produce over the next year and thereafter until the matter is concluded?
4. Can another firm take over the case without financial prejudice to the client?
   a.) If we spend our time to educate the next firm, or
   b.) If we refund all or part of the client's fees?
5. How much of our money and time have we already wasted on the case and how much have we received in fees?
6. How much time and money have yet to be put into this case and how much more can we expect to receive in fees?

All of the above factors, and possibly many more, should be considered by you in deciding whether you want to keep a case in the office or refer it out to another lawyer.

The 100 Percent Refund:

When you have a totally miserable client or case that you really don't like, you should seriously consider the 100 percent refund. That is, you offer to refund all of the money the client sent to you and let the client make another lawyer rich. Think of the many times you would have been much better off had you done so before the loss got any bigger. As a general rule, bad cases only become worse, not better, as time goes on. Dump the dogs.

Refund all moneys paid to you including cost reimbursement. No disciplinary authority or ethics entity will fault you if you refund 100% of the money paid leaving the client time to find another lawyer.

M-14
Using the Client's Curve of Gratitude
To Increase Cash Flow

Many lawyers have told me they have used my Client's Curve of Gratitude as a tool to remind themselves and to explain to clients why it is so important for the client to pay a fee at the beginning of the case and the balance the day the case is settled or concluded.

Although I personally have never done so, attorneys tell me they photocopy the chart and actually show it to clients when they discuss fees. I personally simply use it to remind myself that people do prioritize their legal bill paying as follows:

1. Their first priority is to pay for legal services they desperately need but don't yet have.
2. Their second priority is to pay for legal services they desperately needed and just received.
3. Their last priority is to pay for legal services they desperately needed and have already received.

I developed my version of the Client's Curve of Gratitude in 1975. It is based upon a chart entitled "Patient's Curve of Gratitude," which appeared in a 1934 magazine for doctors. It is also based upon an Australian doctor's telling me that he often justified high fees to patients by saying of the treatment: "Just pay me half of what you were willing to pay me when you came in sick."

The facts in the Client's Curve are from an actual case in my office.

In 1976, I learned that *Law Office Economics and Management* had printed a similar chart in 1966 and claimed credit for adapting the medical concept to lawyers. Their chart contained no wording or numbers. We had each independently created a similar concept (adapting the medical chart for lawyers) although only mine was detailed.

Subsequently, many authors have copied my chart and others have copied *LOEM's*, so that various people have claimed creation of the chart.

In any event, the important thing is for you to be aware of the concept and of possibly using a copy of the chart when you discuss fee payment with your clients.

The Client's Curve of Gratitude

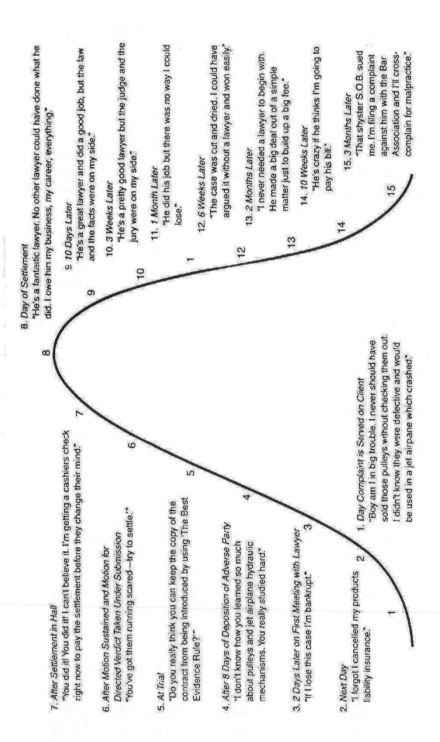

8. *Day of Settlement*
"He's a fantastic lawyer. No other lawyer could have done what he did. I owe him my business, my career, everything."

9. *10 Days Later*
"He's a great lawyer and did a good job, but the law and the facts were on my side."

10. *3 Weeks Later*
"He's a pretty good lawyer but the judge and the jury were on my side."

11. *1 Month Later*
"He did his job but there was no way I could lose."

12. *6 Weeks Later*
"The case was cut and dried. I could have argued it without a lawyer and won easily."

13. *2 Months Later*
"I never needed a lawyer to begin with. He made a big deal out of a simple matter just to build up a big fee."

14. *10 Weeks Later*
"He's crazy if he thinks I'm going to pay his bill."

15. *3 Months Later*
"That shyster S.O.B. sued me. I'm filing a complaint against him with the Bar Association and I'll cross-complain for malpractice."

7. *After Settlement in Hall*
"You did it! You did it! I can't believe it. I'm getting a cashiers check right now to pay the settlement before they change their mind."

6. *After Motion Sustained and Motion for Directed Verdict Taken Under Submission*
"You've got them running scared—try to settle.'"

5. *At Trial*
"Do you really think you can keep the copy of the contract from being introduced by using 'The Best Evidence Rule?'"

4. *After 8 Days of Deposition of Adverse Party*
"I don't know how you learned so much about pulleys and jet airplane hydraulic mechanisms. You really studied hard."

3. *2 Days Later on First Meeting with Lawyer*
"If I lose this case I'm bankrupt."

2. *Next Day*
"I forgot I cancelled my products liability insurance."

1. *Day Complaint is Served on Client*
"Boy am I in big trouble. I never should have sold those pulleys without checking them out. I didn't know they were defective and would be used in a jet airpane which crashed."

© 1976, 1984, 1986, 1990, 1991, 1994, 1999, 2004, 2007
Jay G Foonberg, Beverly Hills, California

M-15
Using Lawyer Demographics to Set or Justify Fees Setting a Fee in Specialty Work

I've used the following approach on several occasions when discussing fees. "Look, there are more than 200,000 lawyers in this state. About 60 percent are young lawyers. The young lawyers claim they are unemployed and under employed. That means they lack experience. A lawyer who has been a lawyer for four to five years may effectively only have two or three year's experience. These young lawyers are absolute geniuses at test taking. They all got good grades as students in college. Unfortunately, they don't have any practical or professional experience dealing with the real world as our state doesn't require any internship or clerkship to get a law license.

"On the other hand, there are only about 850 Board Certified specialists in this state. That's less than one percent of the lawyers. If you want a Board Certified Specialist, you'll have to pay the price.

"Consider that only about 15 percent of the Bar of this state has more than 10 year's experience. If you want an experienced lawyer, you'll have to pay for it. Also, only 800 or so of the lawyers in this state are CPAs. I'm one of them."

You should ask the following question, "What do you want: experience or cheap?" If you want cheap, go to the phone book and the internet and start with "A." Eventually you may find a lawyer who is willing to work at the price you want to pay, The client will usually interrupt you at this pint insisting they want you.

Find out the lawyer demographics in your state. Try to place yourself statistically *vis-à-vis* other lawyers in any relevant terms you can find, whether it be language ability or undergraduate education, or whatever other factor you can find, then use this percentage in your conversation when you quote fees.

M-16
Increasing Your Cash Flow and Reducing Uncollectibles By Matching Your Billing to Your Client's Cash Flow

You can increase your cash flow and reduce your uncollectibles by asking your client about his or her cash flow and then matching the client's payments to you with the client's cash income.

I can best explain the theory of this technique by demonstrating its use in other situations.

As a new lawyer, I had a client who acquired distressed apartments in low-income areas. A building where the rents were $600 per month would be 60 percent vacant. My client would buy the building and change the rent from $600 per month to $150 per week and the building was 100 percent full with a waiting list to get in, even though the rent had been raised from $600 per month to $650, per month. My client patiently explained to me:

> "Jay, you don't understand people. People don't budget. $600 per month is just $600 per week once a month. They don't put aside $138.46 every week to meet their $600 per month obligation. These people get paid weekly or get their welfare checks every two weeks. As a matter of fact, they pay me an extra week in advance when they have the cash from their checks. I simply make it easier for them by matching their cash income to my rents."

Later in my practice, I began doing collection work for banks. I might ask working person debtors if they could afford to pay the bank $350 per month. Often they would say "No." When I asked if they could pay $100 per week from their weekly check, they would say "Yes," even though $100 week was $433.33 per month. If they were paid semi-monthly, I asked for $200 each pay period, if they could manage it. With commercial borrowers, I would find out if they had a pending property sale or were expecting a tax refund or payment on a receivable and I would then match their payment to the bank with their cash flow income.

A major client was in the rubbish collection business. He got paid by the cities he serviced every other month. He told me, "Jay, I get paid every other month. I know how much will be available to pay for this case. I can pay you a fixed amount every other month until paid in full. It might take a year or two to pay in full, but you will get paid. Other lawyers wouldn't do this. They wanted payment in full monthly, which I can't do. Work with me and you'll get paid in full."

His business grew in a growing Southern California. My practice also grew. Over the years I received more than a million dollars in fees by getting paid every other month. His company went bankrupt after a 25 year plus relationship with me. I even got the last cent as a claimant in the bankruptcy proceedings. I simply budgeted his cash flow to my cash flow.

These same principles apply in my law practice and will work in yours as well.

Payment of legal fees in the corporate world is nowhere near as traumatic as it is to small business and individuals. Legal fees, especially large legal fees, usually are not anticipated or budgeted for. Accordingly, you may have to work with your client to get your bill paid. You may have to get your legal fee in part from the client's future cash flow. When your clients indicate that they "can't afford" you because they don't have the cash to pay, it's time to find out where their cash flow comes from to see if part of it can be used for payment of your fees. Typical sources of cash flow could be:

1) Regular income such as wages, interest, bonuses, dividends, etc.
2) Sale of assets.
3) Borrowing against or refinancing assets.
4) Settlement of a lawsuit or legal claim.
5) Inheritance.
6) Borrowing(s) from relatives.

The important thing is to make payment to you an *AUTOMATIC* event. As soon as your client gets cash, you need to get cash immediately without even sending a bill. The client must agree to send you *automatically* the prearranged amount when the client receives the cash. For example, if a client agrees to pay you $200 from each paycheck, then the client could give you post-dated checks to be deposited when the pay date arrives. If the client is refinancing property, you can arrange with the lender to send you part of the proceeds automatically when the loan is funded and disbursed.

Don't hesitate to discuss your client's finances in order to match the client's cash flow to his or her payments to you.

THE AUTOMATIC WEEKLY CHECK. Even in the corporate world, budgeting for legal fees can be a problem. Many corporate clients have the' same problems as individual clients and you may have to help them, too, with their cash flow problems in order to get paid.

I have found the automatic weekly check to be a good solution. The client has the company accounting or payable clerk automatically send a check every week to apply to the bill. For example, if a client requires major litigation that will continue over a period of two years and you estimate the legal fees will amount to $100,000, you should have the client send $1,000 per week automatically without an invoice. When you do invoice, credit all payments received. You should try, if possible, to do legal work at about the same rate as the payments so that you are never far ahead of or behind the client. A missed check is a sign for you to make an inquiry as to what is happening and two or more missed payments can be a signal to slow down or to stop working on the case.

These scheduled weekly payments for the unusually large case must be in addition to, not instead of, the payments for other normal work.

When a client needs legal work and obviously is willing to pay for it, you may help make the deal by working out a program with your client where your payments coincide with the client's cash flow.

THE AUTOMATIC CREDIT CARD OR BANK DRAFT. I have never used either of these methods, but pass them on to you. Instead of a periodic check the client authorizes you to submit credit card charges at regular intervals as though the client was making a new credit card payment at periodical intervals using "signature on file," where the charge slip ordinarily would be signed. It is also possible to do this with automatic bank drafts.

M-17

Support Bar-Recognized Legal Aid or Poverty Law Centers And Send Them the Cases That Don't Belong in Your Office

This book emphasizes getting and keeping clients who can pay their bills to you so that you can pay your bills in the office and at home. This book also suggests that you limit your free legal work and *pro bono* legal work to 5% of your time before you become a *pro bono* case yourself.

The reality of our society, however, is that there are poor people who do need legal work they can't pay for. Often these people have so little money that if they had to pay lawyers, there literally would be no money for food.

I feel that the needs of these people can often best be met through lawyers who are specialists in poverty law. Poverty law, in my opinion, should be a recognized law specialty. When I did debt collection work for banks, I learned that the typical law firm could not, or would not, properly represent a debtor in a debt collection case. I won a lot of cases I might have lost because the attorney just didn't know the law relating to what to do. Sometimes the lawyer wasn't doing anything because he or she wasn't getting paid.

By supporting Bar-recognized legal and poverty law centers, you can accomplish the following:

1. You will limit the amount of free legal work you handle without having to choose between your family and feeling guilty;
2. You will have more time for your family and paying clients;
3. Your net income and free time will rise;
4. The indigent client will obtain competent representation from a lawyer experienced in poverty law;
5. The indigent client will get the needed legal service free or at an affordable price;
6. The Bar, as a whole, will receive recognition for providing the service.

M-18
Feel Good, Not Bad,
About Doing Free Legal Work

The concept of *"noblesse oblige"* is deeply rooted in our profession and will never disappear regardless of a changing world. It has lasted for centuries and will continue to endure.

Almost without exception, every financially successful lawyer I've ever known or met is a lawyer who really wants to help people *and* at the same time be successful.

Every lawyer, for various reasons, does some free or discounted work to help people. Your reasons may arise out of sympathy for a particular person who needs quality help but can't afford it, some concept of social justice, a desire to change the system so that it's fairer and more just, or simply because you like the person who needs help. There are many good reasons.

I do some free legal work and encourage other lawyers to do so. There is one basic rule that I recommend be followed.

THE LAWYER, NOT THE CLIENT, SHOULD DECIDE ON WHICH CASES THE LAWYER WILL WORK WITHOUT GETTING PAID. THE DECISION SHOULD BE MADE *BEFORE* THE WORK IS DONE, NOT *AFTER* THE WORK IS DONE AND A BILL SENT.

When a lawyer does free or discounted legal work for a client, he or she should be able to say, "I feel good. I helped somebody who needed help. I did $1500 of legal work for Mrs. Jones and didn't charge her a penny," and not, "I feel cheated. I did $1500 of legal work for Mrs. Jones expecting payment, and she stiffed me. She's a rotten person for cheating me. Whether she needed help is not the issue. She was supposed to pay and she didn't pay."

Doing free legal work should be an uplifting experience for the lawyer. The lawyer should be able to go to church or synagogue and tell the minister or rabbi that he or she has done a social good on a willing and voluntary basis. The lawyer should feel that the free work will be counted as plus points when the final balance takes place.

On the other hand, if the lawyer has been cheated or tricked into doing free legal work by a non-paying client, the feelings of the lawyer may be negative points when the final balance of good and evil is made.

In the preceding material, I have borrowed heavily from concepts of Harris Morgan of Greenville, Texas. Harris is, in my opinion, the most knowledgeable and personable human being in the world on the subject of Law Office Management. He gives of himself heavily to help the profession and the American public. You should never miss the opportunity to hear him speak or to see one of his video tapes or DVDs or read one of his articles. He and I have been evangelists in the field of Law Office Management; he for more than five decades; I for more than four decades. As of the time of writing this chapter I have done a program for lawyers in every state of the Union, in every province in Canada, and on every one of the 7 continent including Antarctica. Harris has done programs in every one of the 50 states at least twice. An hour of being with Harris Morgan can enrich your life greatly.

In summary, the lawyer and not the client must decide when the lawyer is going to do free legal work.

You should communicate to clients and potential clients that in appropriate cases you or your firm does free legal work but that the amount that you do is limited. This will communicate to the client or potential client your concern for people.

M-19
Barter
Is Half a Moose a Fair Price for a Will?

A lawyer at a program in Burlington, Vermont once asked me, "Mr. Foonberg, is half a moose a fair price for a will?" I thought this was some sort of joke. I asked, "Which half?" Again thinking this was a joke. He answered, "Either half front or back." I asked, "How do you cut a moose in half?" He answered, "With a chain saw." I asked, "Isn't that a bit messy?" He responded, "Not when you shoot the moose. You wait a few hours and he becomes like a block of ice and you saw the frozen moose in half." The lawyer was serious. He wanted to know about barter.

Although I personally am opposed to barter, the practice appears to be widespread among other lawyers, particularly in smaller communities.

I have surveyed audiences of lawyers and found, much to my surprise, that the bartering of legal services for goods and services was not involuntary but rather was voluntary on the part of the lawyer. I found lawyers trading their legal services for the following, among others:

A. Pets and pet services
B. Artwork for the home
C. Personal jewelry
D. Hunting guns
E. Personal clothing
F. Food
G. New cars for family members
H. Medical and dental care

The reason these lawyers willingly traded became apparent to me on reflection. They were trading away fully taxable fee income for non-deductible personal items. The bartering, if not reported to the Internal Revenue Service, resulted in a great tax advantage to the attorney. If the bartering lawyer is in the 40 percent combined state and federal tax bracket (easy to be if you include Social Security taxes), then the lawyer would have to earn $164 to have $100 remaining for non-deductible purchases. If the lawyer is in the 50 percent bracket then obviously the lawyer must earn $200 of taxable fee income to purchase $100 of non-deductible items.

As a tax lawyer and a CPA, I am shocked when the bartering attorneys give me a big grin when I ask if they report the fee income. Most don't! Those who do report the income, normally put a very low fair market value on what they receive on the basis (which is probably true) that the goods and services received do not have readily ascertainable fair market value. In addition, they claim (probably not true) that they really didn't want the barter situation. Detailed records are kept to balance barter received among the partners of the firm, so no one gets left out of the "off-the-books" income.

Typically, the non-lawyer parties to the barter receive non-deductible (for income taxes) services; such as divorce, wills, criminal matters for self and family members, personal injury fees, etc. Accordingly, there is no tax deduction on the clients' tax return and this reduces the likelihood of the clients' taking a direct tax deduction on their books or tax return. However, the client, if in business, may in fact be taking a non-deductible deduction by not adjusting costs of goods or services sold for personal non-deductible items, or not showing as earned income the value of the legal services received.

If the attorney did not report the fee income, it goes without saying that the lawyer is exposed to the possibility of client blackmail at a later date.

Former IRS agents who audited tax returns in rural areas have told me that it was a standard practice when auditing professionals to ask about barter. I have heard of the IRS's serving summonses on commercial barter services to get the names of the barter club members so the IRS could do audits of the members.

I personally am opposed to barter, as outlined above, but I feel duty-bound to report to you that, based on my working with good, reputable lawyers all over America, bartering for legal services appears to be rampant.

M-20
The Cluster Concept of Evaluating
the Profitability of Affiliated Clients,
Recommenders of Clients and Types of Cases

The Cluster Concept is a concept I refer to frequently in various places in this book.

From time to time (at least once a year), you must analyze those clients and referrers of clients who send you business. You must also analyze the cases by type of case.

Each of us has one or more people who sends us lots of business. Sometimes these people are clients and sometimes they are not (friends, relatives, etc.).

We naturally tend to want to take every case we get from "Old Joe" because we don't want to risk offending him and losing him as a client or his referrals of clients.

We tend to take these cases without periodically evaluating the profitability of the cases by referrer or by type of case (litigation, tax, bad faith, corporate formation, family law, etc.).

The Cluster Concept is simply the technique of putting all types of cases into a cluster.

You may wish to analyze, for example, all cases referred by Old Joe, all auto accident cases, all family law cases referred by the Smith Firm, all corporation formations, etc.

It is very easy to make the economic analysis if you have the basic information.

You simply divide all the net fees collected on the closed cases by the total hours spent on the cases of the types you want to analyze.

Examples of this method follow:

Cases Referred by Homer Smith

Case Name	*Net Fee Dollars Collected	Hours Spent On Case	Hourly Rate Earned
A VS. B Auto Accident	$4,500.00	15	$300.00
X Corporation Formation	650.00	10	65.00
R.E. Closing	750.00	2	375.00
R vs. Slip & Fall	-0-	100	(Loss)
TOTAL:	$5,900.00	127	$46.46 Per Hour

Thus, while analyzing the cases Homer Smith sent to you, you should evaluate *all* cases sent, not just the few "winners." We all remember our winners but sometimes forget our losers. The Cluster Concept will help you be realistic in evaluating cases.

Analysis of Slip and Fall Cases

Case Name	*Net Fee Dollars Collected	Hours Spent On Case	Hourly Rate Earned
R v. S	$-0-	100	$ Loss
L v. M	6,500.00	50	130.00
P v. Q	8,000.00	40	200.00
A vs. 0	25,000.00	250	100.00
J vs. T	30,000.00	30	100.00
N vs. Z	-0-	200	(Loss)
TOTAL:	$69,500.00	670	$103.73 Per Hour

You can analyze the cases on an annual basis (all cases completed during the previous year) or on a moving basis (for several years).

The principal value of the Cluster Concept is to make an economic evaluation of case source and type based on facts rather than "gut reactions."

*Dollar figures are by way of example only and not necessarily actual case amounts.

M-21
An Accounting System to Help You Analyze and Increase Client and Case Profitability

It is relatively easy to get the accounting information you need to spot the "winners" and the "losers" in your practice. Your word processing operator or accountant can install this simple system if you don't have the patience.

In order to increase your practice profitability, you need to know what kinds of cases you can or cannot handle profitably, and you also need to know whether the cases you get from a given client or through a given recommender of clients are profitable.

It is obvious that you should target all the work you can get in practice areas where you can practice most profitably and to get all the work you can from those clients and recommenders of clients who send you that kind of work.

When you find you have less profitable or losing types of work or sources of work, you must analyze why you are not making money and either correct your deficiencies so that you can become profitable or stop accepting the work.

To get accurate accounting information, you can code every case file with an identification system which can contain as much of the following information as you need:

A. *What the Client Sees.*
Case Number 07527. This is all the client sees. By using a numeric system instead of an alphabetical (alpha) system, you add new cases at the end rather than in the middle, and you remove files as you close them. This conserves filing room space. The first two digits are the year you opened or renumbered the case. (When a case gets too old you may wish to renumber it so it is not apparent that the case has been dragging on for six years.) The next series of numbers is the file as the case was opened in that particular year. I recommend starting with number 501 in January so that clients won't realize they have the third case of the year in August.

B. *What the Client Does Not See.*
Almost all word processors and computers have a "suppress" system. This means that information is in the system but is not printed out unless you want to print it out. You can print as much, or as little, of the rest of the case number as you wish the client to see on correspondence, bills, pleadings, etc.

C. *Coding or Accounting System.*
What I am presenting here is conceptual in that you have to modify this to fit your own practice.

D. *Types of Cases.*

A two-letter system (alpha) is recommended. A telephone directory lists 64 different fields of law; I will suggest a few here just to get you thinking. You should make your own system to reflect your actual practice. One practice may simply lump all litigation into one category and another practice may wish to refine the field of litigation into several specific subcategories. Some sample codes to designate the types of cases are:

BF:	Business Formation	CD:	Criminal Law-Driving Under the Influence
RC:	Real Estate Closing	CM:	Routine Corporate Record Maintenance
FL:	Family Law	CF:	Corporate Formations
CL:	Criminal Law	PF:	Partnership Formation
PI:	Personal Injury-Plaintiff	TX:	Taxation
BI:	Personal Injury-Defense	CT:	Criminal Taxation
BL:	Business Litigation	LL:	Landlord and Tenant Landlord
CF:	Criminal Law-Felony	LT:	Landlord and Tenant Tenant
CM:	Criminal Law-Misdemeanor		

Obviously, the possibilities for classifying the kinds of work you do are infinite. You must pick your own.

E. *Firm Member Who Brought in the Case.*

Two digits is adequate. A sole practitioner with no partners or associates won't need this. The information enables the firm to evaluate both the amount of business a practice brings in and the profitability of what is brought in.

F. *Client.*

When a given client sends you many different cases, you want to analyze case profitability by client. Perhaps when you average the winners and losers together, you'll find that the particular client is more, or less, profitable than you think. I recommend a three-place alpha numeric code. The first letter is the client's alphabetical designation and the next two are numbers for the client.

G. *Source or Recommender of Clients.*

Here again, I recommend a three-place alpha numeric code identical to the client code above. You'll be able to tell whether this person is sending you winners or losers.

H, *Supervising Attorney.*

Where there is more than one supervising attorney, the ability to manage associates, paralegals, clerks and other timekeepers economically may vary from one attorney to another.

I. *Fee Arrangements.*

A firm may find it is doing well or poorly, depending on the fee arrangements. Typical classifications could be:

CC: Contingency Cases-Collect at End
BM: Bill Hourly-Monthly
BQ: Bill Hourly-Quarterly
FF: Fee Fixed by Firm
DH: Hourly Against Advance Deposit
FC: Fee Fixed by Court
FS: Fee Fixed by Statute

J. *Who in the Firm Set the Fee or Decided to Accept the Case.*

K. *The Sample Case Number.* A sample case number could be:

07-527 BF MR L26 T12 JT FF MR. The client sees only the 07-527. But the case number indicates that this is a Business Formation case brought in by Mary Rainmaker. The client is Longhorn Electronics and it was recommended by Tex Puffer. John Tecnicha is the supervising attorney. The fee is a fixed fee determined by the firm, and Mary Rainmaker set the fee method and decided to take the case.

L. *The Cash Method.*

This system assumes you keep time records. You simply divide cash received by the number of hours to analyze your profitability on the cash basis of accounting. The system (the Cash Method) automatically subtracts out the bad debts because you never collected the cash. The cash method of accounting does not take into account build up or decreases in your work in progress. The accrual method is much more accurate but requires adjustments for beginning and ending work in progress and bad debts. (If you want to see examples, read the chapter on "The Cluster Method of Analyzing Profitability.")

M. *Using the Information.*

Once you have the information, you must act on it. You must determine why certain kinds of cases are not as profitable as others or are losers. You must then take steps to correct your deficiencies or stop taking those types of cases. You should expand your practice in the areas where you are profitable.

M-22
Should You Accept Small Cases at a Loss
Or
Low Profit to Get or Keep a Good Client?

The question suggests the answer. The answers are yes, you should handle small or unprofitable clients to keep a good client, and no, you generally should not accept small or unprofitable cases from new clients to get or keep good clients without a clear understanding of why you are accepting such cases.

I will give you three success stories in point. One is from a Canadian lawyer (The Greenhouse Matter), one from a Minnesota lawyer (The Small Matter), and the other from my own experiences (The Clear Understanding Matter).

A. *The Greenhouse Matter.*

A major real estate developer in Toronto used a well-known downtown Toronto law firm to do his legal work. The developer's wife had a small greenhouse which had been badly repaired by a local contractor. The amount of money involved was small, but the amount of aggravation involved was great. There was very bitter correspondence and other communication between the contractor who repaired the greenhouse and the developer's wife. The developer took the file to his big downtown law firm. The partner in charge took one look at the very small amount of money involved and the large amount of work which would be involved and suggested to the developer that the wife either should forget the matter or find some young, hungry neighborhood lawyer who might handle the case more effectively and economically than the big firm could.

The developer returned the file to his wife, related the conversation about forgetting the matter or locating a young neighborhood lawyer. She was enraged at what she perceived to be a personal insult and she, indeed, went to a local lawyer. She explained that what she wanted was justice and she didn't care what it cost her. The young lawyer worked hard and billed the client at a rate fair to the lawyer, which the wife knew in advance would be uneconomical to her *vis a vis* the amount involved. The young lawyer went to trial on the case and the wife told her side of the story. The judge rendered a compromise judgment. The wife was happy with having had her day in court and receiving a small, albeit uneconomical, victory from the court.

The wife then nagged her husband to stop giving work to the downtown Toronto firm which she felt had insulted her, and instead, to give some of the corporate work to the young neighborhood lawyer who had worked so hard for her. The developer decided at least to try the local neighborhood lawyer, who was conveniently located for early morning meetings prior to the developer's going to job sites.

Consequently, the young neighborhood lawyer received more and more of the developer's business, added two more lawyers to his firm to handle it, and eventually received all of the developer's business. Ultimately the practice grew into a very profitable four-lawyer firm in which the developer was the biggest and most important client. The developer expanded into international real estate construction acquisition and development and the law firm, too, expanded. Now it is one of the most prestigious in Canada.

The lesson to be learned from this long, true story is obvious. The big firm never should have suggested the use of another firm to do the work they could have done. They opened the door for the good client to try out another lawyer and, indeed, encouraged it. They planted the seeds of their own self-destruction as far as the developer's business was concerned. They may have meant well, but it was the wrong thing to do. They should have offered to do the work without any fee discount (the client never asked for a price break) or at a reduced rate (see the chapter on the Cluster Concept of evaluating the profitability of affiliated clients and cases).

B. *The Small Matter.* This story was told to me by the senior partner of a major Minnesota law firm. When he was a sole practitioner, he had a small business client for whom he did mainly litigation work but also some contract work. When the client needed a small matter handled, the client said he wanted only a small amount of work done and was willing to pay only a small fee. The lawyer replied that he would do his best to keep the fee low, but would not work at a loss or do less work than required or do shoddy work merely because the client didn't want to pay a reasonable fee for the work required. The lawyer said he was perfectly willing to take the case but insisted on a reasonable fee, even though the matter was small.

As a result, the client went to another lawyer for the small case. The second lawyer did the work at a loss, hoping thereby to get the good business and litigation work. Twenty years have gone by. The client still gives the good work to the original firm and still farms out the small unprofitable matters to lawyer after lawyer, who take the nonprofitable work, hoping to get a foot in the door for the good work. The client claims he would never give responsible work to any firm stupid enough to work at a loss.

A lesson to be learned from the succession of firms who took on unprofitable matters. Don't take work at a loss from a new client, hoping to get the profitable work later. Later rarely comes.

C. *The Clear Understanding Matter.*

The following are one success and two failures from my own experience. Early in my career (within three years of finishing law school), a former fraternity brother and a law school classmate recommended me for three different types of work:
1. Small collection cases for a bank;
2. Uninsured motorist subrogation cases for an insurance company;
3. Small collection cases for a finance company.

The bank had divided its collection department into three divisions roughly corresponding to court jurisdiction: Municipal Court (then up to $5,000), smaller Superior Court (then up to $30,000) and Superior Court (then more than $30,000). I told the bank I very much wanted to represent it for the prestige and honor, but would only do the small cases on a profitable basis and if I'd be given a chance to do the larger cases after I had proven my ability. I expressly told them, "If all you want is a small lawyer for small cases, the answer is 'no'. If you are looking for a good lawyer who, upon proving himself with the small cases has a 'clear understanding' that he'll also gets some medium cases, and after proving himself with the medium cases gets some large cases, then I'm very interested in being a part of your legal team." They agreed.

I told the insurance company, too, that I would do only its subrogation work if it turned out to be profitable and if it meant that after proving myself in the subrogation area, I had a "clear understanding" I would get a chance at the defense work and be given the opportunity to handle larger and larger defense cases. The insurance company agreed.

I treated the finance company the same way as the bank. The work had to be profitable and I had to have a chance at the larger, more-profitable work.

In all three cases I refused to take on work at a loss, but was willing to take on the smaller cases at a profit if it would lead to larger, more-profitable cases.

It turned out that the bank was serious. As I proved myself, I got larger and larger cases at higher and higher profits.

The insurance company and finance company did not keep their end of the bargain. I later learned that they had a track record (and still do now, as far as I know) of exploiting young, and eager but gullible lawyers. They gave the young lawyers unprofitable work, always dangling the carrot of future, more-profitable work. As soon as I learned that I couldn't make any money on the small cases (which had been "creamed" before I got them), and learned there were no larger matters to come, I dropped them as clients.

To summarize my experiences, you should do only small or less profitable cases to get a foot in the door on the basis there is a "clear understanding" that:

1. The smaller work must in and of itself be profitable, even if at a smaller profit than usual. Under no circumstances will you accept any work at a loss, hoping to get more profitable work later.

2. The smaller work must lead to the bigger, more-profitable work after you prove your ability.

3. If the larger, more-profitable work does not come along after you feel you have proved your ability, discuss your "clear understanding" concerning larger work with the client. If you are not satisfied with the response, drop the client and let some other fool lose money.

M-23
How to Get a Paying Fee From Someone
Who Tries to Get Free Legal Advice at a Party

From time to time at a party, wedding, Bar Mitzvah or other social event, a social friend or a relative (sometimes even a stranger) will try to get some free legal advice.
Typical opening lines are:

"Say, you're an attorney. Let me tell you what happened to me," or "Say, I have a friend who has an interesting legal problem," or "I'm curious as to what you think a judge would do in this situation." Sometimes the person will say candidly, "I'd like your legal opinion on something, but I don't want you to charge me."

You can respond in one of three ways:

1. Respond angrily. Growl out something to the effect of, "Can't you leave me alone? I want to enjoy my social life like you do. Call me at the office if you want legal advice." This is a good way to alienate a potential client, although on occasion, the person will apologize and will actually call you at the office and you might get some sympathy from those around you who hear you growl.

2. Listen attentively and do your best to give an "offhand" answer. You will have lost any possibility of getting a fee from the matter and you will expose yourself to malpractice liability because you've done no "double checking" to see if the law, as you remember it, is still the law; and because you have no notes or other data in your files to confirm what advice you did or did not give when you are served with a malpractice complaint three years later. It continually amazes me that lawyers don't understand they can be responsible for malpractice even though they never charged or received a fee.

3. Listen attentively and then say, "That sounds like a very interesting legal situation." Or, if true, "I do a lot of work in that area of law," or "My partner is an expert in that area of law. You (or your friend) may have a very serious legal problem. Here is my card. You (or your friend) should call me first thing tomorrow for an office appointment or else call another lawyer right away. To answer the question properly, it is important to get more information than what you have given me. For any lawyer to do a good job, the lawyer has to think about the problem a bit in a quiet atmosphere. Sometimes, in a quiet atmosphere, a lawyer can turn what seems to be a complicated problem into a simple problem after mulling over the facts. Also the law changes daily because of new statutes and new case decisions. It is important for a lawyer to double check the current state of the law to assure that your answer is as accurate as can be"

By telling the person "You have a very interesting problem," you have complimented him or her by implying that he or she has the ability to select something important and did not insult you with a "stupid" question.

By telling the person you want him or her to come into the office, you are implying that you are a professional who functions in a professional surrounding.

By saying "You may have a very serious problem" (remember, you have implied also that the person may *not* have a serious problem), you have "gotten even" with the person for spoiling your otherwise pleasant social event. Let the person "stew" and worry all night over the fact that he or she may be in serious trouble. Let the anxiety level rise. The person will be even more grateful when you or some other lawyer tells him or her that the problem really wasn't so serious after all.

The third response provided is totally true and accurate. You will be better able to give good advice after you've had a chance to get all the facts, think about the issues presented and double check the law. In this way, you will be protecting both yourself and your client.

How you do or don't charge for the first consultation is, of course, an extension of your marketing policy. Even if the person doesn't call or come in for an appointment, you have convinced the person you are truly a professional and have left your card with him or her.

M-24
"Cars Can't Run Without Gasoline"

This phrase was given to me by a client. I had to ask a client to get another lawyer when the client couldn't pay my bill. I felt badly about it but I had no choice. This particular client had given me a $2500 retainer and owed me $3500 more and needed much more legal service and simply couldn't pay.

I asked the client to come into the office and handed him a $2500 check and told him I couldn't afford to be his lawyer. I told him that I liked him and found his case interesting and challenging but he simply wasn't paying and I simply couldn't keep him as a client.

He said to me, "Mr. Foonberg, I know that cars can't run without gasoline and law offices can't run without cash to pay for secretaries and rent and equipment."

I have since used that saying many times. I use it before I accept the client and I use it to collect bills when clients are slow to pay and I use it when I have to drop clients. For some reason, clients relate to this expression. They become understanding rather than hostile and they pay their bills.

This expression works for me and I recommend that you try it and see how it works for you.

M-25
How to Reduce a Bill in a Fee Dispute And Still Keep the Client Happy

Techniques

In this chapter, I have included a few fee dispute techniques that I have found to be successful over the years.

The way you handle fee problems is crucial, both to your profitable relationship with the client who is giving you the problem and to the future clients which that client will, or will not, refer to you.

One of the biggest problems you must avoid is the problem of the client's thinking you *deliberately* overcharged or tried to cheat the client. If you lower a fee out of kindness or sympathy or whatever motivating reason, the client may interpret the adjustment as an admission that you were cheating and that you got caught in the act. You will probably lose the client, whether or not you get paid. You will also lose the client's future referrals and, in addition, the client may complain about you to the person who recommended him or her, endangering yet another source of referrals.

Fundamentally, there are two *major* areas of fee problems:

1. The amount of the fee. This is primarily the client's problem, since he either can or cannot afford your services. It is only your problem to the extent you don't want a client to leave you over a fee dispute if the client can afford to pay you.

2. The collection of the fee. This is your problem because you need cash, not promises, to run a law office and support your family. This was covered in a separate chapter entitled "Increasing Your Cash Flow and Producing Uncollectibles By Matching Your Billing To Your Clients Cash Flow" (Chapter M-16).

There are three major times that fee problems occur:

a) Before the work has begun;
b) While the work is being done; and
c) After the work has been done.

The best time to set a fee and to convince the client that the fee is a fair and reasonable one is *before* you do any significant work. A clear understanding of how the fee will be charged and collected is healthy both for you and for the client.

All clients, even major financial clients who are accustomed to large legal fees, occasionally have fee disputes that arise during the course of the work.

The fee dispute problem that arises while the work is being done comes about when a client gets a progress billing and claims that he or she had no idea the fee would be so high. When this happens, you have a potentially more serious problem because, unless the problem is resolved then and there, the client either will go to another lawyer, become an uncooperative client or possibly want to terminate the matter.

Your first response to the client could be, "Thank you for calling me about the bill. I really mean that. If I know there is a problem, we can work it out. I'd much rather that you call me than simply grumble and be unhappy. I take it as a compliment that you're taking the time and trouble to call me."

This usually sets the stage for a cooperative discussion of the bill. No matter how this is resolved, you must be sure that each of you understands what the situation is for the work still to come.

If you are going to make an adjustment downward, you should never adjust more than 40 percent of the amount. You can say, "Look, I'm willing to make an adjustment (never say 'lower the fee') but my gross profit on legal work is only 40 percent. I have to pay salaries, rent, etc., just like any other business. If I adjust the bill more than 40 percent, I'll be operating at a loss and I don't think you'd want that." Most bona fide clients won't want you to work at a loss.

A fee dispute after the work has been completed is the most serious problem. Remember, that fees received or not received after the work is done is 100 percent profit or loss. You've already made your major investment of time and money. Since the work is finished, you've lost your most significant collection tool, which is the work to be done. Don't run away from the problem. That only makes matters worse. Face it head on.

After the work is done, you should make any necessary adjustments by giving the client more time to pay your bill rather than adjusting the total fee downward.

When you simply have no choice but to adjust downward or else risk losing the fee and the referrals, you might consider using one of the following explanations which I have on occasion used:

1. "I see on reviewing the time records that, at various times, we had more than one person working on your case to give you full coverage. There could have been some duplication of effort, so I'll adjust downward for the work of the second lawyer if that'll make you happy. In the future, I won't assign any backup lawyers to the case. This will reduce your fees a bit but means that the case may move a bit more slowly because there won't be a second lawyer available when the lawyer handling the case (you) is in trial."

2. "Look, we have a written agreement setting out the fee. I honor my commitments and I'm sure you honor yours. Do you want to pay the bill to date in accordance with the agreement and then perhaps have us stop working on the case?"

3. "Look, I've reviewed all the work done. It was good effort and the fee is in line with our written fee agreement. If you're asking me for a reduction or discount because of your financial abilities (or financial problems), I'm willing to do so to keep you as a client so that you'll use our offices on your next matter, but I want to reassure you that the bill, as charged, is correct."

I repeat, if you make an adjustment downward out of kindness or sympathy, your client may take this as an admission that you've done something wrong or that you got caught cheating on the bill. Handle this problem sensitively and carefully and you may still salvage some of the fee and a client whose next case or referral may be a good one.

M-26
How to Adjust a Bill or Write off an Uncollectible Bill Without Losing the Client

When clients owe you money that they cannot or will not pay, they often are afraid or embarrassed to use you for the next legal case that comes up. They may take a good, paying legal matter to another law firm rather than face the embarrassment of contacting you. Accordingly, if you recognize that the client can't, or won't, pay you on this matter, but you do want the next good matter the client has, or the next good referral the client can send, then you don't want to leave hanging the fact that the client owes you money. You want to soft-pedal this so that you maintain a good relationship with the client.

From time to time, there will exist either a bona fide dispute or difference of opinion between yourself and the client over a bill. In some cases, the client simply will not have the capacity to pay the bill, no matter what you do. In other cases, the client doesn't want to pay the bill because of a perceived error or perceived overcharge concerning the services rendered or results obtained.

In either case, the plain and simple fact is you're not going to get paid. Accordingly, you have to decide whether you ever want this person to come back as a client, even if he or she does have a paying or good matter. If you do want this person to bring good future cases, or refer good future clients, then you may have to make an adjustment. If you never want to see this person or his referrals again, then you don't need to read the rest of this chapter.

You should always make any necessary adjustment in the form of a letter. You should never simply stop billing the person. If you do so, the person may feel that you, indeed, were trying to cheat or overcharge him or her and that you were caught either in a mistake or a dishonest act. Your discontinuation of billing may be interpreted as an admission by you that you were in error.

Your letter of adjustment should be along the following lines:

Re: *Adjustment of Balance of Bill*

Dear Client:

For the last several months (or as appropriate) we have been billing you for the balance of $12,345.67 for the work done in the Jones matter. You have indicated that you cannot pay or that you will not pay.

We value you as a client and do not want to lose you as a valued client. Accordingly, we are making an adjustment in your account to reduce the balance to zero as a gesture of good will. Therefore, according to our records, you now have no balance due. I am enclosing an extra copy of this letter. Should our billing department erroneously bill you in the future on this matter, simply return the bill with the enclosed photo-copy of this letter and they will immediately make the adjustment.

We are truly sorry about the difference of opinion over the balance of this bill and we trust that you will accept this adjustment in the spirit of mutual cooperation now and in the future.

I wish to emphasize that we do value you as a client and welcome any comments which you may have at any time.

Sincerely,

Joe Doe,
Attorney at Law

Sometimes a client will have a bona fide dispute with you (at least from the client's point of view) over the value of the work done, or for whatever reason and doesn't want to pay for your services. Clients generally are not dishonest people, and clients generally want to do "the right thing." Accordingly, if you can segregate your records so that you can clearly distinguish between hourly fees and out-of-pocket costs incurred, you can sometimes maximize your recovery of the costs, which otherwise might be an uncollectible sum.

In such a situation, you might send a client letter along the following lines:

Dear Client:

We value you as a client. At the present time there is a problem over the balance of your account in the amount of $_____. An analysis of the time and of the charges incurred in this matter indicate that over the course of the case we have expended funds in the amount of $_____ for out-of-pocket costs as follows:

Paid to Corporation Commissioner:	$152.00
Paid for Corporation supplies	184.00
Paid for recording notices	40.00
Long distance telephone calls	52
TOTAL	$428.00

In view of the fact that we have, in fact, expended these funds, we are confident that you do not wish or expect us to suffer a loss, and will remit the above sum.

Please be assured that we value you as a client and wish to keep you as a client, and anticipate that in the spirit of fair play, you will remit this sum.

In the event that you cannot pay even this sum, we are still going to write off the balance, in a spirit of cooperation.

Please be assured that we do wish to include you in our list of valued clients.

I am enclosing a copy of this letter, (etc....).

If you have any questions, please don't hesitate to contact us.

In some cases, the client simply does not have the ability to pay. You have no realistic expectation of being paid, but, on the other hand, should the client have the capacity to pay in the future, you want to get paid. Accordingly, you may wish to send a letter along the following lines:

Dear Joe:

We recognize that you presently cannot pay the balance of your bill. Accordingly, we are concerned that when we send you monthly statements indicating that there is a balance due, we may be irritating you or causing you to hesitate to contact us should you have a legal problem. Therefore, we are going to stop billing you for this sum. We are hopeful that if in the future, you have the capacity to pay this sum, you will do so of your own accord.

Please be assured that we do wish to continue to include you among our valued clients.

Sincerely,

The most important thing is that you do not simply stop billing the client without a cover letter, as the client may take this as an admission that you did something wrong in the billing process.

Chapter N
Big Firm Techniques That
Can Work for a Small Firm

N-1
The Difference Between Sole Practice and Small Firm Practice Development As Opposed to Large Firm Marketing

It has been said that a medium size firm is a collection of solo practitioners and a large firm is a collection of medium size firms. Individual lawyers whether solo or in large firms can use the same marketing techniques.

There are differences, however, between practice development techniques for small firms and for large firms. A sole practitioner is not always willing to layout hard-earned cash to invest consciously in practice development. He or she may be hesitant to risk money or to "find time" for this activity. Day-to-day reactions to client emergencies and personal problems will take priority.

On the other hand, a larger firm will take a chance and make a $25,000 or *$50,000* investment in an outside consultant. A $20,000 investment to a 20-lawyer firm is only $1,000 per lawyer, but its a lot of risk and uncertainty for a solo practitioner or three lawyer firm to invest the same sum in an outside consultant. Some consultants recommend that as much as 7% of revenues be devoted to marketing in a mega firm of 1,000 or more lawyers.

A small firm may not believe it can devote the internal resources or that it has the talent to communicate periodically and continuously with clients.

This book recognizes the fear of the sole practitioner and smaller law firms of investing significant amounts of time or money into practice development and, accordingly, I have outlined and emphasized techniques that can cheaply and easily be installed and utilized.

The advent of computers, which are used by all law firms, makes possible much of the practice development on a systematic or automatic basis without any investment of lawyer time.

Indeed, many of the techniques of this book require no lawyer time and no outside consultants. Lawyers simply have to be made aware of some of the things they are already doing right and those things which they are doing wrong. Little or no money has to be invested to utilize the techniques of this book.

In summary, the techniques are valuable and practical for any lawyer or law firm, but are especially good for the solo practitioner or small firm because so little time or money need be spent in implementing these proven techniques.

N-1A
Advertising Your Firm During Employment Interviews

The employment interview is an excellent opportunity for you to hard sell your firm to every applicant, including the ones who are obviously not qualified for the job sought.

Just because applicants aren't qualified to work for you doesn't mean they are not qualified to send you legal work in the future. These people may eventually end up in another firm that doesn't do the kind of work you do or in a corporate department which deals with outside counsel. By knowing what kind of legal work you do or want, they may have an opportunity in the future to send you business even though you don't hire them.

At the beginning of the interview process, you should state to the applicant:

"We are a firm that practices law in the areas of X and Z. We are actively seeking clients in the businesses of A and B work. The particular position we are interviewing you for is in the department."

You can also put this in writing in the package of paperwork you ask the applicant to fill out.

When applicants leave the interview (or before the interview, if you are mailing information to them), they should be carrying the following information with them:

1. The firm brochure or a firm newsletter describing the firm's practice and attorneys.
2. The professional card of the attorney or other person who interviewed them.
3. A pre-printed Rolodex card or a DVD with the firm's name and website on it.
4. A letter explaining that the applicant's name is being added to your "friend's and clients" list and they may receive information in the future about the firm.

It would be unrealistic to expect a large amount of legal business from this source. However, you will get some business over the years and the investment is minimal, thus making this activity very cost effective.

I've heard of one firm that does business litigation, and periodically advertises and interviews lawyers and non-lawyers for a non-existent general corporate law department. In the interview process, they claim they are considering creating a general corporate law department even though they presently specialize in business litigation. Their purpose in doing all this is to communicate to corporate lawyers that they do business litigation work and are available. I don't know for a fact that the law firm does this only to get business, and I wouldn't do it, but they claim it is very cost effective in getting litigation business and therefore, I pass their technique on to you.

N-2
Dirty Espionage to Steal Major Clients

I personally have never done what is being reported in this chapter. Other lawyers have told me that their firms do what is described and that the techniques in this chapter are regularly practiced by large firms, but I have no first-hand knowledge of whether or not large firms in fact do this kind of espionage.

The steps are as follows:

1. Determine the kind of work you want from a given client, (for example, litigation or tax work).
2. Determine which law firm is presently doing this kind of work. You may be able to find out from public records such as court pleadings, documents recorded with the county recorder, documents filed with the Secretary of State, documents filed with the Securities Exchange Commission, annual reports, etc. It may be as simple as calling up the targeted client and asking who their lawyers are for the kind of work you're interested in.
3. "Pump" employees from the firm that does the work in employment interviews obtained through advertising in the local legal newspaper or through headhunters. Offer an outrageous salary or position for a non-existent job. Try to tailor the ad and job description to "tailor-fit" the firm which is presently doing the work.

Suppose you wanted to do the collection litigation for a major bank and have identified a West Side Law Firm as being the firm now serving the bank.

If you could identify the attorney or attorneys in the firm who are the principal client contacts, a headhunter hired by you could call the attorneys directly (preferably at home) and come on with, "Our client is a major firm which is looking for a lawyer who knows UCC law, attachments, executions, law and motions, secured transactions, bankruptcy and has principal client contact. The starting salary is into the middle six figures with full partnership. Can you recommend someone?" Obviously, you want the lawyer whom the headhunter is talking to, but headhunters must be subtle when they try to steal attorneys.

The headhunter will be programmed to pump the "candidate" for proof that the candidate really has the qualifications and will ask as many questions as possible designed to get information, such as, who at the client's place can he or she suggest as a reference; what are the hourly rates the "candidate" can command from the particular client; what mix of senior attorneys/junior attorneys, paralegals, etc., will the client accept; who are the people at the client's law division or general counsel who decide on attorneys to be used; what are the client's philosophies on what they expect from outside counsel, etc. The list is endless.

We are depending on the candidate's eagerness for the job to cause him or her to be indiscreet and oversell his abilities to try to get the fabulous position (which doesn't exist).

The same approach can be made to secretaries, paralegals, librarians, office managers, accountants, etc. The method is to offer an incredible job with huge compensation that just fits the description of the job the person already has at the targeted firm. You are depending on the "candidate's" personal greed to disclose firm and client confidences.

One good reason you can give for your failure, in fact, to hire the candidate is his or her demonstrated inability to protect client confidences.

I truly don't know what causes of action, if any, the targeted firm would have. They would be in the unenviable position of trying to complain that one of their lawyers or staff was indiscreet.

N-3
How a Professional Consultant Can Help You

I have nothing against professional PR firms or other consultants doing big, expensive PR campaigns for law firms.

Don't delude yourself into believing that you simply write a check and they invent publicity that gets you clients. A professional campaign run by professionals requires a substantial commitment in terms of firm time, firm resources and firm money, because these people don't "sell you"; they help you sell yourself.

This book is intended to teach you specific things you can easily do in your own law firm with very little commitment of your time or money. If you start something recommended in this book and then drop it, you will not have expended a significant amount of money or time. If, on the other hand, you start with a professional PR firm and change your mind, you might have spent a lot of time and money.

Some of the things a professional PR expert may do with you, for you, and to you include:

1. Do in-depth analysis of your people.
2. Do in-depth analysis of your legal strengths and weaknesses.
3. Analyze present and past client base cases and find strengths and weaknesses.
4. Help you design stationery, cards, announcements, letterheads and logos.
5. Help you design and circulate a firm brochure.
6. Set up a series of press releases and press conferences for you.
7. Set up articles for publication, get them published and circulate them and the reprints where they are likely to do you the most good.
8. Set up an open house or reception and get notable people to attend and mingle with your clients and potential clients to impress them.
9. Help you develop and/or buy mailing lists, according to your marketing goals.
10. Help you set up paper and electronic newsletters and blawgs.
11. Help get you TV and media exposure.
12. Help you write news releases and get them published in the appropriate publications.
13. Get old speeches, articles and research "repackaged" and newly printed and distributed.
14. Critique and improve your client interviewing and surveying techniques.
15. Test various types of media advertising for cost effectiveness for your practice.
16. Help your IT people or others to design your website.

All of the above activities and others are very worthwhile activities, but using a PR firm instead of doing it yourself is simply beyond the scope of this book. I list these merely as some of the typical things you could expect from a professional public relations firm.

N-4
The Law Firm Marketing Administrator from A to Z

Most good lawyers would rather practice law than allocate energy or time to administer a marketing effort, and accordingly many firms are hiring marketing administrators. Since the concept of a full time marketing administrator is a relatively new one, the nature of the qualifications for being a marketing director seem to range from a non-lawyer having an interest in the subject matter with no legal experience to experienced lawyers having decades of experience in directing their own firm's marketing efforts.

There has been a huge increase in the number of full time law firm marketing administrators since "How To Get And Keep Good Clients" was first written. This growth has occurred primarily in firms of 25 or more lawyers, although I've seen marketing administrators in firms of five lawyers and I've seen smaller firms, including sole practitioners, use part time marketing directors on a consulting or staff basis.

As large firms vie with each other on who can be the largest in a given geographic area or who can pay the highest starting salary to new associates and lateral transfers, firms have come to realize the importance of a continuing backlog of work from existing clients and new work from existing clients and new clients to support the huge overhead and to support specialized or departmental practices.

I frankly was surprised to learn how many medical groups have been using non-professional marketing directors for years to hard sell the medical groups. They do everything from cold calling people off mailing lists to giving direction to the medical group. Apparently, the ethical restraints on direct solicitation that lawyers have either don't exist among physicians or they are simply ignored without negative consequence to the doctors. I mention the medical profession specifically because many of the newly created positions of marketing director for law firms are being filled with people from the medical profession and a firm should not overlook this source.

In approximately 1986 an organization called NALFMA (National Association of Law Firm Marketing Administrators) was created consisting of people who are employed as marketing administrators or who want to be employed as marketing administrators. They have periodic national & local meetings(I've addressed them at their National Convention) and they serve as a job clearing house center for members. I recommend that you include them in your search for a marketing administrator.

As this new position is brought into firm after firm, both the firms and the marketing administrator are learning how to live with each other in a mutually profitable manner.

I advocate that firms should consider the utilization of a marketing administrator in the marketing efforts as follows:

1. Call the position marketing administrator or marketing director. Remember that they are hired to administer the marketing policy of the firm after the firm decides on the kinds of clients and cases it initially wants rather than telling the firm how the firm should practice law.

2. If you use a non-lawyer to be the administrator remember that you must teach that person current professional responsibility (or ethics, if you prefer to use that designation). The non-lawyer may have little or no prior understanding of the role of the legal profession in society or of the current specific advertising, marketing and ethical restraints on lawyers in your jurisdiction. A recent publication of a marketing organization stressed that firms are confused as to the "criteria for SOLICITING new clients" (emphasis added). The author apparently did not understand that "SOLICITATION" is universally regarded as unethical and grounds for disciplinary actions in most jurisdictions.

   Our legal profession has been organized since the GUILDS and the Inns of Court in the Middle Ages. As a marketing administrator learns more about the legal profession he or she undoubtedly will become more sensitive to our self imposed ethical and professional restrictions. They must learn that law is a fiduciary – beneficiary profession and not a cavaet emptor business. The firm must obligate itself to train the marketing administrator as to legal ethics, and must closely supervise and monitor and control what is being done so that the firm and its partners don't find themselves the object of a state bar disciplinary proceeding.

3. Make a decision as to whether the administrator is to function under the control of the managing partner and firm administrator or whether it will be an independent bureaucracy. The marketing administrator may want to work outside of the general control and administration of the firm. They may want their own budget and to do their own hiring, firing, wage administration, etc., outside of the total administration. They may prefer to work under a marketing committee rather than under the firm administrator. This can create a smoothly running independent unit or it can create a serious morale and administrative problem for the firm as a whole.

4. Be sure to get a non-competition clause in your agreement with the administrator (if your law permits). Remember that the marketing administrator will learn all about your strengths and weaknesses and your clients likes and dislikes. A marketing administrator is in a unique position to harm the entire firm if the administrator defects to another firm. (Conversely, you may wish to "steal" an administrator from a firm that secures the types of clients you want in order to get the advantage of what the administrator knows about the other firm's weaknesses and clients.)

5. Be sure to educate the marketing director as to the do's and don'ts of fee splitting with the administrator, distinguishing between open fee splitting and "performance bonuses" based on new clients and fees obtained.

6. Let the administrator do the myriad small things that a practicing lawyer cannot do well or efficiently.

    a. Work with printers and designers on your stationery designs, logos, etc.
    b. Work with attorneys and printers and mailing houses in publishing firm's newsletters for targeted mailings or emailings.
    c. Work with attorneys and the accounting department to develop a data base of clients and referrers of clients.
    d. Prepare and distribute press releases.
    e. Work with public relations firms to get articles printed and reprinted and distributed to clients and potential clients.
    f. Develop sources for mailing lists for targeted industry groups.
    g. Decide which ads to purchase for which events.
    h. Get control of and supervise distribution of firm tickets for athletic events, theatre, rock concerts, etc., to be sure that firm money is being used for firm marketing purposes. Obtain tickets from brokers when needed.
    i. Do all of the detail work on setting up and following up on seminars.
    j. Do all of the detail work for setting up open houses.
    k. Keep firm brochure(s) current (if you're going to have one or more brochures.)
    l. Obtain information from attorneys and the accounting department to cross sell the firm.
    m. Work with IT personnel and attorneys to design and maintain websites.
    n. Engage specific consultants as required.
    o. Arrange for speaking engagements for firm members and handle all the details of travel, audio-visual needs, handouts, etc.
    p. Set up and staff hospitality suites at conventions and invite targeted people to the suites.
    q. Help decide which charitable activities and contributions produce the highest returns to the firm.
    r. Work with accounting or data processing to develop systems to track cases and clients by source.
    s. Teach both attorneys & staff the basics: (returning phone calls & emails, copying clients with information, etc.) and more importantly how to do these things critical to keeping existing clients and getting new clients.
    t. Decide which law directories should be used for advertising.
    u. Work with a public relations firm or a press firm to develop firm exposure in the appropriate media (TV newspapers, etc.)
    v. Track conventions and meetings or targeted industry groups to get firm members into the speaking or education part of the convention.
    w. Give recognition to efforts and successful marketing results by firm members.
    x. Monitor reception and telephone answering activities to ensure proper client relations.

y. Work with accounting and management on poor pay clients to determine how to get paid and whether to keep the client.
z. Be the firm historian.

It has been said that being the firm's first marketing administrator can be a "suicide position" doomed to failure. There is some truth to this. The firm and the administrator must have a clear understanding of what is expected from each or the likelihood of failure may be high.

It is my opinion that a marketing administrator is most likely to achieve long term success when he or she sincerely tells the individual attorney, "I am here to help you develop marketing skills which will benefit you and benefit the firm." I believe the marketing director who believes they have been hired by the firm to tell the attorneys what they must do is not likely to succeed over a long period of time. I base my opinion on what I have been told by practicing lawyers and by managing partners in firms where the first marketing administrator was successful and in firms in which the experience was a bad one for both the firm and the administrator. It certainly makes sense to me.

N-5
Having an Open House to Attract Clients

An open house, if properly done, can do a lot to improve your firm's reputation with your existing clients and possibly with potential clients.

The most successful open houses I have participated in are those which start off being tours of the office and office facilities and end up as a social event, thus combining business and pleasure. Some clients will be more interested in the tour and others the social aspects.

The lawyers should take the clients through the office showing them the physical facilities such as word processing equipment, computer-assisted research, library facilities, partners' offices, video conferencing and communications equipment, printing equipment, and conference rooms. (Remember that clients are always more impressed with the equipment when they see it operating.) The clients should be met at the elevator or door, escorted to a nice conference room and then taken in groups of 5 or 10 on the tour, ending up in the "social area." You may or may not wish to hand out or make available firm brochures. I personally would not invite total strangers or the general public with whom I have no relationship, unless they come with someone I know, but you might wish to do so.

I recently invited all the tenants of my office building to an informal open house holiday party. I invited them for a "3 to 6 wine and cheese" party. It was very inexpensive - no big deal. As a reason for the party, I indicated that we all saw one another in the elevators, the hallways, the washrooms, etc., and that we should all become acquainted. The response on the part of the other tenants (most of whom I didn't know) was quite good. Many of the tenants didn't even know that we were attorneys. Several asked intelligent questions about the kind of work we do.

One of the tenants accidentally discovered that he had gone to high school with one of the associates in the firm and we are now doing legal work for that person's company. The investment of a few dollars for wine and cheese and a few hours of time has already paid off handsomely.

At one time in Cleveland, the Bar Association arranged once-a-month office tours of big firms for small firms. The bigger firms showed the smaller firms their procedures, technology, systems, etc. The smaller firms were able to create and maintain relationships with the larger firms, and vice versa. The larger firms were simply using the open house and tour to establish their ability to handle the larger or specialty cases which were beyond the capacity of the small firms. The smaller firms received some referrals of matters where the larger firms didn't want to refer the matter to another large firm. These tours worked to the benefit of all involved and I recommend this concept to other Bar associations. I personally have done small firm marketing seminars for invited law firms which sent them specialty work to the firm that hire me.

N-6
Firm Brochures as a Marketing Aid
and Their Website Replacements

This chapter covers both printed brochures and their website replacements. In my opinion, the internet and law firm websites have fairly well made printed brochures almost obsolete and rarely worth the time and money devoted to them. Most of what an individual lawyer or a firm could accomplish with a brochure can more easily & cheaply be accomplished on the internet. The modern printed brochure need not be much more than a few pages with references to the firm's website

Some firm brochures are simply monuments to the egos of the partners who pose for stiff, unnatural photos.

A chief house counsel told me he gets so many unsolicited firm brochures that he simply throws them in the garbage unread. Firm brochures are given the same attention as unsolicited resumes.

A different chief counsel told me he glances at the unsolicited brochures to see what areas of law they practice and where the firm or lawyer is geographically located. If the company happens to need a lawyer or firm in that specific geographic area or with that specific area of expertise at that specific moment of time he will forward the brochure on to the lawyer handling a matter requiring outside counsel, unless it meets a specific need it gets trashed unread.

Formal, slick firm brochures of more than a few pages are beyond the scope of this book because they are rarely used due to the cost of time and money of putting them together. A professional brochure may involve a PR firm's meeting with the attorneys and even some clients. A huge amount of otherwise billable time is spent in interviews; a large amount of time is spent by many partners in reviewing the text. Which photos to use or not to use is also a source of controversy. The biggest argument often centers about how to use the brochure.

Most of what can be accomplished in a glossy brochure by a large firm can be accomplished by a sole practitioner or small firm in a client newsletter which can be undated and sent at any time or in a simple black and white leaflet or on a timely updated website.

Whether you opt for the slick brochure or the simple newsletter, you should simply communicate the kind of work you do, where you are located, how long you have been in business, and include a few words about the lawyers and non-lawyers in the firm.

For example, a small firm might put the following in a client newsletter:

"We encourage our clients to bring us all their legal problems. The firm has a reputation primarily in the areas of taxation, business, tax litigation, and international law. Among the members of the firm, we have the ability and we can properly represent clients in many areas of law. If we cannot properly handle your legal problems, we will bring in (or refer you to) a specialist in the area(s) you need.

"Some of our lawyers and staff are graduates of local schools and local law schools. These members of our firm are from this community and are deeply committed to local issues and institutions as well as to areas of national and international interest. Some of our attorneys are from prestigious national universities and law schools and bring new ideas and approaches to the firm.

"The firm's senior member has been practicing since 1964 and is nationally and internationally known for the quality of the work done by the firm. He is also a CPA and has a broad experience in the practice of law."

Try not to be specific with the lawyer names because of turnover. Similarly, photos often become embarrassing when the person in the photo has left the firm and you are stuck with 5,000 brochures. Some firms identify personnel with two separate inserts which they can change from time to time.

Some firms do not describe specific attorneys or partners on their websites for fear head hunters will search the firm's website looking to entice specific attorneys with specific qualifications away to a different firm which has hired them.

The subject of firm brochures has been so beaten to death that I'm hesitant to say anything about them, but after listening to the raging debates, I've discovered two great truths:

1. "Experts" who are in the business of selling advice on how to do a firm brochure are adamant that lawyers should leave the brochures to the "experts" who, for a fee, will offer their great expertise;
2. Lawyers who have done their own firm brochures are adamant that you don't need an outside "expert" at "outrageous" fees and that there is enough talent in a law firm to turn out a creditable brochure.

In this debate over who should prepare the brochure, and the debate over how plain or fancy it should be, people seem to have lost sight of WHY a firm would want to have a firm brochure.

It is meaningless to argue over what kind of brochure to have or not have until you make three major decisions:

1. How much of your time and your money and the time of the staff people are you willing to spend? In doing a "thorough" job, a consultant will interview you, your people and your clients (at the expert's hourly rate).
2. Why do you want it?
3. How are you going to use it?

It is my experience that most lawyers look upon a brochure as some sort of marketing aid, but lawyers are generally uncomfortable over how to use them effectively.

In my opinion, the greatest value of a brochure is to inform your existing and new clients of all the different services your firm can perform. Clients normally come to you for a specific type of legal work. They usually don't know what other kinds of legal work you can do. Indeed, often when clients or potential clients come to you, they are not even sure that you can handle the legal problem they already have, much less the ones they or another person might have in the future. This type of information is often difficult to put in an appropriate newsletter.

A brochure or website may do other things such as discuss fees or what the lawyer will or won't do during the course of the representation. Many of these things, I submit, could just as easily be covered in a form letter from word processing

Brochures, or the same information in undated client newsletters or on a website, can be used effectively as follows:

1. To be placed in the reception room for potential and existing clients;
2. To be mailed to people who have given you their card;
3. To be sent to new clients; and
4. To be sent to existing clients.
5. To be sent by email via a "click here" to get to the website or by a printed website address (URL).

In summary, the most important message that either a firm brochure or client newsletter or website should communicate is the kind of work and clients you want.

You must know your local rules to determine whether sending brochures is considered "legal advertising" and whether a website is "legal advertising" or otherwise regulated by the rules.

N-7
Analyze Where Your Good Clients Come From With a Client-Intake Form

A client-intake sheet can be very simple. If you regularly fill it out at the beginning of the case, you can get extremely valuable timely information which can be of great help in upgrading your practice. If you get a program to handle the information, the resulting client-intake reports will be very illuminating.

A simple sample form client-intake sheet follows. You can, of course, modify this to fit the needs of your particular practice. It won't take more than a few moments of your time to fill in your part. Your secretary, file clerk or bookkeeper can fill in the rest. Naturally, you should update the list report periodically, preferably quarterly, but not less than annually. A new file should not be opened without completing section 1 and the file should not be closed without completing sections 2 and 3.

CLIENT-INTAKE ANALYSIS FORM

1. Fill in when opening file:

_____

CLIENT NAME   FILE # OR MATTER #

Type of case: (modify for your practice)

Probate	_____	Real Estate Closing	_____
Litigation, Plaintiff	_____	Litigation, Defendant	_____
Probate	_____	Criminal	_____
Family Law	_____	Other	_____
			_____
			(fill in)

Recommended by Client   _____
                             (fill in client name)

Recommended by Lawyer   _____
                             (fill in lawyer name)

Recommended by Other   _____
                             (fill in name of referrer)

Repeat Client   _____
              (fill in name of former case)

Responded to Yellow Page Ad or Website   _____
                                          (fill in book where ad seen or website)

2. Fill in when closing file:

On Closing case _____

At future date $ _____

Don't send $ _____

3. Send Follow-up Questionnaire Survey

On Closing case _____

At future date _____ (fill in date)

Don't send _____

N-7A
False Telephone and Mail Surveys To Get New Clients

I do not know of any law firm which has actually used this technique, but I have been approached by CPA firms using this technique. I'll pass it on to you as though it were used by a law firm. I frankly do not know whether this technique does or doesn't violate any rules concerning soliciting or pretexting.

The method of operation is relatively simple. A target list of potential clients is prepared or purchased and the telephone solicitor starts calling.

The purpose of the call is to expose the potential client to the law firm and to communicate what type of work the firm wants from that particular target. For example, a litigation defense firm could call on claims managers. A personal injury plaintiff firm or worker's compensation applicant firm could call chiropractors or orthopedic surgeons. A tax firm could call the controllers or CPAs. A family law firm could call marriage counselors. There could be a slight variation in each of the calls, but the general theme would be as follows:

You may assume that all of the following questions or statements are being made by the "interviewer" calling on the telephone or sending a questionnaire through the mail.

1. I'm calling from XYZ Market Research on a survey which could be of financial concern to Dr. Jones.
2. Dr. Jones, I'm calling from XYZ Market Research to ask you 10 simple questions as part of a market research project for one of our clients.
3. Dr. Jones, I'm going to name four law firms which do applicant's worker's compensation and plaintiff's personal injury legal work. Please listen to all four names and then tell me which names, if any, you recognize.
   A. Bungle, Bungle & Stall? (The best-known plaintiff's personal in jury firm in the area.)
   B. Catchem, Holdem & Skinnum? (The best-known applicant's workers compensation firm in the area.)
   C. Dewey, Cheatem & Howe? (The best-known personal injury defense firm in the area.)
   D. The Law Offices of Marilyn Smith (The lawyer who is looking for legal business and who has hired the "market research" firm.)
4. Dr. Jones, which of those names do you recognize?
5. (This question is meaningless. It is purely to give the appearance of a bona fide survey.)
6. Dr. Jones, have you heard of any of these firms and, if so, do you remember where? (Again, this is a meaningless question.)
7. Dr. Jones, do you know that some law firms do protect the doctor's fees in a case and some do not? (This question should pique the doctor's interest.)

8. Dr. Jones, do you know that the Law Offices of Marilyn Smith not only protects the doctor's fees but also sends periodic status reports on the status of the case and when payment can be expected?
9. Dr. Jones, would you like a representative of the Law Offices of Marilyn Smith to send you or your office manager more information and possibly set up an appointment?
10. Dr. Jones, is your mailing address still Gree D. Jones, M.D., Suite 1234, Medi-Bucks Building, 9876 Pill Hill, Ultrasonics, Pennsylvania 11111? And is your email address still DrJones@abc.com?

"Thank you, Dr. Jones, for your time. Your office will be contacted by a representative of the Law Offices of Marilyn Smith."

The reason for naming three well-known firms is to include yourself in good company with an outside possibility that the doctor will, in fact, recognize one or more of the other names.

The purpose of using the "market research" firm is to avoid the crudeness of cold turkey telephone solicitation.

The purpose of asking the doctor if he or she wants to be contacted or to be sent information is to avoid the appearance of unsolicited information being sent.

As indicated, this "survey" could be done by mail and the questions would lead to the specific business you are seeking.

As mentioned earlier, I know that this approach is being used by CPA firms because I have received these calls. I strongly suggest that you check out your local ethics rules and laws before using it, however, and I hope that you'll communicate with me as to your success or failure.

As of the updating of this chapter in 2007, various governments are considering laws against "pretexting" (using false identity to get information). This method should not be used until it is determined that it does not violate any criminal or civil laws.

N-8
Split Up Firm Members at Professional and Social Meetings
When the Firm Pays the Bill
(Separate Tables for Firm Members)

When two people from the same firm want to be together socially, it is for them to decide with whom they sit and with whom they wish to talk. The rules of the game should change when the firm's time or money is being used.

It can be a waste of firm money or of firm time and a lost opportunity when two people from the same firm talk to each other when they could be talking to potential clients and referrers of clients.

Make it a rule for yourself and your firm members that they sit at separate tables and that they try not to talk to each other if there is an opportunity to meet and talk with potential clients and referrers of clients.

Two people from the same firm have plenty of opportunity to see each other and talk to each other in the office. They don't have to leave the office to communicate.

Typical events where the firm subsidizes outside events with time and/ or money would be:

A. Bar-sponsored continuing education
B. Non-bar-sponsored continuing education
C. Charitable events
D. Client or potential client sponsored social events
E. Service Organization lunches and meetings
F. Firm open houses, parties and seminars

In addition to losing good marketing opportunities, lawyers often give off negative signals when they talk only to each other instead of to potential clients. The attorneys can often be perceived to be:

A. Stand-offish ("They think they're too good to talk to us.")
B. Unethical - Two attorneys talking to each other often end up using client's names in public, which leads potential clients to worry about the firm's ability not to disclose client (and their) confidences.

N-9
Network the Networkers

In prioritizing your efforts you should first "Network the Networkers." A Networker in my definition is someone who can send you legal work from their clients rather than send you their own legal work.

For example, if you take the owner of a business to lunch that owner can only send you his own legal work and from time to time refer you someone, but a high volume of referrals is not possible.

On the other hand, Networkers such as CPAs or lawyers have hundreds of their own clients whom they can refer to you even though you never did any work for the Networker.

The following are illustrations of typical Networking:

Type of Networking	*Type of Cases*
Accountants, Financial Planners	wills, estate planning, business
Physicians	accident cases
Insurance Agents	accident cases, estate planning
Marriage Counselors	family law
Banks	business and probate clients
Religious Leaders	family law and probate
Friends or Relatives	all of the above
Other Lawyers	all of the above and more

Over a period of time, every lawyer finds Networkers who tend to send the lawyer the kinds of cases and clients they want.

The highest and best return on your marketing efforts and time is as follows:

1. Existing Networkers
2. Existing Clients
3. Potential Networkers
4. Potential Clients

In summary, Network the Networkers.

N-10
Getting and Keeping Clients Through
Inplacing and Outplacing

The purpose of "inplacing" and "outplacing" (two words I believe I invented) is to infiltrate a client or potential client in order to keep the client or to get the client. These techniques are more commonly used by larger firms, but can on occasion be used by smaller firms with great success. I used inplacing to expand my banking practice to a 15-lawyer practice when I started with a two-lawyer firm.

Inplacing consists of your hiring a lawyer or non-lawyer (don't overlook law clerks, paralegals or other non-lawyers) who are, or who were, employed by house counsel or legal departments or other departments of larger clients, or whose parents can send legal business. You hire the person for your firm in order to try to get, or keep, legal work from the client who is the employer, or former employer, of the applicant whom you hire. If you are extremely aggressive, you can even advertise non-existent jobs to get applicants whom you would hire if they can bring the business in.

After you hire the person, you can then offer your firm as having someone who knows the internal procedures, personnel and corporate policy of the client, facilitating the use of your firm because the client can save time, money and mistakes by having someone in your firm who understands the inside workings of the client. Additionally, this person can be represented as having first-hand work experience in the particular industry of his or her employer.

Don't overlook night law students who have passed the Bar. Typically, they are older graduates of the second- or third-level law schools. They sometimes wouldn't be considered for an interview with some law firms. If you hire them and give them a chance as a lawyer, they'll be completely ingratiated to you and will realize that their getting or keeping their job with you will depend on their getting or keeping their previous employer as a client of your firm.

As specific cases in point, I can refer to the following case histories from my own experience.

A. Mr. X, a 46-year-old new graduate of a night law school. He was working as a collector for a bank (when he wasn't studying). I was then doing a small amount of collection work for that bank. I believe he was totally unemployable as a lawyer in a "megafirm." He claimed that another law firm hinted at a job offer and let's give him the benefit of the doubt. My junior partner (Mr. B) was totally opposed to hiring him, believing he was too old to take direction from the younger partners (I was then 33 and my partner, 29). I insisted that we at least try him out. When Mr. X came to work for us, we got a huge increase in the quality and quantity of work from that bank client. Our hiring Mr. X led to that bank's becoming a six-figure per year client. Mr. X's buddies in the collection department wanted to help him "make it" as a lawyer after his sacrifice of four years of night law school. They gave him (us) so much legal work we had to hire more people.

Frankly, my original goal in hiring Mr. X was only to prevent his opening his own doors and taking the smaller work I was getting. He opened my eyes to the possibility of getting more and better work from clients by inplacing.

B. Mr. Y was a personable new lawyer who, in my opinion then, was strong on personality and weak on legal experience. He had the desirable quality of having worked as a junior trust officer in a bank before becoming a lawyer. I hired him in an attempt to infiltrate or get some of his former employer's trust business. He told me he could get the business (it turned out he couldn't). I touted him to our potential banking clients as a lawyer with "banking experience" (I never said his banking experience was as a lawyer - let people assume what they will).

I was marketing myself, Mr. X and Mr. Y as being lawyers who had banking experience and who, therefore, could more easily relate to banks and bankers. (Mr. X had been a collector, Mr. Y a junior trust officer, and I had worked nights in a bank while in high school). The marketing technique worked.

Although we never got the trust business from that bank, we eventually got more collection work from our other bank clients.

C. Mr. Z was a finance company house counsel doing small-time consumer collection work. He had been my college fraternity brother. I gave him a part-time job reviewing our files nights and weekends and promised him a job "when the time was right to make a move." He was a bird dog for us. He sniffed out clients and potential clients when he went to meetings of finance company and banking lawyers which were closed to us. We never got his company as a client, but we got a lot of his referrals and, when the time was right, I brought him on as an associate and later made him a name partner.

There is a hazard when you inplace people for their ability to bring in business. They may eventually realize that the business followed them, not you. They may then become greedy, leave you, take your clients, and set up their own practices.

As indicated, you should not limit your inplacing to lawyers. Paralegals, legal secretaries and non-legal secretaries can often bring you some of their former employers' business when they come to you. I have successfully inplaced associates and others from accounting firms, banks, finance companies, trade associations and many other sources.

During the interview with someone who works for a potential client, ask the following question:

"If we hire you (or if you come to work here), do you think you can get your present (or future) employer to try us for 'some' of their legal work?"

Note the use of the word "some," so as not to appear greedy. You obviously are using this candidate as a potential "in" to make a contact within the prospective client's law department. You can use the occasion of "reference checking" to get the "in" to make a sales pitch. You can casually mention the possibility of your "dropping by" to see their operation.

FAMILY LEGAL BUSINESS.

It often happens that a job applicant has family which can send some legal business to the firm which hires their son or daughter or other relative. The person who can direct legal business is often happy to help the relative get a job by sending legal business to the relative's new employer. The rationale is that, as long as they have to send the legal business somewhere, they might just as well send it where it can help a relative get or keep a job. Again, while lawyers are the people who first come to mind, you should not overlook law clerks and nonlawyers. It doesn't hurt to ask the question:

"If you are employed by us, is it likely that you can bring any family legal business with you?"

In some foreign countries, a lawyer who does not contribute some family business has absolutely no chance of getting a job.

FOREIGN LAW CLERKS AND LAWYERS.

This technique generally is worthwhile only for the larger firms. The large firm hires a lawyer or law clerk from a foreign country. Typically, that person :is already employed by a large foreign law firm and is on leave to study or work for a year in a U.S. firm to improve his English and "learn a little about U.S. law." The hiring of this person is almost never cost effective from a production point of view, for several reasons.

As a rule, the foreign lawyer will be around for only six months to a year, so you can't involve the lawyer deeply in a matter which will go on for years. The lawyer's English probably will not be good enough for drafting documents and often will not be good enough to do superior legal research. (Unlike many other languages, every word in English has multiple meanings, depending on how it is used. Also, foreign students often learn British English in school rather than American English.) Their work requires intensive supervision and review due to language problems and general unfamiliarity with local laws and social and business customs and practices. They often expect a lot of social "baby sitting" and help in everything from where to find an apartment to how to find a social friend. Often they are relegated to administrative jobs in the firm which is still of some value to them in learning how U.S. firms function.

One foreign lawyer from Brazil told me that he was one of 10 foreign lawyers from 10 different countries hired for internships ranging from 3 months to a year. They were paid well and had very little to do except an occasional translation. They came in at 9:30 or 10:00 a.m., read advance sheets and some periodicals till noon, took two-hour lunches with partners and senior associates in the firm, and then did one or two hours of work in the afternoon. The U.S. law firm was simply making a long-range investment, knowing that one or more of these foreign lawyers would someday send them a significant legal matter where the profit on that one matter would more than cover their investment in all the lawyers hired.

Occasionally, the foreign lawyer will work for free "to get experience" and to avoid problems with U.S. Immigration and Naturalization. They want to come back to the U.S. in later years for business and don't want to get on a black list for violating their student or tourist visa status. The U.S. law firm sometimes gives them the option of working for free or for money, and they sometimes voluntarily work for free.

ETHICAL PROHIBITIONS ON INPLACING.

Be careful. Remember the person who in fact comes to work for you, promising to bring in business, may be precluded from doing so by conflict of interest or confidential information rules or contractual restrictions of their present employer.

OUTPLACING TO GET AND KEEP CLIENTS.

Outplacing is a technique used by many larger law firms to dump the lawyers they don't want as partners and at the same time cement relations with existing clients. On occasion, a small firm has the opportunity to use this method.

The process of outplacing consists of your placing a lawyer into a job, preferably as house counsel, with an existing client. The person placed owes his or her job to you and, as such, is likely to be grateful to you. Additionally, outplaced lawyers perceive that if you are influential enough to get them hired, you are also influential enough to get them fired if they try to replace your firm, or if they complain about your bill. The placed person becomes an extension of your control over the client's placement of legal work.

In addition to outplacing lawyers, you can also outplace paralegals, legal secretaries and others, if there is enough time available to do so and if you're willing to keep them on the payroll while you try to outplace them.

Be careful when outplacing that the person you are outplacing is grateful for the placement. If the person is angry at being outplaced, you are planting a time bomb which can cost you a client if the former employee turns against you.

OUTPLACING TO JUDGESHIPS.

I've been told, but don't know for a fact, that law firms, particularly the Wall Street firms, outplace excess lawyers, including partners, to judgeships.

The typical time for this outplacing to judgeship is when there has been a close "rainmaker" relationship between the outgoing partner and a client which has left the firm for a new firm. The client's new firm doesn't want the partner because it doesn't need him or her. To make matters worse, the new firm's lawyers probably have "bad mouthed" both the partner and the partner's former firm, a condition which could well lead to friction. Additionally, the partner's salary may be excessively high, based upon rainmaking ability rather than upon technical legal ability or billing capacity. The partner was receiving the high compensation to hand-hold a particular client and since that client has left the firm, it can no longer justify the high salary.

Outplacing to judgeships is also used when a lengthy litigation matter has been completed and there is no longer a need within the firm for the lawyer or lawyers who had worked on that one case. Through working on a single long case the lawyers became totally out of touch with the current affairs of the firm or the current state of the law.

I am told these lawyers tend to be outplaced through the political process to specialty Federal Judgeships or to specialty administrative positions where there is likelihood that the firm's clients' legal matters would come before that lawyer, now a judge.

The firm can then market itself by saying to a client or potential client that the client would be well advised to use their firm because they know how Judge So-and-So thinks and what he looks for, and that, while he will do his best to be even handed, when the weight of evidence is exactly the same and it boils down to who is credible, the judge is likely to believe his or her old partners rather than a stranger.

Again, I wish to reiterate that I know of no first-hand cases of this happening, but I've been told that it's commonly done by the larger firms and at least one judge have been identified to me as having been appointed by this process, sometimes accompanied by a significant financial contribution to a political campaign which of course was purely coincidental.

Certainly I would advise any firm which has had a partner who is now a judge on the bench to advertise it and, if possible, to show that fact on its stationery. This, of course, is subject to your local rules.

N-11
Getting and Keeping Clients Through Assisting with Job Getting

You can get and/or keep good legal work by running an informal employment agency. This technique is an offshoot of the outplacing and inplacing techniques. You must be very careful to be discreet and not to alienate existing clients who would lose a good employee to a potential client whose work you want.

Your goal is to help people get jobs where they can direct you to more legal work from an existing client or to new legal work from a new client.

You have to let it be known discreetly that you can help place employees of existing clients. You do this in a reverse way. You tell your existing clients' key people that from time to time you get requests on a discreet basis from good people for assistance in seeking new employment and that you would like to be able to refer those people to the client. The subtle message you want to convey is that you not only are able to transmit information on applicants *to* the key employees, but also *from* the employee to others on a discreet basis. If you can succeed in getting the new job for the employee, the employee will be indebted to you and hopefully bring you in as the legal counsel.

When I did bank collection work, I often assisted employees of our banking clients' collection departments to find jobs in the collection departments of other clients or in the collection departments of banks that were not yet our clients. We were privy to information as to which bank was going to increase its staff and which was going to decrease its staff. We helped many collectors get new jobs. These collectors became our close allies and referred us work in gratitude for assisting them in getting their new jobs.

Besides serving as a clearinghouse for job availability information, you can assist by writing letters of recommendation, making calls to the prospective employers or offering to act as a reference on a job application.

Again, you must be very discreet so that your existing clients do not realize that you are "raiding" their good people and getting them jobs with potential competitors.

N-12
Giving Gifts to Clients and Their Employees
As an Incentive for Using Your Firm

Gifts are an excellent investment in terms of business development and are extremely cost effective. Gifts must be given (or received) with extreme sensitivity and care. Giving a gift to the wrong person or under the wrong circumstances can be interpreted as a form of bribe or kickback. On the other hand, properly chosen and given, a gift can be a expression of friendship, respect and regard.

Gifts should be given only to existing clients and their employees. Never give a gift to a *prospective* client.

The best gift is one which the client will display in his or her business surroundings. The client will see the gift constantly, will think of you each time the object is seen, and will be near a telephone to call you when a need arises.

A nominal gift can result in a single legal matter worth thousands or tens of thousands of dollars in legal fees. The client may use you during the year just to stay on your gift list. Often I have received only one matter from a client during the whole year, usually around November. I believe the client sent me the single matter just to stay on my Christmas gift list.

Gifts are especially worthwhile when dealing with middle-level and lower-level employees of large corporations (assuming they have some authority or decision-making power in assigning out legal work). These people often feel (with or without justification) that they are underpaid for what they do. They see what lawyers' bills look like and feel they should be getting something for selecting the lawyer who earns the fee. A nominal gift often satisfies those feelings.

Tax laws may limit the amount of a gift which can be given and deducted. It's not a violation of tax laws to give a gift exceeding that amount. It's simply that the gift may be partially or totally non-tax deductible for you.

The list below includes gifts that I have successfully given to clients over the years. With a little shopping around, they can be obtained in bulk quantities at low cost.

1. Desk clocks
2. Desk radios
3. Desk pen or pencil sets
4. Desk calculators
5. Pocket calculators
6. Pocket pen/pencil set
7. Legal pad holders
8. Plants (not fresh flowers)
9. Terrariums

The possibilities are endless. The important thing to realize is that all of these items are likely to remain in the client's office and be a constant reminder of you to the client.

Generally, I don't like to give a gift which will end up at home because a client is not likely to call me from home with a case. Additionally, I don't want the gift ending up in a closet where it is out of sight and out of mind. On occasion I have had favorable responses on gifts which ended up in the house, such as:

1. Wine or liquor.
2. Cheese boards (with or without cheese).
3. Airplane carry-on luggage.
4. Fresh cut flowers.

I suspect the reason I had favorable responses from those gifts is that the client's spouse pressured the client to stay on my gift list to get another gift next year.

I also give magazine subscription to a client for their favorite hobby. The magazines go to the house where they can be read at leisure and can arrive 12 times/year instead of only 1 time/year.

Gifts can be personalized by engraving, photo engraving, etc., with:

1. The client's name.
2. The client's personal business card (by photo engraving) with the client's firm name.
3. Your personal business card (by photoengraving).
4. Your firm name.

If I am superstitious on any one subject it is the subject of plants. Whenever I get an announcement from an attorney acquaintance or client who has just moved to a new location, I always send a plant.

A plant will stay in the client's office and remain highly visible over the years. Some people believe that plants bring good luck, and I don't argue with them.

I've had situations where an attorney in a distant city referred me clients as much as 10 years after I sent him a plant. I had totally forgotten about the attorney until I received a phone call and a statement that the attorney thought of me every time he saw the plant and finally had the chance to refer a matter to Los Angeles.

Plants, like other office gifts, will follow the client wherever he or she may go.

N-13
Client "Perks" for Using You as a Lawyer for the Company

Remind the decision maker of the "perks" of using you as a lawyer for the company.

There are other chapters in this book on gifts to clients as well as other techniques. In this chapter I simply wish to remind you that individuals should receive a "perk" for using your firm.

Tickets to professional athletic events, the theater or concerts may be what client expects of you as a perk. They are not likely to be so obvious as to ask you outright for them, and you can't be so crude as to say that if you get chosen they'll receive them as a matter of right. You should find out the interests of those qualified to receive tickets. Try to determine whether they simply want tickets to the events or whether they merely want someone to go with (some people like to go to these events without their spouse or family, just for a change of pace).

Don't say, "The firm has tickets for clients for these events," because they may think you are offering a bribe or may feel they will have a claim on the tickets if the company becomes a client.

Tell an individual interested in attending an event that someone in the firm has tickets or has a friend or other client who has tickets. Say that because of travel commitments or other reasons the tickets often cannot be used and sometimes are given away. Offer to keep this person in mind if the tickets become available. This establishes that tickets may or may not be available because the purchaser normally uses them. It also creates the impression that the person is doing you or your friend a favor by taking the tickets to prevent their being wasted.

Be sure to say something like there would be no charge for the tickets because they're simply giving away something that would otherwise go to waste.

If you are going to buy season tickets for clients, decide whether you want your firm name printed on the tickets. On one hand, it establishes your importance and reminds the client and others who go with the client where the tickets came from. On the other hand, this client will realize that you *always* have these tickets, and may be angered or insulted if he or she wants to see a particular game from those particular seats and you have to say "no." The client may feel that you favor another client and become angry or hostile.

1. *Tickets to athletic events.* It is my experience that good tickets to college and professional athletic events, especially football and basketball are the most sought-after perks that a decision-maker may expect from a lawyer.

I personally don't like to accompany the client to the athletic event. It's not my style. It's not a technique that I like to use. I want to spend my spare time with family or in personal pursuits. Other lawyers do like to accompany the client. I even have known situations where there is a tacit understanding that they discuss a case and that the lawyer record the time and send a bill for time at least equal to the cost of the tickets. This is especially the case when it is necessary to buy the tickets through a broker at a premium. Other lawyers simply call the client after the game or wait for the client to call, at which time they discuss both the game and a case in process in order to get billable time equal to or greater than the ticket costs.

2. *Tickets to rock concerts.* If the individual you are trying to develop has teenage children, then some tickets to a rock concert will make an instant hero both of you and the client. You can depend upon the children's pestering the parent to return to you for more tickets in the future.

3. *Tickets to cultural events.* I like to go to plays and outdoor concerts. I like to go with my wife and don't mind bringing a client and spouse along because our attention is devoted to the event and not business conversation with the client. I don't do this often, but on the rare occasions I do, I enjoy it; this is my style and a technique with which I'm comfortable. I find that good seats for this type of event are highly prized by clients and prospective clients.

4. *Other activities.* You'll have to find out from the individual just what activity that person enjoys but considers it a luxury to attend.

I have on occasion simply called the person's secretary to inquire about the boss' favorite spectator sport or activity.

In summary, tickets are an excellent client "perk" for the small firm to get a foot in the door and to stay in the door when going after the larger company.

N-14
Other Client "Perks" for Using You As
Company Lawyer - Clubs and Restaurants

Private Country Clubs and Golf Clubs. I don't belong to any country clubs, primarily because I don't play much golf or tennis, and if I did, I wouldn't want to use out-of-office time for heavy business discussion. However, many lawyers use golf starting times at private clubs on weekends as a client perk, and they are highly valued. There is no question of the desirability of golf at a private country club, as a client perk for getting and keeping the corporate clients good will.

Golf has been described as "the last refuge of the white male," where white males will not be overheard by females or persons of color. Obviously the reverse could be true. White males can be excluded by others. A friend of mine was hired by a major U.S. company to work in sales. She was immediately sent to learn golf. As a very attractive woman she had no difficulty in getting men to play golf with her at an expensive exclusive membership club. She had been playing for about a year when one of the golfers noticed she was left handed and asked her why she didn't use left handed clubs. She had been playing for a year and never knew there was such a thing as a left handed club.

I repeat this story to pint out that in this particular corporate setting, golf was so important they hired a person who knew nothing about golf and sent her to learn. She knew so little about golf that after one year she didn't know there were left handed clubs for left handed people like her.

I know of several lawyers and CPAs who build their entire practices from a single country club where they played golf or tennis.

Private Eating Clubs and Expensive Restaurants. I suspect that many corporate people have never bought their own lunch. They expect to have a firm vendor (in our case, a lawyer) take them to lunch. Accordingly, you should suggest that you meet in your office or their office about 11 :30 and then go to lunch. Pick an expensive place or private club so that the individual will know they can expect this as a perk. It is a very interesting phenomenon to me that many times I've had a sandwich across the desk of a corporate president at a 40-minute lunch because neither of us wanted to waste time and we munched as we discussed the problem at hand. However, the lower down the decision maker tree, the fancier the place the client's employee wants to go and the more time they want to spend.

They choose the two- anq three-hour lunches: at the most expensive restaurants. This is a fact of life and I accept it. I always ask them where *they* would like to eat lunch and also suggest that I can "get in" to a private eating club. I don't say "I belong" in case they have social prejudices against private eating clubs.

I personally enjoy taking prospective clients to the Magic Castle in Hollywood because it is a private dinner club with magic shows nightly. It is unique in all the world. I tell prospective clients that I can arrange for them to use the facilities for themselves and their friends by arranging it through me. Many of my clients ask me to arrange it for them to go with their friends. My wife gets "magiced out" and I often go without her. The Magic Castle is a pleasurable place I am comfortable with, so I use it.

N-15
Miscellaneous Client Perks for
Using You as Company Lawyer

I list these miscellaneous perks for you to be sensitive to in the event your prospective client drops a subtle hint that he or she is receptive to one.

Travel. Some attorneys take clients and prospective clients with them on trips, ranging from weekenders to *30-day* cruises.

Condominiums and Resorts. Some attorneys arrange for prospective clients to use the firm condo or resort facility.

Gifts. There is an entire chapter in this book on gifts. Christmas gifts are often a good perk.

Parties. Wild, extravagant, plush parties can be a worthwhile perk. They may be presented as a seminar rather than a party.

Seminars. Inviting people to seminars at expensive restaurants or resorts is a good perk. (See chapter on seminars.)

Stamps and Coins. If I know my client is a stamp or coin collector, I'll try to find out their area of special interest and them give them a stamp or coin from time to time as a "souvenir" of my traveling.

Magazine Subscriptions. Buying magazine subscriptions for a client based on the client's hobbies or interests is a cheap way to develop loyalty. The client gets 12 reminders of you every year and the amount is so nominal you are not likely to create any problems over the amount of the gift.

These are simply wide-ranging examples. You have to listen carefully to get a feel for the perk the particular individual will prefer.

N-16
Don't Lose Clients Through Improper Delegation
Delegate for Higher Profits - Don't Abdicate

It makes economic good sense for all work in any law firm to be delegated down to the person at the least compensated level who is competent to do the job. It is in the client's best interests for attorneys to delegate to lower level attorneys and to non-attorneys for several reasons, including:

1. They are cheaper
2. They get the job done faster
3. They are usually more available to the client
4. The law firm (lawyers) earns greater profits.

If you properly communicate this to the prospective client, the client not only won't object to delegation, but will usually welcome getting the work done cheaper and quicker.

You can say things such as, "I don't type my own letters, nor file my own papers, nor make my own photocopies. I use other, lower-cost people to help me get the job done quicker and cheaper. This lowers costs for you and increases the number of people I can personally help. I compare it with surgery, where the surgeon is head of the team but is there only for the cutting. I will make the important decisions and supervise what is being done, but I won't be doing everything on the case."

You should then introduce the client to the other people with whom they may have contact, face to face and by name, including secretaries, word processing operators, associates and legal assistants (call them legal assistants rather than paralegals, which can be a confusing term).

However, you cannot abdicate. The client came to see *you* (or your firm) because *you've* litigated cases like theirs before or done deals like theirs before. They want your personal involvement. They don't want to be "turned over" to someone else and then abandoned by you.

You absolutely must maintain some personal contact and you must let the client know that you are the decision-maker and/or you approve the decisions made. This will keep the client happy. You also must make periodic personal contact to ensure client satisfaction. If you don't maintain some personal contact with the client, the client will follow the associate if the associate leaves the firm; or the client may stop referring work to you because the client perceives you as being "too busy" or "too big a shot" to help with his or her problems.

Instruct the associate to review the client's files before calling the client for information. Clients can get angry when an associate calls the client to ask a question that is already answered in the file. It may be permissible for the associate to call to confirm information in the file.

In summary, "DELEGATE-DON'T ABDICATE!"

N-17
Successful Seminars

In general, seminars are a bit too ambitious for solo practitioners and small firms unless they are done on a very narrow, very specific and very limited basis. The investment of staff time and money and hard dollars in printings, mailings, follow-up, etc., is more than a small firm might care to make. Seminars can be a profitable client-pleaser and source of new business, but small firms typically are afraid to make the investment.

This chapter is really most applicable to firms with five or more lawyers, for the reasons stated above. However, I will show you how to do the seminars and you can decide whether you want to invest the time and money.

I did my first client seminars when I had a five-lawyer firm back in 1970, and they were immensely successful. Each succeeding seminar was bigger, fancier, costlier and produced better results.

Seminars at Clients' Places of Business.
My first client seminar took place at my client's offices. The client was Union Bank. Three of us went to the conference room and met with the head of the Loan Adjustment (Collection) Department and six of the Adjusters (Collectors). Each of the three of us spoke on a specific area of collection law (which, as I remember, were bankruptcy, bank executions and prejudgment attachments). The seminar began at 2:00 and each of us spoke 20 minutes. At 3:00, we took questions and at 3:30 it was over. We left our printed outlines behind for the adjusters.

Immediately after the seminar, we got an increase in assignments from Union Bank in those three areas, for two reasons:

1. We demonstrated that we knew the law;
2. We demonstrated that we wanted their business. (Their outside general counsel had never done this for them.)

Each time we wanted to expand the nature of the work we were doing for this client, we simply gave another in-house seminar on the area of law in which we wanted the business and we usually got it.

Seminars for Clients and Potential Clients at Restaurants and Fancy Hotels.
The in-house seminars worked fine, but I was eager for more business on a faster growth basis, so I began doing outside seminars.

I put on our first outside seminar at a restaurant commonly used for group meetings (Roger Young Auditorium). My partners were afraid that doing a seminar in a public place was too aggressive. (They had previously been afraid that going to the client's place of business was too aggressive.) I also invited the collection department of another bank we had just begun doing work for (our second) and one person from the collection department of a bank we did not represent. I told them I wanted their comments on the level of the presentation (which was true) but, truthfully, I was using the seminar as an excuse to promote them. They had been recommended to me by a employee of one of the two banks which we recommended and I made the initial contact using the recommender's name.

What happened at this seminar set the stage for all the seminars which followed and also became the basis for getting bank after bank after bank into the firm as clients until I had 19 banks and financial institutions as clients grossing millions of dollars in legal fees.

While I was standing near the bar (which was open), one of the collectors asked for a scotch and soda. When the bartender turned down the payment pointing out that it was hosted, I heard the client say, "Well, in that case, make it a Chivas Regal and soda." I realized then and there that these guys wanted a free dinner party. Fortunately, I had been the convention chairman of a lawyer group and was a real expert on dinner parties. The format which I followed very successfully and recommend to you is as follows:

1. Your seating arrangements are extremely important. Don't allow people to choose their own seats.

    A. *For existing clients:* Spread them around to different tables. Put the higher-ups in the seat next to a partner level person on one side and a friendly person of the opposite sex from your firm on the other side. Before drawing conclusions, see section on who should attend.

    B. *For potential clients:* Put the highest-level person you can from your firm on one side and a satisfied, enthusiastic client on the other side. Tell your satisfied client you are trying to get the potential client. The satisfied client will praise you wildly to the potential client.

2. The location is extremely important. Go top of the line. Pick a hotel or very fancy restaurant. After the first seminar, we immediately began using the most expensive hotels and restaurants such as the Hilton, the five-star restaurants at the Bank of America, etc. When we wanted to move into San Francisco, we used the Fairmont Hotel, the Mark Hopkins, etc.

3. Select the best liquor and food. These people are looking for a great party, if they enjoy it, they'll talk about it. You want them to look forward to coming to the next one. I instructed the hotels to use only high-quality, name-brand liquor and to be generous in pouring it. The waiters served round after round of hors d'oeuvres. The menu was top quality with lots of wine.

4. Title of the seminar is important. We always titled the seminar in such a way that it suggested a periodic program. "What's New in Collection Law?" or "New Changes Affecting Collection Law." The title of the program was important because it suggested:

    A. We were experts on the subjects.
    B. The employees of the existing and potential clients could justify coming to the seminar for educational purposes rather than just to party it up.
    C. The invitations were going to people we didn't represent and I wanted to impress them with our expertise.

5. The schedule of the seminar requires thought and preparation. A typical schedule ran as follows:

    4:00 - 5:30 Get-acquainted reception.

    We advertised this as being the time for our clients to meet our support staff and others whom they had talked to by telephone or had heard about by name. I believe people work together better if they've met face to face. Naturally, a certain amount of alcohol and hors d'oeuvres were consumed at this event.

    5:30 - 7:00 Seminar.

    Three to five partners spoke on specific subjects. They spoke from a podium, but immediately after their presentation, they left the podium and returned to the table to be with the attendees. Believe it or not, some people (typically the bosses) actually came only for the seminar. They left immediately following the seminar and introductions. They had no interest in the party or the dinner. This was up to them and certainly we didn't force anyone to come early or stay late.

    7:00 - 7:15 Introduction of attendees.

    We introduced every person from our office, described what they did in the firm and asked them to stand and be recognized. We also announced the name of the highest level person present from each of the various clients. We even included the potential clients. We wanted everyone there to feel they belonged there and if the high level people were there, then it was OK for them to also be there. The clients and potential clients could not always distinguish between who was an existing client and who was an "invited guest" so it made us look more important as having all these people as clients. After the introductions some of the top level people would leave.

    7: 15 - 8:30 Dinner.
    8:30 - 9:00 Questions and answers on the subjects covered.

    Typically, there would be only a few questions, but the question and-answer period provided an excuse to stay for dinner.

9:00 - 10:00 Get acquainted with staff. Coffee and desert available, no alcohol served. Most people left to go home; a few stayed on.

6. Who to invite.
    A. Your attorneys. Make it mandatory for all of your attorneys to attend unless there is some extremely important excuse (middle of trial, etc.).
    B. Your non-lawyer staff. Invite all of them to attend. Make it clear there is no obligation to attend. They should be paid for their time. Let them know this is an opportunity for them to get to know the clients and for the clients to get to know them. Attendance should be absolutely voluntary.
    C. Your existing clients who will be interested in the area of law presented. Address all invitations personally. Include secretaries and the accounting clerk who approves your bill.
    D. House counsel for your existing clients. Invite them. They probably won't come, but invite them anyway. You want to impress them as to your expertise.
    E. House counsel for your potential clients (the ones you're trying to get). They might or might not come, but again, you want to impress them as to your expertise.
    F. Do invite owners and high-level people from your potential clients. Do invite the person who decides which attorneys to use for which subjects.
    G. Do NOT invite outside counsel from your potential clients or other outside counsel. These people are your competitors. They may find real or imagined technical fault with your presentation. They may try to lure your existing clients away from you. If a potential client insists on bringing an outside counsel, be sure you assign one of your people to stick with that person and shield him or her from meeting high-level people if it appears that the outside counsel is trying to get your clients. (This is similar to "fronting" in basketball or "double teaming" in football.)
    H. Do invite other people suggested by your existing clients. You can ask your existing clients if they know of someone in a similar company who might like to attend. Your existing clients will want to show off the kind of party their lawyer throws.
7. Follow-up.
    Make it a point to follow up with every guest in attendance. Your opening line can be, "I hope you enjoyed the seminar. I'm most interested in your opinion on how the seminar might be improved next time. If you like, we can get together for lunch." The response may be simply 'That was one hell of a party," or it may be very detailed.
8. Cost.
    This type of seminar is very expensive in terms of time and out-of-pocket cost. You can easily end up with a cost of $400 or more client and potential client per in attendance.

Also, much lawyer and staff time is required both in preparing for the seminar and attending it. It's a very big investment to make, but well worth it if you get the clients and business you want. A single routine legal case resulting from a seminar can easily yield $5,000 and more. A routine business or tax client can provide you with tens and hundreds of thousands of dollars. The returns can be great if you carefully select the people to be invited.

The seminar plans I've presented will work for you if you have the courage to make the investment of time and money.

N-18
Successful Seminars for Recommenders of Clients And Potential Recommenders of Clients

In many areas of law, your business often doesn't come directly from a client or potential client. Examples of people who refer you work are doctors, accountants, insurance agents, bankers, other lawyers, etc.

Think of your own practice. Can you identify the people who refer you business other than their own work, *per se?*

Most of the rules which apply to seminars for clients and potential clients apply here. All of the sections of that chapter relative to format, the seminar itself, who to invite, follow-up and cost apply here as well. It would be an unnecessary duplication to repeat them here.

The difference will be in subject matter. Remember that the main reason attendees will come is for the party, not for the educational aspects. They will talk about the party long after they have forgotten everything educational you've presented. Additionally, there sometimes isn't enough time or a high enough level of sophistication among those you invite to communicate much technical information. Remember, doctors aren't interested in hearing you speak on personal injury law, but they might have an interest in tax law or estate planning or corporate retirement plans.

Remember, your invitation will go to many people who won't attend. The invitation has to convey to them the kinds of law you can practice whether you convey this information directly or indirectly.

Sample subjects could be:

What happens if you die without a will?
What's new in real estate closings?
New tax laws that affect professional corporations.
The rights of doctors with medical liens in accident cases.
The importance of good written contracts.
The importance of annual corporate minutes.

The list is endless and has to fit your own practice. Keep in mind that the seminar is really the excuse for a party.

As I stressed in the preceding chapter, the costs are great in terms of money and time. Solo practitioners who are afraid to try a seminar should possibly consider a client Christmas party instead.

N-19
Simple, Low-Cost Seminars
Which Small Firms Can Present

In the other chapters on client seminars, I've emphasized that "the party is the thing" rather than the subject matter of the seminars.

Solo practitioners have reported to me that they can get very successful results for limited efforts. They don't wish to spend money but are willing to spend a little time.

Typically, they do one of the following:

1. Go to an existing client's place of business to update the client's staff on correct legal procedures. This is similar to the conference room seminar.
2. Invite existing clients to the office on a Saturday morning or weekday evening for a year-end tax planning seminar. Cookies and coffee and soda can be served.
3. Invite clients to the board room of a neighborhood savings and loan or bank for the type of seminar described in item 2 above. Cookies and coffee and soda can be served.
4. One lawyer reports that his wife bakes the cookies and he announces this to those present. For reasons I don't understand, people comment favorably on this at the seminar. The point is that people expect something to eat and drink, even if it's not brand name scotch and canapés.

I personally prefer the larger, more lavish type of seminar, but I pass this on 'to you for your trial-and-error experimentation.

Don't forget that the invitation announces what you can do for your clients and potential clients.

Chapter O
Assorted Marketing Tips

O-1
The Ethics and Development of
Marketing and Practice Development

At one time there was a myth that a lawyer was supposed to sit quietly like a clam in the office waiting for clients to discover him or her. Just as a clam must remain sedentary and wait for the current to bring in nutrients, the lawyer was supposed to remain sedentary and wait for word of mouth to bring clients. Any lawyer who risked open departure from this fiction risked being called "an ambulance chaser" or a "shyster."

A bit of thoughtful reflection will quickly disperse that myth. We all have images from the movies or from real life of well-tailored lawyers on golf courses, on tennis courts and at country clubs dealing with clients and potential clients. It is important to remember that the lawyer went to the golf course and that the golf course did not wander into the lawyer's office. Thus, the lawyer went to where the clients or potential clients were located, exemplifying earlier history of organized practice development.

Lawyers have always been involved in marketing and practice development. Only the forms of marketing and practice development have changed, with new forms evolving as the world changes. Stationery, professional cards, building directories, telephone directories, etc., have always been recognized as proper forms of marketing a lawyer's name and availability. Television, websites, blawgs, fax blasts, email and satellite broadcasts are simply modern extensions of earlier methods. Using firm names with names of principals long since dead and totally unknown to the lawyers presently in the firm is a form of advertising. Fictitious name firms such as "The Aviation Group," "The Litigation Group," etc. are simply extensions of the use of names with advertising value. My particular favorite is a firm named "4 Bitches From Hell." One can guess what kind of law they practice. Hundreds of hours of legal talent have been wasted debating such theoretical subjects as whether a lawyer could be listed in more than one telephone directory. Debates still rage over exactly what a lawyer should or should not put on his or her legal stationery, as though clients and potential clients in some mysterious manner can obtain copies of the stationery and then select a lawyer based on information on it. The Chinese pictograph for a lawyer is "people who like to debate." Lawyers debate *ad nauseam* subjects they think are important, but which in truth are totally inconsequential and unimportant to non-lawyers.

Most of the restrictions on advertising or marketing originated in Roman law practice and were incorporated into English common law, the English legal system, which traditionally treated the practice of the profession of law as a form of *noblesse oblige*. The world changes, even in England. For several hundred years, barristers did not carry professional cards, considering them to be "hawking by tradesmen." Within the last few years, however, even English barristers (or some of them) now carry and give out professional cards. "Direct access," allowing barristers to accept clients to contact a barrister without an intervening solicitor seems to be growing. The permission granted by the Law Society(roughly equivalent to a Bar Association) is an indication of the changes occurring at the root sources of the restrictions.

Years ago, I predicted in articles, books and lectures that the restrictions on lawyer advertising, lawyer marketing or lawyer availability were unnecessary restrictions on the public's right to know of the availability of legal services. Subsequent decisions of the United States Supreme Court and of various state courts have vindicated my position.

From professional calling cards to television commercials to the internet, advertising is simply a matter of degree. The person who screams "ambulance chaser" at every new development is simply living in the past.

It is my prediction that, ultimately, almost any form of advertising or marketing will be permitted so long as it is truthful.

O-2
Practice Development from the
Inns Of Court to the Concorde

I originally wrote this chapter in 1978 on board the Concorde, which took me from London to New York in 3 hours and 27 minutes. According to the clock, I arrived before I left due to the five-hour time difference.

The day before I left London was very symbolic to me in terms of the progress of law office technology and management and practice development. In the morning I had a conference with a Queens Counsel (barrister) at Buck Court at Grays Inn. I noted that the barrister's briefs were wrapped in the traditional red barrister's tape for delivery to the solicitor (similar to delivering a legal opinion from a trial lawyer specialist to a non-trial lawyer specialist). The tradition of this red tape wrapping goes back to the 1600s and is the origin of the term "Red Tape." The Inns of Court go back to the 12th century. Tied to each of the briefs was a magnetic dictating micro-cassette tape. The magnetic tape cassette was tied with the red tape onto the brief so that a typist or word processor could type the accompanying instructions. It seemed symbolic that there was a joinder of technology and the Barrister's red tape. The tradition of eight centuries was combining with modern technology. Law was coming into the 20th century in the hallowed Inns of Court.

Since 1978, the internet, email, and the cell phone have radically affected how clients find lawyers and how lawyers communicate with clients. One of my personal heroes, John Wooden of UCLA basketball fame, was asked his opinion about the changes in professional and college sports. Coach Wooden, then 94 years old with an audience of 2,000 people who had paid to see and hear him, opined, "You cannot have progress without change. This does not mean that all change is progress, but you cannot have any progress without change."

It is my personal belief that most, not all, but most, of the changes in marketing and practice development are progress because they increase the knowledgeable access of the public to needed legal services.

As I sat there at 60,000 feet, traveling 1,400 miles per hour (mach 2), sipping champagne, I reflected on the progress of our entire common law system from the hallowed Inns of Court to the age of law office technology and practice development. To paraphrase a then-current commercial, "We've come a long way, Baby."

As I revise and update this book in 2007, I am reminded that the Concorde no longer flies. The remaining airplanes are in museums. Millions, perhaps billions of dollars were spent to design and operate the Concorde. In the final analysis it simply was too expensive to operate and did not meet the needs of its clients. It went out of business. The same phenomenon may occur in the legal profession. The fanciest, most expensive, largest law firms may become obsolete and go out of business, being replaced as the Concorde was replaced by other more economical airplanes – not all change is progress.

O-3
Ways that Win:
Lawyer Marketing In the 19th Century

Long after I wrote *How to Start and Build a Law Practice*, someone sent me a photocopy of a 46-page pamphlet entitled *Ways That Win*. The pamphlet is a report of a speech given at Phi Delta Phi legal fraternity, Columbia University Law School. As of 1949, only two copies of the original pamphlet were known to exist. The following is a statement from the speech delivered by a lawyer, Walter S. Carter, on April 8, 1898:

"On advertising. . . as a general answer I will say the world moves. When I came to the bar, forty-three years ago this month [1855] very few, if indeed any, good lawyers advertised. Today, all that has changed."

In this chapter, I shall paraphrase some of what attorney Carter told that law fraternity so long ago. Incidentally, his 1898 address preceded the Canons of Ethics of The American Bar Association.

I won't necessarily agree or disagree with what Mr. Carter said, but rather will only repeat the advice he gave on practice development.

1. Law school graduation orators should not be lecturing on honesty, truthfulness, high-mindedness and honor. All of the foregoing are to be assumed. The lecture should cover where to locate, how to start and how to succeed.
2. In picking a location to practice law, stay away from large cities. If you want to go to the large city, start in a closely knit, small or medium-sized community and then, after getting some experience and a name, move on to the larger city.
3. Those who practice in a smaller community will get more out of life professionally and socially than those who practice in large cities.
4. Settle in the place where you have the most family and friends of influence who will "make your success their cause. "
5. If you have a choice, get some clerking experience (such as hewer of wood and drawer of water) before opening a practice.
6. Avoid large firms where you would have to specialize.
7. If a good opportunity (job offer) comes along, take it; if not, start your own law practice.
8. A two-name or three-name firm sounds good. The principal partners should be as different as possible-religiously, socially and politically.
9. In a three-lawyer firm, one should be the court lawyer, one the office lawyer and the third the outside lawyer. The outside lawyer is the most important member of the firm.

10. Your office furnishings should be at least as nice as your home furnishings. The office should be conducive to lawyer comfort and should make a good impression on clients and callers. The office should tell a client that you are on the high road to prosperity. The lawyer spends half of his waking moments in his office. The client will equate your office with your success. You cannot afford not to have a nice office.

11. Don't be afraid to ask for work. Mr. Carter related the story of an attorney who went to the president of a local bank which owned an office building. The attorney offered to rent the entire floor of the building if the bank would hire the lawyer to do the bank's collection work. The offer was accepted and both the bank and the attorney prospered.

12. Show off your law books. Make sure your clients and prospective clients know you have these "tools of the trade". Even if you have only one book, put that one book in a conspicuous place where your clients can see it.

13. Use only engraved, high-quality calling cards, stationery, letterhead, etc. Even bank checks and billing statements should be engraved rather than printed. He recommended putting the scales of justice on checks.

14. If you don't make a connection with an established practice, start your own.

15. Get all the letters of introduction you can to people where you will be practicing. Don't be concerned as to whether the people you will meet are influential. You don't know which letters will do you good. A very important person may be contacted by so many people that you are just another lawyer to that individual. On the other hand, a person of lesser importance may feel honored and he will do everything possible to help you get clients.

16. Meet all the people you can and remember the names of those people you meet. People are flattered by others' remembering their name.

17. Clubs and secret societies are a waste of time.

18. Be active in one of the two major political parties. Choose the one which most agrees with your political views. Support the party's nominees and attend the political meetings and conventions of the party. You will meet the people who make things happen.

19. Do your legal work so well that your client becomes your friend; indeed. in some cases the opposition's client will like your work well enough to use you. As the author wrote, "The sounder the beating you administer to your opponent, the better the friend you may possibly make of him."

20. Always stand up for what is best in the community.

O-4
Treating Other Lawyers as "Competitors"

For more than a third of a century I've been trying cases against other lawyers and I've negotiated deals with other lawyers and I've often considered that other lawyers were my opponents on a legal matter, but I've never regarded another lawyer as a "competitor."

The word "competitor" has crept into attorney marketing largely as the result of some non-lawyer consultants and administrators who treat legal marketing as a classic case book competition for market share as though legal service was beer or cigarettes to be gained by gimmickry or clever logos and slogans. They and their customers may be more interested in snagging the fast buck by any means than in giving clients excellent service. Lawyers who follow this pied piper may win a battle or two but will ultimately lose the war. They typically leave the law when they smell more money somewhere else. It is true that multiple attorneys or firms may wish to serve the needs of the same client. I believe that the client ultimately will stay with the firm that doesn't take the him/her for granted as a client. Attorneys or firms who ignore their good clients and who take them for granted are likely to lose clients when they seek out firms due to the neglect of their current firm. Clients normally initiate the search for new counsel when they perceive they've been mistreated or ignored by present counsel. The "new" attorney can't come in and take a client away unless there is already client dissatisfaction with the old firm.

Accordingly, I personally object to the use of the word "competitor" in the attorney vs. attorney sense. They are only competitors in the sense that each attorney wants to fulfill the client's perceived legal needs. Reputable ethical attorneys needn't "do" anything to another attorney. The competition I believe is and should be a competition to best serve the client and not a competitor to best secure the attorney at the expense of another attorney.

Successful attorneys don't have to stoop to bad mouthing another firm to attempt to create client dissatisfaction. Attorneys have enough to do just to serve clients well without directing energy to attacking other lawyers as "competitors."

I advocate that we attorneys do not refer to each other as "competitors" but rather always maintain control over the marketing effort, and that we always regard each other as professional colleagues recognizing our professional obligation to serve the client.

O-5
Yellow Page Ads Work, Make Your Ad Unique

Yellow Page ads work. A study done by the America Bar Association's Commission on Yellow Pages Advertising demonstrated how well they work. The Commission was disbanded after the report was delivered.

Yellow Pages are especially effective because they are in the potential client's home 7 days a week 24 hours a day. Most people who use the Yellow Pages do not know a lawyer or cannot reach the lawyer they know.

On average, Yellow Page ads return $3 of fees for every dollar of cost. Full page ads returned 8 to 1. 24% of blue collar America found their lawyer in the Yellow Pages. 11% of middle class America found their lawyer in the Yellow Pages.

Yellow Pages callers must be screened. I have been told but have not verified that 100 calls will produce 10 calls that a lawyer should connect with and that 3 of these calls will produce an economically viable matter, but these 3 cover the cost of all 100 with a big overall profit.

A female lawyer from Arlington, Virginia, in her first year of practice, related that she was overwhelmed at the large amount of criminal work, as opposed to other types of cases she received from her quarter-page Yellow Pages ad. Many other lawyers were listed in the Yellow Pages. They, as she, advertised that they did criminal work in addition to other areas of law" Since she was a new lawyer and grateful for the business, she was reluctant to ask the clients why they selected her over so many other lawyers listed. Finally, when she summoned the courage to ask, clients told her she was the only woman lawyer in the directory who listed criminal law as a practice area. There were plenty of male lawyers who listed criminal law and plenty of female lawyers who listed the other areas she listed, but she was the only woman who listed criminal law. (See the chapter on special advantages and disadvantages of being female.)

The moral of this story should be obvious. Look at the other Yellow Pages ads in the book(s) where you will be listed. Analyze them. See if there is something you can put in your ad which makes you unique. The purpose of Yellow Pages display ads is to call attention to yourself. If your unique characteristic is important to you, it also may be important for someone seeking a lawyer.

In summary:

1. Analyze the existing ads in the Yellow Pages where you intend to advertise.
2. Prepare a mock-up of the ad you wish to place.
3. Analyze the mock-up and modify it to list and emphasize something that makes you unique.

Some items which may set you apart could be:

1. Location in or near a particular shopping center
2. Location near public transportation (important to elderly people)
3. Foreign language ability (be sure to include your staff's abilities)
4. Special areas of law
5. Photo or wording to emphasize your gender or ethnic characteristics.

Unfortunately, Yellow Pages advertising often must be contacted for well in advance of the printing and distribution date. It may be several months until your ad reaches the public.

O-6
Cost-Effective Classified Newspaper Advertising

In this chapter, I express my personal opinion based on asking questions of my audiences in cities all over the country. Classified newspaper advertising in specific types of newspapers seems to be cost-effective, producing both inquiries and immediately profitable cases and clients. These might include:

1. Neighborhood newspapers;
2. Shopping news throw-aways;
3. College newspapers;
4. Newspapers that reach military personnel on military bases;
5. Ethnic foreign language newspapers.

Newspaper advertising, whether display or classified, in a metropolitan newspaper is not normally cost-effective and should be avoided. People who read the larger newspapers often skim the newspapers and do not pay attention to the details of advertising, particularly attorney advertising.

On the other hand, people who read the smaller-circulation, local or neighborhood newspapers seem to study them carefully and remember what they read, including the classifieds. I am continually amazed by the effectiveness of small-circulation local newspapers. I have had coverage of my activities in national and international publications such as the *Wall Street Journal,* the *Los Angeles Times,* etc., without much response from clients or potential clients, yet when a simple one- or two-line item appears in a local or neighborhood newspaper, I am deluged by people's sending me copies of the article.

For example, I once gave an address on "Doing Business in The Peoples Republic of China" before the Export Managers Association. The talk was well publicized in the *Los Angeles Times,* the leading international law and foreign trade publications, as well as in mailings to members of many foreign trade groups. Although the talk was well publicized and well attended, I did not receive any legal work as a direct result of my address.

On the other hand, I received a call from a man who noticed my speech in a one-line mention of it in the local neighborhood newspaper. He said he was sorry he missed the talk and would have attended if he had been aware of it. He also wanted to discuss opening a joint venture in China for his company. I earned a fee from his work.

Apparently, this man was too busy to read his mail or the larger newspaper, but found time at home to read the local newspaper.

Many lawyers have told me that local neighborhood newspaper advertising is very cost-effective, and from my own personal experience, I believe it.

College newspapers and military newspapers are read by young people away from home and away from their parents (as well as by the college or military staff and instructors). These readers have their usual share of youth type problems such as accidents, driving under the influence, divorce, annulment, inheritance, etc. These people often don't know anybody locally, and may call a name they have seen repeatedly.

Ethnic foreign language newspapers are a very good market for immigration and buying and selling businesses. Most lawyers advertise their immigration work in this type of advertising.

As with all advertising, the newspaper advertising has to be continuous to be cost effective. You should plan on exposure over many months, not just over a short period of time or just a one-shot deal.

I frankly don't know anything about the cost effectiveness of display advertising.

The following cases and clients seem to be the types of cases that one can expect from classified advertising.

1. Divorce
2. Accidents
3. Worker's compensation
4. Social Security claims
5. Driving under the influence
6. Purchase and sale of a business
7. Wills and inheritance rights

Several lawyers have told me that 24-hour telephone availability is important to the people who respond to newspaper advertising. People will telephone at odd hours and over weekends, and if you or some other person from, the firm are not available, they will call someone else.

O-7
Cost-Effective Lawyer Media Advertising

Most of this chapter is based on information that other lawyers have shared with me. I'll preface this chapter by admitting that I've never used media advertising. This information is based on my discussions of advertising with thousands of lawyers from every state of the United States.

Lawyers who practice in the same community differ greatly in their assessment of the cost effectiveness of similar advertising. In fact, I have received totally contradictory information as to cost-effectiveness from lawyers practicing similar law in the same communities who have used similar advertising in the same media.

It is easy to waste a lot of money and energy putting the wrong ad in the wrong place. Think long and hard about exactly what you are doing before you spend a lot of money.

There are no simple formulas for instant success. There are, however, some general rules that may help you accomplish cost-effective results. It is common that ads that are extremely cost-effective in one community or medium are a total waste of time and money in another. Whenever possible, you must plan your advertising campaign based on facts rather than hunches.

1. Don't be afraid of trial and error. If your first ad or series of ads is not successful, you should change the ad content and design. Many lawyers have reported initial failure followed by success once they have modified their campaign. You may wish to run different ads at the same time to see which are effective and which are not.

2. Track the source of your incoming work. You must know exactly how many matters you received from a particular ad in order to test its effectiveness. Your client intake form should provide this information. Many lawyers will not begin work or open a file on a matter unless they know precisely how the client found out about them. Another excellent way to track ad effectiveness is to use a different telephone number or a fictitious extension for each ad. When a phone rings for an advertised number, it has to be from someone responding to a particular ad. One can also have different addresses for each ad by adding a code to the normal mailing address. A common method of modifying your address is to add a fictitious department or person to the address, such as Dept. PB1, PB2 or PB3 (representing Phone Book Ad 1, Phone Book Ad 2, Phone Book Ad 3, etc).

3. Learn from the winners in your community. Unless you have an unlimited amount of money to spend on experimental advertising, you should learn from the successful advertisers and try to emulate their successes.

   A. Look for ad longevity. Look at all of the currently running ads in the telephone directory, newspaper or whatever other media you are considering using. Refer to back issues or get information on prior ads to determine how long the current ad has been running. It is a safe generalization that at some point, lawyers who get no results will drop their ads, and that the ads that continue over a long period have most likely proven themselves cost-effective.

   B. Call the lawyers who appear to be getting good results based on their ad longevity and ask them their opinion of the cost effectiveness of their ad. Ask them if they know why their ad is successful. Lawyers are generally truthful when helping another lawyer.

   C. Call the lawyers who have dropped their ads to ask their opinion as to why their ad was not cost-effective. Ask them for suggestions as to what they would do differently if they were to resume advertising.

   D. Get help from a professional, but verify their success rate before spending a lot of money with them or through them. Lawyers generally have reported to me low opinions of media salespeople. Many of the salespeople are apparently glib with little or no knowledge of the legal needs of the potential clients or the readership habits of potential clients. Often the salespeople receive a commission on the first ad and no commission on renewals. They don't really care if you waste your money on bad ads.

      Insist on getting from the professional specific references to lawyers who have had cost-effective results with the particular consultant or salesperson. If the consultant can't or won't give you references that you can verify, you should be careful about using the consultant.

4. Be sure you know what kinds of cases and clients you do or do not want to get from the advertising. A particular medium or ad may be cost-effective in one community to get one kind of case or client. The same ad may have a negative effect in another community with different types of clients with different legal problems.

5. Try to make your ad unique in some respect. Although I have recommended copying from the winners, there may not be any winners, so far, for the kinds of clients and cases you want from a certain community. It may be you who has to create the first cost-effective ad. Additionally, although you want to do basically what the winners do, you also want to do something different in an effort to be an even bigger winner.

6. You must be comfortable and happy with the ad. If you don't like the ad, the probability is that the clients won't like the ad either and you'll be wasting your money.

7. Be sure to send a copy of the ad to your Bar Ethics Committee before using it. The rules change daily from jurisdiction to jurisdiction and there is very little consistency in the rules. For example, in some jurisdictions it is considered self-aggrandizement and not permissible for a lawyer to appear in the ad, and models or actors must be used. In other jurisdictions, it is considered false advertising to use an actor, so only the advertising lawyer can appear in the ad.

8. Particular Media. The following observations may help you in working with a particular medium. Bear in mind that what works in one community may not work in another.

   A. *Yellow Pages Advertising.* Yellow Pages telephone directory advertising is probably the most cost-effective advertising, if done properly because the person looking in the Yellow Pages anticipates an immediate need for a lawyer.

     (1) Less cost-effective (or non-cast-effective) advertising is too general and tells the potential client too much. A poor advertisement might read like this:

JOHN DOE
123 Main Street
310-555-1234

Business Law	Probate
Family Law	Workers compensation
Criminal Law	Civil Trials

FREE INITIAL CONSULTATIONS

     (2) Cost-effective advertising lists in simple, one-inch display ads the principal types of case(s) you hope to gain from advertising.

JOHN DOE	JOHN DOE	JOHN DOE
Drunk Driving	Divorce and	Auto Accidents
310-555-1212	Family Law	310-555-1212
	310-555-1212	
JOHN DOE	JOHN DOE	JOHN DOE
Wills and Estates	House Purchases	Purchases of
Sales	310-555-1212	Business
310-555-1212		310-555-1212

Lawyers who use one-inch specialty display ads say they are extremely cost-effective. I haven't done any marketing research into specialization, but I believe the American public wants lawyers who specialize in their particular problems, whatever they may be at a given time. The one-inch ads are cost-effective because the public can find a lawyer specialist at a glance. The ads produce responses from people who have an immediate problem. And the cost of the ads is low.

(3) Display ads (block ads) vs. columnar ads. It is obvious that a large display ad can communicate more information than a smaller columnar ad, and several lawyers have reported that when there were relatively few ads, the display ads were cost-effective with respect to money spent and business obtained. Apparently the cost-effectiveness diminishes as the number of display ads increases.

One lawyer reported that after five years of Yellow Pages (block ads) advertising, he cancelled his $8,000 block ad and bought a $600 columnar ad (an increased length in the listings.) He said that he has obtained a lot more business for a lot less money. He noted that some of his new clients reported that they didn't want to use the lawyers with the large display ads because those lawyers "needed the business."

I can only suggest to you that you use both a display ad and a large columnar ad. Use different phone numbers and see which produces better results.

(4) Ad position. Some lawyers have reported that ads on the right-hand side of the Yellow Pages are highly productive and that ads on the left-hand side are not productive. They said they noticed increases and decreases in effectiveness when the ads were switched from one side to the other. You might wish to negotiate for right-side placement or try an ad on both sides and see in your community which side is more or less effective than the other side.

(5) Ad category. Some telephone directories list attorneys by area of practice or speciality. The people who look in these categories have a fixed opinion of the kind of lawyer they need and your name will be in the place they anticipate finding you.

(6) Ad content. You might wish to place several types of information in the advertisement, depending on the types of cases or clients you want to get. Illustrative information could include:

   (a) Area(s) of practice. I would suggest that you avoid the phrase, "general practice."

   (b) Foreign language ability. This may create the impression that you have or seek an ethnic practice.

   (c) Photograph. This can be important if you are female. Many people seek a female attorney. Occasionally, a lawyer's name may not reveal she is a woman. Minority group lawyers may wish to use their photograph or wording to identify them selves to those clients who are seeking a lawyer of a particular minority background.

(d) Qualifications. Former prosecutor, judge, administrative agency employment, law school (I've seen only one ad with the school listing, which happened to be a J.D. from Harvard Law School).

(e) Membership is specialty Bar organizations.

(f) Office hours (including weekend availability).

(g) Location (with a map). This seems most common in rural areas.

(h) Proximity to public transportation. This is important for older people, injured people and others who cannot drive.

(i) A statement of your mission statement or philosophy as a law office.

(j) Whether you charge for the initial consultation.

(k) Website and email contact.

(l) Just about anything you want to list that is truthful.

B. *Newspaper Advertising.* Here again one finds both cost-effective and non-cost-effective advertising.

(1) Metropolitan newspapers, generally speaking, are not cost effective. I believe that people who read the thick, metropolitan newspapers skim through them and have little time to study, let alone remember, lawyer advertising.

(2) Small circulation newspapers such as neighborhood papers, shopping news and local throw-aways are extremely cost-effective, according to those who use them. College newspapers, newspapers in college areas and newspapers on military bases are very effective. It is my opinion that the people who have the time or inclination to read this type of publication apparently have the time to read the paper slowly or study it carefully, thereby remembering the lawyer's name.

(3) Type of ad. It appears that display ads in small or large circulation newspapers are no more effective than classified ads. People who have the time to read this type of paper have the time to read them carefully. It would appear to be sufficient simply to state:

JOHN DOE
ATTORNEY AT LAW
310-555-1234

(4) Frequency of ad. Ads are scarcely worthwhile on a one-shot basis. Ads, to be successful, must run over a period of time. People will look for a lawyer only when they need one. Therefore, your ad must run continuously until a potential client needs a lawyer.

C. *Radio Advertising.* I have received favorable reports on 3 kinds of radio advertising.
   (1) Religious radio broadcasts, especially Christian Radio. These stations reach a very narrow targeted audience who may equate religion with honesty or skill.
   (2) Public Service Announcements (PSA). Those ads cost almost nothing to produce or broadcast and the materials can be used along with articles for newspapers.
   (3) "Next Town" Advertising. Lawyers in a small town often advertise in another nearby small town (typically 50 miles away). Many people are afraid the local lawyers are too closely allied to the local power & political infrastructure and will not fight for them against the local "establishment."

D. *Television Advertising.* With a few possible exceptions, TV lawyer advertising is not cost-effective for most small firms and should be avoided. Many lawyers have related to me that money spent on TV advertising was totally wasted. For reasons I don't understand, lawyers don't want to believe the truth about the limited effectiveness of lawyer advertising on television.

   I continually tell groups of lawyers my observations in the area and then immediately encounter reservations or disbelief. When I ask if anybody can report contrary evidence, no one raises a hand. When I ask who in the audience has tried TV advertising, a few hands go up. Their experiences always match those of other lawyers I've talked with. Some exceptions are as follows:
   (1) Sponsorship of a cultural television program. Recently a San Diego, California, law firm spent about $8,000 to sponsor a symphony orchestra program on Public Television. (I believe that, technically, it was a "grant.") The law firm is well known and very respected in the area. The newspaper accounts indicated that the sponsorship was extremely well accepted by the firm's conservative business and financial clients. It is not known whether this ad resulted in any new clients or work.

   If I were to spend money on TV advertising, I would follow the leaders and sponsor a series or a special rather than pay for individual or "spot" ads.
   (2) One law firm I know of does claim that TV advertising is cost-effective for developing new business. They sell what, for all intents and purposes, amounts to a franchise for a neighborhood law office and then promise to spend the investor's money on TV ads (at least they did so in the past). I am not aware of any independent verification of their claims of success. I don't doubt that the investor's money was spent on TV ads, but I don't know for certain if there was any benefit to the investment from a cost effectiveness point of view. Although I have my doubts about the ads' cost effectiveness, I repeat the claim that at least one firm has found general practice TV advertising worthwhile.

(3) Divorce, bankruptcy, and accident work. Late-night TV divorce, accident, and bankruptcy ads seem to payoff in some markets. I'm told that people with domestic relations problems and financial problems and people in pain don't sleep well. They often watch the all-night movie channels. They need a lawyer, see a legal services ad on TV, and respond. The law firm, however, should have someone available to field inquirers' calls at the time the ad is aired. Some firms have a "duty lawyer" to work nights to answer the calls. There is an additional cost advantage to late-night ads because TV time is cheaper during these hours.

E. *Cable TV.* Some lawyers have told me that cable TV is cheap and easy to target to specific geographic and interest markets. A bicycle accident firm advertising before and after a bicycle program for example.

F. *The Internet.* I am not certain that the internet should or should not be included in "media" advertising. The internet is treated more fully separately in another chapter. In my opinion, the internet is the single most cost effective advertising available. Websites cost little to maintain. You don't look for the client. The client is looking for a lawyer. There are 3 basic reasons for websites:
   (1) Reaching clients and prospective clients can and will "check you out" before contacting you. The internet is a cheap and fast way for them to do so.
   (2) Reaching people who have an immediate urgent problem and do not have time or resources to seek recommendations. Those people want something done immediately and will usually pay well for it.
   (3) Establishing yourself as a specialist or knowledgeable in a specific area of law, seeking referrals from, other lawyers.

In summary, I wouldn't spend precious dollars on TV ads when I could spend it on Yellow Pages, small circulation neighborhood newspaper classified ads, and multiple websites.

O-8
Direct Mailings to Strangers

The word "Mailings" as used in this chapter includes US Postal mailings, emailings and faxing.

Direct mailings, postal or emailings, or faxing to strangers (non-clients and people with whom you have no pre-existing relationships) can be very profitable if properly done, or a waste of money if improperly done.

Direct mailings to strangers will require an investment of time and money on your part. You can control your out-of-pocket costs by making a smaller mailing, but your (the attorney's) time investment would be the same. If you don't want to spend time or money on practice development, this chapter is not for you.

One of the by-products of doing a mailing is that it forces you to think about the clients and cases you want and to give consideration to some type of firm brochure or description of the services you can or cannot deliver.

In this chapter, I'll relate the experiences of a sole practitioner and of a three-lawyer firm who successfully (cost effectively) used direct mailings to increase their practice profits substantially. These two experiences will exemplify the importance of the two most important aspects of direct mailings, which are:

1. Careful definition of the people you want to reach to serve as their attorney; and
2. Careful design or preparation of the materials you are going to send.

You mayor may not want to spend money to get professional assistance in either area. Let me relate the two experiences.

1. *THE FAVIL BERNS EXPERIENCE*

Mr. Berns was a compassionate, sharing, caring attorney who practiced with his son and one associate in downtown Chicago and in North lake, Illinois, a suburb of Chicago. He opened the branch office anticipating his son's joining him after law school. Mr. Berns bought a mailing list of 7,000 homeowners within a radius of a few miles of his suburban Northlake offices. This targeted the mailings to people who: a) had enough money to own a home (thereby qualifying his market on ability to pay) and b) lived close enough to the office for it to be convenient. He sent a mailing that included an announcement of a new Illinois Living Will Law and a one-page letter describing the kind of work the office did. The response and influx of new clients was overwhelming. He wrote me, "This is the first time in my 35 years of practice that I ever mailed any advertising material. I think I will have to hire another attorney to carry the load." People kept the letters and, two years after the mailing, continued to call in response to it. A copy of the mailings (in a compressed form of printing to conserve space) follow this chapter. The envelope and letter were both on blue paper clearly stating "advertising material," and postage stamps were used instead of a meter. Mr. Berns was a nice, caring person who gladly answered questions other lawyers may have on the subject. He passed away and his firm continues receiving the benefits of the ads.

2. *THE MICHAEL GRODSKY EXPERIENCE*

I first became aware of direct mail advertising when a letter arrived at our home for my son, who was a student. The return address was a lawyer's and printed on the outside of the envelope was "Important Legal Information." Since my son: a) had no need for a lawyer (that I was aware of), and b) would use me if he did need a lawyer (the price was right), I assumed correctly that the letter contained an advertisement.

The advertising lawyer, Michael Grodsky of Torrance, California, was a very affable lawyer, who was building an estate planning practice. He offered to share his experiences through my books and programs with a view toward helping other lawyers. It is worthwhile to study the "Grodsky Experience" Oversimplified, the steps in either method are as follows:

1. Carefully select the audience of potential clients and referrers of clients you want to reach;
2. Buy mailing lists from responsible, reputable vendors who have a good proven track record. (In my son's case, there obviously was an error because Mr. Grodsky thought he was mailing to homeowners in a certain Beverly Hills mailing zip code with incomes of $150,000 or more. Obviously, there was at least one inappropriate name - my son, who was a student, not a homeowner, and who earned *less* than $150,000 per year.)
3. Give much attention to the envelope because you want people to open and read the message inside.
4. Give much thought to the enclosed materials to be sure the potential client knows what you can do for them.

    Grodsky uses a 1st class postage stamp rather than a meter and he prints *"Important Legal Information"* on the outside of the envelope. He feels that affluent people don't open or read all their mail, especially when it might be advertising. Accordingly, you must stimulate them to open and read their mail. (Note that Mr. Berns also clearly stated "Advertising Materials" on the envelope and contents.) Meter bulk rate mail is often trashed unopened.

    Mr. Grodsky invited the addressees to a free seminar on "How to Save Taxes." He got a response of about two percent in that 20 people would go to the seminar for every 1,000 addressees. From these 20 people he gained one high-fee-paying client. This one client's initial fees paid for the entire cost of the mailing and seminar and left Mr. Grodsky with a good-paying, high-income client.

    Mr. Berns successfully defined the clients and practice he wanted as a neighborhood general practitioner; Mr. Grodsky successfully defined the clients he wanted as high-income people who needed tax help. In each case, the home-owning aspect qualified the targets and eliminated indigents. In Mr. Grodsky's case, the requirement of being a homeowner in Beverly Hills guaranteed that the person had enough assets to have estate tax problems. The $150,000 income also qualified the people as needing income tax help.

In each of these two cases, the mailings went directly to the end user of the legal services. If the mailing reached a CPA, attorney, insurance broker, orthopedic surgeon or family counselor, it was purely a coincidence. Attorneys have told me that direct mailings to referrers of clients rather than directly to potential clients are not as cost effective.

A. *ACQUIRING YOUR MAILING ADDRESSES*

The best way to get your mailing list is to buy it from a responsible source with a proven track record. (Mailing lists technically are rented, not purchased.) Some "experts" recommend that you copy names from Yellow Pages, from association membership lists or from commercially printed lists which were sold to others. Before you do this, you should get a legal opinion on your local law of unfair competition or the law of copyright infringement. It is common for publishers of lists to "salt" the list by including false or "dummy" names at addresses where the publisher will receive the mail. If you blindly copy a list without permission, you'll send mail to this dummy name. You'll probably receive a letter from their lawyer inviting you to pay for the rental of the mailing list as an alternative to being sued.

B. *DESIGNING THE ENCLOSURES*

You may "do it yourself," drawing upon your own experiences, or you may use an expert for slogans, graphics, etc. You may test mail three or four different enclosures and see which ones produce the best results.

My own personal beliefs are that you should enclose:

1. A letter which addresses a specific need of the target market; and
2. A firm brochure (if you have one) or simply a letter describing *WHAT YOUR FIRM CAN DO* for a client.

   I personally would not spend a lot of money on "experts" unless they have a track record of success or unless you want to be a pioneer with some new, untried method.

   I welcome hearing from you as to your experiences (successes and failures, or both).

C. *BAR & STATUTORY RESTRICTIONS.*

Sending postal mail, email, faxes, inserts in publications (called "Blowins") may be regulated or even prohibited by statue and by attorney regulation. Be sure you are not violating the rules or law. Reputable list brokers and copyright lawyers can be a good investment for avoiding trouble.

FAVIL DAVID BERNS & ASSOCIATES
ATTORNEYS AT LAW
NORTHLAKE PROFESSIONAL BUILDING
24 SOUTH WOLF ROAD
NORTHLAKE, ILLINOIS 60164
———
(312) 562-1076

Favil David Berns
Sheldon C. Garber
Louis A. Berns

Dear Neighbor:

Governor Thompson signed legislation (effective 1-1-   ) allowing a person the right to have a LIVING WILL DECLARATION, more commonly known as a "DECLARATION FOR DEATH WITH DIGNITY". This is a document directing a patient's attending physician to verify when one is terminally ill and should not be kept alive by mechanical life sustaining procedures which serve only to postpone the moment of death when death is imminent. However, medication and sustenance is to be administered mercifully to alleviate pain and suffering.

Our law firm can now provide you with a LIVING WILL DECLARATION in conformity with the new law. If you believe that this will satisfy your convictions and be of benefit to your family if the need ever arises, then the preparation of such a document is strongly recommended. All previously executed LIVING WILL DECLARATIONS (prior to 1-1-84) have doubtful validity because there is no 'grand-father' carryover clause in the new law and, therefore, they should be re-executed. Our office charge is $35.00 for each DECLARATION, and appointments are requested.

Please note that a LIVING WILL DECLARATION is a separate document and is not a substitute for a LAST WILL AND TESTAMENT. Everyone concerned with the welfare of their family should have their own individual WILL AND TESTAMENT. Further, it is sometimes advisable to have a POWER OF ATTORNEY, which usually nominates a close relative to act for you in the event of an affliction causing physical or mental disability. Your inquiry as to these matters will be answered promptly.

Our office has, for free distribution, the Illinois State Bar Association's pamphlet on WILLS. A copy may be picked up at our office upon request. Also, if you are interested in having your existing WILL or estate plan reviewed without cost, please call for an appointment.

Very truly yours,

[signature]

FAVIL DAVID BERNS

FDB:sl

(Advertising Material)

FAVIL DAVID BERNS & ASSOCIATES

ATTORNEYS AT LAW

NORTHLAKE PROFESSIONAL BUILDING

24 SOUTH WOLF ROAD

NORTHLAKE, ILLINOIS 60164

_____

(312) 562-1076

Favil David Berns
Sheldon C. Garber
Louis A. Berns

Dear Neighbor:

This letter will acquaint you with our law firm.

<u>Legal Services</u>: We have been serving the Western Suburbs since 1961. We provide to individuals, businesses, and not-for-profit organizations a full range of legal representation, including services for the following purposes:

* Real Estate - buying and selling of any property, advice and representation for Mortgages, Title Insurance, Land Trusts, and Leases;

* The preparation of Wills, Trusts, Powers of Attorney, and Living Will Declarations;

* Estate problems, Probate and Guardianship proceedings;

* The preparation and review of Contracts and closing documents for the sale and purchase of a business;

* The formation and maintenance of Corporations and Partnerships;

* Domestic relation problems, representation or defense in Divorce actions, Pre-Nuptial Agreements;

* Personal injury, automobile accidents, and worker's compensation;

* Serious traffic tickets (D.U.I.), and driver's license hearings;

* Bankruptcy;

* Income tax preparation for individuals.

<u>Philosophy</u>: Clients are best served by the prevention of legal problems through careful and thorough advice given prior to their entering into transactions and business arrangements. When a legal problem does arise, clients will be assisted in finding the most practical and cost-effective solution, which may or may not include litigation.

(Advertising Material)

<u>Standards of Practice</u>: All work is done timely and skillfully. Clients are kept informed at various stages by copies of relevant correspondence, documents, and pleadings that we produce, send, or receive on their behalf. Telephone calls are answered as promptly as possible. Information given by clients is held in strict confidence. Our goal is to see that clients receive quality legal services.

<u>Fees and Costs</u>: We have reasonable set fees for many items of standard legal services, such as a Will and Testament, Power of Attorney, or Living Will Declaration. Other fees are based on the amount of time spent, the complexity of the case, skill required, and similar factors. Fees are discussed in the initial conference. Personal injury, worker's compensation, and similar cases are generally handled on a contingency fee basis.

Regular Evening and Saturday office hours for appointments are maintained. Your inquiry is invited.

Very truly yours,

FAVIL DAVID BERNS

FDB:sl

- "Getting The Legal Help You Need When You Need It" -

O-9
Directory Law Lists as a Source of Business

In my opinion, directory law lists are a necessary evil. In all of my years of practice, I've never gotten a client or case from a law list. That is, no one ever selected me by going through a law list looking for an attorney. I am distinguishing organizational membership lists and other directories.

On the other hand, I do know that clients have been recommended to me and then checked in law lists (especially Martindale-Hubbell) to find out more about me. I believe that if I hadn't been listed in the law lists they might have gone on to another attorney listed.

In other words, I don't think anybody is going to select you merely because you're in a law list, but on the other hand, if you're not in the law list, you could miss out on some worthwhile business. Therefore, on balance, I do recommend listing in law lists as a necessary evil.

If you practice in a small community, you may get some referrals by virtue of a geographic listing, especially if you are the only lawyer listed. I have not had any positive feedback about any law list except Martindale Hubbell. I don't mean to downgrade or be negative about any other law lists, I simply don't know anything about them as a cost-effective source of business.

I would appreciate learning about any of your experiences with law lists as a source of clients.

To a large degree, the internet has replaced printed law lists in terms of getting new matters from both clients and other lawyers, yet some lawyers still get some referrals from other lawyers who use the printed lists instead of the internet. Many of the publishers of printed lists also make online lists available.

Directory law lists will probably continue to exist, but in my opinion will be of decreasing significance as the lawyers who used them in the past retire or leave practice.

There are many internet law lists. Some lawyers have reported to me of limited success. Most lawyers have told me they have not gotten any new clients through the internet law lists.

O-10
Maintaining and Using Mailing Lists

You should maintain an email and a postal mailing list for every person you know, and subject to legal or ethical limitations, the mailing lists of members of the organizations you belong to or represent.

The mailing lists should be used at the minimum for the following general purposes:

1. *Client announcements of new laws which may affect them.* (A mailing should go out at least once, but preferably twice a year). If you have (or hope to have) enough clients in a given area of law, you can subdivide the list by legal subject. The following subjects are always of value to clients:

   A. New tax laws
   B. New case decisions involving auto ownership or auto insurance (most clients have cars)
   C. New estate tax or will interpretation cases (these can also serve as a reminder to review a will or estate plan for updating).
   D. Any law which you think could affect them.

2. *Christmas or Season's Greeting Cards.* Christmas cards are a good way of keeping in annual contact with your clients. They are also profitable. Every year when I send cards, I get several telephone calls along the following lines:

   "Jay, when I got your card, it reminded me to update my wills. . ."

or

   "My brother and I bought two vacation condos together and your card reminded me that we need some sort of agreement between us in case one of us wants to sell."

Many people need a lawyer only sporadically and your annual Christmas card is a reminder that you still consider them your clients even though you've not currently doing any legal work for them.

I personally dislike divorce or dissolution work, but I know that families often stay together until after Christmas and then split-up. Your Christmas card is reaching them when they are thinking of seeing a lawyer.

If you have non-Christian clients (Jewish, Muslim, Buddhist, Shinto, etc.), consider using "Season's Greetings" cards instead of those expressing religious sentiments.

Consider making a special list for clients, colleagues, etc., that you know are not Christian and send them appropriate cards. You may wish to use non-religious UNICEF cards or cards which acknowledge a contribution to your favorite charity. I leave it to your local situation as to whether you should or are permitted to enclose your professional card or a family-type newsletter with the greeting card. [For more data on using Christmas cards see also Chapter K-18.]

3. *Birthday Cards.* I've never sent birthday cards, but I'm told by lawyers who do that they are a very effective means of client contact. I am told by lawyers with large probate and trust practices that they are especially appreciated by the elderly ladies who, in turn, show them to their friends resulting in both happy clients and referrals of more clients. I don't have first-hand experience in sending birthday cards and I don't like receiving them (a phenomenon that affects many people when they reach a certain age), so I can't personally vouch for this technique.

4. *Announcements.* I always enclose a professional calling card when I send an announcement. I believe that people are more likely to stick the card in their wallet, purse, desk drawer, card file, or client database than they are to take the time to update their address records. Some lawyers include Rolodex cards with the announcement.
You might wish to send an announcement (and card) for any of the following reasons:
1. New location
2. New telephone number
3. New partner
4. New associate
5. New email address
6. New area of practice
7. New website(s)
It should not be difficult to send a bona fide announcement at least once a year.

5. *Lawyer Advertising Restrictions.* The rules with respect to "lawyer advertising" are in a constant state of flux. You are advised to consult your local Bar rules as to what is permissible in your jurisdiction. If your mailing is determined to be "solicitation" or non-media advertising, or "client communication" you may have restrictions. Note the enclosed samples of mailings.

6. *Other Restrictions.* Email & fax sending may be regulated by federal & state law.

7. *Buying Mailing Lists.* List brokers technically rent mailing lists. Effectiveness of these lists vary, but should be considered.

8. Making your own mailing lists from search engine results or printed directories should be considered. Be sure to clear what you intend to do with a copyright lawyer.

LAW OFFICES
FOONBERG, JAMPOL & GARDNER
A PARTNERSHIP INCLUDING PROFESSIONAL CORPORATIONS

JAY G. FOONBERG*
ALAN R. JAMPOL*
DAVID S. GARDNER**
LESLIE E. CHAYO
NOLAN F. KING
CHRISTOPHER POLK

*A PROFESSIONAL CORPORATION
**LICENSED AS A SOLICITOR IN ENGLAND

8500 WILSHIRE BOULEVARD
SUITE 900
BEVERLY HILLS, CALIFORNIA 90211
TELEPHONE (213) 652-5010

LONDON ADDRESS
14-15 FITZHARDINGE STREET
MANCHESTER SQUARE
LONDON, W.1. ENGLAND
TELEPHONE 01-935-3651

NEW TAX LAWS AFFECTING THE PURCHASE
AND SALE OF SMALL BUSINESSES

The New Tax Law will have a very significant effect upon the purchase and sales of small businesses.

To begin with if a small business is incorporated and the seller can convince the buyers to purchase the shares, the maximum capital gains tax may be as low as 15%. Unfortunately, the person who buys the shares will have great difficulty in arranging their corporate affairs to get advantage of any stepped-up basis of the underlying assets of the equipment.

There is inherent in every purchase and sale a probable depreciation recapture problem and a probable investment credit or other credit recapture problem. It will be critical to know when all investment or other credit carry-forwards and all operating loss carry-forwards arose or expire. Additionally, it will probably be necessary to do an evaluation or an appraisal of the equipment as the book value of the equipment may not be a meaningful figure.

One can anticipate that in order to purchase or sell a business it will be necessary in effect to re-compute or re-structure the profit and loss figure and the evaluation of the assets by using appraisals and by calculating profit and loss by using depreciation rather than the accelerated cost recovery systems.

Careful calculations will have to be made projecting the probable tax consequences of a purchase of the corporation followed by dissolution of the corporation as opposed to simply buying the assets of the corporation. The seller on the other hand will have to be very careful with respect to sales of equipment due to the problems of depreciation recapture and investment credit or other credit recapture. Any operating or other loss carry-forwards and investment credit carry-forwards must, also be carefully analyzed to determine if they will be lost or preserved.

Additionally, UCC searches will be important where assets sold or purchased may have been "stripped" of investment credit or of depreciation and then leased back. It may be necessary to make special provisions to comply with the anticipated non-disposition terms of the sale lease-back agreements if applicable.

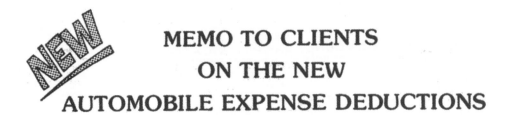

MEMO TO CLIENTS
ON THE NEW
AUTOMOBILE EXPENSE DEDUCTIONS

USE OUR 4-PAGE MEMO TO INFORM CLIENTS OF THE NEW
RECORD-KEEPING REQUIREMENTS FOR AUTOMOBILE EXPENSE DEDUCTIONS

In just a few short weeks, your clients will subject to a new set of
rules on the deductibility of automobile expenses - a subject near and
dear to their hearts.

You know about the new auto expense regs . . . and chances are you've
already mentioned them to clients. But do they really understand that
they've ~ to comply with strict record-keeping requirements in order to
et a deduction?

If you don't set them straight now, they'll soon be flooding you with
calls on the new requirements. Worse yet, they may not call at all and
wind up with no contemporaneous documentation . . . or learn about the
new rules from a competitor and wonder where you were when they needed
you.

We've prepared a special four-page "Memo To Clients" on these new
automobile expense record-keeping requirements that your firm can mail
to clients and prospects alike. It's a concise, clear explanation of
the new rules that includes a sample log. It answers their questions
and serves as an excellent practice development tool.

Reproduction rights for this client memo are $35 for firms with less
than 10 offices. (Larger firms write for prices.) You will receive a
Master Copy suitable for correct reproduction by photocopy or printing
on your letterhead. Our name does not appear on the document. You can
use the copy furnished "as *is*," have it typeset or make any extracts or
revisions you wish. You may reproduce an unlimited number of copies
under your firm name.

To get the client memo for your firm, just complete the form below and
return it to us with your check or credit card payment. Don't wait,
anticipate their needs; send *in* the coupon below today!

PROFESSIONAL PUBLICATIONS, Inc.
3690 North Peachtree Road
P.O. Box 80280 . Atlanta, GA 30366 • (404) 455-7600

O-11
Four New Marketing Tips

1. If you see the name or photograph of someone you know in a newspaper or other periodical, clip it out. Send the clipping (include the name and date of the publication) to the person, along with your business card and a brief personal note. They may be unaware that they appeared in a publication and will be grateful to you for sending a copy of it to them. They may want it for their own purposes.

Your personal interest in the person (or client) will be thought of highly.

2. When you receive an announcement, mail it back to the sender with your card stapled to it and a few hand written words on your card. For example: "Congratulations on your. . . (new association, location, specialty area of law, fax number, etc.). We've noted the information in our records."

The sender will be pleased that you read the announcement and recorded the information, and may remember that you were one of the few people to acknowledge receipt of it. It is best to send the announcement back in one of your own envelopes. (If you don't have extras, order some next time.)

3. Use your announcements to re-emphasize the areas of law you practice. Announcements are an excellent opportunity to cross-market. And you may wish to put an insert in the announcement describing your practice areas.

4. Call clients and attorneys from the airport when you're killing time between plane connections. If you can't get through on the first call (a 50% to 75% probability) leave a short message: "passing through the airport - called to say hello." The fact that you thought of the person will be appreciated.

FROM

ESTHER O. KEGAN:

AS THE HOLIDAYS APPROACH

I AM PLEASED TO SEND YOU SEASON'S GREETINGS

AND TO ANNOUNCE THAT

DANIEL L. KEGAN

CYNTHIA L. SCOTT

HAVE JOINED

KEGAN & KEGAN, LTD.

WITH **MARVIN BENN**, OF COUNSEL

TO CONTINUE OUR LAW SPECIALTIES OF

PATENTS, TRADEMARKS, COPYRIGHTS, COMPUTERS,

FOOD, DRUG, MEDICAL DEVICES, UNFAIR COMPETITION,

LICENSING, LITIGATION IN THE FEDERAL COURTS

79 WEST MONROE, SUITE 1320
CHICAGO, IL., 60603-4969 U.S.A.
TELEPHONE *312/782-6495*   DECEMBER 1

You are cordially invited to attend

a very special guest lecture featuring

Michael E. Grodsky, Tax Attorney

"HOW TO PAY LITTLE

OR NO INCOME TAXES

- LEGALLY"

to be held at the Torrance Holiday Inn

Pacific Room

21333 Hawthorne Blvd., Torrance, Calif.

7:30 p.m.

Monday, December 5th

and Wednesday, December 7th

R.S.V.P.

By reply card or call 310-373-9595

LAW OFFICES
FOONBERG, CHAYO & GARDNER
8500 WILSHIRE BOULEVARD
SUITE 900
BEVERLY HILLS, CALIFORNIA 90211
TELEPHONE (213) 652-5010

JAY G. FOONBERG
LESLIE E. CHAYO
DAVID B. GARDNER*
*LICENSED AS A SOLICITOR IN ENGLAND

AFFILIATED OFFICES
14 HARLEY STREET
LONDON W.I, ENGLAND
TELEPHONE 01-636-1600

9 CAVENDISH SQUARE
LONDON W.I, ENGLAND
TELEPHONE 01-631-4757

December 9, 20XX

To: All Members of the California Rental Association

As the year draws to a close, all taxpayers are facing complex roles and major tax-saving opportunities as a result of tax laws enacted in the past. The Economic Recovery Tax Act and the Tax Equity and Fiscal Responsibility Act added more roles to an already complicated tax system.

With all these changes, it's easy to overlook tax-saving opportunities and fall into one of many tax traps, such as the new alternative minimum tax that took effect this year and the role allowing you to expense currently $10,000 of otherwise depreciable equipment. Also, if you lease assets to your corporation, be sure you have net the requirement of paying Section 162 expenses at least equal to 15% in order not to lose your investment tax credit.

This letter is intended to touch upon some of the opportunities and to help avoid the dangers. It also discusses some of the traditional year-end tax-planning techniques that can reduce taxes.

While effective tax planning is a year-round proposition, some of the suggestions in this memo must be acted on now for example. To assure the continued qualification of your company's retirement plan, it should be reviewed by your tax advisor in light of new rules.

We hope that this letter will also stimulate you to consider doing next year sate of the things you intended to do this year but didn't do, such as wills, buy-sell agreements, leases, etc.

The complexity of the Internal Revenue Code requires that you consult with your tax advisor before deciding how to implement any last-minute tax-planning ideas. A custom-tailored plan created with professional consultation is the only way to assure maximum tax benefits.

If you have any questions, please call us or have your CPA or tax advisor call either Les Chayo or myself.

Sincerely,
FOONBERG, CHAYO & GARDNER

JAY G FOONBERG

JGF/atd
Enc.

LAW OFFICES OF
FOONBERG & CHAYO
PENTHOUSE

TELEPHONE (213) 652-5010   8500 WILSHIRE BOULEVARD   (800) 4-CALLAW
FACSIMILE (213) 652-5019   BEVERLY HILLS, CALIFORNIA 90211

September 6, 20XX

TO: All Clients and Professional Colleagues

RE: 1. New Tax Law Requiring Decisions to be Made;
        2. Our New 800 Number to Give Toll-Free Statewide Service to Clients

The President just signed a new tax law which is the third major tax law in the last four years. We believe there will be another tax law signed shortly after the elections which will raise taxes. There are many changes in the new law which you or your tax advisor should be familiar with, both with respect to your business taxation and your personal income taxes.

The law is theoretically a "deficit reduction act" with the intention of reducing the national debt. As things turn out, it   appears as though the increase in taxes will not be sufficient to cover additional interest costs on the national debt, and accordingly it is our opinion that taxes will be raised again next year. Accordingly, you may wish to make some decisions before the end of your tax year.

We suggest that you read very carefully the enclosed summary of the new law and that you circle those parts which you feel may require further explanation as applied to your own situation.

You may note from the letterhead that we now have a special telephone number, 1-800-4-CALLAW. This California toll-free number is intended to make our offices and personnel more accessible or available to our California clients. Please note also that we have a new E-Mail address for those lawyers and clients who prefer email. We find that the E-Mail facilitates communication with our out-of-state clients where there are problems in time differences.

We welcome your comments or questions.

FOONBERG & CHAYO

Jay G. Foonberg

Jay G. Foonberg

JGF:dh

LAW OFFICES

FOONBERG, JAMPOL & GARDNER
A PARTNERSHIP INCLUDING PROFESSIONAL CORPORATIONS

JAY G. FOONBERG*
ALAN R. JAMPOL*
DAVID B. GARDNER**
LESLIE E. CHAYO
NOLAN F. KING
CHRISTOPHER POLK

*A PROFESSIONAL CORPORATION
**LICENSED AS A SOLICITOR IN ENGLAND

8500 WILSHIRE BOULEVARD
SUITE 900
BEVERLY HILLS, CALIFORNIA 90211
TELEPHONE (213) 652-5010

LONDON ADDRESS
14-15 FITZHARDINGE STREET
MANCHESTER SQUARE
LONDON, W.I. ENGLAND
TELEPHONE 01-935-3651

January 12, 20XX

To: All Clients and Colleagues:

Re: 1. New Tax Law
        2. London Seminar
        3. Your Will
        4. Special Enclosure

Our office has prepared an analysis of the new Tax Law including an analysis of the Estate and Gift Taxes as well as the Income Tax changes. If you wish a copy of the analysis, please return the stub at the end of this letter.

Your Will may be obsolete as of January 1, due to new estate tax laws. We most strongly recommend that you contact your tax adviser concerning a new Will. The Will should take into account the new tax laws and your current situation.

There are also significant changes in the gift tax laws. You should be aware of the following:

1. Spousal Gifts and Bequests - There is no tax on gifts or bequests to a spouse.

2. QTIP Trusts (Qualified Terminable Interest Trust) - You can leave property to a trust with your spouse getting the income during his/her lifetime and others receiving it at their death. There is no estate tax on the death of the first spouse.

3. Tax Free Gifts - You can give $12,000.00 per donee, per donor, per year (formerly $10,000.00) with no tax consequences.

4. Gifts and Bequests to Non-Spouses (After the $20,000.00 annual exclusion) - The unified credit is being increased over a period of years so that estate could pass tax free to non-spousal beneficiaries.

5. Tax Rates – Are being decreased over a period of years.

www.Foonberglaw.com

FRANCIS L. PUGH
ATTORNEY AT LAW
DOS CAMINOS PLAZA
2460 PONDEROSA DRIVE N., SUITE A-110
CAMARILLO, CALIFORNIA 93010
(805) 987-5719

January 23, 20XX

Jay G Foonberg, Esq.
8500 Wilshire Boulevard
Penthouse
Beverly Hills, CA 90211

Dear Jay:

It is that time of year again to think about last year's income tax returns and tax planning for this year.

Enclosed is a booklet entitled "This Year Pocketax" which should be of some assistance to you.

Please contact me if you would like to review your tax situation, or would like me to prepare your returns, or would like to obtain tax planning counsel.

Should you want me to prepare your returns, please contact my office so we can send you an income tax questionnaire. This will assist you in compiling your tax data for return preparation.

Very truly yours,

FRANCIS L. PUGH, Esq.

FLP:plb
Encl.

POCKETAX ®
FOR RETURNS OF   INCOME

BUSINESS
CORPORATIONS - TAXATION
PENSIONS

AVIATION
ESTATES - TRUSTS
WILLS

FRANCIS L. PUGH
ATTORNEY AT LAW
DOS CAMINOS PLAZA
2460 N. PONDEROSA DRIVE, SUITE A-110
CAMARILLO, CALIFORNIA 93010
(805) 987-5719

O-12

Estate Planning for Financially Catastrophic Illness - Letters to Send Upon Client's or Client's Parent(s) Attaining Age 65

In your will interview or other interview information, you should have gotten the birth date of both the client and the client's living parents. Calendar for about six months after the targeted person's reaching age 65 to contact them about estate planning for illness. (I have taken it upon myself to label this area of law as "Estate Planning for Illness.")

Depending upon your own personal political and financial philosophy, you may think that it's morally right or wrong to counsel one to give one's life savings to one's family rather than to the medical industry.

Since I have created the name for the new area of law, I ask the reader to indulge me by reading about why I think you can help your clients and simultaneously earn a legal fee.

The traditional *raison d'etre* of the lawyer was to help the client conserve the estate for passage to the next generation. This "new" area of law fits in perfectly with our traditional function.

Many years ago, I used to joke that I specialized in "Estate Planning for Indigents." This is no longer a joke. A new area of law is developing which allows people of modest (and large) savings to give away and divide their wealth before they become sick with a long-term, financially draining, terminal illness sometimes called "Spend Down". By giving away the wealth, they might qualify for various governmental programs which pay the costs of the long-term care. (This area of law is constantly changing due to political and economic factors.)

When I travel outside the United States, the most common criticism I hear of the American way of life is not our racial problems, politics, leaders, corruption, or crime, but rather our medical system.

Foreigner after foreigner has asked me to confirm or deny that in America people have to lose their life savings when, through no fault of their own, they become sick. It is totally incomprehensible to foreigners that we force people who have worked and saved all their lives to spend their life's savings and become indigent before they can receive adequate medical care through government assistance. To foreigners, this system is barbaric and cruel. It punishes most those who have contributed the most to society and rewards most those who have contributed little or nothing to society.

I have no answer to their criticism, other than to say that in America, these are the rules of the game and that the elderly who have worked and saved can give their property to their children to play the game within the rules.

The following letters relating to estate planning for financially catastrophic illness and living wills, can be sent at any time. I have chosen age 65 only because most people begin to take Medicare coverage at that time and lose their company medical insurance through retirement. You may feel more comfortable (I do) discussing catastrophic illness face to face during will interviews. I have never sent these letters, but I know that one lawyer who had fantastic results with the living will letter.

A. *Catastrophic Illness*

Dear John:

This is not a pleasant letter to write, but we feel an obligation, as your attorneys, to send it.

According to our records, you (your mother, etc.) became 65 last March. We sincerely hope that you are (she is) enjoying these years. If you have not already done so, you (she) should have applied for your (her) Medicare card by now.

Modern medicine and machines can keep a person alive for many years. Unfortunately, this can be a very expensive situation. Medicare, Medi-Cal and Supplemental Security Income and private policies often do not adequately cover many long-term chronic illnesses such as Alzheimer's disease or stroke. We have had the sad experience of seeing a family's entire life savings be dissipated in a short time for convalescent hospitals, doctor bills, private nurses, etc. The result is to impoverish the surviving spouse unnecessarily and to diminish the life's savings that could have gone to the children and grandchildren for their education or to enrich their lives.

It may be possible to arrange your (her) financial affairs legally in such a way that Medicare will pick up the costs at some point. In this way, some of your (your mother's) funds can be preserved for the rest of the family.

We do not consider it to be asking for charity to prepare one's financial affairs in such a manner as to enable one to receive funds for medical bills from Medicare. You (your mother and you) have paid taxes all of your working lives to the trust funds which pay for these programs. You are simply drawing upon the reserves that you paid for over your working life.

There are ways to divide the marital property legally without actually getting a divorce or separation. This can remove the share of the healthy spouse from the medical creditors of the chronically ill spouse.

Additionally, your mother could give away to her children all but the legal maximum which she is allowed to keep. If this is done sufficiently in advance of her becoming sick, it legally removes the funds from her creditors and legally qualifies her for Medi-Cal. Nothing prevents the children from voluntarily giving gifts back to her in the future if they wish to.

This is a very difficult subject to broach with a healthy person and there can be tax and probate and other consequences to the conveyance.

Please let me know if you wish us to discuss the subject further with you or your mother.

Sincerely,

B. *Living Will*

Dear John:

This is not a very pleasant letter to write, but we feel an obligation as your attorneys to send it.

Modern medicine and machinery can keep a person alive for long periods of time. Unfortunately, a person is often kept alive in great pain or under circumstances that render him or her unconscious as to everything around, them, while causing pain and anguish to the family.

Our state has passed a "Living Will" law, often called a "Death with Dignity" law, which allows a person to direct that heroic measures not be taken to prolong life in these unhappy situations.

This "Living Will" is not a substitute for a regular will which affects property rights. The "Living Will" is an independent document to be signed in addition to your regular will.

Please let us know if you wish to discuss this subject further.

Sincerely,

To date I have not personally used either of these subjects as speech materials, and have no success or failure to report.

Favil Berns of Northlake, Illinois, achieved a tremendous increase in business when he sent the three-page letter in Chapter 0-8 unsolicited to homeowners from his suburban office (he also has a downtown Chicago office). Favil has volunteered his letters as a guide for others to follows.

O-13
How to Get International Clients

One of the questions most commonly asked of me is how one can get international clients. To the average lawyer, the world of deluxe hotels and exotic airlines to and from exciting locations seems to have a special appeal. I don't know whether the questions are simply expressions of curiosity or are serious inquiries into how to expand one's practice into this area.

I believe, but am not certain, that the interest in international clients is more a matter of interest in travel to and from exotic and interesting places than it is an interest in increasing one's net income as a lawyer. Possibly, the people who ask this question want to combine the two by having some income and some tax-deductible travel to go along with the otherwise nominal income. (On balance, you can make more money sitting behind your desk for 32 hours than you can make sitting on an airplane for 16 hours in each direction to and from Sao Paulo, Brazil, or Hong Kong.)

In this chapter, I have listed several different client- getting techniques. Each of the techniques has produced at least one international client with a reasonable fee with or without the exotic trip (in a few cases the exotic trip without a reasonable fee).

1. Indicate your international prefix on telephone and fax numbers (currently 01 for the United States), in addition to your non international number. List email contact information on your card.

2. *Have a foreign language version of your website.*

3. *Join the local chamber of commerce of the country or countries in which you have an interest.* Go to the meetings. Meet the people who are involved in industry and trade with the areas you are interested in. If you can't find a chamber of commerce that is involved with the area you care about, then start a chamber of commerce.

My involvement with Brazil began when I became a founder of the Brazil California Trade Association. At that time, I spoke no Portuguese and had been to Brazil only once for a few days as a tourist. Local business people needed a lawyer to form a non-profit corporation for the association and asked me to help because I was a tax lawyer. More than a decade later I'm still helping the trade association. I have served three times as the president, and I have traveled several times to Brazil and I have done a lot of work throughout the world (as well as in California) helping Brazilian individuals and businesses. I have been to the White House for a meeting between the President of Brazil and the President of the United States. I have received two of the highest decorations the Brazilian government can bestow on foreigners and have met some of the most interesting people in the world. Receiving the decorations put me in *Who's Who in the World*. I have also earned a few very good fees in this area.

4. *Meet foreign lawyers in their home town.* It is easy to meet a foreign English-speaking lawyer. (It is even easier if you speak the lawyer's native tongue.) Ask your bank manager to contact the bank's correspondent bank in the country where you are going. (Almost every bank has a 'correspondent bank; alternatively, your bank may use the international banking facilities of another larger bank which has a correspondent bank in the country and city to which you are going.) For varied reasons, most foreign lawyers are eager to meet and host a visiting American lawyer.

5. *Hire a foreign lawyer or law clerk.* This is not generally a *very* cost-effective technique for small law firms. You simply hire a foreign lawyer or clerk who is doing graduate work at a local law school. They will often work for free for "experience" because they don't want to risk violating their student or tourist visas. I have covered this subject rather extensively in the chapter on "How to Get Clients by Inplacing and Outplacing," and recommend you refer to that chapter if you are interested.

O-14
Building Minority and Ethnic Client Bases

With the possible exception of immigration work, I don't know of any lawyer who has developed a profitable practice by concentrating only on minorities. On the other hand, I know of many lawyers (including myself) who have done well by serving certain minority groups in addition to, or as part of, a regular practice. In other words, you can earn good fees by serving the needs of minorities as part of your total practice development, but it is difficult to build a good practice based only on minorities.

It is not necessary for you to be a member of a minority to get minority business. It is, however, good to have members of the minority group working in your office or available to communicate with minority clients. There are many subtle cultural differences that you simply won't be sensitive to.

Let me give you an example of how I've done this in a specific instance. We represented an individual African American man who was rather poorly financed. He was representing a business located in an emerging country which had a colonial background prior to independence. The foreign business was well financed but had no American lawyers, although it, of course, had African American lawyers in its own country. We frankly wanted to represent the company in the U.S. (subject to conflict of interest rules and waivers, etc.). Our African American client had forewarned us that the company frankly did not care to be represented by white lawyers, generally, and white American lawyers specifically. The principals of the company came to Los Angeles to sign the deal. While the principals were in our conference room negotiating, late in the evening, I asked an African American secretary and an African American administrative assistant to work overtime. I explained frankly that these people did not care much for white people, generally, and that working with African American office personnel might put them more at ease. Both employees were thrilled to stay. (The "delegation" included a cabinet-level minister from the country and an internationally famous African athlete.) The group got along quite well. They had a working dinner together and met again the next day. The administrative assistant and the secretary were invited to attend an international press conference at a prestigious location to announce the deal and, again, were thrilled to be part of the activities. The African American company now uses us as its lawyers in the United States.

By being sensitive to the feelings of the minority, we gained a good client, two of our non-legal staff were exposed to a Cinderella-like experience they'll never forget and the African American foreign company is comfortable with its newly found predominantly white lawyers firm in the United States.

Because of my language abilities, I have spoken on television in Spanish to Mexican-Americans. I also have relied heavily on my Portuguese with Brazilians. Over the years, I have lost most of my Japanese clients to Nisei and Sansai lawyers. I've lost most of my Armenian clients, who told me frankly that they were leaving me after many years of good relations because the local Armenian Culture Organization had pressured them to use Armenian-American lawyers who belonged to the Armenian Lawyers Club.

Although I don't wish to define the word "minority, II it can include national background, race, religion, language grouping, gender preferences or any number of classifications.

In my opinion, the simple truth is that potential clients who are members of minority groups prefer to deal with a lawyer, or at least an employee of the firm, of the same minority background.

I tell Hungarian people that one of my grandfathers was Hungarian. I tell people from the British Commonwealth countries that I played cricket in college. Although I have clients from Australia, South Africa and Hong Kong, I have few English clients because they prefer to deal with English lawyers. My English law partner has built up a very successful following of ex *patriate* Englishmen as clients. I tell born again Christians of my liking and following of Billy Graham and of my family involvement with Oral Roberts University in Tulsa.

You don't have to be a member of a minority group to get clients from that group, but you do have to be sensitive to their differences and their concerns. If you want the minority business badly enough, be prepared to hire a minority lawyer or non-lawyer for your firm. When I learned there were 350,000 Koreans in Los Angeles and only four lawyers who could speak Korean. I tried without success to find a Korean-speaking lawyer or paralegal to add to the firm.

In my opinion, members of minority groups need lawyers like anyone else, and feel more comfortable with members of their own groups.

O-15
Getting Minority Work and Money

In this section I can only suggest a concept about "minority work." The particular fact situation is so complex that all I can do is make some general suggestions and give you a few examples, and then it's up to you to start making telephone calls and writing letters. The availability or non-availability of what I call "minority work" varies according to your particular locality and the politics of each particular minority or company.

What I call "minority money" is also called "set aside" money, "affirmative action" money and by other names. Many governmental agencies and many private companies and semi-public entities such as public utilities set aside funds in their budgets to use minority firms.

Many city, county, federal and state appropriation bills contain clauses that a certain percentage of the work in connection with the appropriation must be awarded to minority-owned or operated businesses. (This mayor may not include awarding work to minority law firms to do some of the legal or other professional work.) Sometimes this minority legal work is awarded as a matter of policy rather than a matter of legal requirements, so you'll have to dig around until you find the person in the government agency or the company who is responsible for "affirmative action" programs. You may find that the company or agency has a well-defined policy or program that includes outside attorneys, or you may have to convince the company or agency that you should be the first attorney firm hired under a new program which you will help design.

Often banks, as a matter of policy, or the Small Business Administration or other agencies loan or guarantee loans to minority businesses. I've heard of white lawyers going into partnerships with African American lawyers or lawyers with Hispanic surnames to get access to the money for starting a law practice.

If you are a minority lawyer or know a minority lawyer, you should consider this avenue of financing. Unfortunately, you'll have to do the leg work to get more information.

I suggest doing some homework on identifying the companies or agencies involved and on whom within the companies or agencies you should communicate. You can then send them the form letter which follows this chapter or make your own letter.

O-16
Sample Letter Advising of Availability
for Minority Work

(To Be Sent to Large Companies Which Contract with
Various Government Agencies and to Public Utilities)
(Send Two Identical Letters)

Chief Legal Officer
ABC Company
123 Main Street
Anytown, USA

Affirmative Action Officer
ABC Company
123 Main Street
Anytown, USA

This law firm is a "minority" law firm as that definition is commonly used.

The purpose of this letter is to advise you that we are available to provide legal services. We understand that you may affirmatively set aside a certain portion of your legal services budget or other budget to comply with applicable laws and/or corporate policies requiring such set asides. We would appreciate your forwarding this letter to the appropriate attorney within your company responsible for the administration of these policies.

A brief description of our firm personnel is enclosed. (optional) We shall be calling in a few days as a follow-up to this letter. (optional) Perhaps you would like to consult with us concerning your compliance with the law. (optional)

Very truly yours,

Minority Lawyer

By:

NOTE: I strongly suggest the following:

1. Call the company to find out the exact name of the person(s) to whom to write (to show you've done your homework).

2. Whenever possible, write to an attorney either by name or by position (to avoid solicitation charges)
3. Use high-quality stationery and word processing.
4. If possible, read the annual report to see if the corporation has, in fact, expressed a policy.
5. If you can find the specific federal, state or local law, refer to it. (They may not be aware of their need for your services.)

O-17
Tips From Women Lawyers

The tips contained in this section have been furnished by women lawyers at the seminars and workshops in which I have participated. Some of these programs were done with and for women lawyers.

Don't be misled by the title of this chapter. I recommend it to both male and female attorneys. I recommend it to female attorneys to help them get and keep good clients. I recommend it to male lawyers to make them more sensitive to the problems some women attorneys face. I hope that if male attorneys are more sensitive to the situation of the woman attorney, the male attorneys will be able to avoid unintended offensive conduct or comments. Remember that male lawyers want female clients and referrals from women lawyers. There is no point in alienating women and losing their potential business and referrals.

This is a book on increasing and upgrading your client base. This is not a book on women's rights. I personally would be considered by most people to be a Women's Libber. My suggestions are not intended to create, perpetuate or dignify sex discrimination by potential male clients against female lawyers, or vice versa. I am attempting to deal with realism rather than idealism.

Some women lawyers have some special problems and some special opportunities that some male lawyers just don't have. It is utopian and unrealistic to pretend that all male and female attorneys have exactly the same problems and opportunities. This may be good and this may be bad, but it is the real world.

A female attorney in private practice must expect intentional and unintentional discrimination and must be prepared to deal with it in order to succeed.

The remarks of this chapter mayor may not be applicable to feminist law firms or to militant feminists of either sex. They will have to develop their own rules. On some occasions when I asked for suggestions from female attorneys, I have received criticism even for suggesting that some female attorneys might have special problems and opportunities. I've been told I am perpetuating discrimination and perceived differences by commenting on it. To me, this is like blaming air turbulence on the "Fasten Seat Belts" sign or blaming a fever on a thermometer. Accordingly, this section does not purport to contain suggestions made by or acceptable to radical feminists. On the other hand, I have received valuable input from many female lawyers and judges who are sincerely interested in assisting female (and male) lawyers to succeed and to render good legal services. Similarly given the option of not giving special attention to women lawyers or giving special attention to women lawyers, I believe that I can be of the most value to our profession and to the American public if I *do* give special attention to some women lawyers.

O-18
Marketing Differences Between
Male and Female Lawyers

There are some marketing differences between male and female lawyers. Whether there should be is beyond the scope of this book. Whether articles like this, by acknowledging the differences, are perpetuating the problems is also beyond the scope of this book. The purpose of this book is to recognize realism rather than idealism and offer possible solutions to turn the problems into successful events.

The problems are as follows:

1. Female lawyers generally are no better or worse as lawyers than male lawyers.
2. Female lawyers sometimes are discriminated against in law firms in terms of case assignments, client contact or working conditions. This problem is beyond the scope of this book.
3. Female lawyers are sometimes intentionally or unintentionally discriminated against in court or in public while in the presence of a client or potential client. Dealing with this discrimination to the marketing advantage of the female lawyer IS within the scope of this book.
4. Female lawyers receive both favorable and unfavorable advantages and disadvantages in terms of client acceptance and employment. This is within the scope of this book.

There are many women's networking groups and organizations where women lawyers and potential clients get together for the express and singular purpose of rainmaking. I do not know if a female lawyer attending these meetings receives more, less, or the same amount of legal work as would have resulted in going to a similar mixed gender meeting.

O-19

How a Woman Lawyer Can Take Advantage of Being a Woman in Getting Specific Types of Clients And Cases

In this section, I am repeating what women lawyers have related to me. Some women lawyers relate that a female lawyer can get a competitive edge over the male lawyer in certain cases. I make no comments to condemn or condone the practices related. I am simply passing them on to you.

A. *Rape Cases*. One female lawyer from Tucson has a successful practice representing defendants in rape cases. She has convinced male lawyers they should refer their male clients in rape cases to her because juries are more likely to acquit rape defendants represented by a female lawyer since the jurors believe a female lawyer wouldn't represent a man who actually committed a rape.

I don't know whether it's true that juries are more likely to acquit rape defendants represented by women lawyers. I do know that she has convinced many male lawyers this is true, and she gets a large number of referrals and associations on rape cases.

B. *Family Law Cases*. Here again, some female lawyers have convinced some male lawyers, and some potential clients, that a female lawyer is more sensitive to family needs than a male lawyer and can do a better job of presenting the case to the judge.

C. *Sex Discrimination Cases*. Some female lawyers have convinced potential clients and referring attorneys that an employer accused of sex discrimination will do much better if the employer uses a female lawyer for the defense.

D. *Older Male Clients*. Supposedly (according to the female lawyers), older men like young female lawyers and will look for an excuse to have a younger female lawyer represent them. If this is true. a young female lawyer should spend her time at the social engagements of older males if she is trying to obtain new clients.

E. *Lawyer Referral and Information Services*. Let the LRIS know you will accept clients who insist on a female lawyer. LRS's do get specific requests for female lawyers. Your name may come up more frequently than it would otherwise" if you pass this information to the LRIS.

F. *Representing Children on Court Appointments*. Many judges believe that a female lawyer is more sensitive to the needs of children in litigation. (We are dealing with perception, not necessarily reality.) Many judges are more likely to appoint a female lawyer if the female lawyer communicates availability to the court.

G. *Getting Divorce Clients.* A woman lawyer told me how she successfully gets new divorce clients. She goes into the courtroom where the divorce master calendar is called. She always wears a black suit and sits at one of the counsel tables. She waits until the room is full with clients and their attorneys. She then stands up and yells in a loud voice. "If there are any witnesses here for Mrs. Smith, I'm her lawyer, Mrs. Jones. If you're here, please meet me in the hallway." She then goes to the hallway carrying a yellow pad and waits. This lawyer related to me that invariably one or two women will come out of the courtroom and ask her for her card. These women normally relate something like, "My present. lawyer is a man and just doesn't understand." Or, "My lawyer is a man and I think that subconsciously he has anti-wife feelings." This lawyer related to me that many women don't like being represented by a male lawyer but don't know any female lawyers. When the lawyer announces that she is a lawyer representing a woman they feel they may have found the right lawyer to handle their case because this lawyer is not afraid to open her mouth loudly in a room full of attorneys. This lawyer also told me she is careful to make her announcement before the judge or clerk enters the room for fear of being in contempt of court if any court personnel are present.

Now comes the great "denouement." This woman lawyer uses this technique on days when she has no cases. Her only reason for going into the courtroom is to be "found" by clients unhappy with their lawyers.

O-20
How Women Lawyers Can Take the Initiative with Males
To Avoid Situations or Incidents

According to women lawyers, there are several things a woman attorney can do when dealing with male attorneys, clients and potential clients which will help prevent unnecessary awkward incidents.

1. Indicate how you want to be addressed.

Well-meaning, well-intentioned male attorneys are often perplexed because they don't know how to address a woman lawyer.

For written correspondence, tell the male attorney whether you want to be addressed as Miss, Mrs., Ms. or something else you might prefer. Do not make the attorney guess. When giving your name over the telephone, you might want to say, "I prefer to be called Ms. (or Mrs. or Miss) but I am not uptight over it"; or, "I am not married, so please do not call me Mrs., although I don't care if you want to use Miss or Ms."; or, "I am married but professionally I still use my former name, Miss Jones."

On written correspondence, help the court and other attorneys by indicating how you prefer to receive your mail. You might indicate on your correspondence (Miss) or (Ms.) or (Mrs.) after your signature so people will know how to address mail to you.

2. Obscene language.

(a) By male attorneys. Occasionally, female lawyers are frustrated when they hear obscenities spoken in front of a woman lawyer. You will have to use your judgment when you hear obscene language. If you say nothing, you may unnerve the other attorney or make him think he unnerved you. If you are not insulted, you can say something like, "I've got older brothers; I've heard worse than that."

(b) By female attorneys. I've heard female lawyers use vocabulary that would belong in the lowest of street language. I am not shocked anymore, but I used to be. Some men clients or attorneys cannot handle foul language by females, whether they are attorneys or not. They sometimes react cautiously or very negatively. I believe that the potential benefits of a woman's lawyer using obscene language with males is so small compared to the potential alienation of a client or potential client or attorney, that women (or men) lawyers should deliberately and consciously avoid foul language. I have never heard of a client's choosing a woman lawyer because she used obscene language, but I have heard of female attorneys losing clients and potential clients because of using it.

3. Convince the potential client of your aggressiveness in handling legal affairs. Traditionally, little girls and young women were raised to be people pleasing. Unless they participated in athletics in school, they were not trained to be aggressive or competitive. The potential client should be told by you of your ability and desire to fight aggressively and hard.

4. Portray yourself as a revengeful, back-biting, dirty fighter. I was surprised to learn from women lawyers that they think their being perceived by potential clients as revengeful, dirty fighters in a case is an advantage to them. These women have told me that the male client wants this type of lawyer. I think these women lawyers are wrong, but if they are right and it works for them, then you might be advised to portray that image. I don't know how to advise you on this. I pass the information on to you without warranty.

5. Convince clients and potential clients of your willingness to work hard even at the cost of personal and family sacrifice. A woman lawyer told me that potential clients are afraid women lawyers are not willing to give up their personal life if the case demands it. They tell me that potential clients believe women lawyers wouldn't, or couldn't, skip going home for dinner in order to work on the client's case. Some potential clients are also concerned that a woman lawyer's child-rearing responsibilities would prevent her from working on a case nights and weekends or going out of town.

You can convey your devotion to client matters by saying something like, "Be prepared to give up any personal or social life just before and during trial." Tell the potential client that the case might require you to work on Saturday or Sunday and evenings, and that you want the client to be ready for the interruption in his or her personal life.

O-21
How the Female Lawyer Can Distinguish Herself from Non-Lawyer Females to Avoid Awkward Incidents

The "Dress for Success" rules are extremely important when you are in the office with a client, and even more important when you are in a confrontation situation in a court house. It will severely damage your client's image of you when, as you are standing in or outside a courtroom with your client, another lawyer, bailiff or court clerk asks, "Which one of you is the attorney?" Your client may subconsciously think, "She doesn't even look like a lawyer. What kind of lawyer do I have?"

Stand outside a courtroom and you will soon verify that male lawyers are better dressed than their clients and can usually be distinguished immediately from the client by their clothing and by their briefcase. Male lawyers don't get asked "Which one of you is the attorney?" as often as female lawyers.

This is another tip from a woman lawyer. If you are going to keep personal cosmetics such as lipsticks, combs, brushes etc., in your briefcase, put them inside a purse in the briefcase. It is embarrassing to open your briefcase and have your client or other lawyer see those things.

If you refuse to carry a briefcase, at least carry a yellow legal pad to distinguish you from the client.

It is my impression that some women lawyers truly do not like wearing a suit. They do not feel "comfortable" or "natural." As little girls and as a young woman, "dressing up" meant a nice dress, not a suit. A suit may be new and unnatural for some women. Men, on the other hand, grew up as little boys and young men knowing that "dressing up" meant a suit, or at least a jacket, with tie. The suit is a natural progression for a male, but may be something new for a female who has to start wearing suits on a regular basis for the first time in her mid-20s.

Some women lawyers make an accommodation by wearing suits only on those days they know they are going to meet with clients, go to court or go to a meeting, and to wear more comfortable clothes in the office.

O-22
How a Female Lawyer can Handle the Reaction "You're a Lawyer?"

Female lawyers may sometimes have people at social and business affairs react with surprise when they say that they are a lawyer. Sometimes, the potential client or referrer of clients may mumble something like, "You're a lawyer?" or, "You seem so young to be a lawyer," or "You are so good looking, you just don't look like a lawyer." Few males would be subjected to those comments, but female lawyers sometimes have to handle it.

Be gracious, no matter how steamed up you may be on the inside. Turn adversity into opportunity. Smile and respond with something like, "Thank you for the compliment. I'm a lawyer and my clients and opposing counsel tell me I'm a pretty good lawyer, at that," or "Here's one of my cards in case you find yourself in need of a good lawyer."

Hostile reactions such as, "You wouldn't say that if I were a male," may make you feel better but they are not likely to lead to new clients. Openly hostile reactions will simply get the potential client or referrer of clients angry at you without subsequent referrals of work. Additionally, a heated or excited response may subconsciously cause a client to wonder how you'll react under fire in a courtroom or a negotiation.

If you can't sublimate yourself to be gracious and polite, then just ignore the comment as though it had never been said. Remember that no one ever won an argument with a client or potential client.

O-23
Courtroom Demeanor for Men and Women Lawyers

In this section are tips I have heard women lawyers give to other women lawyers. I pass them on to you without comment.

A. Don't ever go into the judge's chambers alone unless you leave the door open. Unsophisticated clients or others in the courtroom may be suspect as to what you are doing or not doing behind closed doors with the judge.

B. Before you enter the judges chambers, explain to the client that you may be going to discuss the technical aspects of the case. If the client knows what you will be doing, he or she won't be suspicious. Explain to the client that it an honor to be asked into chambers and that the judge's clerk and opposing counsel will also be there.

C. Present your card to all court personnel as soon as you walk into the courtroom, or in advance of calendar call. Give your card to the court clerk, the judge's clerk, the bailiff and the reporter, and announce, "I am Miss Jones and I am the attorney for the petitioner on the Smith case." This will avoid any problems with these people's referring to you as anything other than an attorney in the presence of your client. I personally do this before my client enters the courtroom, or tell my client to wait outside the courtroom while I go inside to be sure the file is ready. I then enter the courtroom and hand out my card or at least introduce myself to these people. Later, if they address me in front of my client, they may say "Mr. Foonberg" instead of "Hey you" or "Counsel." My client will think they know me and respect me because of the large number of cases I handle in that courtroom. This, of course, makes my client feel more comfortable and in good hands.

D. Sexist comments from judges or opposing counsel.

The same general rules pertain to sexist comments in the courtroom as sexist comments in other situations. You are in court to argue your client's case, not yours. Do not let anything dissuade you from the case at hand. If you devote your talent and energy to thinking up clever ways to put down offensive comments or waiting for an opportunity to hit back, you will be diverting your efforts away from the your client's case.

On the other hand, if you don't react to the comments, your client may wonder why you didn't react and may be concerned that you didn't know what to do.

You should ignore the comment and make some comment about the case at hand.

You can respond, "I'm sorry, I didn't hear what you said as my mind was on the case. Would you please repeat what you said?" A person will rarely repeat the comment and will usually back off at this point. Additionally, you will have put this sexist comment or person off balance, diverting his or her attention away from the client's case and to his or her own problems.

You will have succeeded in reversing the problem and the perpetrator of the barb becomes the victim of the response.

Chapter P
Taking Clients When Leaving
The Firm

P-1
Taking Clients When Leaving A Firm
Hope For The Best - Prepare For The Worst

The subject of taking clients when you leave a firm is complex and the rules vary greatly from jurisdiction to jurisdiction. One size does not fit all.

In this section I am highlighting the areas of concern of which you must be aware.

I will cover many of the questions which require answers and then you will have to do your own research and reading of the rules or consult an ethics lawyer as to what is and what is not permissible in your particular jurisdiction. You must also learn the consequences, if any, of violating these local rules. This should be done as rapidly as possible, even though you have no present thoughts of leaving the firm, so that if you ever have to make a sudden move or response, you will be ready.

This chapter replaces in its entirety another controversial chapter in previous editions of the book. The previous edition's chapter should be disregarded.

A great many associates have told me how they approached their managing partner to give notice of leaving and share information concerning their leaving the firm. Their principal purpose was simply to protect the clients and their cases.

Unfortunately, the response of the managing partner in many cases was often an immediate, "No need for notice, you're fired now." Their computer access key and their office door pass key were immediately deactivated before they even walked out the door of the managing partner's office. A security guard or other person sometimes met them at the door to the managing partner's office and escorted them to their office to empty their desk and offices of their personal property.

Accordingly, the associate must think about timing and the likely reaction when he or she announces their intention to leave the firm or go out on their own.

In an ideal world, an associate would announce his or her intention to strike out on their on and to prepare for an orderly departure. Status of cases and clients would be discussed, the taking of clients or staff by the associate would also be discussed and an orderly schedule for departure would be prepared. Fees on work in process for matters being taken by the associate would also be discussed. The associate and the firm would work together to prepare an appropriate joint announcement to clients and the public. This scenario still exists in many firms and is more or less what most ethical opinions call for.

Unfortunately the real world often is very different from what the ideal ethical rules call for, especially in the larger non collegial firms. Associates get fired for reasons having nothing to do with them or their performances as a lawyer. The loss of a major client, the defection of a major rain maker, making a position for the son or daughter of a major client or a firm member, a temporary cash flow problem or other non performance related reasons may result in an associate being fired.

So long as firms hire and fire based on day to day or short term profits, associates will have to be prepared for sudden firing without prior notice.

A young lawyer once said to me that when firms became more interested in the business of law than the profession of law, students then became more interested in jobs in the law than careers in the law. In order to be in the best position to get a good job or good new job in law, associates will have to demonstrate client getting or keeping ability.

The taking of clients with when one leaves a firm is an area where ethical and financial interests overlap and often are in contradiction to each other.

I must repeat that the taking clients is both fact specific and local rules specific. Additionally one must understand that while something may or may not be ethical, there may or may not also be civil consequences.

It is my general opinion that clients will "follow the file" on existing matters when a lawyer leaves a firm. They will want to be represented without having to pay a lawyer a second time to learn what another lawyer already knows. After following the file, they will follow the lawyer, especially as to future work. According to one major survey, clients will stay with the firm only about 1/3rd of the time when a lawyer leaves the firm.

There are several overriding general legal and ethical considerations as follows:

1. A client is not property and does not belong to anyone.

2. The contents of a client's file may belong to the client or to the firm or neither or both in whole or in part, depending on the local law.

3. Neither a lawyer nor a firm may do anything which restricts the clients' right to choose a lawyer of their own choosing. Thus a firm may not refuse to turn over the client file to a departing or departed associate if the client requests it.

4. In most states a lawyer or firm may not claim a "charging lien" on the clients' files for unpaid legal fees.

5. Covenants not to compete signed by associates generally will not be enforced, and even asking for one or agreeing to one may in itself be unethical. There can be local exceptions, depending on the specific facts.

6. One should distinguish between ethical consideration and commercial considerations. With the growth of firms in size, many law firms consider themselves just another form of money making business and will do all they can to protect their client base and client relationships. Agreements considering the taking of clients may have no enforceability as an ethical matter, but may be enforceable in court as a commercial matter. Thus an associate, or even a partner may be required to pay "damages" to a firm for taking a client, but there would be no ethical problem in accepting the clients who want to stay with the lawyer who leaves the firm. In many states, the ethical concepts are superior to the commercial interests and courts will do nothing to reward a firm or punish an

associate who leaves a firm and subsequently agrees to represent a client who requests representation on either existing or future matters

7. The rules may differentiate between contacting a client, orally or in writing, depending on whether the associate and the client did or did not work together on the clients' matters in the past.

8. The rules may differentiate between contacting the client before or after departure.

9. The rules may be very different for associates and partners who leave a firm. A partner may have a fiduciary responsibility to the firm, the other partners, and the clients. An associate may have no fiduciary responsibility to the firm or the partners or possibly in some cases even to the clients.

10. A civil court may be more willing to take action where a group of lawyers secretly conspires to "steal" a client or group of clients and firm's staff. Regardless of how much the associate prepares for the possibility of a sudden forced leaving, there are certain "rules" to be considered.

There are several classes of clients to be considered:

   a. The firm clients whom the associate personally brought into the firm.
   b. The firm clients with whom the associate has worked together closely on matters.
   c. The firm clients where the associate and the client never worked closely together on a matter, but did have some incidental or temporary contact.
   d. The firm client with whom the associate never has worked on a matter.

An associate who is planning to leave a firm and who hopes to take clients with him or her, should, in my opinion, hope for the best and prepare for the worst.

The following should be done as soon as possible and certainly BEFORE announcing the intention to leave:

1. Read the local rules and/or get an opinion of an ethics lawyer as to potential ethics or civil responsibilities and method of announcement.

2. Make a list of all firm clients, contact persons' names, addresses, etc. In some cases it would be permissible to do a computer run depending on any agreements signed by the associate or any indication in the computer that the list is confidential or a trade secret.

Even where doing a download or photo copy might not be permissible, hand writing the information onto one's own paper in one's ones own hand writing from ones own memory , might be permissible.

3. Download or prepare copies of work done on client matters for purposes of application for board certified specialty or malpractice protection. This information could also be used to immediately begin representation of a client if the firm will not cooperate in timely turning over the file to the client or to you as the new lawyer representing the client.

4. You may need the information concerning the cases and clients you have handled to get your certification. Malpractice suits or disciplinary proceedings may take place years after you leave. The firm might not even be in existence or the files may have been destroyed when you need them.

5. Prepare a proposed joint letter and also prepare a proposed individual letter to send to clients announcing the departure. If the firm stalls in agreeing to the wording of or in sending a joint announcement, be prepared to immediately send your own announcement.

6. Do not say or write anything derogatory about the firm to clients, or staff. This will only work against you. You will look bad for working for a firm which does wrong things and may subject you to civil or ethical liability that otherwise might not exist.

There is a joke about the two law schools in a city which had an intense rivalry. It was said that when a student of one failed out and enrolled in the other, the academic level of both schools was raised. Hopefully, the firm you will be leaving will welcome your taking some of the lesser level clients with you in order to raise the level of both practices.

Remember, at least read the rules and cases in your jurisdiction and seek an ethics lawyer's opinion if you are still uncertain.

P-2

How to Prevent Partners and Associates From Taking Good Clients When They Leave the Firm

This is a chapter on how to fight fire with fire. Good locks can't prevent all theft, but they can save some things from being stolen which otherwise would be stolen.

The root causes of why a lawyer would want to steal your clients or to steal firm clients are complex and many. Ego, greed, jealousy, spousal pushing, real or imagined injustices, and many other factors cause a lawyer to leave an organization with the premeditated goals of taking the firm's clients with him or her, rather than simply leaving the organization with the occasional result of some of the clients following that lawyer for any number of reasons.

This is not the place to address the root causes of why lawyers leave. That subject is better left to psychiatrists, psychologists, penal codes, etc. I would also be very careful about using the firm's consultants to address these causes. Consultants may have the unintended result of "stirring up" problems where none exist or where the problems are small. The same consultants who are hired by you to avoid split-offs may be hired by other law firms who are seeking split-offs of lawyers who can bring clients with them.

1. You must be ruthless. A thief steals for profit and because he or she thinks he or she won't get punished. (Getting caught doesn't deter them; it's getting punished that deters them.) You cannot negotiate with a thief. You must lock up your possessions and then bodily throw the thief out with no advance warnings. Fire the culprit and lock his or her office door with no pity. Give the culprit no opportunity to copy files. Deactivate computer codes and entry codes immediately. Have a security guard present while the lawyer cleans out his or her desk. A cancer must be cut out or it can only grow. It is a fatal mistake to believe that your partners are ethical businesspeople, just because you are.

2. Recognize that no one will help you in your fight. In the main, you will have to do it yourself.

Although some law firms now have in excess of 1,000 employees and have millions of dollars of trade secrets, good will, equipment, etc., courts and police authorities do not consider law firms as "businesses" and they will not get involved. If one of your computer client's employees loaded up a truck with your client files, disks, customer information, etc., a call to the police department would result in arrests and a subsequent penal prosecution for theft. The employee and the new firm to which the employee was going or which the employee started would be liable for compensatory and punitive damages and injunctive relief.

If the same series of events happens in a law firm, no one will want to get involved. The police will not get involved in a fight among lawyers. Their attitude is that lawyers are big boys and should take care of themselves. The courts will not want to get involved. Their attitude is that clients have an absolute right to choose lawyers, and therefore the client should be the judge of whether the theft shall be punished or rewarded. You will be totally on your own.

3. Safeguard your files from theft. Understanding how the files can get stolen is critical to the protection of your firm's clients.

I have thought many times about the best way to protect the files from theft and offer the following suggestions. If you know better ways, please let me know.

A. Add a chapter or section to the firm's manual along the following lines:

Firm Files and Confidential Information Rules: All client files are firm's property and all information within them is confidential. This includes not only paper files but also files stored on media such as word processors or computers. The information in the files is confidential and valuable both to the client and to the firm. Improper disclosure of information in the file is unethical and may in fact be a crime or other misdemeanor as well as grounds for disbarment or other disciplinary proceedings, including civil litigation. In order to protect the client's confidentiality and trade secrets, and the FIRM's confidentialities and trade secrets, the following FIRM's rules pertain:

a. All files and their contents are the property of the Firm. This extends to everything relative to the client within the Firm's possession, including but not limited to, documents and other information whether it originated within or outside of the Firm. This also includes all financial data relative to that client. There are no exceptions based on the fact that the same information may be obtainable from public sources such as court files, libraries, public agencies or from third party sources such as accountants or financial institutions. In the event the client leaves the Firm or for any reason wishes to obtain "their file," or any part of it, the entire file must be screened only by the senior member of the Firm in order to give to the client the appropriate information required by the State Bar Act and in order that the conduct of the client's case will not be prejudiced. In almost all cases, not all of the information or documents in the files should be released. The Firm must keep that information whether by way of original documentation or copies, which is necessary to protect the Firm and the members of the Firm from liability or responsibility in the event that the client subsequently decides to allege unethical conduct or malpractice.

b. *The Unnecessary Copying of Files.* No entire file may be copied for any reason unless previously authorized in writing by the client or the senior partner of the Firm. Copying increases the possibility of unauthorized disclosure of client confidential and trade secrets or the Firm's confidential and trade secrets. Additionally, all necessary copying of files in whole or in part must be recorded, whether done in the office or off-premises, so the clients may be properly charged and so that a written record exists of copies made and the distribution of these copies.

c. *Removal of Files from Premises.* No file may be removed from the office premises at any time unless essential to the client's case. In such cases as trials, hearings, etc., only as much of the file as necessary may be removed. The office file facilities are properly designed for security safeguarding and fire protection. Off-premises files are subject to higher risk of accidental destruction and unauthorized disclosure of confidences. The loss or misplacing of file information may prejudice a client's case and result in increased costs to the Firm or client for reproducing or recreating lost or misplaced information.

d. *Clients' Requests for Files or Information from the Files:* The fact that the client requests or demands the files or the information in the files either directly or through an attorney does not excuse or alter these policies which are intended to protect both the best interests of the client and the best interests of the Firm.

e. *Consequences of Disregarding These Rules:* The Firm places the highest possible priority on protecting the client confidences and secrets and the Firm's confidences and secrets. Any person, whether or not employed by the Firm, who violates these policies concerning protection of files and the information in the files faces the following actions by the Firm:

    1. Immediate dismissal.
    2. Forfeiture to the extent permitted by law of all employee benefits.
    3. Criminal prosecution to the extent permitted by law for theft and theft of trade secrets.
    4. Civil suit for damages.
    5. Injunctive relief for immediate return of the files and destruction or return of any copies made of the files and/or any part of them.
    6. Appropriate notification to the State Bar licensing and disciplinary authorities.

All Firm employees and members, whether attorney or non-attorney, regardless of their status being associate, partner, of counsel, associate counsel, co-counsel, full-time, part-time, temporary, or permanent, and regardless of whether they are professional or non-professional, consent to the above terms of employment and authorize the above as their terms of employment. No person is authorized directly or indirectly to waive or modify any of the above terms.

B. Get a warning stamp or sticker to be placed on file folders with words to the following effect:

INFORMATION CONTAINED IN THIS FILE IS CONFIDENTIAL TO BOTH THE CLIENT AND THE FIRM. ITS USE IS GOVERNED BY THE FIRM'S POLICIES MANUAL. ANY COPYING OR DISCLOSURE OF THE INFORMATION IN THE FILE IN VIOLATION OF THE FIRM'S POLICIES MANUAL WILL BE SUBJECT TO CRIMINAL PROSECUTION, CIVIL DAMAGES, AND INJUNCTION AND DISCIPLINARY PROCEEDINGS.

The above rules do not guarantee you either a criminal prosecution or a basis for civil relief, but they might help.

C. Place this notice on the employee's computer access and require an "I agree" to be clicked in order to open the files.

D. Refer to your Firm's Policies as part of your standard "exhibit" to your new employee "deal letter."

4. Be sure the employee sings a receipt for the manual & update the receipts when you update the manual but no less than annually.

5. Maintain periodic telephone or face-to-face contact with the good clients. Out of sight, out of mind. If you have no contact with good clients, they think you don't care about them and they will be ripe for being stolen.

6. Be aware of what matters are being handled for the clients by associates in the firm and communicate frequently to the clients that you are aware of the cases and their progress. Tell them you are involved or available in the major decisions affecting the cases, or that you are, in fact, making the decisions or are involved in making the decisions affecting their legal matters. Clients want to know that top people are involved in their case.

7. Rotate "partner in charge" of the client or of the case. Let the clients know they have more than one lawyer handling their case. Try to eliminate the impression that "the firm" is handling the case.

8. Be aware of "over zealous" client promotion. When a lawyer who previously was rarely able to work nights or weekends because of "family pressures", suddenly has lots of time to take clients to football games, the theater, ski trips, etc., be alert. It's time for you to re-establish or increase contact with the client.

9. When the opportunity avails itself, ask the clients if the associate is available enough to the client. The answer is usually a good tip-off to whether the client is being hustled.

10. Watch out for the attorney who ignores new case assignments and new client assignments. This attorney may be devoting all of his or her time and energy to developing the few good clients he or she wants to take when the big move is made.

11. Insist that all time records include promotional time spent with clients, even if non-chargeable. Insist that attorney time expended out of the office on weekends and time expended on the telephone at home be recorded on the time records. This is good malpractice protection. A client may claim that he or she was given bad legal advice at a social event with a lawyer. The standard practice of recording all promotional time expended may negate such claim. If no advice was given or if no meeting occurred, you should be able to pick out of the time records any apparent increase in promotional activities over what is normal.

12. Watch out for a sudden drop in billable activities or lack of case progress for a given lawyer on a given case. The lawyer may be setting up a backlog of work for his or her new firm.

13. Amend the office secretarial manual and insist that the lawyers and attorneys use the word "we" instead of "I" whenever possible, and similarly to use the words "our client" rather than "my client" whenever possible. Similarly *your* antenna should go up as a warning signal when the first person singular rather than the third-person singular is used.

14. Ruthlessly fire and exclude from the office attorneys who are obviously trying to set you up so they can steal a client. Don't waste your time negotiating with them or threatening them. While you in good faith try to preserve your relationship with them and with the clients, you merely tip them off that you are aware of what they're doing, and they'll probably accelerate doing exactly what they intend to do. You should be mentally and physically prepared to do the following if necessary:
   a. Change locks on doors, deactivate all security codes of the lawyer which would give access to computers or premises.
   b. Hire a private uniformed security guard service to be on the premises 24 hours every day until matters are settled.
   c. Notify the associate or partner by phone that he or she is fired and should not enter the premises. Tell the associate you'll clear off the desk and mail personal effects to him or her after reviewing what's in the office.
   d. Answer all calls for the discharged lawyer by saying:
   "A" has been fired and is no longer with the firm. Don't worry, all of your files are safely here. We're up to date on your case; have no fear about the conduct of your case."

Make it absolutely clear that the attorney has been *fired.* Do not give the impression that the attorney quit or left by mutual agreement. If asked why the attorney was fired, don't give specifics. Just say, "We don't wish to discuss this. For various legal reasons we can't say more. You are, of course, free to ask the attorney why he was discharged. Do you have his home telephone number or do you wish us to advise him to call you." (The probability is that the clients which were being set up already have the home telephone number.)

While the above may seem ruthless and perhaps overreacting, you must remember that the lawyer who steals your clients is stealing from you, your family, your lifestyle, etc. This person wishes to steal from you to enrich his or her own standard of living.

Over the years I have had many associates and even some partners leave (or I left them) with smiles, handshakes, the farewell luncheon and dinner, and I've done my best to refer business to them after they left the firm. I especially tried to send them business when they went out of their way not to steal the existing clients. This has been mutually beneficial. On the other hand, those attorneys, whether associates or partners, who want to steal your clients are thieves to the same extent as if they were stealing cash out of your wallet, and should be dealt with accordingly. I must emphasize that mostly you will be working alone and will get little or no sympathy or help from the legal system should an associate or partner steal files and try to steal clients.

While the foregoing chapter seems rather cruel and ruthless, it is the case that the courts and penal authorities simply don't recognize law offices as businesses. In my opinion, this benefits clients. A few courts in isolated instances have granted injunctions against lawyers stealing files or clients or cases in process, but this is the exception, not the rule. I predict that within a decade or two, courts, both civilly and criminally, will begin to respect the good will and rights of law firms to the same extent they would recognize the good will and rights of other business firms. Until then, however, you must understand that what happened to the attorney in the example given could happen to you. It has taken many years of retrospective analysis to think of all the things the attorney could have done or should have done before the act occurred, especially in view of the fact that after the act occurred the attorney could receive no assistance from anyone.

Again, if you have any thoughts or suggestions, I would most welcome hearing from you.

Chapter Q
A Quick Review Of Your Current Marketing Practices

Q-1
Foonberg's Favorite 70 Rules of Good Client Relations for the Busy Lawyer and the Busy Law Firm

This list is designed for busy lawyers and staff. These rules can easily be followed by lawyers and staff in the day to day practice of law.

This is a list which you can read in a few minutes or study and think about as long as you wish. The rules in this list require little or no money and very little lawyer or staff time or effort to implement. You can easily add to this list based on your own personal experiences. Hopefully you are already following many of these rules. You should seriously think about those rules you are not now following and why you are not following them.

Why 70 Rules? 70 is the number representing all 10 Canadian provinces, all 50 US states, the District of Columbia, Puerto Rico, the US Virgin Islands, and all 7 continents where I have done presentations for law firms, bar associations, law societies, law schools and others. (50 plus 3 plus 10 plus 7 equals 70.) I believe I am the only person in the world to have had this opportunity to teach and learn from other lawyers what does and what does not work.

In June of 2003, I had the honor of addressing the Law Society of Newfoundland-Labrador, Canada; hereby reaching a milestone on a journey that began 37 years earlier, when I began doing Marketing and Practice Development programs for CLE and law firms. At each program there were questions and other panelists. I not only taught, I learned what works and what doesn't work. I have learned that these Rules apply in many languages, many legal systems, and many cultures. Fads come and go, but basics remain the same. These 70 rules are among the basics.

I receive large numbers of "thank you's" from those who attended my lectures and read my books. Many of these lawyers and their spouses have thanked me years later for what they learned from me and my books. It is interesting to me to note that many of those whom I taught while they were still in law school, are now retiring. They credit what they have learned from me for much of their successes.

On my more than 40 year journey as a practicing lawyer, which still continues, I have learned that these 70 rules work. They have worked for other lawyers and firms throughout the world and they can work for you.

1. Always carry high quality professional cards.
2. Always offer clients and other visitors coffee or a soft drink while they wait in the reception area.
3. Be sure your reception area contains periodicals indicative of the kind of practice you want people to think you have.
4. Be careful when you answer the question, "What kind of law do you practice?" Don't limit yourself or your firm.

5. Always send thank you letters when someone refers you a client.

6. Always send thank you letters to the witnesses who testify for your side (if the local rules permit).

7. Either return all calls yourself or be sure that someone returns them for you. Return all calls before the end of the day and preferably within 2 hours.

8. Always send clients copies of all "correspondence in" and "correspondence out."

9. Dress the way you would expect your lawyer to dress if you were a client paying a fee.

10. Always get as much cash up front as possible from new clients. This is known as "Foonberg's Rule" and is a modification of Lincoln's statement that when a client has paid cash up front, the client knows he has a lawyer and the lawyer knows he has a client.

11. Always be sure that your fee agreement is in writing.

12. Always send your clients Christmas cards or Seasons Greetings cards.

13. Remember that your invoices are a factor in your clients' opinion of you.

14. Dump the dogs. Get rid of the "Bad News" cases and clients as soon as you know you have a problem before they really give you problems.

15. Learn how to convert "social consultations" at weddings, etc., into paying clients by being attentive, letting the person know they may have a serious problem and suggesting they come into your office where you have facilities for helping them.

16. Remind the staff in the firm that they can also refer their friends' legal matters to the firm.

17. When a staff member refers a client, give the staff member a praise in a memo that goes to everyone in the office to remind them that they can also refer clients to the firm.

18. Remember that availability is the single most important factor in your being selected or not being selected after you are recommended.

19. Always send a tax news letter in November, reminding clients of new tax laws that might affect them. Be sure you remind them that cash basis taxpayers can only deduct legal fees if they pay them before December 31st. Show the client how a bill can be tax deductible if possible.

20. Send clients "no activity" letters when a case is inactive for 90 days or more.

21. Always discuss fees and payment schedules at the first meeting.

22. Always remind the client that the firm has a good reputation in the community.

23. Always reassure the client that you have handled similar cases to theirs (if true). Clients don't like being used for educational purposes.

24. Calendar ahead and remind clients of the need for annual minutes of shareholders or directors meeting, lease renewals, judgment renewals, etc.

25. Recognize and appreciate that clients have a high anxiety level when they go to see a lawyer. Be prepared to meet it.

26. Be careful if you adjust a bill downward that the client doesn't think that you were deliberately overcharging to begin with.

27. Be sure that you and not the clients decide, before you do the work, which clients are going to get free legal work before you do the work.

28. When collecting fees, try to match clients' payments to you with clients' receipt of money or cash flow.
29. Always be firm and in control in your manner with clients when discussing the case or discussing fees. If you act wishy-washy or wimpy, your clients will quickly lose confidence in you and stop using you and stop recommending you.
30. Don't complain about how hard you're working.
31. Always use high quality legal stationery for client communications with your address clearly legible. Use large size fonts for correspondence with senior clients.
32. Always have some hard back, firm chairs in the reception room for injured or elderly clients.
33. Always introduce your clients to your secretary and to paralegals and/or associates who will be working with them or on the case.
34. Always get new clients into the office to meet them before giving them any legal advice whenever possible.
35. Be wary of clients who have lots of complaints about their former lawyers. It is probably just a matter of time until you are on that list of lawyers.
36. Always communicate to a new client that what the client tells you is normally covered by attorney-client privilege and that you won't discuss the client's affairs with other people.
37. When an interview is over, stand up, walk to the office door, and tell the client that the interview is over and walk them back to the reception area or elevator.
38. When the case is over, send a letter to the clients thanking them for the opportunity to have been of service to be sure they are not expecting you to do more work on the case.
39. When a case is closed tell the client in writing that the file will be removed to a closed file storage area and may be destroyed without further notification to the client. Non response may be deemed acquiescence to file destruction without further notice.
40. When a client offers you a cash fee saying, "nobody will know," don't forget that the client knows and may be setting you up for blackmail.
41. When a case is lost, be simple, direct and honest. Tell the client by phone or in person as soon as possible and follow up with a letter.
42. When quoting settlements, be sure the client understands the difference between gross settlements and net settlements after fees, costs and liens.
43. When quoting fees, be sure to cover (in writing) the difference between fees and costs and what the fee does and does not cover,
44. When collecting fees, remember that people are more willing to pay for what they desperately need and don't have now than for what they used to desperately need and already have. Clients are more eager and willing to pay before the work is done than after the work is done. They will feel better and you will feel better if you get the advance retainer check before you do the work.

45. Always ask a client whether to send mail and e-mail to the home or the office or if the client wants to pick up the mail (to keep information from getting into the wrong hands).

46. Keep a photo of your children or family on your desk facing you to remind you of unpaid bills and your need to be sure that the clients clearly understand and can meet their financial obligations in the case.

47. Have someone call your office for you while you listen in and see if you are satisfied with the way your phones are handled. See if the receptionist projects a helpful attitude or is simply functioning as a human answering machine. Remember, people can and do hang up and call other lawyers when they're not happy with the way their call is handled.

48. Remember to give the client a road map of the matter at the first meeting, telling the client what will happen, when it is likely to happen, and what it is likely to cost.

49. When estimating completion dates, double the estimated time required and finish before that date if you can.

50. Remember that clients want you to listen to them tell their story not vice versa. Remember you have 2 ears and 1 mouth. It was intended that you listen 2/3rds of the time and only talk 1/3rd of the time. Otherwise you would have two mouths and one ear.

51. At the end of an interview always ask the question, "Is there anything you want to ask me or tell me?" Tell the client, "I don't want you to leave here feeling that you didn't have an opportunity to tell me something or ask me something."

52. Limit your pro bono work to 5% of your time or you may become pro bono your self. Tell clients and potential clients that you do pro bono work, but must limit it to 5% of your time.

53. Be very careful of conflicts when you represent more than one client in a matter. Be sure to get appropriate waivers and consents to avoid being conflicted out of the matter without getting paid. Clients will appreciate your strict compliance to ethical rules. If there are two or more people in the room, ask yourself, (and them) "Who is the client and why are the others in the room?" Have forms ready to cover the various situations.

54. Be flexible and creative in helping the client figure out ways to pay for the legal services they need. They will appreciate your working with them and both you and the client can avoid unreasonable expectations. They might appreciate and be receptive to alternate billing methods.

55. Be sure you have a web site. When you are recommended, clients will often check you out on the Internet before deciding to call you. Include your areas of practice. Try to include your full name in your web site URL and in an e-mail address, so that clients can contact you by simply remembering your name.

56. Consider having more than one web site which includes your geographic area of practice for potential clients looking for a lawyer in a particular city, county, state or neighborhood and another for potential clients who want to "check you out."

57. Be sure to promptly respond to web site generated email contacts.

58. Be sure a caller can immediately reach a live operator without several minutes of voice automated hell. Clients are often nervous or upset and often do not have the patience for voice automated prompt systems. If you are not in the office, the receptionist should ask callers if they wish to speak to another person or leave a voice mail. This may deter a potential client from calling another lawyer when you are not immediately available. If a voice automated system is used, give the caller the immediate option of "dialing" "0" to reach an operator.

59. Remember that a client or potential client is more likely to choose you based on your friendliness and demeanor than on your legal skills.

60. Remember that Yellow Pages are extremely effective in attracting certain types of work in certain communities. Do not advertise in the Yellow Pages unless your staff is trained on how to handle the calls which the ads produce.

61. Add clients' names to your spell checker to reduce the possibility of misspelling their name.

62. Keep a written list of who refers clients to you and to whom you refer clients and review it at least once a year.

63. Calendar client birthdays, anniversaries, or other important events to send cards or e-mail greetings when appropriate. Be sure to have the names of your own spouse and children and client's secretaries on the list.

64. Prepare a written document to be given to the receptionist on duty listing the most important clients and the difficult clients and how to work with them. Include how the clients' names are pronounced. Indicate who covers for whom when the called person is not available.

65. If you have not spoken with a client in 90 days, call the client just to say hello. Start the call with: "I'm not calling on any specific legal matter. I'm just calling to see how things are going as we haven't spoken in a while." These calls often result in a new legal matter that needs attention.

66. Protect your mailing addresses (postal and e-mail) if you move or your zip code or domain are changed. Have mail forwarded even if you will also get junk mail and spam. Clients get very upset when they get mail returned "return to sender" or "undeliverable." Be sure to renew the forwarding services and notifications when they would otherwise expire and keep a stack of notices to send out every time you receive a forwarded item.

67. Protect your phone number and fax number if you move or if the area code changes. Have your phone calls and faxes forwarded to the new numbers. Clients get upset when they hear "This number is no longer in service." They may simply call lawyer #2 on their list rather than spend time and money calling information to get your new number.

68. Remember, you have a "marketing force" consisting of yourself, your firm, your family, your friends, those who refer you clients and your former and existing clients. You are only one person. They are hundreds. Utilize the leverage of your entire marketing force instead of trying to do everything yourself.

69. Send clients alerts as to new laws and cases which may affect them or their business. Utilize e-mail or fax blasts to be the first person with the news ahead of printed formats.
70. Always shake hands with a client when saying hello or goodbye. Touching by way of handshake, cheek to cheek kiss, or other means appropriate to the client's age, gender and station is a basic human expression of friendship.

Q-2
Check List for Creating and Implementing an Effective Marketing Plan

In this chapter I am presenting a framework for creating and implementing an effective marketing plan. In the future, I shall write an entire book on this subject.

My general approach in writing is to present stand alone "bite size" chapters that can easily be read and absorbed in a short time and then immediately put to use. I deliberately avoid writing in a sequential fashion; i.e., you must read and understand Chapter 1 before going onto Chapter 2, etc. This "bite sized" approach is not possible in creating and implementing an effective marketing plan. Planning is a "ready-aim-fire" approach and one must proceed sequentially to be successful.

If you are ambitious you can go back over each of the previous chapters and fit them into the outline I've given you in this chapter.

Subject to the caveat that this chapter is not a "stand alone" chapter like most of the others in my books, I hope you'll be able to use this approach in your practice.

I. Find out everything you can about your own firm and all the people in it, including the non-professionals. You have to know what you can do and what you can't do before you actually market.
    A. What are your collective legal skills; i.e., what kind(s) of legal work can you do competently and efficiently including work that has never been done by your firm.
    B. Identify your collective legal weaknesses. What kind of work do you do incompetently, inefficiently and at an economic loss to the firm.
    C. Identify which of your people enjoy working with the public and the client vs. those who regard the client as a necessary evil. (The kind of lawyers who say "The practice of law would be enjoyable if it weren't for clients.") Be sure you consider the non-lawyers in the firm.
    D. Identify which people are willing to "put out" that little extra something for the firm or the client and which are the 9 to 5'ers who will only entertain a client on firm time at firm expense.
    E. Try to determine which people want to acquire or improve client relations skills and those people who regard practice development as "too commercial" or "beneath their dignity."
    F. Does the firm have lawyers or non-lawyers or departments who are super specialists in an area of law where there is a shortage of good lawyers?

G. Does the firm have lawyers or non-lawyers or departments which are super specialists in understanding a specific industry? This will take a great deal of person-by-person analysis because often this asset is hidden due to the fact that the people who have industry knowledge often don't understand how valuable the skill can be when properly marketed. (It has been said that after knowing your own business the next most important step is to know your client business.)

    1. Is there anyone in the firm with experience in putting out a house organ or school newspaper (to utilize for a client newsletter or internal firm newsletter).

II. BUILD A MARKETING DATA BASE FROM KNOWN DATA

A. List every client (past or present) the firm has represented over the past 10 years.

B. List every key individual at the client's organization including secretaries, assistants and staff with whom anyone in the firm has done legal work, whether or not the people still have a relationship with you.

C. List every vendor with whom the firm is doing business.

D. List every bank or banker with whom the firm has done business over the last 10 years.

E. List every referral or networker from whom the firm has received a referral in the last 1 0 years (lawyers, bankers, accountants, physicians, etc.).

F. List every relative of every person in the firm and the spouse of every person in the firm to the extent of about two links (parents, grandparents, aunts, uncles, first cousins). This is also a good way of identifying those firm members who are embarrassed about marketing, afraid of failure in marketing or who are embarrassed about the firm (as these people won't turn in the names).

G. List every social or service organization which has been a source of clients during the last 10 years.

H. Get the alumni list of each lawyer's law school classmates.

I. Build a list re "special service" recipients of greeting cards (birthdays, Rosh Hashanah, Thanksgiving, other).

J. Code every existing case and reference with control numbers to identify type of work, source of business, etc.

K. Add any other comment you wish to each name on the list.

L. Other _____

III. TARGET YOUR MARKETING

A. Identify the kinds of businesses and clients you now have that you want to keep.

B. Identify the kinds of business and clients you want to get rid of.

C. Identify the kinds of business and clients you don't have but want to get.

IV. IDENTIFY YOUR CLIENT RELATIONS SUCCESSES AND FAILURES
(You may wish to hire an outside public relations firm to do this.)
A. Survey present clients to find out what they like about your firm.
B. Survey present clients to find out what they would like to see changed in your firm.
C. Survey past clients to find out why they left the firm.

V. IDENTIFY YOUR PAST MARKETING TECHNIQUES' SUCCESSES AND FAILURES, IDENTIFY WHICH TECHNIQUES PRODUCED CLIENTS OR FAVORABLE COMMENTS AND WHICH PRODUCED NO RESULTS OR UNFAVORABLE CLIENTS.
A. Bombarding clients with information on their case.
B. Visiting client's place of business or scene of an accident.
C. Telephone reception techniques.
D. Office location and furnishings.
E. Making opportunities to give professional cards.
F. Media publicity or advertising.
G. Other publicity or advertising (telephone listings, etc.)
H. Frank discussions of fees and payment reduced to writing with cash up front.
I. Sending greeting cards.
J. Sending thank you notes and letters.
K. Trade association activity.
L. In-house training of how to market.
M. Firm brochures.
N. Firm newsletters.
O. Scheduling future anticipated work for clients.
P. Telephone return call techniques.
Q. Seminars.
R. Open houses.
S. Christmas gifts or other perks.
T. Internet.
U. Other _____

VI. IDENTIFY CROSS MARKETING OPPORTUNITIES FOR EXISTING CLIENTS
A. List every existing client.
B. Determine the legal work the firm does do for that client.
C. List all legal work of existing clients the firm does not do because it is being done by house counsel or other outside counsel.
D. List every lawyer and non-lawyer in the firm.
E. List every legal skill and all special industry knowledge of every person in the firm.
F. Ascertain which legal skills and special knowledge already existing in the firm could be utilized in informing the client that you can have the ability to offer more services to that client.

G. Ascertain whether it would be worth the investment to add a lawyer or non-lawyer to the firm in order to have the capacity to do more work for existing clients. Consider having "Of Counsels" to do specialized work you can't do or won't do.

H. Decide which person(s) from the firm should be introduced to which person(s) from the client's office to present the firm's ability and interest in doing the client's legal work.

I. Decide the best time and place to make the contact (often called a "presentation").
1. Firm offices
2. Client's place of business
3. Presenting a seminar for the client or inviting client to a firm seminar.
4. Athletic or social setting.
5. Other _____

J. Follow up initial contacts with repeated short term (days or weeks) and long term (monthly) contacts.

K. Decide when to try to "close the deal" (ask for and get the fee paying work).

L. Post mortem both successes and failures to improve successes on future attempts with same or different clients.

VII. IDENTIFY THE ROLE EACH PERSON IN THE FIRM IS WILLING TO ACCEPT AS THEIR PERSONAL CONTRIBUTION TO, THE FIRM MARKETING EFFORTS.

Require as a matter of firm policy and condition of employment that each professional (and appropriate non-professional) make specific contributions to the firm's marketing effort by choosing from among the following activities (or comparable ones). These activities are in addition to billable time requirements and not in lieu of billable time.

A. Turn in information requests for marketing database on monthly basis _____
B. Take existing client to lunch _____
C. Take prospective client to lunch _____
D. Visit a client's place of business _____
E. Teach a class _____
F. Become active in trade association _____
G. Form new trade association _____
H. Send more season's greetings cards _____
I. Rewrite an existing research memo into an article for publication _____
J. Prepare personal cross-marketing list _____
K. Serve on firm's speakers' bureau _____
L. Work on firm newsletter(s) _____
M. Other _____
N. Other _____
O. Other _____

VIII. MAKE A FUNDAMENTAL RESOURCE-GOAL DECISION
    A. Do you want to seek additional legal business or eliminate existing legal business based on the skills and limitations of the existing people in the firm?
    B. Do you want to add (or delete) people in the firm based upon the legal business you want to keep or seek?
    C. Both A & B above?
    D. Other _____

IX. DECIDE WHO IS GOING TO CREATE AND IMPLEMENT THE FIRM MARKETING PLAN:
    A. Marketing Committee should meet at least once a quarter.
    B. Marketing Partner must devote 200 hours per year.
    C. Marketing Administrator, full time job.
    D. Part-time Marketing Administrator, experienced or novice.
    E. Outside consultants (as necessary).

X. SET REALISTIC "BITE SIZE" FIRM GOALS WHICH ARE ACCOMPLISHABLE WITHIN FIRM'S EXISTING ABILITIES
    A. Decide upon three things which will be done in next 90 days.
        1. Train receptionists on proper telephone techniques   _____
        2. Develop uniform answer to question "What kind of law does the firm practice?"   _____
        3. Get cards for every eligible person in the firm.   _____
        4. Other   _____
        5. Other   _____
        6. Other   _____
    B. Decide upon three things which will be done in next 180 days.
        1. Develop marketing data base   _____
        2. Develop Christmas and special card mailing list   _____
        3. Survey former clients   _____
        4. Other   _____
        5. Other   _____
        6. Other   _____
    C. Decide upon three things which will be done in next year.
        1. Firm in-house marketing seminar   _____
        2. At least one open house   _____
        3. At least one client seminar   _____
        4. Other   _____
        5. Other   _____
        6. Other   _____
    D. Keep your goals well defined and attainable. Replace accomplished goals with new goals. Success will engender enthusiasm, participation and profit. Failures due to unrealistic goals will engender defeatism.

Chapter R
The Internet and the Future

R-1
Foonberg's Rules from A to Z for Internet Marketing

The internet empowers the client to decide in minutes which lawyers to use (or not to use) from the comfort of their home or office or wherever there is wi fi. The experience and qualifications of the lawyer as well as the likely personality of the lawyer can be quickly learned, and the client can compare those findings to other lawyers. The client can also decide on whether to go to non lawyers for help or to use "self help" for legal services.

The cost of creating and maintaining a website is tiny and the potential results are huge. I personally have earned hundreds of thousands of dollars of fees from clients who found me on the internet.

Clients have engaged my services from thousands of miles away and from other continents by finding me on the internet and conducting all communications via email.

Other lawyers conduct their entire practice over the internet, getting clients and rendering services to clients from all over the world.

It is not the intent of this chapter to provide a treatise on the internet.

Many volumes have been written and more volumes will be written on the use of the internet to attract and keep many clients.

Based on my own personal experiences and what I have learned from others, I offer the following guideline to the use of the internet to get and keep good clients.

A. Decide what you want your website(s) to do.
   1. Get the viewer to immediately click through to email you at that moment.
   2. Convince potential clients that you can provide your service Better or Faster or Cheaper.
   3. Convince lawyers and other professionals that you are a learned expert who can be consulted with, or engaged for, major matters.
   4. All of the above.

B. Consider having more than one website and domain name based on areas of law practice sought and differing demographics of clients or potential clients sought as clients.

C. Decide before you design your website(s) what kind(s) of clients and matters you want. What will be a success in one geographic or economic market of clients and potential clients might be a total failure in another market. Multiple websites appealing to different clients may be the best solution.

D. Only hire web design consultants who have a track record of success for lawyers with similar practices and check their references. Alternatively, be willing to experiment to be different. Be willing to pay for click throughs. Be willing to pay for technical help to modify your website. The cost of technical help is likely to be far less than what you could earn as a lawyer for the same amount of time.

E. Be willing to update and fine tune your website(s) by providing your own search engine to determine what the users are seeking. Updating with "what's new" brings visitors back.

F. Have in house procedures to rapidly respond to emails, even if only to reply that you will reply later. Failure to timely respond will suggest failure to timely do the work. Failure to timely respond will also encourage the potential client to use a lawyer who does timely respond.

G. If you wish to attract non English speaking clients provide them with pages in their language. Be careful in choosing translators. There may be significant differences, national and regional, in the meaning of words. Slang words and words with double or triple meanings are especially a problem with people with little or no education. When in doubt, go for professional translations or ask for reverse translations. (Give your foreign language page to a 3rd party and ask them to translate into English what they see in the foreign language.)

H. Try to minimize or avoid graphics. They require time to download and people looking for a lawyer often are in a hurry and are not looking for entertainment. They may just go back or to another website rather than wait for the download.

I. Understand that the dynamics and economics of search engines and links is a rapidly changing field. Payments for "click throughs" are increasingly common. The use of links to and from other sites will bring some more visitors but may also cause viewers to leave your site by clicking the link.

J. Be open minded and willing to experiment with new ideas you think of. No one knows you, your clients, and your practice better than you do.

K. Decide on which area(s) of law you wish to emphasize in your domain name(s) for search engine and advertising purposes. Somewhere in your website (not on the front page) list other areas of law practice you want. A line "other areas of law practice" with a click through from the front page may work. Clients or potential clients who want to use you for a particular matter may use you or recommend you for the other matters if they know you want matters in the other areas.

L. Your State Bar Rules may require you to keep copies of the information provided for a certain number of years.

M. The internet provides a measure of equality or leveling the field between solos, small firms and big firms. The well done (the clients and potential clients use it) site of a small firm will prevail over the poorly done site of a larger firm. Many large firms hide the names and qualifications of their lawyers for fear (often justified) that search firms and other law firms will look for lawyers to be offered higher paying positions with other firms.

N. In my opinion, even a poor , badly done, website is better than no website. No website will be a turn off for those who want to know something about you before calling to hire you.

O. Time Requirements. Don't fool yourself, maintaining a website will require some of your time to periodically review it for accuracy or change. If you are going to make the changes yourself, decide if you really want to invest the time to learn. I personally do not maintain a blawg to go with the website for two reasons:
    1. The amount of my personal time which would be required to continuously update it and review what others add in the postings.
    2. Blawgs frequently contain opinions about current events. The contents of the blawgs may contain inaccurate postings or reactions to the wrong set of facts. Information which seemed accurate and appropriate at the time may turn out to be in error or inaccurate with the benefit of hindsight. What you write or allowed others to write may come back to haunt you years later. As a trial lawyer one told me, "You can't be cross examined on what you never said."

P. Looking at other lawyers' websites to get ideas is not a waste of time. Do not make the mistake of believing that something that appeals to you will also appeal to clients and potential clients. Remember that how the bait tastes to the fish is more important than how the bait would taste to the fisherman.

Q. Be sure you have a contact line on your front page with a click through to a page with all the ways to contact you including phone(s), fax, email, street address, etc. Be sure to have your website and email address and phone on every page in case someone downloads and prints a single page.

R. List geographic areas served including cities and counties. People from out of state or out of your community may not know that you do litigation in a certain county or that they need a lawyer in a city which is across the street from your office. You may also wish to list the courts agencies and governmental bodies in which you do work. The potential client may need a layer experienced before a specialized body.

S. Provide a place for people to indicate they want to be on your email list (guest book) and a place for "comments."

T. Reproducing a list of articles written by you or speeches given by you, or to be given by you, may impress professionals or prompt them to ask if you in fact really practice law as well. Other lawyers may or may not read them, but most people won't spend the time.

U. List clubs, organizations, and pro bono achievements if you feel they are important. Be careful about listing religious or political affiliations, unless you feel they are important. What appeals to one group may offend or repel another group.

V. Look at your web pages on your computer screen. How much of your page can appear without the need to scroll will depend on how you set up your page and how the viewer has set up his or her computer. Ask a technical person the most common settings now being used. Your pages may appear differently depending on the monitor size and settings of the clients and potential clients. Don't be afraid to try different settings to find the right sizes for your content.

W. Don't hide your website(s), list them on stationery and professional cards. They are more important than your logo. Include them in your Yellow Page ads and on your fax cover sheets. Add them to your email signature.

X. Disclaiming. Somewhere on your website, and possibly on your first reply to an inquiry, you need language to the following effect. "This website is intended to give general information and does not give legal advice. Appropriate legal advice depends on specific facts and circumstances and specified applicable laws. Neither reading emails nor replying to emails is intended as giving legal advice nor establishing an attorney-client relationship. We do not accept professional responsibility or liability for any matter unless, and until, there is an appropriate fee and representation agreement between us and the client. Our firm is licensed to give legal advice only in the State of California. Certain individual lawyers are also licensed in the states of Colorado, Nevada, New York, Illinois and Texas."

Y. Search Engine "Experts." There are many individuals or companies who for a fee, will claim to get you "discovered" or "pushed up" the list of search engine lists. The "secrets" of being found by search engines change rapidly as search engines find people who try gimmicks and in some cases, I am told, actually push them down the list. I can only suggest that if the sum of money is small, you may wish to gamble a few dollars. If the sum of money sought is significant, check out references.

Z. The internet is in its infancy. It is increasingly becoming the principal way lawyers and clients find each other and the way people offer, obtain or exchange the information needed for legal representation.

R-2
Anticipating the Future

Allow me, in this chapter to reflect on the past, comment further on the present and opine on the future.

I have been teaching client the relations and related ethics for more than 4 decades. I have previously studied the history of lawyers and their clients and of client relations covering a period of more than 5,000 years of recorded history.

There has always been and there always will be lawyers or people who do what lawyers do. Whether they are called lawyer, or attorney, or barrister, or advocate, or judge, or justice, or notary, or legislator, or tribal leader, or monarch is not the determinative factor. As Shakespeare wrote, "A rose by any other name...." Lawyers write and administer laws for the benefit of people in order to solve their problems and then interpret, and apply the laws to and for those people. This will never change.

There have always been and always will be clients. Clients have or anticipate having problems caused by rules or lack of rules, and lawyers help the clients solve problems.

Client satisfaction or client dissatisfaction, present or anticipated, will always be a factor in the selection of lawyers. In some instances client dissatisfaction with those who write and administer and apply the laws has led to violent revolutions and warfare.

The future of the legal profession will always be dependent upon 3 factors:

1. The needs of society.
2. Who will fulfill those needs? and
3. The means by which those needs are fulfilled.

In reverse order, the means of the delivery of legal services have changed over the centuries but most of all during the last 50 years.

Wax tablets with engraving tools, parchment and quill pens and manual typewriters have been replaced by the computer and its word processing abilities.

Letters that took months to cross a continent or an ocean were replaced by letters delivered by trains, and airplanes, and then further replaced by the fax machine and currently by email and the internet. Voice recognition may someday replace the keyboard as we now know it.

Electronic digitalization has made possible equipment and tools, in everyday use in homes and offices, that were considered science fiction a few decades ago.

The changes in transportation of people allow people to expand beyond the 50 mile range of the horse or the 1,000 mile range of the train when they want to be somewhere to see their lawyer or the lawyer needs to go somewhere to represent a client.

My father crossed the Atlantic on a ship that took 10 days to sail from Europe to America. I made the same trip in 3 ½ hours on the Concord. Yet the Concord no longer exists, except in museums, because it was not economically viable in meeting the needs of the air traveling public.

WHAT THE FUTURE HOLDS FOR THE PRACTICE OF LAW

Who Will Fulfill The Legal Needs Of Society

What was once the unauthorized practice of law by non lawyers has increasingly become the authorized practice of law by non lawyers.

Increasingly people have been turning away from lawyers to fulfill their legal needs. The commercialization of law and lawyers has impaired or destroyed much of the personal relationship that in the past existed between the lawyer and the client. Legal services have, in many cases, become commercialized to the point that people really don't care who timely fulfills their legal needs at costs they can afford. Legal services have in many cases become a commodity with decisions based on price alone.

Increasingly clients don't care if their contract for their house purchase and sale is prepared by a lawyer or a real estate agent. Their will may come from a form book or the internet or a bank instead of a lawyer.

Increasingly they totally avoid lawyers when going to court using instead court prepared checklists and free services provided by the courts to assist them. The trial of a major case use non lawyers for jury selection and non lawyers who determine how to entertain and convince jurors with acting performances and sound and light tech shows.

The wealthiest of clients go to accounting firms for tax and estate planning and avoid court and court delays by using private arbitration.

The list of legal services which no longer are the exclusive domain of lawyers is rapidly increasing. As law practice, in many instances, becomes a commercial commodity in which price and marketing determine where the public goes, the lawyer must be able to convince the public that the lawyer can produce the needed services better, faster and cheaper.

It is my prediction that the lawyer who can use technology and staff most effectively will thrive. Those who cannot will see their clients go to lawyers who can or to non lawyers providing institutionalized legal services.

Better, Faster, Cheaper was the mantra of those of us who started the Law Practice Management Section of the American Bar Association more than 3 decades ago.

Better, Faster, Cheaper must become the mantra of the lawyer who wants to succeed and thrive in the providing of traditional legal services.

The lawyer who cannot provide legal services Better, Faster, Cheaper must look for new areas of legal practice or new areas of unfulfilled legal needs to avoid competition based on price alone.

The areas outlined below are the ones most likely, in my opinion, to be what our public will need and want over the next decade(s).

The Internet & Email

For those who think the internet has already significantly changed the way law is being practiced, I can only say, "You haven't seen anything yet."

Clients will find their lawyers on the internet. If a lawyer is recommended, clients will go to the internet to check on that lawyer's apparent qualifications for the matter and the client. Clients will, in the not too distant future, have their first meeting with the lawyer via internet with inexpensive video cameras on each computer transmitting a real time interview.

A lawyer in Honolulu and a client in Boston will be able to examine the scene of an accident in Iowa, in real time, by using satellite images which both the lawyer and the client can see at the same time.

Legal research that took hours and days can be done in minutes. Forms or other documents can be brought up in minutes for adapting to a particular situation or person.

Parties and witnesses can be examined without being physically in the court room.

Clients and their lawyers can be separated by continents and still effectively work together.

English is already the language of communication in the legal and professional worlds and will increasingly be so world wide, thus further enabling lawyers and clients to communicate in a common language, which is not the native language of either.

Specific Areas of Law

A futurist does not predict which of 8 horses will win the race. The futurist predicts that one of the eight will win and the others will finish after the winner, but they will finish. The futurist states that one should be prepared for the fact that only one will win and to prepare for the fact that all eight will finish.

Thus, I am predicting which horses will finish the race, although not necessarily in the order given. I am also predicting that something may happen to one or more of the horses causing it to be scratched, and one or more may be replaced by a new horse at present unknown.

Here are my predictions based in my perceptions of societal needs. A specific person or group may have a specific need not addressed in this list.

Always keep in mind the mantra of "Better, Faster, Cheaper" as you review the list.

1. *Elder Law*

In my opinion this will be the biggest growth area. The population of the world is aging. Modern medicine and procedures and devices prolong the quantity of our years of life. In many, if not most, cases they also extend the number of years during which the person will require medical, general functions and financial care and help.

Protecting the person, and assets of the aged and aging, will be an increasingly important and needed area of law. Elder Law is my #1 choice to win the race. The next 8 choices will also finish, but in unknown order.

2. *Probate and Trust Law*

Historically, one of the principal reasons for the need for lawyers has been the supervision of the passage of property from one generation to another. This will continue to be an important task of the lawyer.

3. *Environmental Law*

The natural resources of our planet are being depleted at a faster rate than they are replaced. There already are, and there will continue to be, huge fights between those who will benefit by exploitation and depletion, and those who want to preserve and protect the resources for future generations.

There are huge amounts of money involved in both the battles between the exploiters themselves, and between those who wish to exploit and those who wish to preserve.

4. *Energy Law - Traditionally, Oil and Gas Law*

Energy law now includes all forms of energy including wind energy, hydro-electric, bio mass fuels, etc., and other forms still in the infancy state. The nation of Brazil was able to change from 100% gasoline to 100% alcohol for automobiles. Various economic and political interests are preventing this from happening in the United States.

I am predicting that at some point, the needs of the population will force major changes which will only come about by litigation and legislation.

A lawyer who does not now include energy law within his or her knowledge would be wise to learn some of the buzz words in order to be prepared.

5. *Poverty, Insolvency and Bankruptcy*

I express no opinion on the benefit or detriment to a society where the rich get richer, the poor get poorer, and the middle class disappears. Suffice to say that as the gap increases the poor also suffer lack of education. Lack of education combined with a decreasing income make the poor relatively easy prey for financial predators. The financial predators are able to influence legislatures and judicial appointments to a greater extent than the poor. The financial predators are able to maintain their legalized ability to exploit the poor.

Representing the poor is, and will continue to be, an expanding area of law as individuals and businesses need assistance. The lack of ability of the poor to themselves pay for assistance or to obtain assistance from government or insurance will make it difficult for the private sector lawyer to represent the poor. The lawyers who can use management of technology and other resources to lower the cost of representing the poor may have an unlimited potential future.

6. *Communication Law & Intellectual Property Law*

Governments increasingly want to control and tax communications via telephone, the internet and satellites. The public want low taxed or untaxed forms of communications.

There are ongoing battles over control of content. It is reported that the governmental fine for the showing of one female breast for a moment, during the half-time of a televised football game, exceeded the fine on a coal mine for safety violations which resulted in the multiple deaths of the miners.

The battle over communications law and intellectual property law is huge because the money is huge, and there will continue to be throngs of lawyers on both sides.

Television networks and other means of communication depend on the advertising income from political candidates and parties. Candidates spend millions to get jobs that pay thousands.

Electronic, and digital, and other rights may involve many millions of dollars. Owners of various copyright licenses spend millions to protect their rights from those who would give it away for free or low cost.

7. *Criminal Law*

If prevention of crime is a means of judging penal systems, then our system does not seem to function well. The prison population is swelling beyond the willingness or ability of the nation to pay for prisons. Laws are increasingly being passed with criminal sanctions for violation.

As with poverty law, the ability of those accused with crime to pay for the legal help they need is a severe problem.

Governments threaten seizure and forfeiture of legal fees paid to a lawyer as a method of preventing effective legal representation for the accused. There is a huge need for criminal defense lawyers if the defense lawyer can determine how to get paid and keep the money.

Prosecution lawyers are also needed to reflect the huge increase in criminal prosecutions. Payment is rarely an issue for the prosecutor.

8. *Mediation and Arbitration*

Abraham Lincoln is reported to have said, "A brand new lawyer with no experience in the law will cause a simple uncomplicated dispute to drag on for a year in the courts. An experienced trial lawyer can drag it out for 3 years." Whether or not Abraham Lincoln actually said this is not important. The simple truth is that the population is weary of the costs and delays of the court system. The public is increasingly turning to mediation and arbitration as an alternative to the existing court system.

Being a mediator or an arbitrator or representing clients in mediations and arbitrations is an area of law which will continue to grow.

Niche or Specialty Practice

The medical profession has done an excellent job of promoting the words "specialist" and "specialty." In the medical profession, in many states, as in law in many states, a person may call themselves a "specialist" with no special qualifications, experience or examinations or education while being held to the standard of care of a specialist. Accordingly, I am avoiding the use of the word "specialist" or the words "practice limited to" or "areas of practice" or other terms.

The American public now prefers "specialists" to general practitioner. I avoid the word "specialty" because that word has many different legal meanings in terms of lawyer regulation. I use the words "niche practice" to cover abilities in given area(s) of law which may or may not include "specialists."

I do believe in niche practice whether or not it is called "specialty." Every lawyer has one or more areas of law which they truly enjoy practicing. The lawyer should develop these areas into niche "areas" of law.

Being a "gatekeeper" for non niche areas can also be profitable to the lawyer. In those jurisdictions in which a lawyer can receive "forwarding fees," a lawyer can do well for himself or by getting the clients to the right lawyer for their matter, and practicing the niche areas while referring those non niche areas to others.

In those jurisdictions which do not allow forwarding fees, the lawyer can accomplish the same result by being an of counsel or a member of another firm other than his own, and receive "client origination" percentages of the fee with disclosure to the client if required.

THE ECONOMICS OF LAW PRACTICE

In 1973, I participated in the creation of the Economics of Law Practice Section of the American Bar Association. We were dedicated to providing more economical legal service to the American public, with technology and the efficient use of personnel and resources.

We believed that if we could produce and deliver legal service "Better, Faster, Cheaper" we would be able to serve more clients at lower fees. We prophesied that unless the legal profession could provide legal service Better, Faster and Cheaper, non lawyers would do so.

It was never our purpose to use "Better, Faster, Cheaper" to be able to increase our net profit with no benefit to the American Public.

Over the years we pioneered the use of computer legal research, word processing equipment and systems, creation of a new occupation called "legal assistant," copy equipment to replace carbon copies, electric typewriters and word processors and computer word processing to replace manual typewriters, fax and email and messengers to supplement or replace mail, payment for periodic rendered payment by credit card, and many many other innovations.

A visit to a modern law office could find that almost everything done in the office today did not exist before we came into existence in 1973.

Two things have never changed: The skills needed in both of these areas are skills only a lawyer can fulfill. Everything else is support for the lawyer.

The entire medical team and the hospital and those who work in the hospital all exist to help the patient and the surgeon holding the scalpel or prescribing the treatment. In law all exist to help the client and the lawyer with the client.

In the late 1980's the world of law practice began to change. Law schools expanded rapidly as they learned they could charge (and collect) huge tuition fees by letting the student sign a student loan. Law schools became, and still are, a very profitable business generating untold amounts of student loans.

The students, on graduation, needed and demanded and got increasingly large amounts of money to enable them to repay the loans, and larger law firms began paying larger and larger amounts of money to get the students from the prestige schools. In many cases the newly hired lawyer earned more than the junior partner.

The increased size of law firm increased the use of non lawyers to do the administration required in any large organization. Human resources, finance, insurance, and training all became additional functions performed by non lawyers. Some law firms even have art curators on the staff.

These non lawyers also increased the need for income.

Eventually, the need for more and more clients to support the larger and larger firm brought about the need for marketing directors to assist the lawyers in fulfilling the need for new clients and keeping existing clients.

The American Bar Association Economics of Law Practice Section which was devoted to the lawyer and the client, in the practice of law, became the Law Practice Management Section which increasingly became devoted to the management of the money and profit aspects of the firm. The section decided to declare itself devoted to the "business of law" rather than the 'profession of law."

As some of the larger law firms acted like businesses, rather than professionals, the American public began treating lawyers as money oriented business people instead of professionals dedicated to assisting people. Lawyers and the legal profession began being treated with dislike and as the objects of anti lawyer jokes. This societal dislike of lawyers is increasing and makes the marketing of legal services more difficult. It is difficult to prophesy the long term effects of large firms acting like money enterprises and being treated as money enterprises.

This book is about how lawyers market themselves and their firms and how the entire office can support the lawyer on his or her effort to bring clients to the firm and satisfy them.

Lost in the furor and noise is the statement, "It's not about you it's about the client."

Despite publicity to the contrary, the "Selling" of lawyers by cold calling, paid and unpaid media advertising, "branding," and other buzz words to designated targeted audiences still require a lawyer to gain and keep the confidence of the client.

Despite all attempts at economic restructuring, patients still want to talk to the doctor, penitents still want to talk to the priest, and clients still want to talk to the lawyer. Trying to convince the patient or the penitent or the client to talk to someone else to save money doesn't go very far when only the professional can solve the problem or when the person has the money to pay for what they need.

The point I am making is that the successful lawyer always has been, and always will be, the person who successfully gets and keeps the client.

The best way to predict the future is to create it yourself.

R-3
Acknowledgments to the Pioneers

One of the problems of an acknowledgment section of a book is that one can inadvertently omit a person who is greatly deserving of an acknowledgment but who somehow got overlooked in the pressures of meeting a publisher's deadline.

I readily admit that much, if not most, of this book consists of concepts that I learned from others and then tested in my own practice. Some of the concepts, I did not use, but have passed them on for the reader to consider. Accordingly, I must admit that I will never be able to give credit on a name by name basis to every person who gave me concepts which are repeated in my words in this book.

On the other hand there are people who recognized the need for disseminating this information to the lawyers of America and who encouraged me to do so while others were afraid of "being involved" in the then controversial area of good client and public relations and its effect on practice growth.

In 1968, several California Attorney-CPA's worked with me to put together the program "How to Start and Build a Law Practice." Those programs, done four times a year, became the starting point for this book and the book "How to Start and Build a Law Practice." Included in these Attorney-CPA's were Burton Rosky, Arnold Magassin, Richard Berger, and Jerrold Kaplan.

On April 27, 1974 I sat in a hotel room in San Francisco, California and voted to create the Economics of Law Practice Section of the American Bar Association now called Law Practice Management Section. I was appointed Chair of the New Lawyers In Practice Committee and a few years later began my six-year term on the Council of the ELP. Through the ELP section I met many of the people who encouraged me to "go national" with my programs and concepts.

In 1976 the ABA Economics Section and the Law Student's Section began to print and disseminate my book "How to Start and Build a Law Practice," which was the first single author work published by the ABA ELP. The 1979 publication catalogue of the ELP contained my book, 4 others; 2 pamphlets, reprints of 8 articles, 7 audio tapes and 4 films and audio tapes. The current ABA LPM catalogue contains more than 100 books. "How to Start and Build a Law Practice" is still there, now in its 5th Edition, and is consistently, year after year, the leader of the ABA Publications Program.

Again, at the risk of omitting some very significant people I'll try here to acknowledge those who encouraged me (albeit at times with some reservations) to do the programs which culminated in this book. Unfortunately some of these pioneers have passed on.

No list can start with any name other than J. Harris Morgan of Greenville, Texas who did so much to encourage me by word and by deed. All of America, lawyers and non-lawyers, have a debt to Harris for what he accomplished often single-handedly and in the face of influential, well entrenched opposition. He has led the lawyers of America to modern systems and technology expanding greatly the access of affordable legal services to the American public.

It is not possible to list every person who, over the years, has "opened the doors" for me, but some of those who helped so much at the beginning include Jimmy Brill and Gene Cavin of Texas, Mitch Miller, Ron Haydanek and Lynn Gold-Biken of Philadelphia, Austin Anderson and Ray Bishop of Ann Arbor, Bob and Rose Wilkins, Al Moses and Del Roberts of South Carolina; Paul Luvera, Dick Reed; and Bob Mucklestone of Washington; Lee and Betsy Turner of Great Bend, Kansas, Tom Brown of Maryland; Lee Taylor and Klein Strong of Salt Lake City, Garth Grissom and Harold Feder of Denver, Arnold Fischer and Steve Maskeleris and Al Ferguson of New Jersey; Fran Musselman, Bob Shack, Herb Goodfriend and Bernie Sternin of New York, Leo Eisenstat of Omaha, Nebraska; Tom Gonser of Boise, Idaho; Dave Link of Notre Dame University; Dick Williams and Tom Ledbetter of Arkansas; Marty Howard of Portland, Oregon; Bob Bigelow and Ted Orenstein of Massachusetts, Ezra Clark of Arizona, Sam Fowler of Tennessee; Dick Tempera, formerly of Des Moines, Iowa, Charles Thompson of South Dakota; Budd Orren of Minneapolis; Ned Parker of Virginia; Duke Nordlinger Stern and Jim St. Clair of West Virginia, Don Rikli and Kathryn Marshall of Illinois, Kathryn Braemer, Joel Bennet and Larry Lapidus of Washington, D.C. Unfortunately, some of these wonderful pioneers have died.

I have only named three professional CLE administrators in the above list, namely Gene Cavin of Texas, Tom Gonser of Idaho, and Duke Nordlinger Stern, because of their enormous influence and help and support in the early years, when the subject of this book was considered controversial, but I cannot overlook the hard work and ongoing efforts of the professional staffs of the state and local bars and CLE programs. These cadres of professionals keep the profession on its steady track while the elected leaders ebb and flow.

I have been blessed to be able to work with hundreds of lawyers, Bar Association and CLE staffs, and non-lawyers who have given selflessly to the legal profession. It would take many pages to list them all. Many of their organizations are listed elsewhere in this book. This book truly represents the selective input of hundreds , if not thousands, of lawyers and those who work with lawyers as part of the legal profession.

My assistant Yolanda Ornelas has been with me for more than six years. She painstakingly scanned and reformatted the entire second edition and keyboarded major changes of this 3rd edition, with the difficult task of reading my writing and finding discrepancies and errors.

I must also acknowledge the contribution of my wife Lois and my sons Alan, David and Steven who often accompanied me to the many meetings where I spoke or who were home when I was away.

Lastly, but perhaps most importantly I must acknowledge the American Bar Association professional staff, particularly the Economics of Law Practice now Law Practice Management, and Law Student Division staff. I wish to give most special recognition to the one person who over the many – many years always found the time and means to smooth a ruffled ego and get the job done: the true backbone of the American Bar Association ELP, Donna Spilis.

R-4
Dedication

"A good lawyer finds a solution for every problem. A bad lawyer finds a problem for every solution. Be a good lawyer."

This was the advice my late father gave to me when I announced that I was leaving my successful CPA practice to become a lawyer. I've tried to follow that advice throughout my career. My father died unexpectedly in 1985 at the age of 85. He was a child of the century and saw the introduction and development of the automobile, the airplane, radio, television and space travel. Before I was born he had fought as a soldier in two wars, had been wounded in combat while a cavalryman, and emigrated to America as a penniless immigrant. He achieved millionaire status in Los Angeles before the Great Depression, losing his money when the banks were closed and then becoming a millionaire again during the Depression in Chicago in a new business and losing it again to the industrial sabotage of a competitor.

I was fortunate to have known him for fifty years before he died. He never tired of teaching me the secrets of his success and the causes of his failures. My father taught me that experiencing some failure is the price of success.

My father loved America as passionately as any man loved any woman. He taught me respect and love for America and its institutions of social and religious freedom and economic opportunity. He had lived in Tulsa, San Diego, Gary, Chicago, Philadelphia and Los Angeles. He had been a truck driver, cheese distributor, restaurant owner, butcher, lumberjack, welder, upholsterer and hotel manager. He had lived in slums and mansions.

He knew America and the American people and knew that there was upward mobility and new opportunity for success no matter how many times one failed economically.

He taught me, "Always be nice to the people you pass as you go up the ladder of success because in America you may see the same people again when they pass you on their way up or as you pass them on your way down."

He was at heart a salesman and an innovator who loved people and who loved being with them and helping them.

My father's love for America has been passed on to me and I hope through this book to pass on to others the courage to try new methods and the maturity to accept an occasional lack of success as part of the price of ultimate success.

I dedicate this book to the memory and teachings of my late father Hyman J. (Jimmy) Foonberg (1900-1985). I dedicate this book also to the lawyers of America past, present and as yet unborn who have labored often and who will labor at personal sacrifice to defend and maintain our precious freedom and liberty.